Deep in the Heart

As always, Marilyn King brings a setting, her characters, and their love story blazing to life. I was invested from page one! Prepare for an adventurous ride (on horseback) to a time long gone but not soon forgotten—just like this masterfully written story. A true delight to read.

—Beckie Lindsey, Author, and Editor, *Southern California Christian Voice,* author of the Beauties from Ashes series.

Here's another romance by novelist extraordinaire, Marilyn King. You'll be hooked from page one when you meet John Grigsby in 1841 sensing something is not right with his wife, Nancy, who is carrying their seventh child. King's descriptive talents are at work again as she deals with longings to move west, death, loss, confusion, childbirth, and most of all love."

—Dr. Mary Langer Thompson, Poet and Writer, author of *Poems in Water* and *The Gull Who Thought He Was Dull.*

An artist in the historical romance genre, Marilyn King has done it again. *Deep in the Heart of Love* tells the true story of her ancestor John Grigsby as he navigates the harsh life of the Old West. King has a gift for bringing her readers into the era, from description to dialogue. Her research knows no boundaries, and it shows. A talented wordsmith, she perfectly captures the experiences and emotions John and his family face through their daily challenges, and the blessed hope that comes out of tremendous grief. Filled with exceptional characters and events, King's stories are worth reading many times over.

—Molly Jo Realy, Editor, Speaker, and author of the romantic, location mystery novel, *NOLA*

Poignant, engrossing, and vivid are trademarks of this popular author's novels. King knocks it out of the park again with this compelling story based on family history. Drop everything and read this book!"

—Ann Miner, author of *I Lift My Eyes* and *Bugs in the Baptismal.*

Also by Marilyn King

The Winds of Love

The Winds of Grace   *The Winds of Courage*
The Winds of Promise   *The Winds of Redemption*

Hearts of Home

Isabel's Song

The Call of the West

Deep in the Heart of Love

Anthologies

The Letter   *A Hobo's Thanksgiving*
Everybody Out Here Comes a Train

Children's Book

Tony Finds a Home

The Call of the West

Marilyn King

Deep in the Heart of Love

Crown Leaf Publishing

Published in the United States by Crown Leaf Publishing, functions only as book publisher. As such, the ultimate design, content, editorial accuracy, and views expressed or implied in this work are those of the author.

Deep in the Heart of Love is a work of fiction. All incidents and dialogue, and all characters, with the exception of some well-known historical figures, are products of the author's imagination and not to be construed as real. Where real-life historical persons appear, the situations, incidents, and dialog concerning those persons are entirely fictional and are not intended to depict actual events or to change the entirely fictional nature of the work. In all other respects, any resemblance to persons living or dead is entirely coincidental.

All scriptures quotations are taken from the King James Version of the Holy Bible.

ISBN: 13: 978-0-9967258-6-6 Trade paperback
ISBN: 10: 9780996725866
Library of Congress Catalog Card Number:

Cover design and artwork by Ken Raney, copyright © 2022
Printed in the United States of America
2022–First Edition

To Grandmother,
Tilly May Grigsby
You blazed a trail for our family.
A strong woman who was
truly loved.

But they that wait upon the Lord
shall renew their strength;
they shall mount up with wings as eagles;
they shall run and not be weary;
and they shall walk, and not faint."
—Isaiah 40:31

Preface

Much of this novel you're about to read is purely fictional, yet there are strands of actual history and people braided throughout the story. For instance, the family of John Grigsby most certainly did exist, as did the Shields' family.

Additionally Grovespring, is an actual community in central Missouri with a current population of about 1,200. The Grigsby family, characters in *Deep in the Heart of Love*, did have a ranch near the river with creeks running through their land, as did the Shields's family. Many of the events included in this story were drawn from records of their personal experiences. It was my pleasure to flesh out their lives in my imagination.

In addition to the Grigsby family, fictional characters were created to enhance the story. All of the characters' personalities and actions are of my own creation and should be considered as such.

After four years of research and writing *Deep in the Heart of Love,* I invite you to join me on this journey into the West, where life was hard but the people were strong. Thank you from the bottom of my heart for taking the time to read this novel based on a true story of my third great-grandfather, John Grigsby. I treasure the investment of time put into this novel, and .

In His Grip,
Marilyn

Chapter ONE

Grovespring, Missouri—Early August 1841

JOHN GRIGSBY STOOD AT the entrance of the stable and stared intently at the house. A dark feeling pulled at his gut. Something wasn't right. His wife, Nancy, was carrying their seventh child but this time she looked pale—and something more—worried?

Behind him the horses chuffed in their stalls waiting for their morning oat grains. John stared at the house a moment longer, still troubled by the sense that something was amiss. But he turned back to the stable to tend to the horses. He'd go along in a moment to check on Nancy. She had always been headstrong, it would be hard to get the truth out of her but he had to try. He had to know if she was all right.

NANCY GRIGSBY STARED DOWN at her stomach for a long moment. She'd been stirring eggs when she'd felt a hard kick. The baby seemed to demand her attention of late. Her concentration, however, had been on her husband's latest dream of going West—and her dream of keeping her family's roots here in Grovespring, Missouri.

Why can't we just stay? A creak on the floorboards alerting her that she wasn't the only one who had risen in the early morning hour, pulled her from her deep thoughts.

"Good morning," came a deep voice near her ear just before John snatched the tail of her apron strings, and tugged it loose. He held it in the air with a glimmer in his eyes.

"John Grigsby," she cried as she whirled into his arms. "You sneaked up on me!" She didn't miss the spark of amusement in his gaze. What had gotten into him, this man who next to never showed a playful side? He surprised her this early morning hour. Burdened with working the land and the responsibilities it brought, John rarely took time to play. Tall, broad-shouldered, and lanky from the waist down, he wore the rough-cut print of the land in his features, and he wore it well. So well, that he often took her breath away.

John held her gaze. "Come see the sunrise with me."

"Sunrise my foot. I have breakfast to make before our brood wakes up and wants to be fed," she playfully complained as she wriggled out of his arms.

John looked magnificent in his worn blue shirt, dark pants and his sun-browned features. She had been tempted to stop him from leaving the kitchen, yet, she knew if she did, he wouldn't go back to the barn to finish the morning's work and she'd be late in canning peaches today.

His hand went to her waist. "How long before breakfast?"

"Not long if you move out of the kitchen." Nancy snatched her apron out of his hand. "I thought you and the boys were already out in the barn."

"They haven't shown up yet. I came back to look at your pretty face." He tried to pull her into his arms again.

Her hand flew to his chest. Not that he could get too close with her midriff extended as big as a wash tub. In her seventh month of gestation, this child had grown faster than the others.

"Are you feeling all right, Nan?" John inquired, a note of concern in his voice. He stood to his full six-foot-two height.

Nancy's hands went to her hips. "What's gotten into you? I'm fine."

"Are you being straight with me? You seem overly tired lately."

"It's summer and it's hot. Of course, I'm tired." She looked down at her bulging tummy and splayed her fingers over it. "If anything, the heat's taking a toll on me, but honestly, I'm fine." She put one finger on the top button of his shirt. "Go milk Bossie while I get breakfast."

John dropped his hands. "I'll be back," he promised, his blue eyes shining.

She giggled. "Just like a pesky fly."

John's hand flew to his chest as if she'd wounded him. "Is that what you think of me?"

"Go before I swat you." Her hand went for a dish towel.

When her eyes lifted to his, John saw faint embarrassment mingled with a tinge of pink in her cheeks—and something else. There had been a glow in those warm eyes, the same glow he'd seen every time she'd been with child. He wanted to touch the lovely flush of her cheeks. He took in her long, flax-colored hair already combed to perfection at this early morning hour. At thirty-five, Nancy was still beautiful beyond expression. It was true he'd come back to the house to look at her pretty face, but she'd seemed drawn of late, and it concerned him. Her playful mood lifted his spirit and removed the worry that plagued him.

"I'll be back for breakfast." He kissed her soundly and strode out of the kitchen.

Moments later, the sound of clomping feet filled the stairwell and then the hall as the boys bounded down the stairs to join their father out in the barn. The back door swung open and banged closed, and she smiled to herself.

Nancy thought of John's coal-black hair and lazy grin and shook her head. "If I don't get these eggs into the skillet, they won't be ready when the brood shows up for breakfast." She cracked another egg against the bowl. Scrambled eggs would be ready soon. After that, she'd best get to peeling peaches. The day was sure to be a hot one. The canning would be hot work, and she wanted to get a good start on it while there was still a little coolness in the air.

A twinge of guilt jabbed at her. She *wasn't* feeling her best and worried that she had been more tired than usual with this baby than the others. The first hint of the morning's sunrise glowed through the window and hope leapt into her soul. Everything had to be all right—didn't it?

"OUT! OUT OF THE kitchen now." Nancy glared at two of her sons, Granville and Calvin, and her brother-in-law Franklin, and clamped her jaws shut tight to keep a smile at bay. After all the hours of sweating in the hot kitchen making peach jam, it did her heart good to see the boys' eyes shining from her hard work.

The twelve-year-olds, Granville and Franklin, had a glint in their eyes as they swiped a dribble of peach jelly from the rim of a canning jar.

Nancy watched Franklin, fondly. She avoided calling him her brother-in-law most of the time. It wasn't his fault that John's mother died giving birth to him. With Nancy already nursing five-month-old Granville, it had only seemed fitting for John to bring his tiny baby brother home to live with them.

To the children Franklin was their brother. He and Gran looked like twins with their unruly golden hair and spray of freckles across their cheeks. Having raised Franklin from birth, he had been as much a son to her as the rest of her children. He was a Grigsby—that's all that mattered.

"Hey," Calvin said, squeezing in to get a finger's dab of the sweet jam. At nine, he often followed his brothers' lead.

The kitchen held a strong scent of sugary syrup while a new batch of peaches bubbled in the large pot on the stove. If she didn't shoo the boys out of the kitchen, she and her older daughter, Tess would never get their work done. She gave the boys a stern look. "You heard me. Out!"

Calvin backed away, giggling and licking his finger. "You make the best jam, Mama."

"We'll not have enough for the winter if you keep sneaking in here and sticking your dirty fingers in the jar. Now mind me and scoot!"

Nancy turned her back, amusement in her eye. She loved nothing more than to make peach jam for her family. It was hard work, but hearing their appreciative comments made it all worthwhile.

She gazed appreciatively at five-year-old Mary Jane, who sat quietly at the table, observing all the fuss. She held her well-worn rag doll, her feet swinging beneath the chair. Mary Jane had dark hair like her father, and a head of naturally curly ringlets. Where she got her curls, nobody knew.

"Come on, Calvin," Granville said. "We better get outside before Mama pinches our ears."

"Hold on." Nancy turned back to them. "I want all of you to go back out to the orchard and pick enough peaches to fill another basket. We're nearly done with the first batch."

She turned to eleven-year-old Theresa, whom the family called Tess. "I need you to bring more jars from the cellar. At least a dozen."

Tess's shoulders slumped. "All right, Mama."

Nancy watched her elder daughter, dragging her feet, start out of the kitchen. Her long golden curls were damp from the heat and the trips she'd already made to the cellar for the first batch of empty jars. Tess would much rather be out on the range, riding the mustangs, or in the stables brushing down one of the horses. But truth to tell, she needed her daughter's help on canning days.

Tess looked back with the bluest eyes and said, "It's so hot in here that it's hard to come back. It's nice and cool in the cellar." She lifted her chin. "Why don't you take a break and join me. Then you can cool off too?"

"Because I'm busy putting up jam . . . and because climbing those stairs is hard on my body right now." Nancy's left hand went to the small of her back and kneaded it with closed eyes.

Tess wrinkled her nose. "Then take a break and sit down. Your face is as red as a tomato."

"Speaking of tomatoes, once we're done with the peaches—"

Tess gave her mother a cross-eyed look and disappeared.

"Theresa Angeline!"

The front door slammed shut.

Nancy's hands flew in the air. "Don't wake Wiley and Jefferson from their naps." Nancy cut Mary Jane a look and put a finger to her lips. "Be a good girl and stay quiet."

"I will, Mama. Can I have some bread with jam on it?"

"Not now. You'll spoil your supper."

Looking over the counter flooded with jars, it occurred to her that she didn't see the eggs Mary Jane should have collected from the chicken coop this morning. Turning back to Mary Jane, she asked, "Did you feed the chickens this morning?"

"Uh, I forgot." Mary Jane curls bobbed as she swung her head to look at her mother.

Nancy stared at her daughter. "You need to go out right this minute and feed those chickens."

"All right."

"And collect the eggs. I'll need them for tomorrow's breakfast. I want you to come straight back inside when you're done. It's too hot out for you to stay outside today." Nancy wiped her brow.

"All right, Mama." Mary Jane scooted out of her chair and ran out the back door. When she reached the chicken coop, she lifted the wire holding the gate shut and slipped through between the gate and the post. Since they'd been having trouble with coyotes killing their chickens, for now they had to stay in the chicken yard. Mary Jane wiped her sweaty hands on her blue gingham dress and gazed at the excited chickens gathering around her. The cackling chickens followed her as she stepped inside the wooden enclosure and grabbed a small sack of dried corn.

When she went out to the chicken yard, she called, "Here, chick, chick,

chick," as she tossed out a handful of dried corn. Mother hens, followed by little yellow fluffs of baby chicks, ran over to scratch at the corn kernels in the dirt. Mary Jane's brows rose and her mouth formed an "O" as she watched the chickens run about pecking the ground. "You're sure hungry little ones, aren't you? Here, chick, chick, chick," she said again as she tossed more kernels to the ground. Her mother had told her not to throw too many kernels, but she couldn't resist. She grabbed another handful of corn and scattered it on the ground.

Tossing down the last piece of dried corn in her hand, Mary Jane clapped her dusty hands together and then wiped them down her pinafore. She took a basket off the wall hook in the chicken coop and gathered nearly a dozen eggs. Her mother would be thrilled to see how many eggs she'd gathered. Some of the eggs were soiled, but her mother would wipe them off before she put them in the springhouse. Mary Jane set the basket on the ground as she hooked the wire over the wooden post to keep the chickens in their pen, and then lifted the heavy basket. She trod back to the house more carefully than she had come.

NANCY FELT HOT AS a tea kettle whistling with steam. It was more than the heat of the kitchen with the peach jam boiling in the pot. Mood swings came and went with this baby. But even this didn't seem to be what troubled her.

The rattling of wagon wheels filled the air, interrupting her thoughts, and she glanced out the window in time to see that an unknown visitor had arrived in their drive. She knew at once what really nagged her. The town had filled with covered wagons and John wanted to join them and move out West. He'd talked to her about selling their land to come up with the money to buy supplies and start all over again in Oregon.

She'd watched John's best friend, Charles Matthews, a wealthy cattle rancher, climb down from his wagon. He'd looked longingly at their family home as if he'd snatch it out from underneath of them if she'd agree.

John's heart had been on a mission to buy more land. And yet, four-years ago he'd built this ranch from scratch. He had a gift for making something out of nothing. He could envision the bigger picture in the scope of things when he planned and mapped out his dreams. He had wanted their home to sit on acres and acres of land and had imagined the house filled with children when the land nothing more than prairie grass and riverbed. He wanted cattle grazing and mustangs roaming the range. And it had all came to fruition. With time all that existed on the Grigsby ranch fell into place because of hard work and his vision.

Their house bustled with seven children whose noise and laughter filled her heart with joy. And yet—John wasn't content. He had been antsy—too antsy. She could see it in his eyes. Thinking, planning, and working on ways to move out West—to start all over again.

And here they were again—the town full of wagons, the streets filled with strangers buying supplies and trading out stock and horses, preparing for the next leg of their journey that would move them farther West.

She'd be glad when the wagons were gone and the town grew quiet again. Only then would the fluttering in her chest dissipate—if only for a little while. But she knew it wouldn't be long before the next group of wagons converged on their small community to eat everything in their wake—the way the locusts do.

Nancy swallowed and turned back to the cook stove. She checked on the pot of chicken and dumplings simmering on the back burner of the stove. "Supper will be ready soon." She gazed at the counter cluttered with bowls of peaches, sugar, and canning jars. Sighing at the idea of so much work still to do, her mind shifted to her neighbor. "What I wouldn't give to have Mahala's help right now."

Mahala Shields lived on a ranch a mile down the road, but she wouldn't be home this time of day. She worked at Mr. Thompson's tailor shop, as a seamstress. Right now she had her hands full making dresses for the upcoming harvest dance. Nancy wouldn't be surprised if her friend showed up in the next day or two. In the four years they'd lived in Grovespring, she and Mahala's friendship had grown.

An hour later, the table set and the children waiting for their father, Nancy looked out the window for John. *Supper's ready,* she mused. *Are you going to be late again?*

Besides selling stock to the flow of travelers, this was the season for branding cattle and getting ready for fall. John's days were long and hard. He'd hired cowhands to work the cattle range and to get the rest of the hay cut and stacked in the barn. With her days full of canning, housework, and tending the children, she felt hard pressed to keep up with all her husband did.

The back door slammed and John Grigsby came through the kitchen door, whistling a tune. His black, unruly hair was smashed from his wide-brimmed hat, but a lock of hair tumbled over his slick forehead. His shirt was dark and damp in a V-shape across his muscled chest, and a growth of beard shadowed his rawboned features. John stopped whistling as he strode across the floor and opened the wooden, insulated icebox. He brought out a pitcher of water and set it on the counter. "Smells good in here." With a forefinger, he swiped at a dab of peach jam that had spilled onto the counter. "Umm. Tastes good too."

"Supper's ready." Nancy wiped her hands on her apron. "Wash up."

"I can't sit down just yet. There's a couple of men riding out to look at our cows."

"Again?"

"Don't look so put out, Nan. We raise them to sell. Remember?"

"But your supper's getting cold."

"It'll keep." He kissed her forehead, and glanced out the kitchen window. "Town's full of wagons heading for Independence. I expect a few more folks will come by for stock."

"Why would folks want to leave their farms and live in wagons for months on end?" She couldn't look John in the eye. She knew what she'd see. Her hand went protectively to her swollen belly. "I love it here, every inch of it."

"I know, Nan." He tilted her chin and kissed her nose.

"Oh, go on. But don't sell Bossie. She's mine."

"I won't." He started out the door and stopped to look at the jars of peaches lined on the counter. "When I come back, I'd like a piece of bread with some of your good jam." Eyes twinkling, he disappeared out the front door.

Nancy spun around at the sound of the children giggling.

"Get to eating . . . now."

She sat down next to three-year-old Jeffrey, who wiggled impatiently in his chair. She broke off a half-slice of homemade bread and set it before two-year-old Wiley, who sat in a highchair. With such a large family, the seating was tight in the kitchen. They could eat in the formal dining room, but Nancy reserved that table for when they had company. She like their family crowded together in the kitchen.

"Aren't you going to say grace?" Mary Jane asked.

Nancy looked at Granville. "You do the honors since your father isn't here."

"Bow your heads," Granville said. The prayer was short and before long the sounds of serving spoons clinking against containers filled the room. Laughter and chatter soon took over. Then all went quiet as the family set to eating the good meal.

"Can I go out to see what cows Dad's selling? Please?" asked Calvin.

"No. Stay put and finish your supper. You can go after you've eaten."

"Yes, ma'am." His lips formed a thin line as he forked a bite of dumplings.

The family had nearly finished eating when John came through the kitchen door once more. He stepped around Tess, who was helping to clear the table. "Well, that's done." He pulled his hat off and sat down. "I sold two heifers and a bull calf."

Nancy filled his plate and sat down again. "I can't imagine why these folks are on the road this time of the year. They're leaving far too late in the season to get to Oregon before winter sets in."

"They've been warned. They're coming from New York and the journey's been slow. We told them they should hole up in Grovespring for the winter."

"They won't hear of it?"

"They don't have the money and supplies to stay through fall and winter. They need to get to their destination before their funds run dry." John lifted his glass of water and took a long drink.

Nancy shook her head. "This smells bad no matter which way the wind blows."

"You're right." John chewed his food a moment and then said, "Well, at least you can rest assured I won't be talking about moving out West for the moment." He eyed her with amusement and tipped back his chair.

"If you never brought it up that would be fine with me." She wiped Wiley's mouth and hands with a damp cloth and lifted him out of the highchair. He ran out of the kitchen to join his siblings in the front room.

"Come watch the sunset with me," John said, reaching for Nancy's hand. He led her out to the front porch. She leaned her back against his hard chest, her flax-colored hair falling over her shoulders. The evening sun blazed across the sky, reaching out in rivers of red, purple, and gold, reclaiming what it had lost at daybreak.

Nancy looked out over the corn fields, silhouetted against the blazing sun, and then to the back side yard. Peach trees lined the orchard, and the fields were speckled with cattle. A vast contentment filled her as she stood, embraced by John's strong arms. When she looked at the sky again, the red had faded to rose and pink and a soft hue of blue. In her mind their ranch had been a little piece of heaven. An ache seeped into her soul. She wondered—and prayed—could she talk John out of his wild dreams of moving out West?

Chapter TWO

THE FOLLOWING AFTERNOON, NANCY looked out the kitchen window in time to see Mahala ride into the yard in her black buggy. As she alighted, she called out, "Hello, anyone home?" Her voice drifted across the yard.

Nancy went onto the porch. She wiped her hands on her apron and gave her friend a hug. "Mahala, it's so good to see you. Come inside."

Mahala's dark brown hair was held back in a loose bun, but a few wisps floated around her face. In her thirties, Mahala was quite an attractive woman. She still had a trim waist. Nancy often wondered why she'd never married. Her friend had been one of the kindest people she knew, and she could find no fault in Mahala's appearance, so what would keep a man at bay?

"I heard you were putting up peaches. I came to help." Mahala said.

The two women went into the house. The sound of the children playing in the back yard filled the air behind them.

"Whew! It's hot in here." Mahala waved at the air in front of her.

"I know. I've got all the windows raised, but it isn't doing a bit of good. The stove has been going nonstop all morning." Nancy pointed at the rows of peach-filled jars. "We've too many peach trees. I can't keep up with them."

Mahala pulled an apron off a wall hook and tied it on. "Mother wondered about that. She said to ask if you'd be willing to sell some of your peaches. Our family thoroughly enjoyed them last year."

"Pfft! Sell them? You canned half of them last year. I'll send some home with you." Nancy turned back to the stove, where she picked up the tongs and began lifting jars out of the boiling water and setting them on the counter. "How's work?"

"Oh, Nancy, it seems half of the women in Grovespring have decided to have a dress made for the upcoming Harvest Festival. And you'll never guess who came to the shop needing a seamstress." A mischievous smile turned up her lips.

Nancy held the pot steady as she spooned hot jam into the first jar. "From the look on your face, she must not be one of your usual customers." She tilted the pot and moved to the next jar.

"Give me that. You shouldn't be carrying that heavy pot in your condition." Mahala took it and proceeded to ladle the sweet-smelling jam into the rest of the jars.

Nancy wiped the sweat from her brow and picked up a peach.

"Flora Benson has never come into Mr. Thompson's tailor shop until today," Mahala said.

Nancy stopped peeling the skin from the peach and held her paring knife in the air. "Flora Benson? She's going to hire *you* to make *her* dress?"

"One and the same. And her daughter Caroline is supposed to come into the shop Monday morning for measurements. This is truly a first for both of them."

"What on earth has gotten into her? I can't count how many times she's gone on about having her clothes made in Springfield as if you're not good enough for her."

"I know. It was all I could do to keep my jaw from hitting the floor when she walked in. At first, I thought Mr. Benson might have hired Mr. Thompson to make a suit for him. But when she scurried past him and walked straight to my sewing table, I nearly dropped my pin cushion."

Nancy picked at the peach she'd been peeling. She pulled back the fuzzy skin with a little more vigor. "So . . . did she choose a dress from Godey's fashion book for you to make?"

"She did. It's far too fancy for a barn dance, but I didn't say as much." Mahala wiped the last jar with a damp cloth and placed her hands on her hips. "You look flushed. Have you given yourself permission to take a break?" Her eyes went to Nancy's belly.

"I've taken several breaks, but my feet are swollen something awful. I'm afraid my shoes are cutting off circulation."

"Sit down. I'll peel," Mahala said, taking the paring knife from Nancy.

Nancy didn't argue. She sat on the kitchen chair and took her shoes off as she watched her friend take over the process of canning the peaches. "I'm going to write Mother and see if she'll come out and help with the children when the baby comes." She ran a hand over her large bump.

"Nonsense, Nancy. I'll help."

"You've got your seamstress business at the tailor shop. I need someone who can be around full time for at least a week, preferably two."

"I said I'll do it. What are friends for? By the time the baby makes its appearance, the harvest dance will be over and things will have settled down." Mahala swiped at the sweat beading her brow. She filled the pot with the cut-up peaches and stuffed more wood in the stove.

An hour later, the counter was filled with new jars of jam and both women eyed their work with satisfaction. "That creek behind the house is calling us," Mahala said. She looked wistfully at Nancy.

"I can't wade in the stream like this." Nancy placed both hands on her tummy.

"Why not?"

"I might fall." She wrinkled her nose.

"I'll hold your hand. Come on. You've been canning for a week. You deserve it."

"But the babies—"

"Go on, Mama," Tess said, coming into the kitchen. "I'll watch Wiley and Jeffrey. When are you going to quit calling them 'the babies?' They aren't babies anymore."

"I know. It's just a habit. And Mary Jane? She can be a handful."

"Yes, Mama. I'll watch all three. They're out in the backyard, playing in the washtub water. I hope you don't mind, because they've been splashing each other and their clothes are soaked." A crooked smile played across her face. "I'd gladly watch them outside rather than being stuck in this hot kitchen."

Nancy looked at Mahala and then at Tess.

"Go on, Mama. It's not often you wade in the stream," Tess urged.

Nancy didn't wait a moment longer. In truth, that creek had been calling her all week. She tore off her apron and scurried out the back door. She moved through the prairie grass fairly well for a woman heavy with child.

Mahala slipped her hand into the crook of Nancy's arm and giggled. "Thank you, Nan. I've been looking forward to this. I don't know if Grovespring's ever been this hot in the summer. If you had refused, I was going to ride home and wade in the creek behind our place."

When they reached the bank, both women tied their skirts and tucked them in at the waist, leaving only their petticoats to get wet. They kicked off their shoes and stepped into the water.

"Ahh, I feel better already," Nancy said, moving carefully into the bubbling creek. "Oh, Mahala. This is heaven."

They waded out to the middle of the stream, letting the current brush past them. They curled their toes around the small, smooth pebbles on the bottom of the creek. Mahala leaned down and let the water flow through her slim fingers. They splashed and laughed until they realized they'd whiled away the rest of the afternoon. When they climbed the cool grassy bank, Nancy looked across the field at the clapboard house and took Mahala's hand. "This has been wonderful, but I'd better get back and start supper. Will you stay and eat dinner with us?"

"No. I have some catching up to do at home. I've got to finish three dresses tonight—just small finishing touches."

"All right." Nancy knew full well how Mahala spent her evenings doing the fine detailed work that gave her dresses that special touch.

They walked on in silence until they came to the drive where Mahala's buggy sat. "I'll come by in the next day or two." Mahala said and raised a hand in farewell.

As she stepped into the buggy seat, John came out from the barn. "Hello!" he called.

Mahala smiled back at Nancy and gave her a second wave, then waved at John on her way out of the drive.

Nancy picked up her steps almost feeling as if she wasn't so burdened with this little life inside of her. Maybe she'd visit that creek more often. For now, she had a houseful of mouths waiting to be fed.

Before she could turn to the back door, however, she saw a wagon roll into their drive. She felt her stomach twist. What was Flora Benson's husband doing here at this time of the day?

JOHN STRODE TO JUDD Benson's wagon and called out, "Hello, Judd. What brings you here?"

Judd wrapped the reins around the brake pole and jumped down onto the ground. He crossed the graveled drive in a casual manner, a hand outstretched. John shook it and stepped back. Judd walked past him and studied the barn and the land beyond toward the creek. "You've got prime property here."

John eyed the man's silver streaks feathered into pitch black hair. The tall man held a swagger that suggested he was superior to others.

"I'm aware of that," he bristled.

"A source tells me Charles Matthew came by and offered a handsome price for your land."

"Now, who might that source be?" John asked.

Judd pulled off his hat and slapped it against his pant leg. "I told him I wouldn't say. I'm a man of my word." He squinted at the barn where a couple of workers raked alfalfa hay.

John clenched his jaw and gazed over his shoulder to see Luke and Brady pitching hay next to the barn entrance. Luke looked up and gave him a nod. John's blood boiled at Judd's comment. "This land's not for sale." *Not to you anyway.* Judd Benson worked on his nerves like a pebble in his boot.

"I heard different. Some folks are saying you're itchin' to go out West, that you plan on letting go of this place—cattle and all." Judd ran a hand across his face. "I sure could use the land you've got here, situated by the river as it is." His eyes slanted back to John.

"Like I said, I'm not selling at the moment." John walked to Judd's wagon with deliberate strides as if indicating it was time for the man to leave.

"I'll tell you what, Grigsby. If you change your mind, I'll up the price Charles Matthew's offered you. I can make it worth your while." He shoved his hat on and turned back to his wagon. Before he climbed into the seat he stretched out his hand again.

Clang! Clang! Clang! The clanging echoed across the yard and both men looked up to see Granville ringing the dinner bell hanging by the back door. The interruption gave John an excuse to step back, avoiding Judd's hand. He pushed his hat off his forehead with the tip of his finger. "I best get inside before supper gets cold."

Judd climbed into the wagon and pulled the reins free. The rig rolled forward, made a wide circle, and came back beside John. Judd gave him a sidelong glance before going out the drive.

John stood for a moment, watching the dust settle. Judd Benson was known for buying available land in the Grovespring area. Some folks were suspicious that Benson was to blame for their cattle missing—or worse, poisoned. When times were hard, Benson showed up to buy their land. He paid little and sold high.

"I wouldn't sell my land to you if you were the last man on earth," John muttered as he watched Judd Benson depart his property. "You can take that to the bank."

Chapter THREE

THE SOUND OF POUNDING hoofbeats cut through the air as four horsemen rode like the wind over the vast countryside. Shouts went out as the men spurred their mounts to go faster. "Don't let up! That posse's hot on our tails!" Jiggs Woodrow bellowed and lashed out a scalding stream of words.

On and on they went, winding through rutted roads, cutting through the woods and coming out the other side, hoping they'd lost the sheriff of Laredo and his posse. With shouts and with dirt flying, the horsemen rode hard to make their escape.

After looking back a half dozen times, Jiggs Woodrow finally called, "I think we lost them." He pulled up his mount and shouted, "Slow the horses down a mite." He ran a hand over his steed's neck where white lather slicked the horse's skin. The stallion snorted and shook his withers, making his bridle jingle.

The four horsemen reined in to allow their mounts to catch their breaths.

Jiggs' saddlebags bulged with cash concealed beneath the latches. The Woodrow gang had stuffed the bags quickly when they were behind the teller's counter at the bank in Laredo. They had threatened to kill anyone who didn't stay down and keep their faces to the floor. Duke had kept an eye on the customers while Otis and Joe filled the bags. Jiggs had stood by the door to make sure no one else came in. When the bags were full, the four men jumped onto their horses and raced out of town. It wasn't long before the law was hot on their trail.

"We'll hole up somewhere ahead until the heat's off," Jiggs said, turning in his saddle to face the three men riding single file behind him. "The last I saw of the posse, it was only about a mile back."

"Let's stay along the woods," Otis said in a deep voice. "If they show up we can easily lose them again."

The outlaw leader known as Jiggs Woodrow—a name chosen to keep his true identity a secret—was known as Alastair Stonewall in Independence, Missouri. Stonewall ran a lucrative cattle ranch, secretly expanding his livestock by means of cattle rustling and further increasing his income by robbing banks and stagecoaches.

He was a tall man in his late sixties, slenderly built with curly white hair that laced over his collar. He'd taken daring risks to enrich himself, at the expense of losing men in his endeavors and endangering his grandson, Duke.

After each robbery and roundup of cattle they rustled in neighboring towns that they herded back to his ranch, he promised himself it would be his last. It was time to put this lawless life behind him and enjoy the fruits of his labors. And he wanted a better life for Duke. Once the gang laid low for a time in the next town, he'd tell the men this was his last heist.

Duke, better known as Clarence Stonewall, lost his mother to typhoid fever when he was a young boy, and he lost his father to a gun fight in Kansas City a few years later. Hard luck had met the boy far too young and far too often.

With Duke having lost both parents, Jiggs took his red-headed grandson under his wing. Duke tagged along during the cattle rustling, but Jiggs encouraged him to keep a low profile and let the men do the dirty work. He wanted Duke to learn the trade of ranching—the right way. Duke had already told him he wanted to break horses and train them to wear a bridle and saddle. It was honest work and he could sell the well-trained horses.

Most of the horses at Stonewall Ranch were stolen. Duke could breed them and fill the corrals with new colts and fillies which, when they were old enough, he could train to be riding horses. Jiggs was glad that in time, Duke would have an honest job. But the truth was, it would still be based on stolen goods. He hated that he'd put his grandson in this position, but the business had been lucrative.

Now, with more people were going West, he knew the time was right to try to make an honest living. In Independence, he saw the endless lines of wagons coming through town, heading out each spring for Oregon. Duke could sell horses to them at a prime rate. Folks driving wagons West would always need fresh stock for the long trip.

Jiggs turned to the Murphy brothers, who also hid their true identities with false names. "Otis" was tall with a head of dark hair, handsome in a rugged sense. He was a looker and the women liked him.

At twenty-five, "Curly Joe" was high-strung. Why he chose the name Curly Joe baffled all of them because his hair was stiff and short and straight.

As Jiggs stared at Joe, a slow burn gnawed at him. The young man had been responsible for the bank robbery going wrong. They had a standing rule that no one would ever shoot to kill. Fleeing Laredo today was the first time they'd left a dead man behind.

Jiggs reined in his horse and let Duke and Otis ride on ahead. Joe started to ride past, but Jiggs moved his horse in front of Joe's steed.

"Something wrong, boss?" Joe asked.

"I've got a bone to pick with you!"

"Why's that?"

"You shouldn't have gun-downed that teller today. We've done good keepin' our hands clean from takin' any lives . . . until now."

"That man was goin' for his gun!"

"With seven people in the lobby, you know better than that," Jiggs barked back. "We had a pact! We agreed not to kill anybody!"

Joe's neck grew red, the color working its way to his face.

Jiggs glared at Joe for a long while. The only sound came from the horses chuffing and stomping their hooves. "You better never pull your gun out again or I'll skin you alive! You hear me?"

The two men held their breaths and waited to see who would back down first.

Finally, Joe muttered. "Yeah, I hear you, boss." The color deepened in his face and he hung his head.

"What are we going to do now?" Duke asked, having come back to see what was keeping his grandfather.

"We're goin' east.: Jiggs said. "We gotta high tail it out of this territory for a couple of months."

"You got a place in mind?" Otis asked.

"East!" Jiggs spat on the ground and his horse shied sideways. "I'll let you know where we'll land when I feel we've landed."

"What about the cattle we left out on the range south of town?" Otis asked.

"I'll telegraph Charlie and tell him to send Felix and the boys to go after them. There ought to be a telegraph office in the next town we come to."

"We'll have to get that done before ranchers figure out their cattle are missing." Joe relaxed in the saddle.

"Yeah, and with the cattle stranded north of the river, we can't waste time. They need water." Jiggs scowled.

Otis loosened his collar. It was high noon and the blue skies were free of clouds. "Talkin' 'bout water, we best find a creek. These horses have been pushed pretty hard." He shoved the brim of his hat off his forehead. "The way I see it, we've got three counties with riders lookin' for us now that Curly Joe shot that teller." He gave his brother a raw look.

After watering the horses at a near stream, Jiggs mounted his horse. "We're wasting time. Let's ride out!"

The men rode on for hours. The Murphy brothers rode side by side behind Woodrow and his grandson as the sun lowered to the hilltops. The charred—orange-red sunset scrawled ominously across the vast sky. It appeared the heavens were on fire. It wouldn't be long before dusk set in.

"It's gonna be dark soon," Jiggs said. "We best find shelter and build a fire. A cup of coffee sounds mighty good right about now." He nudged his mount toward a crest of rocks piled below the rising hills.

Duke appeared sullen as he rode alongside Curly Joe. "I thought you were gonna take me to see one of them girls at a saloon." His ears burned red.

"You ain't ready for nothing like that." Jiggs said, overhearing his grandson. He pulled back on the reins until Duke and Joe came up beside him. He spat on the ground between them. "You're still wet behind the ears."

Joe snickered. "The kid's gotta grow up sometime."

"He's right," Duke said, looking over at his grandfather, amusement in his eyes.

"Drop it!" Jiggs finalized the conversation. He kicked the stallion in the flanks and surged ahead of the other riders.

THE THREE MEN WATCHED dust kick up behind Jiggs' steed.

"Let him go," Otis said, looking over at Duke. "He's just being protective of you." A glint showed in his eyes.

"You've got some learnin' to do," Joe said. "Number one—you don't go advertisin' when you plan to see a soiled dove." He gave Duke a disgruntled look. "Get my drift?"

"Yeah, I get your drift." Duke kicked his gelding's side and rode ahead of the two brothers. The horse ate up the ground as he attempted to catch up with Jiggs.

Proud of his grandfather, Duke thought about the man who had shaped his life. Jiggs hadn't always been a cattle rustler. He'd been a hardworking man in his day. At sixty-nine, he still held his own.

Tall and handsome, Jiggs easily caught the eye of a woman. And being the leader, he carried the weight of the gang on his shoulders. Duke understood his grandfather's anger. They had a hard rule, a pact, about killing a man. Today, that rule had been broken.

Duke reined in next to his grandfather. He saw a look on Jiggs' face that he'd seen only one other time. They rode on in silence.

"It irks me," Jiggs finally said. "I might have to teach that boy a lesson."

Duke nodded, but he kept his mouth shut.

The two continued on, but behind them, Otis and Joe could hear them talking.

"Let 'em go," Joe said. "If we take our time, we'll arrive in time for a warm fire and hot coffee."

"Maybe," Otis said. "Unless Jiggs takes it upon himself to knock some sense into you."

"He wouldn't do that."

"You bet he would. Be lookin' for it when we get to camp."

"Maybe we should head out on our own."

"Not on your life, dimwit. He's got the money in his saddlebags, and if you turn away now, you won't get any of it."

"You'll keep him from hurtin' me, right?"

"We'll see. Come on, a hot cup of coffee sounds mighty good. It looks like we'll be camping for the night."

FOUR HORSEMEN RODE LAZILY down the middle of Main Street. The mid-morning traffic was heavy with wagons and, carts. Pedestrians threaded their way between the slow-moving rigs. The outlaws rode single file as the traffic milled around them.

"Not much to this town?" Duke scoffed. "It's just a hole in the wall."

"My kind of place," Jiggs said. "Small usually means peaceful . . . unless you get folks like us."

"Ain't too bad," Otis chimed in, riding behind the kid. "There's a joint up ahead where we can wet our whistles." They rode past a dry goods store and a mercantile on one side of the street. Horses were lined up at the hitching post across the road in front of the largest building in town. The sign in front read Yates Hotel and Café.

"I could go for a shot of whisky right about now," Joe said, reining his horse off to the side of the road in front of the saloon his brother had spotted.

"No whiskey 'til you boys get food in your bellies." Jiggs kept riding.

"THANK YOU FOR BRINGING in more eggs and milk, Mr. Grigsby. Seems I can't keep enough supplies on hand here at the café," Gertrude Yates said, following John Grigsby out of the kitchen.

"Oh, by the way, my chef said to remind you we're running low on beef. Could you have a hindquarter of beef ready for him to pick up in the next day or so?"

"Sure thing, Gertie. Tell him to come by the first of the week." John carried an empty milk can in each hand. "I'll bring in two more tomorrow. That ought to hold you over the weekend. How's that?"

"That would be wonderful. Eggs too, if you have them," Gertrude said.

John balanced the cans and nodded. "See you tomorrow." He stepped outside just in time to see four men riding down Main Street. He set the containers in the back of his wagon and looked over to see Sheriff Noah Ford standing on the boardwalk in front of the hotel. The four horsemen swung their horses in front of the café and stopped.

John Grigsby moved next to the sheriff. In the four years that he'd lived in Grovespring, he'd observed the older man becoming more complacent. Ford didn't wear his gun and holster anymore, not since he'd lost the use of his right hand. John suspected Noah Ford had been afflicted by a mild stroke. Folks didn't worry much about the absence of his firearms since the need for them rarely occurred. John had put off bringing up the subject of the sheriff not wearing a gun because the man was so darn likeable. Ford was gentle in spirit, but that hadn't kept the sheriff from being quick with a gun in his day. But those days were gone. More often than not, these days John found himself standing in as the sheriff's sidekick when the law was needed.

"Afternoon fellas." Sheriff Ford tipped his felt hat to the four men.

The oldest rider sat lazily on his horse and stared down at them. "Afternoon, yourself." His gaze swung to John.

John touched the brim of his hat and gave a slight nod. "Welcome to Grovespring."

"That be the name of this pee hole?" The red-headed teen asked.

John steeled himself. He wasn't one for obnoxious boys still wet behind the ears, but he restrained himself from knocking the kid off his horse and gave the teen a derisive smile. "You've got a point there. This here's a small town, but don't let its size fool you."

The sheriff laid his good hand on John's arm. "We're peaceable folks, fellas. Enjoy your stay."

"We plan to. Thank you, sir," the white-haired man said.

The other horsemen had been sitting quietly on their steeds, taking it all in. Now, the younger of the two leaned forward and asked, "You got any women over at the saloon?"

"That's enough, Curly Joe," barked the older man.

John gave the sheriff a warning glance.

Ford's mouth thinned, but his only response was a slight shake of his head.

"Grider's Saloon's a respectable establishment. You can get a drink or play a game of cards," John replied curtly. "But no women work there."

"You're outta luck." Joe punched the arm of the redheaded teen.

A woman for the kid? John gazed at the boy. He couldn't be more than sixteen. Annoyed he asked, "You men got business in town?"

"What's it to you?"

"Just asking," John said. "We get a lot of folks come through. But seeing as we're a small community, they don't stick around too long."

"We're lookin' for a room. Been on the road a while," the man said.

John slanted his gaze and sized up the white-haired man with the long lanky legs and slim torso. The man wore a black wide-brimmed hat emblazoned with silver metal around the crown. Hands clenched, John eyed the four men. The way they peered down at him with wary eyes gave him the sense that something wasn't right with these men. Until now, he hadn't noticed they all kept their hands on their holsters.

The oldest man spoke up. "Name's Jiggs Woodrow. We're looking for a meal, a bath, and whiskey—in that order."

A sign hung on the wall behind John, advertising the price of a bath for five cents.

John pointed at the sign then cut his gaze to the riders. "Looks like you're in luck." He looked down at the boardwalk and then at Jiggs, who seemed to be in charge. "Most folks mind their own business around here. See that you do the same."

Seeing the arrival of the horsemen, several curious store owners had stepped out onto the boardwalk and now watched as John addressed the strangers with authority.

"Who are you?" The red-headed teen glared at him.

"John Grigsby. And who would you be?"

"Duke Woodrow. Are you the sheriff?"

"No, just a concerned citizen of Grovespring." He looked over at Ford. "He's the sheriff." John put a hand on Ford's shoulder. "Sheriff Ford."

"He don't wear a badge?" Jiggs asked.

The sheriff glanced down at his dark shirt. "Not always. Folks here know who I am."

"You live here in town?" Jiggs turned his gaze back to John.

"Where I live is none of your business."

"Where I live is none of your business," the teen mimicked and drew his gun. "You'll do well not to get smart with him!"

John hadn't worn a firearm in a long while. Up til now, there hadn't been a need to. He swore under his breath. That was about to change.

Ford grimaced. "No need for that pistol, son."

"Put that gun away, Duke." Jiggs's ordered.

The teenager shoved his pistol into the holster and glared down at John.

"That café got any good food?" Jiggs asked.

"Best food in all of Missouri," John said, wishing the men would move on.

"We ain't got much cash, but we'll check it out." Jiggs dismounted and tied his horse to the hitching post. The others did the same, and the four men strode to the door of the café and disappeared inside.

John's gut twisted. "I don't like it. I don't know who those men are or what they're doing in town. Let's hope they fill their stomachs and then high-tail it out of here."

"We best be ready if they don't," Ford said. "Think I'll mosey on down to the jailhouse and put on my badge."

"I'm going to ride out to the ranch and dust off my firearms." John shot the sheriff a cool smile. "Let's hope those boys ride out of town in the morning."

LATER THAT EVENING, AFTER the sun went down, the Woodrow gang hung out at the saloon. Well after midnight, Jiggs Woodrow and his men stumbled out onto the street and mounted their horses. The moon was high, lighting the ground around them. Not familiar with the area, Jiggs pointed his horse east.

"What now, boss?" Otis asked as the four men rode out of town. "I thought we were going to get a room?"

"We'll camp out tonight. There's a cold nip in the air, but not enough to keep us from sleeping out by the creek." Jiggs glanced at each of the men to see if there were any protests. Seeing none, he continued on past the church and parsonage. They rode out of town at a gallop.

A half mile down the road they spotted a house and corral nestled at the base of a low hill.

"How about that ranch over there? It don't look inhabited." Duke Woodrow turned to his grandfather.

Jiggs reined in his horse at the crest of the hill. Looking down, he could see a large expanse of land, but no animals stood beyond the house and barn. "Don't see any animals out in the field, and come to think of it, I don't see any cattle or horses in the corral near that shack."

"Maybe the place is deserted," Otis said, riding alongside Jiggs.

"Let's check it out," Joe said.

"All right, let's go." Jiggs nudged the stallion and he moved forward, leading the gang down the hillside toward the buildings in the lowland.

The men were quiet when they approached the house and tiptoed to the windows to peer in. They walked to the far side of the building and looked behind the shanty. All was still except for the hoot of an owl in the distance.

The four men strode back to the front of the shanty. "Don't look like much," Jiggs said, trying the door handle. The door opened easily and pale moonlight lit the room. He stepped inside and scanned the rough wooden floor. A table and two chairs sat in the middle, and a stove sat in the corner with a chimney pipe leading out of the ceiling. Jiggs crossed the wooden floor and shoved a curtain aside on the far side of the room to find there were no beds—just empty space. Through the back window, an outhouse could be seen some distance behind the shack.

It was dark, but not so dark that he couldn't see that the house was rundown and needed work. Otis, Joe, and Duke waited to see what Jiggs wanted to do.

"All right, fellas. We'll spend the night here," Jiggs said.

Duke stared at the stark room and back at his grandfather. "There's no beds."

"We'll use our bedrolls." Jiggs said.

Duke strode out the door while the men followed and pulled their supplies off their horses.

Jiggs joined them. "The house is rundown a bit, but we won't be staying long. We've got a roof over our heads, an outhouse out back, and a corral to keep the horses. Everything we need for now."

"Whoever lived here before must be long gone. This place has an eerie feeling to it," Otis said, dropping his things on the floor before the wood stove. "It's a good thing they left firewood outside."

"Won't seem so bad after we get a fire going," Joe said, sinking down in one of the chairs at the table.

Moments later, Duke pushed the door open with an armload of chopped wood. He dropped it on the floor and opened the door to the wood stove. He pushed a couple of twigs onto the grate, and lit the kindling. It didn't take long for the fire to take hold. He added a chunk of wood, and soon the flames heated the room, the light creating shadows on the walls.

The crackling fire had a soothing effect on the four men. They'd had a full meal and a few drinks. It didn't take long before the younger men slept.

Jiggs mind preoccupied, he sat by the fire and gazed at the flames. First thing tomorrow morning, he'd have to see if Grovespring had a telegraph station. He needed to send word to Stonewall Ranch where the rustled cattle were stranded.

They had seen several cattle ranches on their way into Grovespring. Maybe they should round up a few head of cattle to add to his stock. They needed to hide out a few weeks before heading back to Stonewall Ranch. Was it possible they could stay here for a while?

Chapter FOUR

JOHN WENT TO THE house for the noon meal rather than the bunk house where Corky would have a pot of beans boiling in the fireplace, along with strips of beef frying in a skillet. He'd serve warm biscuits, too, but John wanted to check in on Nancy.

He opened the back door and started down the long hall toward the front of the house. He passed their bedroom, his boots clomping loudly on the hardwood floor. Tess jumped out from the living room with Wiley on her hip and pressed a finger to her lips. She pointed to the bedroom he'd just passed.

John stopped and turned around to peer into the bedroom. There lay his wife, sound asleep in the middle of the day. He quietly slipped into the room and hovered over her to watch her breathe. Long lashes rested against her flushed cheeks, and her yellow hair fanned across the pillow. Her breathing came soft and steady. She looked peaceful lying there, unaware that he looked on.

Good. I'm glad you allowed yourself some downtime and off of your feet. John retreated quietly from the room and continued up the stairs to the room that Granville, Franklin and Calvin shared. Their bedroom sat central to the upstairs and allowed a good view of the ranch.

It would be time to brand calves in another month. Six men worked for John on a steady basis, seeing to the cattle and horses, but during branding season, John and two other ranchers—Benjamin Shields and Charles Matthews—always pooled their hands and worked together.

John gazed out of the boys' bedroom window and off to the side at the bunkhouse behind the barn, he spotted Corky, their cook, standing outside. Corky was a wrinkled old man who'd traveled nearly 700 miles with the

Grigsby family from Blount, Tennessee, to Grovespring, Missouri.

John was grateful for Corky's decision to join them on that journey, because 700 miles was a long way to herd cattle without a cook. With all the hired cowhands required to keep the cattle and horses moving, he had needed a cook to feed them all. Once their wagon train had arrived in the small town of Grovespring, most of the cowpokes had gone on to Independence. But two of them had stayed on and moved with John to the ranch. In the early days, they had helped build the main house and stable. Now, Luke and Brady tend the cattle. Eventually, John had hired three more men to keep the ranch moving smoothly.

Back then Nancy and the children had lived out of the wagon and a large tent until the house was completed. Corky and the men had set up quarters in tents out on the range until they built the bunkhouse. One of the first jobs had been putting up the fences needed to mark the Grigsby boundary lines and to keep his cattle in. All hands had been busy that first year of 1837.

Now John stood near the window and looked out over the vast land he'd purchased with hard earned dollars. Gazing out at the Durham cattle grazing behind the barn and stable, and the horses in the corral, he heaved a contented sigh.

Moving away from the window, John glanced around the boys' simple room. A small desk sat before the window with a straight chair tucked beneath it. On each side were beds. Nancy had embroidered colorful, crisscross designs at the edges of their pillowcases. Wall hooks held their Sunday shirts and, on the floor, sat their Sunday shoes. A dresser sat against the opposite wall.

The floor creaked as John left the room and headed down the stairs. This wasn't the first time he'd used the boys' room to look out over the ranch. It gave him a perspective of his spread and the responsibility on his shoulders to keep it running like clock-work.

The land had been good to him, although the winters were harsh. Deep snowdrifts made it hard for the cattle to survive. Two more winters and he'd move his family and cattle to the land of milk and honey. He'd heard Oregon land was lush and green, and there was plenty to be had. He'd cash in on the ranch he'd built and use the money to start a new homestead. He'd replicate what he'd done here—and more. They'd be close to the ocean, where he could herd his cattle onto the wharf for sale. He'd thought it through a hundred times. Now, to convince Nancy it would be a good move.

LATE AFTERNOON THE FOLLOWING day, Calvin entered the kitchen, his face flushed and damp. "Mama. I'm done with chores. Can I go fishing at the creek?"

Nancy was bent over the table, rolling out flour dough. The first layer of pie dough lined a pan filled with sliced peaches. "Are you sure you're caught up with everything your dad wants done?"

"Yep." He slapped at a fly. "If you let me, I'll bring home some catfish for supper." He glanced out the kitchen door, where a pail filled with nightcrawlers sat on the porch. He was itching to get down to the bank and throw his line into the creek.

"All right." Nancy wiped her floured hands on her apron. "I've already got a roast in the oven, but catfish will make a welcome meal tomorrow night."

"Thanks, Mama!" Calvin glanced at the door.

"Don't stay long. You've got evening chores to tend to."

"I know." He grinned at her. "The last time I was down at the creek, those catfish were biting." He inched away. "They're waitin' for me."

"Go on, Calvin. I know they're waiting for you." She smiled down at him and ruffled his hair.

Calvin didn't pause a moment longer. He picked up the pail and grabbed his pole leaning against the door post. He strode across the yard, set the bucket on top of a gate post, and leaned his fishing pole against the fence. Then he went to the corral and led their mustang, Brownie, out to the yard. He mounted the horse and walked him to the post. where he picked up the pail full of nightcrawlers. He laid his fishing pole across his lap and went out the gate that led to the open prairie. Farther beyond the tall green grass, the creek called to him.

Although the landscape appeared flat, a small rise of land hid the water. But he could see the bottomland forest trees that lined the banks. The thick stand of cottonwood, silver maple, and white oak looked inviting on this sultry, hot day. The heat baked his back and his sweaty shirt stuck to him. Calvin gazed toward the shade of the woods. He nudged Brownie's flanks and quickened his pace to the edge of the trees, where he easily found the worn path that led to the creek.

Calvin ducked his head under low-hanging branches as he worked his way through the trail. It wasn't long before he heard the pleasant bubbling of water flowing down-stream over smooth rocks. "Come on, Brownie." He held the reins loosely, and walked his horse toward the mossy banks. The sound of rushing water filled the still air.

All along the banks the tree limbs hung low, creating dark shadows. In the middle the creek ran swiftly, and the water glittered over smooth rocks. He leaned to the side to look for catfish. He found them swimming near the muddy bottom, playing hide and seek with the stones clustered in the middle, their long, black whiskers waving in the water. Several catfish swam downstream as if they knew he was there.

Calvin slid off his horse and tied him to a branch of a cottonwood. Mud sucked at his boots as he reached the cool bank with fishing pole and pail in hand. After attaching a nightcrawler to his hook, he threw it into the water and found a stump to sit on. It wasn't long before he felt a tug on the line. As the water flowed over the slick rocks, he filled his gunnysack with three good-sized catfish.

The creek smelled of damp roots and mud. Black-and-white speckled woodpeckers and yellow warblers flew from limb to limb, and tiny animals ran in and out of the damp grasses and dried brush, rustling the leaves. The water danced merrily downstream, while a small pool circled lazily in a cove nearby. Water-bugs skated across the top, leaving tiny trails behind them.

Calvin's ears tuned in to the chorus of nature. As much as he wanted to stay longer, he knew he'd soon have to head back to the ranch house. He stood—then stopped. A rustling sound in the brush nearby caught his attention. "Who's there?" Calvin peered up and down the creek bank and toward the trees across the stream. A strange feeling slicked up his back, and the hairs on his neck stirred.

Brownie's ears flicked forward. Calvin jumped up and threw the gunnysack over the horse's back and stepped into the saddle. Horse and rider walked cautiously along the bank toward the trail that led back to the fields.

Boom! A rifle shot rang through the air nearby.

Brownie reared and shot forward. The pail flew out of Calvin's hand. The horse whinnied and galloped along the uneven bank.

"Whoa, Brownie!" Calvin clutched the reins and bent low to avoid the low-hanging branches.

Boom! There it was again. Holding the reins tightly, Calvin swiveled in the saddle to look behind him. Brownie shivered and leaped over a log lying in their path. At the same moment, Calvin turned back to watch the trail ahead, but a low limb came at him too fast to duck. The power of the blow sent shafts of pain to his forehead as he flew out of the saddle and splashed into the rocky creek. The world grew fuzzy as water washed over his face.

"H-help!" Calvin cried out. Pain drilled into his skull, and blood trickled into his eyes. Just as quickly, it was washed away by the creek water washing over him. "Help!" He slid farther into the stream. He couldn't find the strength to get up. The current pulled him through portions of the stream that were four-to-five feet deep. He coughed and sputtered, the world spinning out of control. "Dad! Mama!" The last thing he heard was Brownie's whinny and the pounding of his hooves fading into the woods.

Pain throbbed in his head as he slid underwater. He struggled against it but had no strength to fight. The current sucked him along as if he were a drifting log being tossed at will. The sharp pain pounding his skull pulled him under a dark cloud, along with the current. He fell into darkness, no longer resisting the depth. He couldn't fight anymore. He was too weak—too tired.

A WARM TONGUE LICKED his face. The sounds of the creek seemed distant. Instead, he heard a whimper and panting above him. When he opened his eyes, Calvin found himself lying flat on his back in the open field with a rust-colored dog—the ugliest dog he'd ever seen—standing over him. The dog pawed Calvin's chest and whimpered again. He licked his face and nosed Calvin's side.

"Easy boy. Get off of me." Calvin rolled onto his elbow and sat up. He stared at the splotches of red, black, and orange that covered the dog's coat. "You sure are a sorry sight."

The dog backed up and stood on all fours, his tongue hanging out of a happy grin. The stray turned toward the house and barked with his nose in the air.

"Hey, buddy. I'm all right. I just need to find Brownie." Calvin stood on wobbly legs and staggered a bit, his head pounding again. When he reached to touch his forehead, his hand came back with blood on his fingertips.

Calvin gazed at the ground where he'd lain. The grass had been mashed flat where it appeared he'd been dragged from the creek to this spot. Did this mangy-looking stray pull him out of the water?

The dog sat on his haunches and watched him, anticipation in his eyes.

"Where'd you come from, boy?" Calvin patted the dog's head. In the distance, he heard Brownie whinny. The horse ran out of the forest, the reins dragging on the ground. The mustang trotted toward him. The first thing Calvin noticed was the gunny sack of fish was gone.

Calvin groaned. "I guess we're not having catfish for supper tomorrow night." He waited for Brownie. The horse snuffled when Calvin grabbed the reins and began walking. The pounding in his forehead persisted as he walked toward the house. Every time he looked back, the stray was still on his heels. The scraggly looking dog looked as if he hadn't had a meal in a long while.

"I guess you can come with me." Calvin stopped to scratch behind the dog's ear. "We don't have a dog—and for good reason." He looked at the house beyond the pasture. "Mama's not fond of dogs, especially, strays. I guess she got bit by a stray dog when she was a little girl, the way she tells it."

Calvin took a few steps and then stopped again. "She might let you stay when I tell her you saved me from drowning." He patted the dog's head, thinking he'd found a loyal friend. His heart started pounding in rhythm to the pain in his forehead. Would his Mother let him keep the dog?

The sound of hoof-beats filled the air, and Calvin looked across the field to see his father riding his blue roan toward him. John's horse moved alongside Calvin. "What happened to you?" John slid off the horse and strode over to him. He tipped Calvin's chin up and stared at his forehead. "You're bleeding."

"I know." Calvin looked back at the woods. "I fell into the creek."

"How in tarnation did you fall into the creek?" His father's hand squeezed his son's shoulder in concern.

"Someone's shooting a rifle down there. The second shot spooked Brownie. He reared and I fell off. Next thing I knew, I was floating downstream."

"It's a good thing you were able to get out of the water. That's a nasty cut. You could have drowned." His father's brow drew into deep furrows.

"That's the thing, Pa. I didn't get out of the water. I couldn't. I just kept floating down-stream. Next thing I knew, I was laying in the field with this dog licking my face." Calvin patted the dog's head again. "I think he saved me."

"That mangy mutt pulled you out of the creek?"

"I don't know for sure. But there wasn't anyone else around when I woke up. Just the dog."

"When you woke up?" John's hand weighed heavy on his head. "Did you pass out?"

Calvin nodded and glanced down at the stray.

"Well, I'll be." His father stared at the dog with a glint in his eyes. If Calvin didn't know better, he thought he saw appreciation for what the dog had done.

"Well, come on. Your mother's frettin' cuz you're late for supper. She sent me out to look for you." John gazed at the dog. "You can come along, too."

A smile spread across Calvin's face and he squared his shoulders. Now to get his mother's approval to let him keep this mangy mutt.

Granville, Franklin, and Tess stood on the porch when Calvin and his dad came around the corner of the house. "Hey! Where'd you get that dog?" Granville jumped off the steps and ran over to the stray.

"Did I hear somebody say something about a dog?" Nancy stepped onto the porch.

"Look, Mama. Calvin brought a stray home." Tess eyed the rusty-colored dog with curiosity.

"Well, you can just take him back to where you found him!" Nancy's fists went to her hips.

"Nancy." John said.

"No, John. You know how I feel about dogs."

"Yes, I do. But I want you to hear Calvin out." He gently pushed him forward. "Tell your mom what you told me."

"Oh, for land sakes! What happened to you?" Nancy grasped Calvin's shoulders and inspected his forehead. "Into the house right now. I need to get you cleaned up."

Calvin looked at his dad, only to see his dad nod in agreement—and there was a glint in his eyes. "You heard your mom. Go on."

Nancy gently pushed Calvin forward. Before they went into the house though, she looked back. "And get rid of that dog!" She closed the door.

"Um, Mom?"

"Sit down. I want to get a better look at your forehead."

"Can't I keep the dog?"

"No! How many times do I have to tell you? No dogs."

"But Mom!"

"No. And that's that."

Calvin choked back tears. "He saved me from drowning in the creek. We can't just send him away!" The tears he'd held back spilled down his cheeks, and he swallowed the salty sting in his throat.

"What?" Nancy wrung out a rag and lifted his chin. She eyed the nasty cut on his forehead. "Start from the beginning, young man. What happened out there?"

Calvin gulped down the tears and told his story again. Just as he finished, his father walked into the kitchen, the stray close on his heels. Calvin swallowed a sob and hiccupped.

John gave Nancy a steady look, and a slow grin spread across his face.

"This stray saved our son from drowning. Let him stay, Nan. He looks like a keeper to me."

"Oh, John." A crease formed between her brows, and she crossed her arms over her chest. "That's the ugliest dog I've ever seen."

"Tell you what, son," John offered. "We'll keep him on a trial basis. If he proves to be a good dog, he stays, if not . . ." John shrugged.

Nancy's shoulders dropped and she let out a heavy sigh. "All right."

"Thanks, Pa! Thanks, Ma!" Calvin hugged the dog and then scratched him behind the ear. He glanced at the food on the table and said, "He's hungry too."

His mother's hand shot up and she pointed to the door. "He'll have to wait on the front porch until after supper. Then you can give him the leftover scraps. Until then, you best give him a bowl of water."

"Yes, ma'am!" Calvin's heart swelled. "Come on, Rusty."

By now the kitchen was filled with the rest of the family looking on. Franklin said, "That's a good name for your dog." With tongue in cheek, he asked, "Did you catch any fish?"

"You bet I did. I caught five . . . three twelve-inchers." Calvin stretched his arms out wide. "And two big ones." Then he shrugged. "I lost them somewhere down at the creek."

"Sounds like a fish story to me." Granville teased.

Calvin watched his brother struggle to keep a straight face and a giggle from his throat. But it was too late—the room erupted in laughter.

"Well," Calvin giggled. "Whoever's out there in the woods is gonna get free fish."

"Which reminds me," John said. "We best find out who's trespassing on our land."

Chapter FIVE

BY THE TIME NANCY'S swollen feet slid to the rag rug beside her bed, the sun had already risen over the outbuildings. She crossed the floor and brushed the lace curtains aside and did what she did every morning in the summertime. She pushed the window up to let the early morning breeze sift its way into the stuffy room. She gazed out to see the barn doors were open and knew full well that John was inside, milking their two cows, Bossie and Ginger. She looked beyond at the herd of cattle scattered across the still-green pasture, tugging mindlessly at the grass.

She ran her hand over her extended belly. It had grown even more in the past ten days. "Your daddy's a good man, little one. He takes good care of us." A rush of pride washed over her knowing John was a responsible man in every sense of the word. He arose every morning before the sun came up and began his day's work. He worked long hours near the ranch house and outbuildings and in the pastures where the cattle grazed.

The baby kicked hard in her womb, reminding her that he was ever present, ever waiting for the day she would meet this little one. But her body felt different with this baby. More times than not she found herself fretting whether everything would be all right. Would she be able to hold off from giving birth to this child until the due date? Fear of losing the baby consumed her.

Yet she felt reprimanded. The scriptures from the Good Book said, *For God hath not given us the spirit of fear, but of power, and of love, and of a sound mind.* She gazed down and splayed her fingers over her belly. *Lord, I must put my fears to rest . . . or I'll go crazy with all this worry.*

She closed her eyes and took in a deep breath and let it out slowly. *I trust*

You, Father, in whatever You have in store for me and this wee one. When she opened her eyes, she felt relief wash over her.

Nancy breathed in the fresh morning air and looked down at her stomach again. "I better get breakfast started. Your father will want to eat before he goes to town today. And I'll need to collect eggs from the chicken coop and get out my jars of peach jam," she murmured. "He'll be taking them to the general store." Nancy talked to her babies in the womb as if they understood every word she said.

Feet clomping down the stairs alerted her that she wasn't the only one awake. She ran a hand over her stomach again. "I best stop lollygagging. I've a houseful of mouths waiting to be fed."

JOHN THREW HIS HAND over his son's slim shoulder as they stepped outside the house. Calvin's dark brown hair had a tendency to fall over his forehead, and over the long hot summer, a new spray of freckles had spread across his nose and cheeks.

Once they finished the chores and ate breakfast, Calvin would run out to the field to see what he could find.

His son managed to find adventure in the nooks and crannies of the ranch nearly every day. Just this week he found a bird with a broken wing under a bush and a squirrel down by the creek that looked half dead from starvation. He brought them home in his burlap sack and was nursing them back to health. Knowing Calvin's heart for the down-and-out, John was hard put to keep up with him, and to curb the amount of critters he brought back to the ranch yard.

Granville and Franklin crept outside and quietly shut the back door. The four fell into step on the way to the barn. The world was quiet at this hour of the morning. John knew the animals in the stalls would awaken when he opened the barn doors. The cows, their udders full of milk would start bellowing.

"Are you going into town this morning?" Granville asked.

"Sure am," John said. "Why'd you ask?"

"I'm wondering if Mr. Owens still needs a delivery boy at the mercantile. I heard Jake left with the last wagon train that headed out of town."

"Delivery boy, huh." John gazed down at his son. "Are you thinking you want to earn some money?"

"If it's all right with you, sir."

Granville's thick golden hair tousled every which way. Nancy often said Granville reminded her of herself at his age. Not only in appearance but in his stance as well. He could be stubborn as a mule and just as hard to move if he didn't have a mind to. Yet, at the moment, his eyes, so dark a gold they hinted of amber, held a glint of hope that his father would allow him to work in town.

"School starts in a couple of weeks. And you'd still have to keep up your chores."

"I will, Dad. I promise." Granville looked up wistfully.

"Let me think on it." John ruffled the boy's mop of hair. "In the meantime, I'll ask Mr. Owens if he still needs a delivery boy when I drop off our supplies."

"Thanks, Dad!" Granville's eyes lit up as they neared the barn.

John opened the heavy doors. A warm, earthy scent of dirt and stock spilled from the darkness. The familiar smell met him every morning when he walked past the row of stalls. Horses snorted their greetings as John's boots crunched the dry, yellow hay. Something scurried into a dark corner. *Probably a mouse*, he thought, keeping an eye on the ground as he glanced around. "All right, boys. Let's get to work." He eyed Calvin. "The sooner you get your work done, the sooner you can play."

"Yes, sir." Calvin grabbed a metal can and dipped it into the feed barrel. He scooped out oat and dumped them in a bucket of water to make slop for the pigs.

Granville climbed the ladder to the hayloft to throw down clean hay for the animals. He tossed the bales and then clambered down to the barn floor. He and Franklin went to the stalls and began mucking out the old hay.

John turned a bucket upside down and sat on it. The barn kittens scrambled over and lifted on hind feet as they pawed the bucket in a chorus of meows.

"You'll have to wait your turn." John's deep voice echoed through the barn as he gently pushed them away and leaned into the cow's side, tugged on her teats, and began squirting milk into the pail. Bossie swished her tail, swatting away the flies. There was plenty of milk in the house, and there'd be plenty to take to town. The buckets from the night before had been poured into milk cans and stored in the spring house waiting to be delivered to the general store and the hotel's café in town.

An hour later, with the milking done, John dumped a small measure of oats into the grain box in Blue's stall. He stopped to stroke Blue's neck. The roan was strong and muscular, his black coat intermingled with white hairs, creating an optical illusion that the stallion's coat was blue. His lower legs, mane, and tail were pitch black. Blue snuffled and reared his head as if ready to meet the day.

"I'd take you out for a run, but I'm going into town." John ran his hand over the horse's velvety nose. Then he pulled a carrot out of his pocket. "Forgive me?"

Blue leaned over the stall and accepted the carrot, munching loudly, but he kept his eyes on his owner. A splinter of sunlight shown through the rafters and spilled across the horse's face.

"Are you boys done here?" John strode back toward the opened barn doors.

"Calvin's been done. We're gettin' ready to put the cows out," Granville said, dusting hay off his pant legs.

Franklin had stayed quiet the whole time the boy's worked. John eyed him now. *Did he want a job in town too?* John shoved his hat back. "All right. Your mama's sure to have breakfast ready." He watched as Granville and Franklin led Bossie and Ginger out of the barn to graze. Ginger seemed eager to go when Franklin opened the gate, but Bossie just moseyed along.

"Come on you lousy cow." Granville tried to hurry her along, but she wasn't having it. He slapped her black-and-white rump then lifted the gate lock in place after she clumsily ambled through the gate. Ginger hurried on to join the cattle in the field, while Bossie stood still, seeming undecided as to where to go now that the choice was hers. "Dumb animal," Granville said, striding back to where John stood.

"Don't let your mother hear you say that. Bossie's her prize cow." He ruffled Granville's hair. "Come on, breakfast is waiting."

An hour later, John shoved milk cans into the back of the wagon. Then he loaded a box of Nancy's peach preserves. Last, he took the basket of eggs she held out to him and sat them between the wall of the wagon and box of supplies. "Mr. Owens sure is going to be happy to see me." John climbed into the wagon seat.

"Be sure to ask him if there's any mail. I've written a letter to Mother. I hope to hear from her soon."

"Sure thing." He glanced at the blazing sun rising over the buildings and then down at Nancy. "You sure are a pretty sight, Mrs. Grigsby."

She looked down at herself and laid a hand on her swollen belly. "Even when I look like this?" Her cheeks burned red.

The sun shone on her thick, flaxen-colored hair, shedding light on its silky strands. When Nancy pulled it into a tight bun at the nape of her neck, the weight of her hair brought on headaches, so she let it hang loose more often than not, and it cascaded down her back. When it was loose, it was tempting to run his hands through the shiny locks. He shook his head and smiled down at her. "I better get this rig to town. And yes, you're beautiful even with our child growing inside of you."

John shifted on the wooden seat and slid his hand to the gun and holster at his side. With the Woodrow gang in town, he had an uneasy feeling he'd need it. It had been a long time since he'd felt the need to wear a firearm, but good judgment told him to be on guard. The gang's appearance could be nothing, but a man should be prepared. He hoped he wouldn't have to use the weapon.

COCK-A-DOODLE-DOO!

Mahala's eyes snapped open and she slid out of bed at the sound of the rooster's crow. "Goodness gracious! I've got to get dressed and get to work!"

As the pale dawn light crept over the ranch, Mahala poured water into the china washbasin and took a towel from its hook beside the window. She splashed water on her face and toweled herself dry.

She felt as if she hadn't slept a wink after the rough night of tossing and turning in bed. Try as she might, she couldn't rid her mind of the snooty looks cast her way yesterday. Three young women striding down the boardwalk had glanced her way as she left the tailor shop. Their heads were bowed and they spoke in hushed tones, but she hadn't missed the curt remark one of the ladies had whispered. "There's the town's spinster."

Mahala's cheeks had burned red hot as she crossed the road to the other boardwalk, where there was less pedestrian traffic and where she continued on her way to the mercantile.

Little did they know that today she would post a letter to Mr. Alexander Bates, a man who'd placed an ad in the newspaper for a mail-order bride. She had read his ad the day before and, for the first time considered this might be the only way out of being a spinster. Mr. Bates lived in Pennsylvania and was looking for a wife. A father of three boys—ages three, five and seven—the article said he was a widower who could send for a prospect bride by stagecoach. Mahala's heart had thumped in her chest. Should she answer the ad? She had written down the man's address on a piece of paper and set it aside. But after much thought throughout the day, Mahala sat down the night before and wrote a response to Mr. Bates' request. She remembered the words by heart.

Dear Mr. Bates,

I believe I may be just the woman you are looking for. I am a Christian woman, honest and able. I have never been married and have no children of my own. If you are interested in knowing more about me, please send a reply.

Most sincerely,

Mahala Shields

She folded the parchment and stared at the locket sitting on her desk. The framed picture had been painted three years earlier, but it was still reminiscent of her likeness. The silver locket had sat in her vanity all this time in hopes that someday she'd find someone to be endeared by, someone she could give it to. But as of yet, that hadn't happened. She slipped the locket into the folds of the letter and slid the parchment into the envelope. Feeling a bit ridiculous for what she was about to do, Mahala sealed the letter with wax. Today she would deliver the letter to the post office in Mr. Owen's mercantile. She knew it could take months for Mr. Bates to receive her letter, as mail sometimes took months to reach its destination, but as far as she was concerned, she'd taken the first step to ending her life as a spinster. Now it was up to Mr. Bates.

For the hundredth time, Mahala examined her trim figure as she readied herself for work. She stood sideways in front of the long mirror and frowned. *Would she never have a womanly figure?*

"Pfft! I'm as straight as a birch tree, and just as plain. There's not one thing about me that stands out," she murmured. She stepped into her skirt, pulled it to her waist, and buttoned it. "It's no wonder I've never been courted."

She cursed her looks and groaned. Her cleft chin stood out like a sore thumb. Her father, brothers, and *she* had inherited the Shields' cleft chin. How her sisters had escaped the curse she didn't know. Mahala buttoned her starched-white blouse scrutinizing her face. Her mother had berated her for complaining about her features. "Oh, Mahala," her mother often said. "You are a beautiful woman. The cleft in your chin is so slight I don't think anyone even notices it. You're making far too much of it." Well, maybe she was. She bolted for the door. She was going to be late if she didn't hurry.

Mahala crept out the back door hoping not to awaken her mother and sisters. She still lived at home with her parents. Thank goodness she had her job at Thompson's Tailor Shop. The work there was gratifying and kept her hands busy.

Five years earlier she had become a seamstress, and Grady Thompson made men's clothes. Together, they made a good team and supplied their small town's necessary needs for custom clothing.

"Good morning," Benjamin Shields said, coming out of the barn. "You're up early."

"I'm way behind on my work," Mahala told her father. "I may be home late tonight."

"Now don't wear yourself out. You stop when Grady does." Her father gave her a concerned look.

"I can't, Father. The ladies in town will never forgive me if I don't have their dresses ready for the harvest festival."

"You've got four weeks before the event." He kissed her forehead and gently shoved her shoulder. "Go on. You're stubborn as a mule when you want to be."

Mahala smiled. "See you tonight."

Charlie had the buggy ready, the horse, Dan, standing patiently in his harness, when she reached the stable. But he wasn't standing by the wagon when she came through the double doors. She found him hunched low in the corner of the barn, crooning to their barn cat, Blackie. Though she was in a hurry, Mahala couldn't help but peek over the stableman's shoulder to find they had a new litter of kittens. Four tiny fur balls kneaded their mama's stomach as they gorged themselves with milk.

"Oh, Charlie, look at the darling little babies!"

Charlie stroked Blackie's head. "Want to hold one?"

Mahala's hand flew to her chest. "I would love to, but I'm already late for work." She gazed a second longer at the new additions to the barn animals before she turned and stepped into the buggy. A slight breeze blew as she slapped the rein against Dan's broad back and the buggy moved onto the road toward town. Ahead, the Hollow Creek bridge came into view. The covered bridge, painted barn-red, was easy to see in all kinds of weather. The creek bubbled and danced as the buggy wheels echoed over the wooden floor. When she reached the other side a hot gust of wind blew her hair into her face. Tossing her long curls over her shoulder, she grinned. Well, at least her hair was the one true gift God had blessed her with. She'd received many a compliment for her dark silky hair.

"Giddy up!" She flicked the reins and continued down the lane. Far ahead, town was just a small dot. But the dot grew until she finally rolled passed

Thompson's Tailor Shop. Grady was sweeping the boardwalk as the buggy went by. He looked up and she waved. "Good morning, Mr. Thompson." She continued on to the livery, where the stableman cared for her horse during the day.

"Mornin', Miss Shields," Lyle Weaver said as she pulled back on the reins to slow Dan to a stop. "I'll take yer rig from here."

"Thank you, Mr. Weaver. I'm a bit late this morning." She stepped down and brushed the wrinkles out of her skirts. "I'll return late this afternoon."

"Good enough." He stared at her for a long moment.

Mahala quickly walked across the road. She'd known for some time that Lyle Weaver wanted more from her than being his patron. He'd asked her from time to time to join him on a Sunday ride or a picnic. Truth was, she had no interest in him as a prospective husband and had no intention of leading him on . . . even if she was the town's only spinster. She lifted her skirts as she stepped onto the boardwalk and hurried past the general store toward Thompson's Tailor Shop.

Grady held a broomstick in hand and peered down at her. "This is the second day in a row you've come into town late. Is everything all right, Miss Shields?"

"Yes, Mr. Thomson. I woke up late again. And don't ask me why. I don't want to talk about it." She scurried past him and pushed the door open. The cowbell on the door jangled as she went in, and the smell of fabric met her nostrils. Once inside, her shoulders relaxed. She never tired of the scent of the cloth that filled the shelves. She walked to the back where her sewing machine sat on a long table near the window overlooking the street. The table was strewn with a pile of gowns waiting for finishing touches.

Not one for cramped dark spaces, Mahala had requested Mr. Thompson allow her to place her sewing table near the window. Watching the pedestrians as they passed by helped to pass the time while she worked. She had a view of the vast sky and the changes of weather each season, too. If one must be stuck indoors all day, at least getting a bird's eye view of the outdoors helped immensely.

Mr. Thompson gave her ample room in her corner. Not only did she have a long table to work on, but she had also set a tall screen near the back wall for her customers to stand behind for fittings. Along the far wall were shelves with bolts of material of every kind needed for the day's fashions.

At the moment, there weren't enough hours in the day to finish the dresses for the harvest festival. Just yesterday, two more women had scurried into the shop pleading with her to take on the task of making their gowns. *What was going on?* In the past most of the women who needed a seamstress to make a special gown, had traveled the forty-eight miles to Springfield. It gave them the opportunity to visit a larger city and to see the latest fashion of the day. The trip also meant staying at a hotel and visiting a fine cafes with delectable food not available in Grovespring. It was a known fact that Grovespring was a small community and often behind in the times.

"I better get to work," Mahala breathed softly. She picked up the first gown and examined her handiwork. She soon settled into sewing tiny pearl buttons down the back of the dress. At mid-morning, she heard the cowbell over the front door tinkle and looked up to see Flora and Caroline Benson hurrying over to her, looks of concern on their faces. Mahala schooled her features and set down her work.

"I brought Caroline in like I said I would." Mrs. Benson gazed at her daughter as if she were a prize to behold.

"Good morning, Caroline." Mahala stood with a strained smile. She picked up her measuring tape and glanced over the young woman's slim, but curved figure. "Come stand over here where I can get a better look at you." Mahala swept away loose strands of material with her foot. She'd been cutting a dress from a pattern before the two women arrived and bits and pieces of material littered the floor.

Caroline's brows drew together as she stepped forward. "How long have you been a seamstress?" She looked around at the mess on the floor. "I want my dress to be done right."

"Yes," Mrs. Benson said forcefully. "We want Caroline to outshine all the other women at the dance."

"I'm sure she will. The material you've chosen is exquisite and your daughter has a fine figure. You have nothing to worry about." She gently pushed Caroline's arms up and leaned in to wrap the measuring tape around her waist. She jotted down the measurements on a scrap of paper and continued measuring the rest of her.

Mrs. Benson seemed to relax at Mahala's remark, which in turn helped Mahala's nerves to calm.

"Mother." Caroline turned to face the two women. "I asked how long she's been a seamstress. I can't afford to take any chances."

"We don't have any choice, dear. We've run out of time to go to Springfield. It's a two-day ride at best. Miss Shields will have to do."

Mahala's cheeks burned as she listened to mother and daughter carry on as if she were not there listening to their conversation.

"You *will* make it a priority to get our dresses done, won't you?" Flora's tone held an edge to it as she stared at Mahala.

"First come, first served, Mrs. Benson. That has always been my policy." Mahala's shoulders lifted a tad. She wouldn't allow the Benson women to intimidate her.

"Very well. Caroline . . . we best leave if she's to get our dresses done in time for the dance." Mrs. Benson laid a hand on her daughter's back and the two left the shop.

Mahala moved to the window and watched them make their way down the boardwalk. Just outside the store, a poster advertised the Harvest Dance. Mahala read it again for the umpteenth time.

Saturday, September 25th, at 6:30 P.M.

HARVEST DANCE

TRIPLE M RANCH

LIVE MUSIC 7 P.M.

BARN DANCE 7:00 to LATE

WHERE: 1 Mile West of Main Street

She glanced down the boardwalk where the Benson women were stepping into their carriage and sucked in a heavy breath. "I'm glad that's over." Her brows puckered together. "They'd die if they knew how hard pressed I am to finish the gowns I'm already committed to." Why had she taken on sewing gowns for the Benson women? Of all the women in Grovespring, these two women were the most difficult to please. Mahala's shoulder's tensed. Should she run after them and tell them there was no way she could complete their gowns in time? She hugged herself and tapped the toe of one shoe on the hardwood floor and frowned. No. She'd finish the gowns if it was the last thing she did. She had a reputation to defend, didn't she?

Chapter SIX

JOHN PULLED HIS RIG up in front of Owen's Mercantile. He tied the reins around the brake post and jumped down. He cut a glance over to Clyde Benson, Judd Benson's seventeen-year-old son, who stood on the boardwalk outside the store. Clyde leaned against the building as he listened to idle conversation from his friend Jimmy Radburn. As they talked, Clem Owens swept the walkway in front of his store, pushing the dirt out onto the street.

Clyde stepped away from the building and shoved his hands in his pocket. "Well, looky here. If it isn't John Grigsby." He slanted a look at his buddy with a smirk.

John touched the brim of his hat, pretending not to notice the antics of Benson's boy, and gazed at Clem. "Good morning, Owens."

"Mornin', Grigsby." Clem picked up his broom and carried it into the store. He set it against the wall behind the counter. Then he slipped the neck loop of a sturdy apron over his head and knotted the ties behind his back. "I see you brought goods for sale in the back of your wagon. Let's have a look at what you've got."

The two men walked out to the buckboard. Owens smiled brightly. "Good, good. I was hoping you'd bring in some of Nancy's peach jam. Let me give you a hand with these boxes." Owens reached for the box of jam and John lifted the basket of eggs from the back.

"Do you need milk?" John asked.

"You bet I do. I'd have my delivery boy help you carry in the milk cans, but he left town with the last wagon train."

"Are you hiring?"

"I should. Folks are grumblin' 'bout not gettin' their goods delivered."

He ran a hand over his face. "Do you know of any boys lookin' for work?"

"I do. My son Granville approached me this morning. He wants the job."

"Granville?" Owens glanced out across the street and back. "He's a fine boy. How old is he?"

John chuckled. "Twelve going on eighteen."

"Send him to my store," Owens said. "I'll have a talk with him. No guarantees, though."

"Of course." John followed Owens into the store. He set the basket of eggs on the counter. "Do you have a box I can transfer these into?"

"Hold on, I have a crate to put them in." Mr. Owens wheeled out of the room and disappeared into the back room.

John headed outside to grab a milk can. When he stepped behind the wagon, Clyde glared at him. At seventeen, the boy was a rebel with a cocky stance. He snickered and glanced over at his buddy Jimmy, and ribbed him. Then he gave John another slanted gaze.

Jimmy pushed away from the wall. "You missin' any steers Mr. Grigsby?"

John whipped around and stared at the two boys. "What are you talking about?"

Clyde gave Jimmy a harsh shove and his ears grew red. "Watch your mouth Jimmy."

"He's gonna find out anyway," the young man said defensively.

John shoved his hat back with the tip of his finger and strode up to Clyde. "You got something to say to me?"

"No, sir." Clyde swallowed and took a step back, darting a look at his friend, as he licked his lips. "I don't need this. I'm outta here." He glared at his buddy. "See you later, Jimmy. For now, stay away from me." Clyde stomped away and headed down the street.

Jimmy stared at John then thumbed a finger at the departing Clyde. "Benson's hot. He didn't want me to say anything, but if I were you, I'd look around your ranch. You might find some dead cows." He spat on the ground and walked away.

This wouldn't be the first time Benson and his boy were accused of killing steers in Grovespring. Thing was, no one could prove it. John knew Benson wanted his land in a bad way. And if Judd Benson didn't get his way, things happened. John had 900 acres of prime property with a river and creeks flowing through his land.

John stared at Clyde's back and flexed his fists. He walked back to the wagon and jerked the milk can toward him with more fervor than he'd intended. He heard the milk splash inside the metal container. "No good rotten kids. They better not have touched my steers." He swung the can down alongside his leg and carried it into the store.

Mr. Owens had counted the eggs and stored them in a crate next to the peach preserves on the counter. "I'll take that milk back to the icebox," he said as John walked in.

John let Owens pull the can out of his grip. Seeing the empty milk cans from the last delivery sitting in front of the counter, he picked them up and strode back to the wagon. His gaze searched the road for the rowdy teenagers who had just left. They were gone.

"You all right, Grigsby?" Mr. Owens walked out, eyeing him curiously.

"I'm not sure. My boy heard gunshots out by the creek yesterday. I haven't had a chance to check it out." He gazed down the road. "I think it's time I do."

"Well, come inside. I'll tally what I owe you."

"All right." John clamped his lips tightly together and strode back inside the mercantile. "Any mail? My wife's expecting a letter."

"I don't think so. Let me look." Owens bent behind the counter and checked the cubbyholes where mail would be if it had come. "Not yet, Grigsby." He counted the eggs and jars of peach jam, noted the milk cans and tallied it all on a piece of paper. Then he opened a drawer under the counter and counted out a couple of bills. "Here you go. Tell Nancy I appreciate her making that jam. Folks look forward to buying it."

"Sure thing. I best get on back to the ranch." He shook Owens' hand. "I'll see you in a couple of days." He wheeled around and headed for the door.

"Send Granville in, Grigsby. I could use his help."

"You got it." John strode out the door and raised a hand to wave goodbye. He climbed into the wagon and unwrapped the reins from the brake post. "Dadburn it! Benson better not have killed any of my cattle. If he did, he'll pay!

As John gazed down the road, he spotted the four horsemen he'd seen a few days ago. "They're still here?" he grumbled. He absentmindedly touched the firearm at his hip, and waited for the men to ride up alongside his wagon.

Jiggs gave him a curt smile when his horse ambled near. "Afternoon, Grigsby," Jiggs said.

"Afternoon," John replied. "I see you're still here."

"Got a problem with that?" Jiggs frowned. He shifted and his saddle creaked. "Me and my boys have been keepin' a low profile here."

John perked up at his comment. "A low profile?—Why?"

Jiggs sidestepped his horse and his eyes flickered. John didn't miss the body language of the men sitting on their mounts. Their backs stiffened and they glanced about them as if worried folks were listening in on their conversation. Otis trained his eyes on John.

"Just makin' conversation, mister," Jiggs said in a deep timbered tone.

Gertrude Yates, known to most of the town folks as "Gertie" hadn't said whether the men roomed at her hotel, and John hadn't asked. Narrowing his gaze on Jiggs, John figured now would be as good time as any to find out. "Where're you men staying while you're in town?"

"Got us a place outside of town." Jiggs chewed on a match stick.

John came to attention and pushed his hat off his forehead. "Where might that be?"

"Deserted ranch east of here," Jiggs thumbed his finger to the right. "We came to town for supplies from the mercantile. Now, if you'll excuse us, me and my boys have business to tend to."

Were they holed up out at Judd Benson's deserted ranch that lay a mile and a half out of town? John decided to let it go. He'd meant to see Sheriff Ford while in town. He didn't rightly know why these men disturbed him, but if there was one thing he'd learned from the past, if something niggled him, it was best to get to the bottom of it. Something told him these men were trouble. He had a family to protect and a town he cared about. He wouldn't ignore the caution that prodded him. He wanted to find out more about these men. If they needed to be run out of town, he'd be the man to do it.

"WHOA! BROWNIE!" JOHN BROUGHT the wagon to a halt in the barnyard and climbed down.

Granville ran out to meet him. "Did you talk to Mr. Owens?"

"Sure did, son. He wants to talk to you."

"Can I ride into town now?"

"No. Brush Brownie down and put him away. I'm going to saddle Blue."

"Yes, sir." Granville's shoulder's sagged as he unhitched the horse and led him into the stable.

John ruffled his son's hair as he passed by. "Tell you what. You can go into town after you tend to the horse. Take Star. He needs the exercise."

"Thanks, Dad!" Granville strode over to the wagon to unhitch the horse.

John strode to the row of stalls. Blue spotted him coming and nickered. "I see you, boy. Are you ready for a run?" John opened the gate and led Blue into the spacious breeze way. Blue's ears pricked forward and he snuffled, eager to go outside. "Hold still." John wiped down the roan's back with a few strokes to smooth down the hair. Then he swung a blanket over his back and set the saddle into place. Lastly, he tightened the cinch. "Come on, buddy," John said in a deep voice. "We've got to find out if anyone's been trespassing on our land." He took hold of Blue's bridle and led the mustang out to the yard.

Calvin ran out the back door. "Where you goin', Pa?"

"I'm riding out to the creek to give Blue a good run."

"Can I come?" Rusty ran to Calvin, wagging his tail. "How you doin', boy?" Calvin dropped to his knees and threw his arms around the dog's neck. He looked up. "Can I come, Dad?"

"Not this time, son. You stay here and help your mother. I bet she's got plenty to keep you busy." He gave Calvin a crooked smile.

"All right." Calvin pushed to his feet. "Where's Franklin and Granville?"

"Frank's out on the range, moving cattle with the cowhands, and Granville's in the barn, brushing Brownie down. Why don't you see if you can help."

John swung his horse toward the pasture, nudged Blue's flanks and started out in a gentle canter. He hadn't gone too far before he heard Rusty barking.

John turned in his saddle to see Rusty running behind him, the dog's tail wagging happily as he ran behind.

"Are you coming along, old boy?" John slowed his horse.

Rusty's tongue hung out and he looked as if he had a wide grin and his tail wagged harder.

"Well, come on. I could use your nose while I'm checking out the creek."

His Durham cattle speckled the pasture in red, black and white. They didn't pay any mind to John entering their territory. He rode over the yellow grasses and gazed at the herd, looking for anything unusual. He felt a oneness with his horse. Blue knew what John expected of him and in return John gave utmost respect to this gentle beast.

The path that led down to the creek was just ahead. The trail was worn from years of passage as he and the boys went through the grove of dense trees to and from the fishing hole. A touch of the reins turned the horse into the tunnel of trees.

The leaves crunched under the horse's hooves as they rode on. All the while, John listened keenly to the sounds in his surroundings. He peered through the thick stand of trees to his left and right, his body rigid. Birds flitted overhead and chirped a chorus of songs as he rode Blue deeper into the woods. Rusty followed close behind.

It wasn't long before John heard the sound of running water as he came to the cool bank where the sun's rays sent a million diamonds dancing over the creek. He turned away from the brightness and zeroed in on the opposite bank, looking for anything unusual. Blue's hooves were muffled now as he stomped over the thick, damp leaves scattered on the ground.

A rustle in the bushes on the far side of the creek alerted John. He felt the hairs on his arms rise and he held the mustang steady. Rusty's ears pricked up. John pulled on the reins and waited. A moment passed before a doe and her fawn crept down the side of the bank to the water's edge. The doe drank thirstily and lifted her head to stare at the brush in front of John and his horse. She darted a look his way, and then she and her fawn scampered away, disappearing in the thick foliage.

John relaxed in the saddle and pushed the brim of his hat off his forehead. "Where'd Calvin hear that shooter?" He ran a hand over Blue's neck and patted him. They continued on along the bank, carefully picking their way among the rocks strewn on the ground. A shiny object up ahead caught his attention. He nudged his horse on and then stopped and swung out of the saddle in an unhurried manner and crossed the stretch of ground, methodically pulling off his gloves. He walked over and picked up the bucket that had once held Calvin's nightcrawlers. The gunnysack of fish was nowhere to be seen.

Blackbirds flew high overhead in a circle, sailing in the wind, farther downstream, John mounted his horse again and they walked along the trail. Then he smelled it—a foul, offensive odor filling the air. He bent to peer through the low-hanging limbs blocking his way. More blackbirds flew into the air, alerted by his presence. He nudged Blue's flanks and pushed him slowly, and horse and rider crept near a bush and gazed over the water to see a large mass of birds swarming over the carcasses of two, swollen, dead cows. A vile stench filled the air and hung over the water.

"Ahh no!" John cried.

Rusty growled and splashed through the stream toward the birds that hovered over the dead cows. He barked and barked, scattering the crows, and ran in circles, sniffing the area. He circled the cows and whined.

The two cows lay near the creek, where flies buzzed around them. John tied Blue's reins to a cottonwood and waded across the stream. He stared down at the decaying beasts. Large gaping holes showed between their ribs. Crows crawled over the animals pecking and ripping skin from the carcasses. "Get out of here!" John waved his arms to rid the area of birds. He reached a hand to his back pocket and pulled out a handkerchief and held it to his nose as he examined the ground near the dead animals. Hoof prints led away from the creek and into the woods leading to the boundary line of Benson's ranch. John swore under his breath. Did Judd put Clyde up to this? He remembered the uncomfortable look on Clyde's face at Jimmy's remark earlier that day.

John pulled his hat off and slammed it against his pant leg. "Dadburnit!" The breeze ruffled his sweaty hair. He peered ahead at the creek that wound farther across his land. Shoving his hat back on, he retraced his steps across the water to find Blue munching the green grass.

"Come on, boy. Let's see if there's any more damage." When he'd gone as far as he could along his property line, he nudged Blue and rode out of the forest and back onto open land. He continued onto the road between his and the Shields' land.

Benjamin Shields' family had also traveled from Tennessee to Missouri. The Grigsbys and Shields had made the trip together back in 1837. When they came to the Missouri, they spread out and bought land, some of which butted against each other.

John had a lot of respect for Mahala's father. He was an honest rancher who took pride in his Herefords. Benjamin was in the business of raising cattle to sell to ranchers in the West. He recently sold steers to a Texas rancher interested in his breed. Mahala's brothers worked on their father's ranch. They had homes nearby and rose early each morning to work on the ranch. It was a family affair.

John spotted Benjamin Shields sitting on his horse in the field and waved at him.

Ben rode his horse from the pasture to where John sat with the reins wrapped around the saddle horn and Rusty standing nearby.

"Afternoon, Grigsby." Benjamin sat up straight. "Anything wrong?"

"Sure is. Have you noticed anything suspicious on your land?"

"Not lately. I heard gun shots south of here a few days ago. Seems it came from down by the creek. I rode my horse downstream and checked it out but didn't find anything unusual on my land. Did you find something?"

"I did. I just rode Blue down to the creek. I've two dead steers that are nearly gutted crows. Both of them were shot in the head."

"Oh, no!" Ben gasped. "Are they in the water?" He jerked his head to look toward the edge of the trees and gazed south.

"Luckily, no. They were shot down away from the creek. Good thing, or I'd have to have my men drag them out."

"So somebody shot your steers." He shook his head and ran a hand over his face. Then, almost as an afterthought, he added, "Not good."

John gazed back toward the trees, irritation gnawing at his gut.

"Who do you suppose is responsible for that evil deed?" Ben shifted in his saddle.

"It can only be one person is my guess."

"Benson?"

"You've got that right. I found horse tracks leading toward his property." John sat upright. "Thing is, I think his boy, Clyde did the dirty work for him."

"How so?"

"I ran into Clyde and his buddy, Jimmy in town this morning. Jimmy intimated that I check on my stock to see if I had any dead cows. Clyde scowled at Jimmy and left. It made me suspicious enough that I came home to check it out. Sure enough, I've got two steers down. They'll be skeletons in the next day or two." He frowned and gazed at Ben. "We've got to put a stop to this."

Ben brought his horse alongside John's. "If I find any of my steers shot by Judd or any of his men, there'll be hell to pay!"

"I'm all for making Benson pay for his ill deeds. Problem is, we have to prove he did it."

"Well, you just said Clyde's buddy all but admitted Clyde was the culprit responsible for shooting your steers." Ben's brows drew together.

"That's not actual proof. But if I can prove Benson did it, he won't get away with it. You can bet on that," John said.

"I best get on back to my herd. I'll keep an eye out for anything out of line." Ben touched the brim of his hat.

"Thanks, Ben." John reined Blue onto the road. They galloped toward his ranch, and the horse's mane flared out as the wind blew through it. John didn't know how he'd prove Clyde Benson shot his cows. He'd found hoof prints leading to the Bensons', that ought to count for something. But could he prove Benson was responsible?

Chapter SEVEN

NANCY WATCHED THROUGH THE window as Mahala stepped down from her buggy and approach the house. The autumn wind rustled her dark hair and skirts, telling Nancy she'd better don something warm for today's work.

"Are you ready to work in the garden?" Mahala hugged herself as she came to the edge of the porch as Nancy stepped out to greet her.

"I've been ready since I woke up this morning. We've an abundance of vegetables that need to be picked. I'll be canning for another week after today."

Mahala gently grasped Nancy's shoulders after she'd look down at her belly. "Oh, Nan. You look like you're about to pop. Are you sure you're up to working out in the garden today?"

"I'm fine. Come on." Nancy led the way off the porch and to the side of the house and they walked to the back yard. The kitchen garden was off to the side in front of the springhouse, where they kept their food cool during the summer.

Nancy slanted a look at her friend. She wished Mahala could be married and have a family of her own, but her friend remained sing. Even though it had only been four years, it seems as if they'd been neighbors forever. But the women had known each other longer than that. They had both lived in Tennessee before the long journey to Missouri.

Mahala was considered the flower of her family, so gentle was her nature. But as a spinster, she sometimes had the air and characteristics of a woman who felt unlovely, when in truth she possessed indescribable charm. One saw it in the way she interacted with people, the motion of her hands, her gait.

And then there was the cleft in Mahala's chin. Mahala was sure it ruined her features. Yet what Mahala considered offensive actually emphasized character in her face. Nancy thought Mahala should at least console herself with her fair complexion, keen, amber-flecked, green eyes, and that dark thick hair, more abundant than most of the women in their town.

Mahala followed Nancy to the side of the yard. After the long, hot, and humid summer, the fall weather gave relief from the humidity, but Indian summer had set in. Some days were warm as if summer refused to give way to fall. Today, however, a fresh coolness filled the air. The women wore broad straw hats, and let their hair hang loose.

Now that Nancy was finished harvesting the peaches, there were cucumbers, green beans, and tomatoes that needed to be put up. And the weeds in the kitchen garden had nearly taken over. It looked as if the weeds were trying to strangle the plentiful crop. The two women hoed the ground, pulled weeds, and threw them outside the fenced-in garden. The women filled their buckets with vegetables, all the while watching Jeffrey and Wiley playing in a mud puddle created from the tub of water Nancy had drained from the morning's wash.

Nancy's hair kept falling into her face as she bent and attacked the weeds that fought to gain ground. With the hoe occupying her hands, she tried to puff the hair away from her sticky face. Finally, she stopped and said, "Mahala, braid my hair, and I'll braid yours." She pulled off her hat and sat on a stump they used for a seat at the edge of the garden.

Mahala dropped her hoe and clomped through the rows of leafy vegetables to where Nancy sat. "We should have done this before we started weeding." She gathered the sides of Nancy's straw-colored hair with slim fingers and began plaiting it, picking up strands as she went.

Nancy sat still, glad for the heavy layers being lifted off her neck. When Mahala came to the end of the single braid, she used a string to hold it in place. Nancy pushed to her feet and pointed to the stump she'd been sitting on. "Your turn."

"Gladly." Mahala sat down. "I thought it was going to be a cold day, but the heat has really picked up." Her long tresses were thick and heavy. Once Nancy finished braiding Mahala's hair, Mahala stood up. "We better finish weeding the garden before the sun rises overhead. We still have an abundance of vegetables to pick."

Nancy gave Mahala a wilted smile. "If I have to bend over one more time, I think I'll burst."

Mahala threw a hand to her mouth. "Goodness, Nancy. Have I pushed you too hard?"

"Yes, you have." But she smiled to take the sting out of her words. "Let's take a break." Nancy turned away from the long rows of vegetables and called out to Tess. "Keep an eye on the children. Mahala and I are going for a walk down the road."

"Yes, Mama." Tess sat on a crate and watched Jeffrey and Wiley as they filled old cans with mud and spilled them out on the ground again and again.

Mary Jane knelt on the ground and was busy making round piles of mud in front of her. She patted them flat and stood to examine them. "Look, Mama, I'm making pancakes!"

"Umm. They look delicious."

Mary Jane's blue eyes shone. "You want one?"

"Not now, honey. Save me one for later."

Mary Jane wiped her muddy hands on her dress. "All right, Mama. How about you, Aunt Molly. You want a pancake?" Mary Jane had called Mahala, "'Molly'" from the time they'd met. Neither of the women had any intention of correcting her.

"I quite like it," Mahala had said early on.

"We're going for a walk, Mary. Mahala will have to save her appetite for later." Nancy brushed Mary's curly dark hair out of her face and kissed her nose.

Mary Jane's face brightened. "I'm gonna make a whole bunch of them."

"You look like you've got more mud on you than on the ground." Mahala laughed softly.

"Tess, let Mary play a little longer, and then I want her cleaned up," Nancy said.

"Can I throw her into the horse trough?" Tess's eyes gleamed mischievously.

"Don't you dare," Nancy warned.

"Please, Mama, I want to go swimming!" Mary Jane begged.

The two younger boys chimed in, "Me too! Me too!"

"Now see what you've started." Nancy ran a hand over her extended stomach.

"Come on, Nancy." Mahala pulled her away. "Tess has it all under control."

Once the two women had strolled down the drive and onto the main road, Nancy said, "I wish my mother was here."

"Why? Are you okay?" Mahala asked with concern.

"I've never felt such uncertainty about being with child as I have with this one." Nancy's fingers splayed over her belly. "I've been having early contractions, and I've still a month before the baby should come."

Mahala stared at Nancy's stomach. "Is it safe for you to be out walking on the road?"

"Of course it is. Anyway, I've already told you that I've written Mother requesting she come and stay with us a while." She gazed at the cornfields as they walked along the road. Acres of green and golden corn stalks stood tall under brilliant blue skies. On one side of the road were the cornfields and on the opposite side the rest of the land had turned yellow where the cattle had grazed on the dry grass. Blackbirds flew over the crops, cawing.

The women walked for a while saying nothing, both in deep thought. Nancy seemed absorbed, as if she had something she wanted to say, and Mahala wondered what was on Nancy's mind. Moments later, Mahala asked, "What's eating at you, Nancy? You've been in deep thought since the moment we left the garden. Is it something more than the concern over the baby?"

"Oh, Mahala. I'm sorry."

"So—what is it? Are you going to keep me in suspense?"

Nancy gave her friend a sidelong glance. "Why have you never married?"

Mahala wrinkled her nose and her cheeks grew rosy, but she smiled as she said, "I've never met the right man." She brushed at her sleeve. "I don't *need* a man." She shook her head before she looked out over the cornfields as if to avoid eye contact with Nancy.

"But you'd like to marry someday, wouldn't you?" Nancy wasn't about to let Mahala off the hook. It had taken her forever to find the nerve to ask her friend such a personal question, and now that she had, she wanted to know the truth.

"Of course I'd like to marry. But if it's not too much to ask, I'd like to marry for love." Mahala cheeks flamed a radiant red now.

"Oh, Mahala, I've embarrassed you. That was never my intention." Nancy wrapped an arm around her friend's slim waist and drew her close. "Tell me to mind my own business if you've a mind to."

Mahala pulled away. "I'm surprised it took you so long to ask." She bent and picked a yellow wildflower from the side of the road. "I'm pretty sure I'm the oldest spinster in all of Missouri." She plucked the petals from the stem as they walked.

Nancy was at a loss for words. Her friend was a charming woman. Not only did she have dark, silken locks that flowed down her back, but a slight spray of freckles sprinkled over the bridge of her nose and upper cheeks added a youthful look. "Well, maybe your *Mr. Right* is waiting just around the corner."

"If you're speaking of my boss, Mr. Thompson, he's certainly not my *Mr. Right.* He's a gentleman in every sense of the word, but he's taken." Mahala's cheeks resumed their natural color. "Libby Matthews has her eye on him, and I've seen them together on buggy rides."

"And Mr. Weaver, the blacksmith?"

"Oh, please! I'm not that desperate. But in truth, they are the only single men in Grovespring. The rest of the men in town are either married or too young."

"That's the problem of living in a small community like ours. We just ran out of men," Nancy said.

"I don't understand how Grovespring ran out of men," Mahala said. "And of all things, *I'm* the one who becomes Grovespring's only spinster." She stopped walking and put both hands on her hips, clearly miffed. "How did that happen, Nancy? I know men just don't grow on trees, but still, you'd think there would be *someone . . .* "

"Well," Nancy gave Mahala a lopsided grin. "You could have accepted Daryl Keegan's proposal." She clamped her lips together into a thin line and her eyes glinted playfully. "But you declined his offer . . . just as I would have done if I were you." She laughed softly as she ribbed her friend.

"And to think Ada Mae married that no-good louse who's content to sit on his rear end and drink his life away while his family scrambles to find ways to make ends meet." Mahala's cheeks reddened again. "Thanks for reminding me about Daryl Keegan." She stuck her tongue out.

"And for two," Nancy continued, ignoring Mahala's reaction. "You weren't *always* the only spinster in Grovespring. You forget Isabella Yates never married either."

Mahala fanned her cheeks and pushed her friend away playfully. "You would remind me about her." She kicked at a small stone. "Although it wasn't quite as daunting being a spinster when she was here." She grinned mischievously.

"You lie," Nancy gave her a knowing look. "You worried every minute that Bella would make a catch and leave you—"

"— the only spinster," Mahala finished, wrinkling her nose at Nancy. "Well, she didn't make a catch, and she did the next best thing by leaving for

New York a year ago—even though she left me to face this disaster by myself."

"She comes back from time to time," Nancy said softly. She strode back to Mahala and slipped her hand through the crook of her friend's arm. She turned them back the way they came.

"Bella does come back from time to time, but it isn't because she's husband hunting." Mahala grinned. "If it weren't for her aunt Gertrude, we'd never see her."

Nancy pulled Mahala along. "That poor old woman had that enormous house built a mile out of town in hopes of Bella returning with a husband and taking over the hotel and café."

"Gertie doesn't have anyone else to leave it to," Mahala said. "She's made a good living and has profited well from the hotel. It wouldn't surprise me if Bella didn't keep that thought tucked in the back of her mind."

"I heard Gertrude telling Mrs. Trubridge that she sent Bella a letter requesting she come."

"When was that?" Mahala asked.

"Must have been a week ago."

"Well, if she does, then I won't be the only single woman in town." Mahala kicked at another stone, moving it along as they walked. "I don't understand why Bella hasn't married."

"She's an attractive woman, but so are you," Nancy said.

"If that's true, a lot of good that's done me." Mahala lifted her chin.

"Oh, Mahala, I shouldn't have said anything."

Mahala seemed to have relaxed a bit and turned to face Nancy. "Do you ever wonder why Bella hasn't married?"

"No, not really. Let's just drop it for now." Nancy pulled her arm from Mahala and her steps quickened.

"I understand Bella is a touchy issue, but I have a niggling thought. Every time she returns to Grovespring, Bella seeks John out. I can't remember a time that woman doesn't zero in on him when she's in town. Just so you know, I'm glad she's in New York." Mahala frowned and picked up her pace to keep up with Nancy.

"So am I." Nancy's brows drew together. "And in case you're wondering—I knew." Nancy's cheeks burned. "Every time she comes to town, I see how she watches my John." Nancy laid a hand on her extended belly, feeling big as a cow. "She's such a spoiled beauty."

"I'm sorry, Nancy. I didn't know you knew."

"I knew." Nancy shook her head. "But I'm okay." She quirked a half smile. "Gertrude gave Bella everything she ever wanted, just to keep her in town. But the one thing she wanted, she couldn't have—my John."

"Oh, Nancy. I'm not sure that's really true. She's a flirt, but I don't think she's a home-wrecker.

"Gertie never had children. She sees her sister's daughter as one of her own. When her sister died, she promised to look after Bella. I think much of what Gertie has done for Bella is the reason Bella comes back."

"I suppose. When Bella runs out of money, she has no recourse but to come back and stay with Gertrude for a spell. I often wondered if Gertrude has ever figured out that Bella will never stay for good?" Nancy said.

"I think not." Mahala said. "How that woman can sashay into this hole-in-the-wall and stir up trouble so lickety—split is the town's undoing. The moment Bella steps off that stagecoach, trouble flies through town like angry bees out of a beehive." Mahala swallowed. "I wish she'd stay away for good."

"I'm not worried about Bella." Nancy gave Mahala a devilish look. "And my John's—"

She didn't finish her thought as the sound of horses' hooves arose ahead of them. Four horsemen trotted their horses toward them, the riders coming two by two.

Nancy felt Mahala pull her arm. "I don't recognize those men, do you?"

Nancy pursed her lips and shook her head. "No. They're not from around here."

An older man with snow-white hair that curled around his neck and a red-headed teen were the front two riders.

Mahala lifted a hand above her eyes as if straining to get a better look at the them.

The four men grew nearer. Still not recognizing them, Nancy and Mahala stepped to the side of the road and lowered their eyes.

When the horsemen grew even with them, Mahala looked up. Nancy squeezed her hand. But she too looked up to find the handsome rider in back staring down at Mahala. He pinned his gaze on her as they rode by. Heat climbed up her neck and her pulse raced. *Keep going!*

Mahala seemed frozen where she stood, her eyes seemingly glued to her dark shoes. After the horses went past them, for reasons unknown, both women glanced up one more time to find the handsome stranger staring back at them. There seemed to be a ruthlessness about him—something wild, untamed. The other three men seemed preoccupied with the road ahead, but the dark-haired cowboy with the black felt hat with a feather dangling form it kept his gaze on Mahala. The rider craned his neck to look back one last time before he continued on with the other three riders.

"Mahala!" Nancy whispered.

Mahala looked over at her.

"Let's go!"

"Who do you think they are?" Mahala asked.

"I don't know but we should get back to the house."

"Maybe they're the men folks in town have been talking about."

"What men?" Nancy tugged on Mahala's hand to get her off the road.

"Word has it that four men road into town around a month ago. Nobody knows where they've come from or where they're going. They just showed up," Mahala said.

"I wonder where they're staying if they've been around this long?"

"I overheard Gertie at the hotel telling a customer that the men are staying out at Judd Benson's deserted ranch."

"If they've been here that long, you can't call Judd's place a deserted ranch any longer."

"True." Mahala lifted her shoulders and dropped them.

The two women looked at each other and then stared after the strangers who had disappeared down the road.

Mahala picked up her pace. "You might want to tell John those men were here."

"I will. For now, let's get off the road." Nancy cut through the ditch and strode through the dry stubble in the field. The lane into their place was just up ahead. With the men out of sight, Nancy lifted her shoulders. "Let's go in and get a glass of cold tea. I feel like a wilted weed."

Mahala grabbed her arm. She had to have an answer to what had been eating at her for far too long. "Do *you* think of me as "the town's spinster?"

"Pfft! Stop it! Don't even go there." Nancy protested.

"Well, I am, you know. How many thirty-year-old women do you know who aren't married?"

"Oh, Mahala. I'm sorry I ever brought it up." Nancy took Mahala's hand and they walked toward the house.

"I'm not sorry. Everyone's afraid to say anything." She walked in silence for a moment. "I'm going to find a man if it's the last thing I do. He's out there somewhere. I just have to find him, even if I have to get one from the newspapers."

Nancy slowed her pace and looked sideways at Mahala. "Are you talking about becoming a mail-order bride?"

"If it comes to that. I won't be a spinster forever." She leveled her gaze at Nancy.

"I admire your courage, Mahala. If I can, I'll help you find your special man." Nancy slowed her steps again. She felt another contraction coming on. Would she make it to her due date?

Chapter EIGHT

JOHN SPENT THE MORNING working on a section of broken fence near the barn, while his mind tangled with thoughts of Judd Benson and his harmful ways. Resentment stuck in his craw that his neighbor would go to any length to get his land. Truth was, the more Judd tried to con John into selling his land, the more John didn't want to give him the time of day. Did Judd truly think killing his steers would lead him to sell his land? *Over my dead body!*

John set the wooden post into the hole he'd dug, then shoveled dirt into the opening. When the post looked secure, he pushed on it with his boot to see if it was firmly set. Satisfied, the next step would be to set the new rails in place. With fall in full swing, he needed to spend the next few weeks getting the ranch ready for winter.

John gazed out beyond the fence rails that bordered the ranch yard, to the pastures where the cattle grazed. He scanned the land with sharp and knowing eyes. His cowhands would be farther out, rounding up strays that had wandered away from the herd. It was commonplace to spend half his time building and repairing fences. With a large herd, fence work came with the territory. The stake-and-rail fencing kept the herd from wandering off his property.

The sound of wagon wheels clattered on the graveled drive leading to the road. John looked up to see his younger brother, Jesse, pulling into the yard. He dropped the shovel and lowered the rail he'd been about to hammer into place. He shoved his hat off his forehead and gazed over the yard to see that Jesse had brought his family with him.

"Hello!" John's hand went up.

"Good to see you." Jesse jumped down and went around the buckboard to where his wife, Margaret, handed down their young son, Pulaski, with one hand while cradling the baby with the other. Before she could hand the baby to Jesse, the back door swung open and John's family spilled out of the house.

The air filled with delighted squeals of greeting as they circled Jesse's family. Nancy waved as she waddled over to Margaret, who waited for a hand to help her down. "Give me the baby," Nancy said, reaching up to take one-year-old Trisa. Holding the baby on her hip, she stepped back as Margaret pulled a basket from the floor of the wagon and joined her.

Franklin started to stride over to where his older brothers John and Jesse stood shaking hands, but before he got far, Nancy called, "Franklin, take Margaret's basket of food and set it on the back porch."

"All right, Mom."

Nancy wasn't his mother, of course, but since she'd raised him from infancy, the name came naturally to him.

Franklin didn't waste any time relieving Margaret of her burden and set the basket on the top step by the back door. Before joining his brothers, he picked up a corner of the dish towel that covered the food in the basket. He was just about to poke his fingers in and pull out a hot, juicy fried chicken leg when he heard Nancy cry, "Franklin!" He dropped the cloth with a sheepish look, followed by a crooked smile that crossed his face.

"I thought I might make sure this chicken was cooked just right," he laughed and ambled away from the basket.

"Go on now and join your brothers and leave that food alone," Nancy said.

The women watched as Franklin walked away, amusement flickering across his face. They giggled and shook their heads, then went back to their conversation.

Tall and gangly, Franklin was the youngest of eleven sons. He'd come west with John and Nancy, but they weren't the only Grigsby's who made the 700-mile journey from Tennessee to Missouri. One of his older brothers, George, and his family had come along too. George was a quiet man, more of a loner who kept to his work and family. He seldom came out to the ranch. And then there was Franklin's brother Jesse, who made it a point to drop by often with his young family, just like they were doing today.

Franklin had never known his father, George Sr. who had remarried soon after Franklin's mother, Rebecca died. With nine sons in the house, his father had needed help feeding and caring for the boys. By then, Franklin was already living with John and Nancy.

A year after his father had married his new wife, Margaret, she gave birth to a son, Melcheldek. It seemed George Sr. was destined to have sons. Of the eleven boys, seven of them remained in Tennessee.

Jesse strode over to where John stood and his voice carried over the air. "I promised Franklin we'd come by soon." The men watched as Franklin covered the short distance to where they stood. "He's getting tall," Jesse said, as Franklin neared. He slapped him on the back. "You've already passed up the women. You'll be catchin' up to us before too long."

Franklin gave his brothers a smile. "I'll pass both of you up, too, you'll see." He kicked at a stone on the ground.

The three brothers had broken away from the noise of the women and children and strode to where John had been working. Jesse turned his attention to the fencing lying nearby. "What have you got here?"

"I'm mending fences this morning." John shoved his hat back. "You want to give me a hand?"

"Let's get to it." Jesse followed John to the rail lying on the ground. They each picked up an end and shoved it into place. An hour later, the men joined the women in the backyard where the children were playing.

Franklin left the men to join Granville and Calvin by the barn.

John and Jesse sat at a distance and kept their voices low. "You ever find out who shot your steers down by the creek?" Jesse asked.

John eyed his brother as he pulled out a pipe and a tobacco pouch from his pocket. "How'd you hear about that?" He filled the pipe with a pinch of tobacco then scratched a match against the bottom of his brown boots.

"Small town. Word gets around."

Flames came to life from the wooden matchstick. John squinted as he lit his pipe and puffed several times. Smoke billowed out as the tobacco seared red. John shook the flame from the match. "Yeah, well, I have my suspicions."

"Benson?" Jesse leaned his chair back and swung his ankle over his leg.

"One and the same. He wants my land in a bad way. What with the creek and all, he's regretted he didn't get the land before I did, but I'd already laid claim to it. Blue and I rode out to the river, and I could see the land was prime property. The fact that the creeks veined out from the river to lower land was a bonus. My cattle have good running water and the crops benefits as well."

"Benson's doin' all right with his land and cattle," Jesse said. "I don't know why he's so hell-bent on grabbing up all the land." He swatted at a fly.

"I've had my fill of thinking about that man," John said. "He's one of the reasons I'm planning to go west."

"You aren't going to let that go, are you?" Jesse said. "Well truth to tell, if you ever do it, I'm comin' too." Jesse stared at John and changed gears. "Have you heard about the four men who've ridden into town?" He leaned forward, his next words for John's ears only. "Folks are thinkin' they're a rough bunch and hidin' out. From what—nobody knows."

John lowered his pipe and eyed his brother. "I met them in front of the hotel just the other day. A rowdy bunch if you ask me." John stuck his pipe in his mouth. Tiny red coals lit up when he inhaled.

"Have you talked to Sheriff Ford about them?"

"He was there."

Jesse sat up straight. "Did they say what they're doin' here?"

"No. They're a tight-lipped bunch, and if you ask me, they seemed a little edgy."

"Are they still around? " Jesse pulled a blade of grass and picked at it.

"They haven't left the area, and it doesn't look like they're going anywhere anytime soon."

"So where do you s'pose they're stayin'?"

"They're hanging out at Benson's deserted ranch. Said they wanted to keep a low profile."

"A low profile from what?" Jesse darted a glance at him.

"I don't know, but I'm going to find out."

"Does Benson know those men are stayin' at his place?"

"I don't know, but I don't like it." Pipe in hand, John blew a cloud of white smoke.

"Seems you're in good company. Folks are feeling a bit edgy with them here. Clem Owens seems to think it's only a matter of time before they pull something like robbing the bank," Jesse said.

"I intend to keep an eye on them as best I can. But I've got my hands full here and them being on the opposite side of town it makes it difficult to keep a handle on what they're up to."

John gazed out at his land. He and Nan had come a long way from when they first arrived from Tennessee.

"Missouri's growing." John crossed his boot over his ankle. "More wagons will be arriving from the East every spring. Folks are always looking for new territory to start over again."

"You see that last bunch of wagons that came through Grovespring?" Jesse asked.

"I did." John studied the women sitting on chairs across the yard from them. They were deep in conversation as the children played. He lowered his voice. "I'd give my eye tooth to pack it up and head out to Oregon. It's been said there's prime property that's never been touched, with plenty of rivers and creeks for everybody." He shook his head and frowned. "I'm tired of fighting with Benson."

Jesse laid a hand on John's shoulder. "Don't let him get to you, John."

"I don't intend to. He hasn't seen the bad side of me yet. And if he does, he'll wish he never had."

LATER IN THE DAY, John found Nancy cleaning up the kitchen. Their company had gone and the two of them were alone, something that didn't happen often in their busy household. John pulled Nancy against his chest, her back to him, and wrapped his arms around her. "Have I told you lately that I love you?"

He felt her relax in his hold, her head tilting to his chest. "You might have, but I never get tired of hearing it," she said softly.

"You should let Tess help you." He kissed the top of her head.

"I'm giving her a break. When this baby's born, I'll need her more than ever." Nancy broke out of his hold and faced him, the magic of the moment gone. "How did your visit go with Jesse?" She dropped a plate into the soapy water.

"We talked about the latest development in town." John said.

"And what would that be?" Nancy turned and dried her hands on her apron.

"There's a band of riders who've ridden into town, never seen 'em before." John leaned against the counter. "I meant to tell you about them before now."

"Yes, I know."

"You know what?"

"Yes, I know those men have come to town. They rode past Mahala and me the other day while we were out for a walk."

"Why didn't you tell me?" John pushed away from the sink.

"I meant to bring it up." Nancy wrung out the dish cloth and draped it over the wash basin. "Is something wrong?" Her brows lifted in an inquisitive arch.

"If you see them again, I want to know." John paused, obviously thinking, and added, "So the men have been out and about checking the area." He let out an irritated breath. "I don't like it. Did you get a good look at 'em?"

"Yes, I did." Nancy wiped a bowl and set it on the counter. "There were four of them, and one of them appeared quite a bit older than the rest. There was a young man, maybe in his teens, and two men who hung back. One appeared to be in his twenties, the other, maybe his thirties." She searched his eyes, a hint of concern in her expression.

John stared at her thoughtfully. It was the same men all right.

Nancy dried her hands on a dish towel. "One of the men rode slower and hung back. He made us a little nervous. He couldn't take his eyes off of Mahala—of all things."

"You don't say!"

"I think she liked it, though she didn't say as much." Nancy went to John's side and wrapped her hands around his waist. "I miss being held close." She turned her chin up to him.

"It won't be long before the baby's born, and I'll be able to hold you close again." He kissed her forehead. "Do me a favor."

"What's that?" Nancy asked.

"Don't go out on the roads anymore, not until we know it's safe."

"All right." Nancy's face reddened. "Those men didn't seem to be a threat though, if you're worried about that."

"They're strangers. We don't know where they've come from or why they're here. But I don't have a good feeling about them, Nan." John grabbed his hat off the wall hook and turned back to her. "Dadburnit! Our roads aren't even safe anymore!"

AS MAHALA OPENED THE door and stepped outside, a gust of wind swept along the deck of the front porch, skittering dead leaves across the planks. She walked head down into the biting wind that tugged at her long, dark hair. Out in the yard, the maple trees blazed with oranges and reds, and all day, crimson leaves dropped onto the ground.

Upon entering the barn, Mahala was met with a chorus of meows. Tiny peeps and cries filled the corner of the stable where the kittens crawled on unstable legs. Mama cat had left them alone and gone in search of food. Day and night the black-and-white cat patrolled the barn keeping mice from the feed-bins and her stomach full.

"Well, look at you." Mahala picked up a kitten whose body and legs were black as midnight, but the fur around her pink nose, mouth, and the tips of her paws were snow white. She nuzzled its tiny head against her cheek. "You're so soft, little one, like velvet." The kitten's eyes blinked and began to open, and blue eyes peeked out at her. Mahala thumbed the kitten's fat little belly and put it back on the straw with the other kittens.

Mahala climbed into the buggy and before long, Dan pranced happily along the road toward town. Another day and another dress that would be completed before the harvest dance arrived. She'd kept a steady pace threading needle through fabric, not wanting to let her customers down. Now as she held the reins loosely in her hands, she eyed her fingertips. Her thumb and forefinger were red from pushing the needle in and out of fabric for many hours every day.

The late September weather had turned chilly, not an unusual occurrence for Grovespring. Riding into town, a blustery wind sent crisp leaves scampering down the center of the street and in front of Thompson's Tailor Shop. After dropping off her buggy at the livery, Mahala drew in a deep breath and walked swiftly across the street. She quickened her steps and hurried past the Wells Fargo Express Office and the doctor's office. As she neared the barber shop, when she spotted the stranger she'd seen a few days before, riding past their property. The dark-haired man with the black felt hat strode on the boardwalk ahead, and he was coming her way, the dull thud of his boots resounding on the wooden planks.

The cowboy riveted his gaze on hers at the same time she spied him. She tore her gaze from his and drew her cloak firmly about her. The man was alone this time, his collar raised against the cold. She considered going across the street in pretense of heading for Owen's Mercantile. It unnerved her that he kept his gaze pinned on hers. *So rude,* she thought, and something about the look on his face chilled her.

Despite the wind, he slowed his steps and swaggered down the boardwalk. When she looked again his dark eyes lit up and he touched the brim of his hat.

"How do, Miss Shields? A chance meeting on a day like this."

A chance meeting? "H-How do you know my name?" Mahala lifted her shoulders and pulled her cloak tighter.

He licked his lips and leered at her. "When I see a pretty face in town, I ask around. Folks around here tend to be a tight-lipped lot, but not everybody."

Mahala stared at him not knowing what to say, but eager to get past him and into the tailor shop and to work.

"Aren't you going to ask my name?" He feigned a hurtful expression.

"No, sir. It's none of my business." Mahala gave a slight nod and tried to skirt around him, but before she could pass by, his hand flew out and grabbed her arm in a firm grip.

"The name's Otis Murphy, ma'am. I don't know where you learned your manners, but that's not a way to treat a man who just gave you a decent hello.'"

He towered above her and her breath caught, her heart hammering in her ears. "I-I'm late for work—sir." She kept her gaze straight ahead, not wanting to look him in the eye and wishing someone would come to her aid.

"Well, then, maybe you'd oblige me by having lunch together on your lunch break." His fingers dug in a bit harder.

"Hey!" Sheriff Ford shouted down the boardwalk. "Get your hands off of Miss Shields."

Otis's grip loosened and he stepped away, both hands going up. But he lowered his voice and said, "Too bad he interrupted us, isn't it, Miss Shields?"

Bile worked its way to her throat, and she quickly stepped away from the rude cowboy, wasting no time in continuing to the shop. She passed the sheriff as his boots thundered toward the outlaw. She looked back when she heard the sheriff ask, "How many times do I have to tell you to keep your hands off the women in this town?"

"Twice sheriff, to be exact." The look he gave Ford was cocky. "Once with a little filly who didn't have enough sense to keep her mouth shut and just now with the lovely Miss Shields."

Mahala's stomach lurched before her fingers grasped the doorknob and she flew into Thompson's Tailor Shop. When she closed the door, she stood with her back against it and turned her head to gaze out the large front window where Grady displayed his tweed coats. She could see past a stand cloaked with a jacket, and watched the sheriff berate the offensive stranger. She guessed she couldn't call him a stranger any longer now that she knew his name. What was he doing in Grovespring? And how long would he and his partners be around? Would she have to be on guard every time she came to town?

Mahala looked up to find Grady Thompson staring at her. "Are you okay,

Miss Shields?" He pointed out the window toward the boardwalk where Sheriff Ford and Otis Murphy were parting ways. Otis cut through the crowd of pedestrians without looking back. "The sheriff beat me to it. I was just about to step out the door in your defense when Ford came along."

"I'm all right, Grady. But what's a woman to do when she can't cross the street without being accosted?"

SHERIFF FORD STOOD WITH one boot on the spokes of the stagecoach wheel as Bart Clemens brought him up to speed about the outlaws running loose in their territory. He was suspicious that the gang Bart was talking about was the same men who'd arrived in town. If so, the Woodrow gang had robbed banks all the way from Kansas City to the territory around Grovespring.

"You might keep your eyes open for any suspicious men riding into town," Bart said. "There's a posse looking for the Woodrow gang. It appears they've been hiding out for the last month or so."

"Too late," Ford said grimly. "I think the men you're talkin' about have already arrived in town."

The teamster driver looked out over Main Street. "They're here?"

"They're not in town at the moment. But if we're talkin' about the same gang, four men rode into town about a month back. And they're a rowdy bunch to be sure." The sheriff tipped his hat back and gazed at the driver through his spectacles. "Crazy thing is, they said they didn't have much cash, but it appears they have plenty of it. They show up every night at Grider's Saloon. The bartender tells me they're loose with the bills in the card games. He suspects they're cheatin', too. Grider says those boys go home with far more cash than they come in with."

Ford moved away from the Wells Fargo stagecoach and shoved his hands in his pockets.

"Come to think of it," the sheriff added, glancing over at the hotel. "Gertrude said they all tipped her nicely at the bath house, too."

"You might watch your back, Sheriff. If it's true they're the Woodrow gang, those outlaws are a tough lot."

"Mighty obliged for the information, Bart. Grovespring's always been a quiet town, least till the wagon trains come through. We'll keep an eye on the gang. Some of the folks in the valley have suspicions they're stealing cattle."

"I know you don't usually carry your firearm, Sheriff, but I suggest you keep one on you while those men are in town." Bart touched the brim of his hat, slapped the reins he was holding, and called out, "Hip!" The string of horses jerked forward and the stagecoach moved out onto Main Street. The way station was down the road at the end of town. The sheriff knew Bart would change the horses out for a fresh set, and then hightail it out of town.

In the meantime, Sheriff Ford thought it would be best to seek out John Grigsby and Charles Matthews. He'd share the news Bart had just given him, not that they didn't already have a suspicion what Woodrow and his men could do, but because he knew that of late he wasn't as strong as he used to be and wouldn't be up to the task of forcefully upholding the law by himself. But men in their community looked up to John Grigsby and Charles Matthews. John would know what to do about the gang. And though Ford wore the badge to enforce the law, John Grigsby wore the fortitude of strength and wisdom to do the right thing.

Sheriff Ford headed back to his office, thinking it was high time he put on his gun belt. Would those renegade men end up in his jailhouse before too long?

Chapter NINE

GRANVILLE SET THE BOX of groceries on Mrs. James front porch.

"Thank you, young man," she said as she gave him a few coins and he dropped them into his pocket. This was his second-to-last delivery for the day. He climbed onto the wooden bench of Mr. Owens' rig and flicked the reins. "Let's get the last delivery done, you old nag," Granville called out to the horse. "I've got to get home to my schoolwork."

Twenty minutes later, Granville was headed back to Owens' Mercantile. Just when he turned the wagon off a side road onto Main Street, a horseman cut in front of him. "Whoa!" Granville called as he pulled back on the reins and the wagon lurched to a stop. The rider, a redheaded young man, turned his horse around and rode lazily to the side of the wagon, eyeballing the goods in the back.

Granville gripped the reins feeling uneasy. What could he do if the teenager started a ruckus? The redhead looked to be a good four or five years older than him, and what's worse, he wore a firearm buckled around his hips.

The teen gave him a level gaze and his lip curled up on one side. He nudged his mount closer to the side of the wagon. He leaned over and picked up a loaf of bread wrapped in brown paper and sat it in front of him on the saddle.

"Hey! You put that back!" Granville yelled.

"What are you going to do about it, you little pipsqueak?" The redheaded teen leered at him.

"You can't steal Old Lady Josie's groceries!" Granville wheeled around on the buckboard as he yelled at the redhead.

"You gonna stop me?" Red's eyes lit with a challenging look.

Granville held his breath as he watched Red reach into the back again and grab an apple out of the box.

Red waved the apple in front of him. "Thank you kindly." He turned his stallion back onto the road and trotted ahead. When he looked over his shoulder, his eyes bore into Granville's and then he galloped out of town.

"I'm in trouble now," Granville mumbled to Moses. "How am I going to account for the missing food?"

Stopping in front of Josie's picket fence, Granville jumped down and carried the last box of groceries to her front porch.

"There you are young man. I've been waiting for you." The old woman looked to be a hundred years old, but she was as spry as a young colt. She moved with ease as she came out onto the porch and reached for the box of food.

"I'm sorry, Mrs. McCleary, but someone just stole one of your apples and a loaf of bread from the back of Mr. Owens' wagon."

"Well, for land sakes. What happened?" Old Josie gripped her box of food.

Granville wiped his forehead with the back of his arm. "A fella just up and stopped me on the road on the way here and took your food, free as you please and rode away."

"Well, for goodness sakes! What's this world comin' to when a boy can't make deliveries without gettin' robbed!" She set the box on a chair by her door and reached into her apron pocket and brought out a few coins.

"I'll go back and get you another loaf of bread, ma'am." Granville shuffled his feet while Josie counted out the coins and handed them to him.

"Why don't you bring me that loaf of bread tomorrow, and don't worry about the apple."

"Yes, ma'am." Granville nodded. "I can carry your box into the house for you."

Josie picked up the box easily and smiled at him. "Thank you, son. I can take it in."

"Yes, ma'am." Granville turned back to the wagon and climbed in.

"Mister Owens sure ain't gonna be happy when he learns he's been robbed," Granville told the old horse. Getting robbed put a damper on his day. Before the teen boy had shown up, he'd been thinking he couldn't wait to get back to the mercantile. He'd been eyeballing an item on the shelf in the center aisle all week. But as much as Granville tried to get the horse moving quickly down the road, old Moses trudged along at a beetles pace. Mr. Owens had used this horse for delivery for as long as Granville could remember.

"No wonder Mr. Owens isn't worried about boys taking you out on deliveries. You're slower than an old mule." Granville leaned his elbows on his knees as the horse clopped along in no hurry to be anywhere. "Come on, Moses. I'll give you a carrot when we get back to the store."

Once they arrived in the alley behind Owens Mercantile, Granville tied the horse to the hitching post, went through the rear door, and grabbed a carrot from the bin Mr. Owens used for Moses' treats. He gave the horse the carrot and retraced his steps. When he entered the mercantile, he emptied his pocket of change and set the money on the counter.

Mr. Owens examined the coins. "You are doing a fine job, son. Business is picking up again." He counted the money while Granville watched. Each day Granville emptied his pockets of the change the customers paid for delivery. And each day, Mr. Owens took the money due him for the goods sold. If there was extra change, he scooted the coins back to Granville. Today was no different. "There's your tip, son."

"Thank you, sir." Granville pulled the coins he'd earned during the week out of another pocket. With his weekly pay and the daily tips, he could see his money growing. He wouldn't spend it though. Not yet anyway.

"You count your change every day." Mr. Owens chuckled. "What are you saving for?"

"A new rifle, sir." Granville slid the coins off the counter and dropped them into his pocket. "I saw one advertised in the newspaper."

"Your pa know you're workin' to buy a rifle?"

"No, sir. I want to surprise him."

"Is this for him or you?"

"Me, sir. Dad lets me use his rifle if I need it. But I want one that's all my own."

"You keep deliverin' them goods to my customers, you'll get there." Mr. Owens winked and went back to stocking shelves.

"Uh . . . Mr. Owens?"

Clem turned back. "Whatcha need, son?"

"I need to report two items got stolen out of the wagon, sir." Granville's stomach knotted.

"What do you mean merchandise got stolen?"

"A rider stopped me on the road and took a loaf of bread and an apple."

"Who did that?" Clem Owens growled.

"Never seen him before. He was a teenager, though, 'bout four years older than me, and he wore a gun and holster. But that wasn't what kept me from stopping him."

"Well, what was?"

Granville couldn't look Mr. Owens in the eye. Shame engulfed him. "The way he stared me down, sir. Like he'd pull that gun of his if I tried to stop him." Granville swallowed and dug in his pocket and pulled out the coins. "I'll pay for the bread and apple." He set the money before his boss.

Clem Owens stared at the coins on the polished counter, and concern filled his eyes. "No you won't. You did the right thing keepin' your mouth shut. A loaf of bread and an apple ain't worth your hide layin' dead in the middle of the road."

Granville gulped.

"Don't think nothin' of it. But do me a favor."

"What's that?"

"I want you to report what you told me to the sheriff right now, and when you get home, make sure you tell your dad."

"Yes, sir." Granville didn't move.

"Now." Mr. Owens' made a shooing motion with his hand.

"Yes, sir." Granville ran out of the mercantile and all the way to the sheriff's office.

When he pushed open the door, Sheriff Ford looked up in surprise.

"What can I do for you, Granville?"

"I'm here to make a report, sir." Granville stood at the door, eyeing the jail cells beyond in awe.

"Have a seat." The sheriff waved the boy to a chair.

Granville glanced out the door and shuffled over to the desk. He slid into the chair and stared at the sheriff. He'd known this man to be his father's friend from the first time they'd ridden into town four years ago. He was a gentle man, more like a grandpa than a sheriff. Granville tried to ease the beating of his heart. He'd never had to make a report about anything before.

The sheriff leaned his elbows on the desk and looked over at Granville. "Okay, son, tell me what happened."

It didn't take long to tell the sheriff what had occurred on the road. The more he told the story, the worse it seemed. He watched as Ford scribbled down everything he said on a piece of paper on his desk.

"Is that all?" Sheriff Ford asked when Granville stopped talking.

"Yes, sir." Granville swallowed and stared at the sheriff, his heart pounding in his chest.

Ford leveled his gaze on him. "If he tries anything again, you let me know. But don't go confronting him on your own. I don't want you gettin' hurt."

Granville swallowed again. "Yes, sir."

"I think I got all I need from you for now. You can go."

Granville let out the breath he'd been holding. He headed back to the mercantile in record time.

BEFORE GRANVILLE LEFT FOR the day, he went to a shelf that held a couple of brand-new slingshots. He'd been working at the mercantile for a month now. In that time, their chickens had been attacked relentlessly. Every morning, his mother found more chickens were gone. His father said a fox was responsible for the deed; a dog or a coyote would have left chicken feathers behind. Granville set traps in hopes of catching the culprit, but the fox was a sly one. He avoided the traps as if he knew what they were.

Just this morning, his mother had stormed into the kitchen and complained, "We've lost two more chickens! John, you've got to catch that thief or I will!"

Granville's lips curved up. His mom hated guns. How she planned to get that old fox he didn't know. Now he examined the craftsmanship of the slingshot on the shelf and nodded. It was made from a Y-shaped piece of wood and a strip of the new material Granville knew was called rubber. A plan began to form in his mind. He wouldn't spend his hard-earned money on a slingshot when he thought he could make one himself.

When Granville arrived home, he brushed Star down and put him in his stall. Then he went on foot to a stand of trees that edged the pasture. There were plenty of old branches laying on the ground. He picked up a few and looked them over. Then he spotted the perfect limb lying in a bed of dried leaves. Within an hour he broke off a sturdy section with a Y-shape. Granville didn't have any rubber, of course, but he'd cut a strip of leather that was wider in the middle than at the ends and formed a small pocket in the middle. The branch was fairly flexible, and when he fastened the length of leather to both sides of the Y, there should be enough give in the wood to allow him to pitch a rock a good distance.

Granville held the sling in his left hand and shoved his arm out straight. With his right hand, he pulled the leather strip back as far as he could and then let go. It sprang forward with a strong *swoosh!* "Perfect," he breathed. Smiling, he went in search of smooth stones to practice shooting his new weapon.

Calvin joined him in the field. Rusty followed close, his tail wagging. "Where you goin'?" Calvin asked.

"Nowhere. Go on back to the house."

"What's that in your hand?"

"Nothing. Leave me alone."

"Did you make that slingshot?"

"Yeah. Now go on."

"Why can't I come along?"

"You ask too many questions."

"But why can't I come along?" Calvin persisted.

"I need to learn how to use this thing, and I don't need you interrupting me."

"I won't. I'll be quiet."

Granville let out a heavy sigh. "All right. But stay behind me and don't make a sound." He looked back at Calvin, who shrugged his shoulders.

Granville went in search of things to shoot at. He found a sparrow in a tree. He set a small stone inside the pocket and pulled on the band. With one eye closed, he aimed, and let go. In a flash the slingshot hurled the stone which sailed through the air and under the branch. The bird flapped its wings and flew away. Heat crept up Granville's neck and he glanced back at Calvin. His brother shrugged, his lips clamped together.

"There!" Granville said under his breath. A jackrabbit's long ears poked up above the tall, dried grass. Granville held his arm straight out and aimed for the rabbit. A second later, the stone flew through the air. But the stone fell short of the hare and the rabbit hopped away, his ears appearing now and again above the tall yellow grasses.

Calvin ran and retrieved the stone. He handed it over to Granville, but he didn't say a word.

Granville eyed his little brother with amusement. "What are you thinking?"

Calvin lifted his thin shoulders and opened both hands, palm-sides-up. "You need practice."

"Well, what else can I practice on?"

"Let's set up cans like dad does when you practice shooting his rifle." Calvin's blue eyes lit up.

"Not a bad idea, Cal. Come on. You can help me line the cans up."

The two boys went to the backside of the barn where tin cans were scattered on the ground. They set a long board on two barrels and then spaced the cans along the rough surface. Granville aimed at the cans. On the first few tries, the stones hit the barn wall with a loud thud.

"Can I try?" Calvin held out his hand.

"You think you can do any better?" Granville handed him the slingshot and a couple of smooth stones.

Calvin took several steps back and then dropped a stone in the leather pocket. He straightened his arm with the slingshot held firmly in his grip. Then he stretched the leather strip and held it taut a moment longer. *Swoosh!* The stone sailed through the air and slammed against a tin can, sending it flying against the barn wall.

"Wow!" Calvin spun around and held out the slingshot to Granville. "I hit it!"

"Yeah, you did you dumb cluck. Let me try it again." Granville's heart thudded against his chest. He wasn't about to let his little brother best him. He slipped a smooth stone into the pocket and held it steady. He closed one eye as he aimed for the rusty can in the middle. *Swoosh!* The stone whistled through the air and smashed into the can. The tin can flew through the air and ricocheted off the barn wall.

"Bull's eye!" Calvin ran up to him. Rusty started barking and running in circles with his tongue hanging out and a big grin on his face.

"All right," Granville said, his shoulders relaxed. "Let's try it again."

In the next hour, the tin cans flew through the air time after time.

"I think I'm ready for that sly old fox who's been attacking Mama's chickens." Granville threw his arm over Calvin's shoulders. "Come on, we've got chores to do, and then our homework."

When the two boys rounded the corner of the barn, Granville saw his father riding in with his brother Franklin riding along beside him. He remembered what Mr. Owens had told him earlier that day. "Go on and get started, Cal. I've got something I've got to talk to Dad about."

Calvin stopped and looked up at him "Can I come?"

"No. Not this time." Granville gave him a gentle shove and strode toward the fence railing, his gut roiling again. What would his dad say when he learned one of the outlaws stole food from his work wagon?

IN THE WEE HOURS of the morning, Granville crept down the stairs in his stocking feet. He gripped his boots in his hands and winced as the stairs creaked. Moving stealthily, he tried not to wake the rest of the household. When he reached the bottom landing, he moved swiftly out the back door and sat on the wooden steps, where he shoved his feet into his boots.

When he stood, he pulled the slingshot from his back pocket and ran quietly through the barnyard. Up ahead, the chicken coop was dark and ominous. He lowered himself onto the ground at a distance and waited. Time stood still the longer he sat, and after what seemed hours, his eyes drooped. The world was eerily quiet except for an occasional moo from the cattle in the pasture or a nicker from a horse in the barn, Granville trained his ears for the sound of the sly fox.

He waited.

His father had said patience was the mother of virtue. But could he sit all alone in the dark with only the moon lighting the buildings just enough to give an outline of where they stood? The longer he sat, however, the more he realized the world screamed with subtle sounds that one wouldn't notice during the light of day:—the hoot of an owl, the rustle of leaves in the breeze, and the skitter of mice hiding near the grain bins.

He closed his eyes, but kept his ears awake. His head drooped and he jerked it up. *Come on, Granville. You're never going to catch that dumb fox if you fall asleep!* He sat up straight and shook himself. He eyed the outbuildings again for the hundredth time. Shadows lurked in every corner. Objects against the buildings seemed to emulate still animals or a human form. Granville squirmed and squinted to see better.

Chickens began to cackle in the chicken coop. Granville leaned forward, turning an ear to the pen. There it was again, a squawk and a flap of wings. Granville slowly slipped his hand into his pocket and pulled out a smooth stone. He crept stealthily to the opposite side of the coop, a good ten yards away. The chickens began to cackle frantically.

There! Granville spied a fox feverishly digging under the wooden frame of the chicken coop.

He straightened his left arm, holding the slingshot firmly in his grip. He stretched the leather with the stone in the pocket. He held it tightly a moment longer, his eye trained on his target. *Swoosh!* The stone sailed through the air and slammed into the side of the fox's temple.

"Yelp!" The animal dropped to the ground.

Granville's heart raced as he hurried across the yard to where the fox was crumpled into a heap. He stared at the animal. *He's dead!* Granville jumped in the air. *I did it. Wait till Mama finds out I got that old fox that been killing her chickens!*

JOHN ENTERED THE KITCHEN smiling ear to ear.

"You look like the cat who ate the mouse." Nancy set a plate of pancakes before the children at the table. "What's that look for?"

"I think Granville took care of that fox that's been killing your chickens." He gazed toward the table as if expecting Granville to be sitting there. His chair was empty.

"Really?" Nancy's eyes widened.

"There's a dead fox lying in front of the chicken coop." John turned to the table and winked at his brood. "He's dead as a fox can be."

The children giggled. Their father had their full attention.

Glancing back at his wife, John said, "I found a smooth stone lying on the ground beside his head."

"Yes!" whooped Calvin from the opposite side of the table.

Nancy and John stared at their son and then at each other.

"He must have snuck out of the house last night and waited for the fox to come." Calvin squirmed in his seat.

John shrugged. "I thought I heard a faint sound outside our bedroom early this morning."

"Well, that accounts for why Granville's slept in. I couldn't wake him." Nancy's eyes lit up as she looked toward the ceiling as if she could see beyond it. "I'm going to let him sleep in. He's earned it."

John pulled Nancy into his arms and kissed her forehead. "All right. Just this morning. But let's not make it a habit."

They heard giggling at the table as the children looked on.

"Get to eating your breakfast or you'll be late for school!" Nancy said.

John let Nancy push out of his arms as she turned to face the children, straightening her apron and clearing her throat.

"I'll be back after a while. I've got to bury that fox before it gets too warm." John grinned and winked at the children again before he moved out of the kitchen.

"Can I come, Dad?" Calvin scooted out of his chair.

"No, son. Finish your breakfast." John turned to Franklin. "Come on, I want you to give me a hand."

"Yes, sir." Franklin scooted his chair back and gave Calvin a grin.

Calvin slid back in place with a disgruntled look on his face.

"Do you suppose there are any more foxes out there waiting for my chickens?" Nancy asked.

"I don't know, but if there is, your son will take care of them." John swung out the back door with Franklin on his heels. Proud of Granville for killing the fox, John asked Franklin, "Who would have guessed Granville would have such a good aim with a slingshot?"

THE WIND RATTLED THE front door as Otis Murphy swaggered into the tailor shop. He gave Grady a slight nod and then threaded his way past the dainty fabrics leading to Mahala's work table. She looked up in time to see the outlaw, who was wearing a blue tight-fitting shirt and brown breeches. Suspenders held up his pants and a gun belt hugged his hips.

Mahala's stomach twisted as Murphy's boots grazed the floor. Most men removed their hats when they entered an establishment. But Otis Murphy didn't. His eyes were shadowed under his broad-brimmed hat.

What is he doing here?

Mahala lowered her eyes, and watched his boots as Murphy strode to her table. She jerked when the table shook under his body weight. Broad hands splayed over the material she was working on and her stomach tensed.

"Afternoon, Miss Shields." Murphy touched the brim of his black hat that held a feather tucked in the silver band surrounded the crown.

Mahala sat stalk still. "Are you lost, Mr. Murphy?" She feigned bravery.

"Can't say that I am." He gave her a quirky grin. "I see that your little town is going to have a harvest dance." He jerked his elbow toward the window, where a sign hung on one of the posts along the boardwalk. "I'd be obliged if you'd make me a shirt for the occasion?" He eyed her hungrily.

Mahala was stunned by his request, and she wanted to retreat under the table to avoid his sleazy gaze. She cleared her throat. "The Harvest Festival is for farmers and ranchers who have spent an incredible amount of time planting and harvesting their fields, and for those of us who live in this community." She lifted her chin. "Seeing you don't fit either of those qualifications, I'm surprised you'd want to attend the celebration."

"I— "

"Besides," Mahala cut in. "Grady handles the men's clothing. You've come to the wrong person." She dismissed him by lowering her head and picking up a needle and fabric. She pushed the point of the needle into the material, wishing Murphy would leave.

"You don't understand, Miss Shields. I want *you* to make my shirt." He pushed his hat back. Dark eyes glared down at her with a storm brewing in them.

Mahala glared at the outlaw. "Mister, I've not finished the gowns I'm committed to. What's more—" She squared her shoulders, although her body shook. "I reserve the right to refuse service to anyone I choose." She held Murphy's gaze, but her belly felt like mush.

Murphy's hand shot out and he grabbed her wrists. "You're a sassy little thing, aren't you?" His steely gaze burned into hers and then showed a glimmer of admiration. "You're a little spitfire. That's what I like about you, Miss Shields." He still held her wrist and it throbbed. "Since you won't make my shirt, I'd be obliged if you'd let me escort you to the dance." His fingers cut into her skin.

Mahala jerked her arm out of his hold. "Good day, Mr. Murphy."

"I'm not done." His hand shot out, but before he could make contact, Grady grabbed his shoulder and spun him around. He held a pistol at Murphy's nose.

"The lady's busy, mister." Grady shoved the gun closer, denting the man's nose. "You're not welcome in this establishment. Now get out!"

Murphy's hand went for his holster, but the click of Grady's gun stopped him. Gun cocked Grady said, "Don't make me blow your head off, Murphy."

The two men held each other's gaze and if she didn't know better, Mahala would have sworn she saw a spark of fire rising between them. A slow grin spread across Murphy's face. He backed away and slanted a gaze at Mahala. "I'll see you at the dance, Miss Priss." He turned and stalked out of the shop.

Lowering his gun, Grady heaved a sigh. "You all right?"

"Quite. Thank you, Grady." She heard the edge in her tone, as she leaned her shoulder against the window and watched Otis Murphy step into his saddle. He stared at the store window, touched the brim of his hat and laughed. He reined his steed toward the outskirts of town. Dirt kicked up as he put his mount into a gallop.

"You don't think the Woodrow gang would really show up at the dance, do you?" Mahala's jaw grew tense as she gazed at Mr. Thompson.

"It appears you're like honey to a bear with that man. I wouldn't put it past him to show up. You best keep your guard up with him," Grady warned.

The two of them stared out the window again before Grady went back to his work. Mahala continued to watch Murphy ride out of town.

Good heavens! Surely that man wouldn't show up at the Harvest Dance—would he?

Chapter TEN

THE AUTUMN WIND RUFFLED the water as it flowed lazily downstream. John nudged Blue along the banks, searching for wandering calves. Two of his ranch hands, William and McDuff, rode alongside. It wasn't uncommon to find cattle down by the water, but every once in a while, a calf wandered into the middle of the stream where it was deeper and would have to be hauled out with their ropes.

Today's search was a two-fold ride. They'd look for wandering calves, but he wanted to count his stock too.

After a time, they left the stream and rode back through the dried yellow grasses to count the crop of calves. It wasn't long before concern etched John's brow. "The number of calves aren't adding up like they should," he said, gazing at the cowhands. "It seems I'm missing a few yearlings." His jaw tightened. "Let's split up and count them again. You men go back to the pastures and I'll check the creek."

"Yes, sir," William said, reining his horse aside.

McDuff nodded and rode off toward the east end of the ranch at a gallop.

Not wanting to rush to judgment, John pushed Blue to travel the path back down to the creek. He ambled slow and steady, alert to sounds that might be a bawl from a lost calf. He rode upstream to the Shields' boundary line, and kept his eyes keen to movement in the brush. A half hour later, as he rode back down stream, he felt eyes looking down on him from the knoll to his left. Gazing upward, he spotted Judd Benson sitting on his steed. His neighbor sat rock still, observing him. Irritation grated on him for the time spent hunting for missing calves. He ignored Benson and nudged Blue on.

Benson, however, wound his horse down the side of the hill and waited at his fence line. John let out a deep breath. He'd missed breakfast while he'd been out hunting for calves, and Benson was the last person he wanted to talk to at the moment. Still, John obliged him. He touched the brim of his hat. "Good morning." John nudged Blue over to the split rail fence.

"Mornin', John," Benson looked over John's shoulder to the cool running water behind him. "I've been watching you this past while. You looking for something?"

"Yearlings. What with the Woodrow outfit hanging around, I've been keeping a closer eye on my herd."

"You think that lot would steal your cattle?" Benson gazed at the trees on the other side of the water as if he could see beyond them.

"We're suspicious that they've already stolen a number of cattle from ranches in the valley. Some of the ranchers have seen cattle out in the pasture at your old ranch east of town." John squinted under the brightness of the morning sun. "But we can't do anything about it until we can prove who those cows belong to." His gaze narrowed on Benson. "You're not missing any cattle?"

Benson shifted and his saddle creaked. "Not that I'm aware of, but what're you talkin' about? You sayin' those no-accounts are stayin' up at my ranch?" His jaw dropped.

"Don't tell me you didn't know that Woodrow and his men have been hanging out at your old place? I thought you knew."

Benson paled and his expression hardened. "I hadn't heard where the gang was hiding out—let alone—my place."

John shook his head. "I can't believe you didn't know. They've been there for over a month. You might want to check it out."

Benson removed his gray felt hat and ran his fingers through his silver-and-black hair. "That place has sat empty for so long, I don't give it much thought. It's not as if we have a run of ranchers moving into the area and in need of a piece of land."

John listened to Benson while Blue side-stepped and chuffed.

"Looks like I better find out what's going on. If you'll excuse me, I'll head out." Benson shoved his hat back on and touched the brim as he turned his horse back up the rise. His horse kicked up dirt as it lunged upward.

JUDD BENSON TIGHTENED HIS fingers on the reins as he rode up the long drive to his property. He'd hoped to find someone to buy the deserted ranch at a good price. But he wasn't in a hurry. The land was as good as gold when it came to cattle ranching. The fields were lush and green. It was just a matter of time before the right person came along who'd appreciate that piece of land. It burned his hide to find out that the Woodrow clan had helped themselves to his property.

Pushing his horse forward, Benson rode up to the house and stopped in front of the porch. Two horses were tied to the hitching post, and he'd already spied two others in the corral when he rode over the knoll.

"Hello in there!" Benson called out.

The door shot open and Jiggs Woodrow stepped out onto the porch. "What can I do for you, mister?"

"Well, for one, you can pack your stuff and get off my land," Benson said.

Jiggs ran a thumb over his lower lip and grinned. "This here's your place, is it?"

"That's right." Benson watched Woodrow lean against the porch post, a match stick in his mouth.

"It appears no one's been livin' in this run-downs hack for a long time." Jiggs pushed away from the post. "Why don't you rent the place to us for a spell."

"You're interested in renting it?" Benson's shoulders relaxed.

"Hold on," Jiggs said and disappeared inside the shack.

Benson waited, feeling the morning breeze kick up. He'd anticipated a ruckus with the men—one he hadn't favored. That Woodrow wanted to rent the place surprised him. Things were looking up.

Jiggs reappeared with cash in hand. He stared at Benson for a long moment and said, "This ought to do." He tossed the bills in the air and the paper feathered to the ground. The breeze whipped the money across the yard.

Anger burned inside Judd Benson, and he swallowed the venom of words he wanted to spit at Woodrow.

"You best collect your rent if you want it." Jiggs rocked on his heels, a smirk on his face.

Judd's ears burned as he slid off his stallion and picked up what fluttering cash he could. When he'd collected the money, he stared at Woodrow with contempt. The two men held each other's gaze for a moment, but then Benson strode back to his horse. He climbed onto his mount and glared at the white-haired man. He'd never known anyone to be a bigger bully than him.

He stuffed the cash inside his coat pocket and leaned forward. "If you aren't out of here in thirty days . . . I'll be back."

"You do that." Jiggs smiled and chewed on the match stick.

Judd turned his mount toward town. He rode off with one thought swirling in his head. *I want those men off my land!*

LONG AFTER THE CITIZENS of Grovespring had gone home for the day and retired for the night, the Woodrow gang kept the saloon owner busy serving one bottle of whiskey after another. The restless men were soused when they finally left town late into the night. They rode out of town at breakneck speed, whooping and hollering. The ground thundered with the sound of horses' hooves echoing through the night air.

"Whew!" Joe cried out as his horse ate up the ground. They came to the edge of the road that led down into the valley. Below, Judd Benson's ranch sprawled black and ominous in the darkness. The trees appeared as giant sentries guarding the surrounding oasis.

Curly Joe pushed his horse harder and sweat glistened off the animal's back in the moonlight. Horse and rider thundered on.

Jiggs and Otis rode ahead of Joe and Duke. Joe veered from the main road and cut through the downhill slope, pushing hard toward the dark fields and racing through the weeds and ruts. All at once, the horse lunged head first. A shrill scream seared through the air as the animal's foreleg buckled under the full force of its weight, and a loud snap split the air. The shrill whinny of the steed echoed through the night in a terrifying cry as Joe sailed over the horse's head and hit the ground with a thud. The force took his breath away, as his horse rolled past him with a painful groan. When it came to a stop, his mount's coat quivered and it snorted low in its throat, its eyes white with pain. Both forelegs lay at an angle.

"Dog dang it!" Joe called out as he got to this feet. He stared down the hill at the sickening sight of his horse shivering. He walked in circles and kicked at a stone nearby.

The steed's sides heaved heavily, short puffs of air escaping its flared nostrils. Joe heard the thundering hooves of the gang riding up. Jiggs slid off his horse and pulled his rifle from the leather sheath on the side of his horse. He strode over to the suffering animal and glared up the hill at Joe. "You just wasted a good horse." Jiggs cocked it his rifle then aimed the weapon at the injured animal's head—and fired. The horse quivered one more time and then grew still.

Jiggs stared down at the animal and then at Curly Joe, who'd strode to where the dead horse lay. "That was a mighty fine horse you had. Too bad you haven't learned how to care for a fine animal like him."

Jiggs spit on the ground, shoved his rifle back into the leather sheath, and mounted his steed. He signaled for the others to ride out, leaving Curly Joe standing alone with the still horse.

"Hey! Wait for me!"

Jiggs and the two riders continued on toward the ranch.

Curly Joe stomped his boot on the hard ground. "Come back here!"

The riders rode on with deaf ears.

"Now I've gone and done it!" Joe pulled off his hat and threw it to the ground. He watched the fading backs of the three riders and knew they weren't coming back. He picked up his hat and shoved it back on. The young outlaw trudged over to the horse, and pulled off the saddle and gear, and began walking down the hill, the saddle weighing down his steps.

"Rats in a poke! What am I goin' to do about a horse now?"

THREE DAYS LATER, THE thunder rolled and lightning snaked through the sky. Frightened whinnies from the stable broke through the night. John Grigsby shot up in bed and listened. The horses neighing and stomping intensified in the midst of the great silence that had followed the last clap of thunder. Dulled by sleep, John justified the confusion in the stable to the storm that had awakened and frightened the stock. He listened for more sounds outside. A few low rumbles were heard from the thunderclouds, but the sounds in the stable grew silent. When he heard no more noise coming from outside, he leaned back in bed and went back to sleep. Long before dawn, he awakened again with a start. Again, he heard sounds from the barn.

Nancy rolled over and clung to him. "Stay here."

"You hear the horses too?"

"Yes. It's just the storm making them restless." She snuggled as best she could against his back. "The heat of your body is keeping me warm." She smiled sleepily. "Go back to sleep."

John tried to slumber, but the muffled sound of frightened whinnies broke the still of the morning. He shot up and listened. There it was again. The horses neighed and kicked their stalls, and their cries drifted through the window. This time he felt there was something ominous about the sounds coming from the barn. He couldn't stay in bed any longer. He had to go take a look outside—if for no other reason than to put his worries aside. He climbed out of bed and pulled his firearm out of the chest of drawers.

Nancy rose to her elbow. "What's happening?"

"I don't know. I'm just going to check and make sure everything's all right in the stables. No matter what you hear outside—you stay here." John pulled on his britches and belted on his gun.

"Why can't you wait until morning?" Nancy whispered.

"Because it sounds like someone might be trying to steal our horses." John tossed his shirt over his head and then slammed his body into a chair and shoved his feet into his boots.

Fully awake, Nancy sat up straight. "John, be careful!"

"I will. Don't come outside, and keep the boys in the house."

Nancy slid out of bed as her hands went to her chest.

"Get down. Don't stand by the windows!"

"Oh, John, you're scaring me!"

That's all he heard as he strode from the bedroom and down the hall to the back of the house. He threw open the back door and stepped outside into rain pummeling the ground. His ears were alert to the horses' shrill whinnies, even though the rain poured and the thunder rolled.

John stormed through the mud, spinning the cylinder of his six-shooter. He slid the gun into the holster and pulled the double doors open. The mustangs whinnied and snorted in their stalls until they recognized John. He stood in the expanse of the opening and gazed down the wide aisle, where he found Blue's stall gate open. Blue stood in the aisle, his hoof scratching the dirt floor. He whinnied low in his throat.

"It's okay, boy," John said in a low voice. "Who let you out, huh?" With the whites of his eyes flashing, Blue stomped his hooves and his ears pricked forward. "Easy boy," John said. He listened for sounds that wouldn't come from the horses. Reflexively, the fingers of his right hand tapped against the gun strapped to his thigh.

Blue came forward and chuffed. John ran a hand over his neck. "What's goin' on, buddy?" It was then that he noticed the back door to the stable stood wide open.

John could have sworn he heard horses near the outside of the barn. At the same time the blue roan reared and his nostrils flared. John crouched low to the ground, his pulse racing, his heart pounding in his ears as well. A tremor slicked up his spine. *Don't bolt*, he silently begged the mustang. Blue snorted and took a step backward.

John crawled to the stable wall, listening to the sounds of the rain pelting the roof. He eased his body against the wooden structure and moved toward the opening, where he strained to see who was out there. He waited, his gun cocked. No sign of life moved beyond the building. A moment later, a horse and rider shot out through the darkness and the rain, and he heard a gunshot as the horseman left the ranch. Was that one of his cowhands who shot at the night rider? John moved closer to the opening of the barn, his eyes peeled on the house, the long drive, and the buildings nearby. Was anybody else out there? He heard nothing but the rain drumming on the ground outside.

In the distance, John thought he heard footsteps coming from the bunkhouse. The hairs on the back of his neck rose. The last thing he needed was for one of his men to get shot by whoever was out there.

"Boss, are you in there?" came a raspy whisper on the other side of the wall.

"That you, Luke?"

"Yeah" The voice sounded muffled.

"Go back to the bunkhouse. I've got this!" John ordered.

"No dice, boss. We've got your back."

"Who's with you?"

"Brady." That was Brady's voice.

"All right. Cover me if you have to."

"Yes, sir." Silence followed.

John ducked back to where Blue stood. The mustang stomped the ground with one hoof, the muscles on his shoulder twitching. The other horses snorted as well.

John stepped outside the door, his body hunched and ready to spring. Once he was outside, he heard the sound of boots running along the backside of the building where a door led to the outbuildings behind in the ranch yard.

Who was in the stable?

Only seconds ticked by before someone stepped out behind the building.

John crept to the west side of the barn. When he came to the corner, he peered around the edge, his gun ready. Brady and Luke were nowhere in sight. He moved alongside the barn toward the back door and stood stock still. He reasoned that whoever had slipped out of the barn would have a horse waiting somewhere in the barnyard. He focused his vision on the trees, the side of the spring house, the corrals. Nothing!

John ran from the barn to the nearest tree and strained to see if there was any movement beside the barn. Rain dripped from the leaves above and soaked his clothes.

He saw movement near the south side of the bunkhouse. He aimed his gun and narrowed his gaze. It was then that he saw a horse spring out from behind the building. He leveled his pistol at the departing rider and a shot rang through the air.

The rider swung low over the horse's mane and kept riding out of the drive and onto the main road.

John and his men ran out into the open, their guns firing over and over. The rider fled down the lane until he was too far away for them to shoot at.

"You all right, boss?" McDuff asked, seeming to come out of nowhere.

"Where were you?" John asked, surprised to see him. Rain drenched the men.

"Will and I were back by the tree line. There were a couple of riders in the yard." McDuff said and continued, "I think we shot one of them—but I couldn't tell for sure with the rain coming down like it is."

"Who do you suppose was out there?" Will asked.

It was then that John discovered Will standing alongside the men. "I don't know. Coulda been a couple of Woodrow's men or maybe Clyde Benson." John cocked a grin. "Whoever it was isn't feeling so good right about now." He gazed at his men, thankful for the lot of them. "Go on back to the bunkhouse. I don't think they're coming back."

"Yes, sir," Will said, and the four men slushed through the puddles as they walked back toward the bunkhouse.

Luke turned back. "Want us to start a night watch, boss?"

"That's not a bad idea." John gazed at the men. "I'll meet up with you shortly."

"Sure thing, boss." The men dropped their heads and shuffled back to the cowhands' sleeping quarters.

John went back to the barn and walked inside. Pale light shone through the doors and between the slats of the barn walls. The horses stomped their hooves and chuffed.

He holstered his gun and ran a hand down Blue's flank. "Let's get you back in your stall."

Brownie and Star chuffed and stomped on the opposite side of the aisle.

John ran his hand through his thick black hair and swore under his breath. "It's time to visit the sheriff again! This morning's pranks were likely the works of the Woodrow gang."

A HALF HOUR LATER, the storm clouds were gone. Rankled from the mornings' events, John strode across the yard and sat on the back steps. The early morning sun rose higher, lighting the horizon a brilliant yellow, and with a red blaze emanating from it, and with the trees silhouetted against its brightness.

The back door cracked open and Franklin peered through the slim opening. "Is it safe to come out?" he asked.

"Yeah, come on out, boys." John ran a hand through his black hair.

"Who was out there this morning?" Granville joined John on the steps while Franklin and Calvin looked on.

"Could've been a couple Jiggs Woodrow's boys, or Clyde and Jimmy. It seems they tried to steal one of our horses."

"They already have horses," Granville said.

"Don't matter. There's money in selling horses." John ruffled Granville's hair. "I think one of them has a hankering for Blue."

Granville ducked away but asked. "What are you gonna do?"

"I'm going to catch the rat who tried to steal my horse!" John stared down at the boys. His family depended on him to keep them safe. Raw anger gnawed inside him.

The back door opened a crack and Nancy peered out. "Are they gone?"

John nodded. "They're gone."

Nancy looked frazzled. Her long flaxen-colored hair was tangled, and she still wore her nightgown. She pushed open the door and Granville stood up to make room for her to sit beside John.

"I don't think I've ever been more afraid than I was this morning. Who was out there?"

"I believe it was the Woodrow gang," John said for the second time.

"What are you going to do?" Nancy shuddered.

"I'm going to ride into town and talk to the sheriff." He pulled his wife close to his side. "Don't worry, honey. I've got everything under control."

"Do you, John?" A crease wrinkled the smooth skin between her brows.

John kissed Nancy's cheek. "I do. How about making breakfast while me and the boys take care of the stock in the barn?"

"All right." The worry lines stayed, but she pushed herself up and went back inside the house.

John watched the boys cross the yard.

Lord, don't let me fail from keeping my family safe. He swallowed. *And I'd be obliged if You'd help me get that rat that tried to steal my horse!*

Chapter
ELEVEN

MAHALA'S EYES SNAPPED OPEN at the smell of sizzling bacon. *Today's the harvest festival!* She climbed out of bed and splashed tepid water on her face from the washbowl which sat on a small stand in front of the window. A breeze stirred the lace curtains. Mahala donned her brown skirt and brown dotted Swiss blouse and headed downstairs in record time.

Upon entering the kitchen, she spotted her mother cracking eggs into a skillet. "I thought I heard you from upstairs. You should have awakened me." Mahala tied an apron around her thin waist.

Mary waved a hand as if motioning Mahala to sit down. "You're up early every day of the week. I thought I'd let you sleep in."

"Sleep in on the day of the harvest festival?" Mahala shook her head. "That's not happening." She glanced around the kitchen. "What do you need me to do?"

"Put the bacon on a platter. I sent your father out to the chicken coop to wring a couple of chickens' necks. I'll have the girls pluck the feathers after breakfast."

"Are the girls up?" Mahala asked. No sooner had she asked than Elizabeth, Mary Ann, and Rebecca trailed into the kitchen, rubbing their eyes and yawning. "Morning," they chorused and slid into the kitchen chairs. They wasted no time planning what they'd wear later that afternoon for the harvest dance.

The girls sounded like Blue Jays with their unending chatter. It was obvious they were excited that the day of the festival was finally here. Mahala never tired of their interactions each day, and at times she envied them their carefree spirits. The three girls had features she wished she'd inherited: curves in all the right places, delightful, cornflower blue eyes, and golden hair, which at the moment looked disarrayed from sleep and hung down their backs. But most of all, they didn't have the Shields cursed cleft chin.

"You girls best turn around and march right back up those stairs and get dressed. Your father's killing hens for us to cook for this afternoon's festival. He'll be in shortly and when he does, I want you outside plucking their feathers."

"Oh, Mother!" the three girls whined.

"Do as I say. Now up to your room."

"Can we eat first?" asked sixteen-year-old Rebecca as she slid out of her chair. Rebecca was the youngest daughter in the family. Mary Ann was eighteen and Elizabeth twenty.

"Your plates will be waiting for you after you get dressed. Now hurry up and change, we have a big day ahead of us."

Rolling their eyes, the girls retreated from the room.

Mahala could hear their firm steps as they trudged disheartened up the stairs.

Moments later, Benjamin came in through the back door and hung his hat on the wall hook. "The chickens are ready to be dipped in the boiling pot and plucked." He grabbed a dish towel from the counter and dried his hands. "I knew you'd be busy in the kitchen, so I washed up outside at the water pump." He gave his wife a peck on the cheek and went to the sink to pump himself a glass of water and then sat down at the table. "Mighty quiet out there with the ranch hands taking the day off for the festival. Young Benny and I will have to pick up the slack today."

No sooner was his name mentioned than, Benjamin Junior strode into the kitchen and went straight to the stove, eyeing the food in the frying pans.

"Get your nose out of there before the bacon grease pops on you." Mary pointed at the back door. "Chores are waiting to be done. You can eat when you get back."

Fourteen-year-old Benny backed away. "I'll be back before the rooster crows." His eyes sparkled as he went out the door and he pulled it shut behind him.

"He's a fine boy," Benjamin said proudly. "I don't have to tell him twice what's expected of him."

"He's learned from his older brothers not to cross you. It helps being the youngest and learning from the others."

Mary turned away from the stove. "Mahala, could you collect some eggs from the chicken coop? I've just used the last of the eggs in the house," she asked as she began to set the table.

"All right." Mahala lifted the basket from the pantry shelf and headed out to the barnyard. Meows met her ears when she crossed in front of the stable. Taking a detour, Mahala slipped into the barn and headed to the back corner where the kittens had grown and now scampered and played, chasing each other's tails while the mother-cat slept in the sunshine.

Picking up her favorite black-and-white fur ball, Mahala smiled as the kitten mewed and opened her pink mouth in a wide yawn. Then the baby nestled in the palm of Mahala's hand. Mahala decided then and there that she was going to keep this little kitten in the house as soon as it was weaned from its mama. Eyeing the four white paws, she said softly, "You are now endowed with the name of Boots." She kissed the kitten's small head and put it back on the hay with the others. "I'll come for you another day. For now, I've eggs to collect."

An hour later, the family fed and the chickens plucked, Mary and Mahala set to work on frying chicken and baking pies. Each family attending the harvest festival would bring a main dish, a side dish and a desert.

It was a known fact that the women of Grovespring used the annual harvest festival to show off their cooking skills and display their best desserts. There was no better reward than watching their dessert disappear first. Every year, Mary fussed more about the meal she'd take to the event than the clothes she'd wear.

Humming, Mary wiped her hands on her apron and continued to roll out pie dough. The kitchen smelled of simmering peaches and cinnamon spice, while Mahala placed the flour-battered chicken pieces into the hot grease in the skillet and listened to her mother's soft voice.

They worked well together, but not for the first time, Mahala wished she had her own kitchen, her own house, and her own family. How long before God would allow her to experience so natural a thing as having her own home?

"Your sisters are going to be the death of me," Mary said in a distant voice.

Mahala barely heard her and turned to face her mother's back. "Why do you say that?" She placed the lid on the frying pan and crossed the floor.

"Your father caught Mary Ann kissing one of the ranch hands the other day. He liked to have killed that boy, and he sent Mary Ann to her room. And then your sister Rebecca came home from town, swooning over the delivery boy who helped her at the feed store." Mary waved the knife through the air as she spoke, sending flour dust onto the table.

Mahala couldn't help but grin and placed an arm around her mother's waist. "They are coming to the age to notice boys. Beside, Cord Matthews is a fine young man. Charles and Gretta raised him right. He's only got one more year to work in the feed store, then he'll be out on the range with his father. Like it or not, another year from now, available men will come knocking on your door to court the girls." She gave her mother an extra squeeze

"We'll worry about that next year. For now," she shook the knife Mahala's way, "the girls better mind their manners. They're too young to be ogling boys." Her frown turned into a smile as she cut slits into the pie crust.

"My sisters are little flirts." Mahala elbowed her mother's side. "At least they won't be old spinsters like me."

"Stop that. We both know it isn't your fault you're not married yet."

"Yet?"

"Yes." Mary opened the oven door and placed three pies onto the wire rack. She closed it and said, "They'll be ready in about an hour." She wiped her brow. "Don't let me forget about them. These pies should be just as good as last year's, what with the peaches coming from the Grigsby's orchard."

The big kitchen felt toasty and smelled deliciously spicy. Mahala continued to fry chicken, lifting the lid now and again to turn the crispy pieces over to fry to a golden brown. She added a few sticks of wood to the firebox. Moments later, she placed the pieces of fried chicken into a warmed cast iron skillet that had been cleaned and reserved for this purpose. She spread a dish towel over the top to keep the cooked chicken warm. When done, she lifted the hand pump beside the sink and filled two glasses of water and set them on the table.

"We just about have the cooking out of the way," Mary said, brushing a wayward strand of gray hair from her cheek. "Did you finish all the dresses for your clients?"

"I finished the last one yesterday. Mrs. Benson was hot as a cross hen when she stormed into the shop to pick it up."

"You made Flora Benson wait until the last minute for her dress?" Mary's brows rose with a look of disbelief.

"Wait until you see her gown. The design was fit for a general's dinner, not a barn dance. By the time I finished putting the last touches to the dress, I was glad to be done with it." Mahala smiled slowly. "She may have had to wait until the last moment to pick up her dress, but I believe she was more than happy with my work."

Mary let out a small huff. "I'll be seeing it tonight for sure, and that Flora—she'll be flaunting it in front of all the ladies."

An hour later, Mahala watched her mother get to her feet and cross over to the stove. Taking up potholders, she opened the oven door and stood back to let the rush of heat out. The aroma of sweet peaches and cinnamon spice wafted even more strongly through the kitchen.

"Mmm, that smells heavenly," Mahala said.

Mary removed the three pies and set them on the counter to cool.

"Let's set them in the windowsill." Mahala took two dish towels and one by one she set the pies in the window, where a fresh breeze blew in.

"I just hope those blackbirds don't come peckin' at them." Mary stood with fists on hips, examining her handiwork.

"Well," Mahala said, turning to exit the kitchen. "Now that the cooking's done, I best see to the finishing touches to my new dress."

"Your new dress?"

"Yes. I decided to make one for myself for the dance."

"That's a first. For once you listened to your mother's good advice."

"And I'm glad I did. After all, I may not be here for the next harvest dance."

Mahala started to step through the kitchen door into the front hall but stopped when she heard her mother ask, "What's that supposed to mean?"

"I mailed out a response to an ad in the newspaper. I may just become Grovespring's first mail-order bride."

"You didn't!" Mary's face went pale.

"I did." It was Mahala's turn to put her fist on her hips. "I don't intend to be the town's only spinster next year. I'll be married even it means going back East to a place I've never been."

"Well . . . will wonders ever cease?" Mahala heard her mother say as she sailed up the stairs.

THE SOUND OF THE horses' clop-clopping kept pace to the drumming of Mahala's heart. The family was well on their way to Charles Matthews' spread. As the wagon creaked and bumped along the potholed road, Mahala strained to hold back the mischievous smile that wouldn't hide. Not only had she finished the last gown for the party tonight, but she had also completed a handsome gown for herself.

The full-skirted dress featured an all-over vertical pattern of floral sprays of varied colors. The belt, front placket, and bows, all in green, made a refreshing contrast to the light-gold background of the dress. A sedate lace collar, a brooch at the neckline, and lace inserts in the sleeves toned down the gold, giving the dress a cheerful but not overdone look.

She had wanted to wear her hair pinned up in an elegant style, but after several tries to get her heavy locks to stay put, she gave up, and now her thick hair flowed over her shoulders and down her back.

Her sisters sat across from her, beautifully dressed in long skirts and white, starched blouses trimmed with lace on the collars and sleeves. The girls *had* taken the time to put their hair up in the latest fashion, held firmly with tortoise combs and pins. They had pinched their cheeks so many times earlier that afternoon that they truly had rosy complexions.

Charles Matthews' ranch yard would be filled with wagons, horses, and people when the Shields arrived. In the past few weeks, posters advertising the harvest festival had been tacked to the walls of stores and posts around town. It was the talk of their community.

In the distance, Mahala saw smoke spiraling to the sky. As their wagon drew closer to the Matthews' ranch, she gazed at a group of men surrounding an open fire pit where they were attending the beef on the spits. Beef fat dripped, causing the flames to spit and spurt. Even at a distance, she could tell the men were intent on giving each other advice on how best to barbeque the beef.

John Grigsby was among that party of men. He looked up and touched the brim of his hat as the Shields' wagon drove by.

Mahala nodded in return. Then she gazed past him to the crowd of women setting food on the long tables covered in red-and-white checkered tablecloths.

Nancy was among the ladies, carrying a big bowl to the first table, where she set it down. Mahala watched as she stepped back and kneaded her back with her fist and looked around. Their eyes caught and Mahala waved.

"Can you stop right here?" Mahala asked her father. "I see Nancy and she looks as if she's overdone it again."

Benjamin Shields pulled on the reins to slow the wagon to a halt.

"I'm coming with you." Mrs. Shields climbed down from the wagon and then gazed at the girls. "I want you girls to bring the food to the tables."

"Yes, Mama," chimed the three girls.

"And be extra careful with the pies." Their mother darted a warning glance at the three of them.

Benny sat at the back of the wagon, his legs dangling over the edge. He gave his mother a salute.

Mahala had taken a few steps away from the wagon, but she waited for her mother to catch up. "From the looks of those tables, there's more than enough food for everybody." She picked up her skirts as she walked across the grass.

A few women looked up from the tables at the newcomers. When they saw Mahala and her mother approach, some of them gave each other looks.

Mahala's stomach twisted a bit. She had scolded herself several times that morning for making her dress just as beautiful and festive as the ones she'd made for the women of the community. Even though she was a spinster, she decided it wouldn't hurt for once to not be outdone by the other women at the party tonight.

Every September, the single women of Grovespring had high hopes of meeting an eligible bachelor at the Harvest Festival who would court them. More often than not, the dance was the beginning of the courting season.

Not that Mahala thought there was any chance of being noticed by any of the men from Grovespring. Most of the men her age or older were already taken. And at thirty, she had all but given up hope of ever marrying. Then again, that was before she answered the ad in the newspaper. And though she hadn't received a reply from Mr. Bates, she would not give up hope.

"Mahala!" Nancy walked up and stopped short. Her eyes widened as they trailed from her friend's head to her polished white shoes. Eyelet lacing ran from the toes of her boots and interwove with white ribbons to the top of the fancy footwear.

"You look absolutely stunning!" Nancy said with a mischievous smile. "It's about time."

Taking a deep breath, Mahala said, "Thank you, Nancy, but I believe you're making far too much of this dress." Mahala ran her hand down the front of the gown, pleased that Nancy had noticed her new dress, but partly to calm the jitters in her stomach. "And look at you. That yellow skirt and blouse you've chosen look quite refreshing. They nearly match your hair."

For the harvest dance, Nancy had allowed her tresses to be pulled up high with tendrils of curls falling on her brow, near her ears, and at the nape of her neck. Her swollen midriff couldn't be hidden, but she wore a long blouse that flared loosely in an attempt to make it less noticeable.

Nancy looked down at herself. "Maybe one of these days I'll attend the harvest festival in a slim dress." She patted her brows and cheeks with a lace handkerchief.

Mahala noticed tiny droplets of sweat on Nancy's upper lip and thought again that her friend had overdone it in preparing the food before coming to the festival.

Elizabeth, Mary Ann, and Rebecca strode to the tables, carrying their main and side dishes and the desserts. Their mother was quick to supervise where the food would be placed.

Before long, blankets were spread on patches of prairie grass, while children ran and played. A hive of women hovered over the makeshift tables that were covered with so much food one couldn't see the table tops.

NANCY WATCHED AS MAHALA hung back from the crowd of women gathered around the tables. She could almost feel Mahala's tension, her desire to be a part of them. Mahala's sister Mary Ann seemed to have noticed Mahala's apprehension and walked up to take her hand. Nancy felt a smile tug at her mouth.

"I'll get my food and join you in a moment," Nancy said. She gave Mahala a reassuring look and then began filling her plate. Wondering where John had gone off to, Nancy searched for him in the crowd as her gaze cut through the maze of blankets.

Up ahead Tess sat on the quilt with the three little ones. Nancy had already made several trips with plates for them. She was grateful for her daughter's willingness to help, but she knew there would come a day when Tess would have interests elsewhere at the lively harvest festival. She best enjoy the help while she could.

Mahala took her plate to the Grigsby's blanket, which had been placed next to the Shields' and sat down next to Mary Jane.

"We brought a thousand things to eat," Mary Jane said. "Aren't you hungry, Molly? I am. It's been hours since Mama made breakfast, and she barely let us eat lunch, shooing us out of the kitchen to get ready for this event."

"Yes, I'm hungry darling." Mahala gazed at the curly-headed little girl. "Everything smells heavenly."

Nancy sensed that Mahala was a bundle of jitters with so many women glaring her way. Her friend appeared pleased and nervous at the same time. Why, oh why, had Mahala undertaken the notion to make such a beautiful dress? Not that she didn't deserve it, but she'd drawn attention to herself.

She watched as Mahala gazed beyond the blankets and stared at the low hills surrounding the Matthews' ranch.

Nancy followed her gaze to see three horsemen silhouetted on the rise. She swallowed. "It's them," she murmured.

"I had hoped they'd left town," Mahala said. She stared at the horsemen with a slight frown.

"John's been wary of them," Nancy said. "A couple of riders showed up at the ranch in the wee hours of the morning, yesterday. One of our horses was found standing outside his stall with the gate wide open."

Mahala's hand went to her chest and she leaned forward. "Was it them?" She pointed toward the strangers on the knoll.

"We don't know. It was dark and raining. None of the men got a good look at them."

"Oh my word!" Mahala sat back again.

"What's more," Nancy said, "John said some of the ranchers are missing cattle and they think those riders are responsible for it."

"Father's missing cattle too." Mahala took a bite of fried chicken.

Tess's and Mary Jane's gazes swung to the hill and Tess visibly shivered.

"Come on, girls, eat your lunch," Nancy said. "The party is going to start before too long." She looked over at Mahala and gave a slight shake of her head.

Mahala nodded and they changed the subject. Soon the strangers were forgotten, at least for the moment.

The day wore on and the women cleaned up after the meal. The children ran and screamed in delightful laughter, while the men set up games of horseshoes. A crowd gathered around to cheer them on.

At last the sun went down, and Charles Matthews' barn was lit brightly. Kerosene lamps were set in wall sconces and were lined up at each post and all along the walls. At the far end of the barn, a makeshift platform had been built to accommodate the musicians, who were tuning their instruments in preparation for a night of dancing and lively music. Soon the music floated out from the barn.

Tables had been moved inside the barn and were spread with refreshments. Punch bowls sat at one end of the tables, with an assortment of crystal glasses and plain jars set around each bowl. Rumors had spread throughout town that several of the Grovespring women had been in competition concocting this year's fruit drinks to quench the party guest's taste buds. Another table was filled with cookies, cakes, and pies, sliced and ready to be picked up.

The townspeople flowed into the barn, the men in their Sunday best, the women in colorful gowns newly made, some gingham checked, some with flower prints, and some too lavish for a barn dance.

Chairs were lined on the sidelines for those who wanted to sit and watch the dancers on the wooden floor. Most of the chairs were occupied, but Mahala found her mother seated by an empty chair with her shawl draped across it. "Is this for me?" Mahala smiled as she sat down. "I haven't seen the Bensons yet," Mahala gazed toward the barn entrance. "Do you suppose they've decided not to come?"

"Pfft! Flora Benson is not going to give up the chance to flaunt her new dress," Mary said.—"And if I know that woman the way I think I do, she's late on purpose. She wants to make a grand entrance."

"You think so?"

"I know so."

Mahala glanced at the entrance to the barn where the inside glow lit the opening. Beyond, it was pitch black outside. If Flora Benson arrived like her mother said she would, that glow would be like stepping onto a stage at the opera. Come to think of it—she expected the haughty Benson women to show up at any moment.

Were the Benson women happy with the outcome of their gowns? And if so, would they seek her out the next time they needed a new ensemble? Good Lord! What was she thinking? Hadn't she learned her lesson as to how difficult a customer Flora Benson was? Could she truly go through that again?

Chapter TWELVE

THE MUSICIANS PICKED UP their instruments and plucked at the strings, teasing the crowd. Soon the air was filled with music, the pulse setting the atmosphere for the night. The folks grabbed their partners and hit the floor dancing as the rafters trembled with the sound of music and laughter.

Couples swirled around the floor in rhythm with the music, making splashes of color as the women's skirts flared out. Mahala felt a certain satisfaction as she watched the women pleasantly twirling in the new dresses she'd made for them. She felt swallowed up by the crowd as the floor filled with more dancers and those who watched on from the sidelines.

Whistles and applause rippled across the room as the band played on. The banjo played its plunky tunes while the fiddle shrilled happily, the guitars gave the music the right amount of sway, and the deep bass from the cello set the tempo.

Out of nowhere, Kyle Weaver appeared before Mahala and bowed low. "Good evening, Miss Shields."

Mahala looked up, taking in the muscles layering his arms and chest, and then willed her pulse to slow. The man's voice and manners contrasted with his powerful stature and muscular build. A "gentle bear" is what she thought of the man and, maybe, a little slow. He sported a catfish mustache that extended straight across the upper lip of a wide expanse of mouth. It was sleek, oiled, and glistening. He'd shown up at the dance in a faded cotton shirt and pants. His hair was neatly parted and slicked down, and alert blue eyes were fixed on her.

"Let's see now." He seemed to be working up the nerve to ask her to dance as he tugged at one side of his mustache. "You been sittin' here far too long, Miss Shields, and that purty dress sure do need to be twirling on the floor." His black mustache twitched ever so slightly as he offered her a smile.

Holding her breath and wanting to say 'no,' nevertheless, she held out her hand and stood up. As Mr. Weaver led her onto the floor, she felt eyes on her back from the other partygoers, and the short walk to the middle of the dance floor seemed an eternity.

If the women of Grovespring thought she was interested in Kyle Weaver, they were sadly mistaken. The man was old enough to be her father and slightly off, but he had a heart of gold. Truth was, she'd known the poor man had his sights on her for many years, but he simply wasn't her type. She couldn't imagine spending the rest of her life married to him, much less bearing his children. Would she find herself thinking the same thing when and if she met Mr. Alexander Bates?

It wasn't Kyle Weaver's fault she had no interest in him courting her, but she'd favor him with a dance, and she would see it through. With a lump in her throat, and still feeling eyes on them, she put her heart into the dance as they do-si-doed to the music.

"Allemande left!" the announcer called out. Kyle and Mahala danced to the left, keeping step with the others. "Back to your partner for a right and a left grand!"

Kyle swung Mahala around, and for the first time that evening, she found herself smiling.

"Ace of diamonds, Jack of Spades! Meet your partner and all promenade!"

Hoots and howls went out on the sidelines. Mahala caught sight of John Grigsby twirling his daughter Tess through the dance. Glancing over her shoulder, she found Nancy sitting on the sidelines with young Wiley on her lap.

Finally, the music ended and Mahala brushed a loose strand of curls off her forehead as she headed for her chair. "I thoroughly enjoyed the dance, Mr. Weaver. Thank you."

But the music began again, this time slow, and Mr. Weaver caught her arm. "Miss Shields, I'd be obliged if you'd allow me the pleasure of one more dance."

Mahala gulped and fanned her face. "Thank you, Mr. Weaver, but I think I'd best sit this one out." She looked to her mother, her sisters—someone to help her out of this next dance.

The strum of the guitar was inviting and the deep bass a slow beat. If only

Mr. Wonderful were here to draw her onto the floor instead of Old-Man Weaver.

He held out his hand with pleading eyes.

Mahala took a step toward the dance floor, her stomach in knots.

"Mahala, you should rest," she heard her mother say.

Too late. One last dance.

Their dance was awkward, and Mahala was eager to end it, but on and on the music vibrated throughout the barn as they danced on the wooden floor. When he stepped on her toes, Mr. Weaver said, "I'm clumsy as an ox, Miss Shields. An ox with a gentle lamb," he said gently.

An uncomfortable heat burned up her neck. She waved a hand at him as if to indicate there was nothing to be sorry about. But in truth she wanted nothing more than to be done with the dance and to find her seat again.

The last strum of the guitar faded and Kyle led Mahala back to her seat. He touched the brim of his hat and said, "I truly do thank you, Miss Shields, for allowing me the pleasure of this dance." He walked away with his head held high.

"Goodness, Mahala," her mother said, shaking her head vehemently.

"Don't, Mama. He deserves to have a fun evening as much as anybody else."

"If you say so." Mary Shields heaved a disgruntled sigh.

"I do."

The room buzzed with excitement as the party was in full swing. Mahala looked for Nancy as the dancers cleared the floor at the end of another song. To her surprise, John was leading Nancy back to her chair where Tess sat waiting and holding her youngest brother, Wiley. A smile spread across Mahala's face. "Good," she whispered to herself.

The evening was well on its way when Judd Benson's family arrived. The musicians had just ended a ballad, and dancing partners were finding seats on the sidelines.

A hush fell among the crowd as they craned their necks to see who had just arrived. The women murmured in hushed tones as they gaped at Caroline's and Flora's gowns.

Judd crooked his arm as he led his wife to the entrance. Flora jutted her chin and her eyes sparkled as she stood looking around the barn as if searching for an appropriate place to sit in all her grandeur. Her gown was a mixture of lace in an unusual combination of lilac and moss green. The plunging yoke, framed by a collar of double shirring and contrasting green, was accented with a diamond brooch. The short, gathered-sleeves were edged with netting, and the front of the skirt was gathered with large ribbons, revealing a green underskirt.

A ripple of murmurs hummed across the floor, and the women stared at Mahala, their jaws slack, and then back to Flora. Some of the women squinted jealously, while others gasped with wide-eyed disbelief—and in truth,—Mahala knew neither reaction would do her any good. Yet when Mahala gazed back at the Grovespring women, she was pleased by the stir she'd created. Might there be more women lined up at the tailor shop in need of a seamstress for the next community event?

Seeing the Bensons had arrived, some folks gave up a row of chairs and offered the seats to the family. The Bensons, however, continued into the center of the barn, while everyone waited for the festivities to continue.

Judd touched the brim of his hat and nodded toward the crowd while he led his wife, Flora, to a chair on the far side of the dance floor. He turned then to his daughter, Caroline, who was escorted by her brother Myron. Clyde side-stepped his siblings and slipped away to the shadows at the side of the barn.

A new wave of gasps ran through the room as Caroline stepped forward, her hands holding out the sides of her skirts as if she were truly a princess. And indeed, she looked entirely out of place at a prairie barn dance. Her cerise satin dress was a delicacy of lace and bows, and the full, cherry red overskirt was covered with long panels of lace and ribbons tied into rosettes.

Mary Ann tapped her shoulder and said, "Why didn't you make me a gown like that?"

"Shush, Mary Ann. I would never make a spectacle of you," Mahala said.

Mary Shields leaned close to Mahala. "You certainly outdid yourself this time."

"What did I tell you this morning?" Mahala gave her mother a conspiratorial look. "That," she pointed with her hand lowered on her lap, "is why her gown was last."

The two Benson women sat in their chairs and spread their gowns, which flowed grandly around them.

Mary patted Mahala's arm and crossed the floor to the refreshment table. Moments later, she returned with a glass of punch. "I think you need this," her mother said in a low tone. "If looks could kill, you'd be dead. I've never seen so many jealous women under one roof at one time—"

Mahala laid a gentle hand on her mother's arm. "You mustn't worry, Mother. I'm fine. I really am."

"I watched the color drain from your face. Drink this."

Mahala took a sip of the fruit punch and looked up mischievously. "Thank you, Mother, and don't fret—I can handle the gaggle of chickens in this coop."

Her mother's hand flew to her mouth. "Well, I believe you can." She gave Mahala a conspiratorial grin. "You were never one to take too much guff."

THE SUN HAD LONG since gone down when pounding hoof beats from beyond the barn cut through the sound of the lively music. It appeared the bold intruders were determined to change the outcome of the evening's event. Startled, Mahala's thoughts were diverted as the men and horses arrived outside.

Mary Ann ran in, a look of terror on her face. Her mouth opened as if she wanted to say something,—but not a sound came out. She closed her mouth and tried again. "There's . . . m-men coming on horseback," she stammered.

"Don't worry." Mahala laid a hand on Mary Ann's arm. "We've plenty of men here to protect us. Just stay inside." She glanced beyond Mary Ann. "Where's Elizabeth and Rebecca?"

"I didn't see Elizabeth—but Rebecca's outside!"

"Lord have mercy!" Mahala shoved her sister toward their mother and went to the entrance of the barn. She searched the grounds near the stable where a halo of light from the barn fanned on the ground. She spotted Rebecca hunched behind a wagon,—terror-stricken. Mahala ran out of the barn and skirted the nearest wagon.

"Mahala get back here!" barked her father.

Mahala looked over her shoulder but kept running. The horsemen were coming toward the barn at a gallop. She swerved behind a wagon next to the one where Rebecca hid, and called, "Rebecca!"

Rebecca turned her head, and Mahala crouched lower. She motioned for Rebecca to come and mouthed, "Come here!"

Rebecca shook her head and lowered her body. She peered at the arriving marauders over the front brace of the wagon.

A shiver ran up Mahala's spine. The men galloped their horses back and forth and in circles around the yard and in front of the lit-up barn. The darkness made it difficult to see the faces of the men.

Shots cracked like fireworks as the riders whooped and hollered, scaring the crowd, who gazed out of the barn with stricken faces.

The blaze of torches along the fence-line and the flash of gunfire coming from the Woodrow gang lit up the sky.

Soft fingers gripped Mahala's arm. "Where's Rebecca?"

Mahala jerked back to see her mother crouched behind her. "Get back inside! It's too dangerous out here!"

"Where's Rebecca!" Her mother wasn't going to be put off.

Mahala turned back to where she'd last seen her sister. She was gone! "I don't know," she cried. "She was here a moment ago."

Benjamin Shields came from behind them and dragged his wife back toward the stable. He gave Mahala a sharp look. "Get inside!"

Just then Mahala spotted Rebecca crawling on the ground between the wagons. She was nearly in front of her, peeking from under the tailgate. "Rebecca!" she whispered loudly.

The gunshots continued to pop through the air, and the partygoers hid anywhere they could. Rebecca held Mahala's gaze, and in an instant she fled from her hiding spot and ran to where Mahala crouched. Mahala threw her arm around Rebecca's shoulder and whispered loudly, "Good God, Rebecca, you scared the crickets out of me!"

"Sorry," her sister whimpered, hovering close. "I couldn't run."

"I know. It's okay. You're here now." Mahala hunched behind the wagon wheel, and gauged the situation of the rowdy men galloping their horses in the open space between the barn and the row of wagons parked against the fence. Could she and Rebecca get back to the barn safely?

When she looked out again, several ranchers were shooting rifles in the air. The riders' attention averted, she grabbed Rebecca's hand, and the two ran between the nervous horses. Their snorting and stomping the dirt was a sure sign that the roughnecks had not only disturbed the folks in the barn but made the stock uneasy too.

Mahala gripped her sister's hand and pulled her swiftly to the barn. Once inside, Mary grabbed her daughters as if she'd never let them go. "Your father's outside with the men," she cried. She searched Rebecca's face. "Are you all right?"

"Yes, Mama." Rebecca trembled.

"Move away from the door, Mother." Mahala gently shoved her mother farther into the stable. The three women went to the back wall, where most of the other women shrank behind tables.

Two bullets zinged through the stable's opening. One ripped a gash in the door-jamb, another sliced through a high wooden beam. Terrified, the women screamed in unison and shrank closer to the floor.

"Where's Nancy?" Mahala inched her chin over a table and spotted Nancy across the floor and crouched behind the tables with her children. The children huddled beside her, shaking, and Nancy covered them with her arms like a brood hen. "Stay there," Mahala whispered, even though she knew her friend couldn't hear.

All at once the shooting ceased and an immense silence followed. After long moments, Mahala stood and crept to the door. In the distance, John Grigsby pointed a gun at Jiggs Woodrow, and he and his men were holding their hands up.

The yard was filled with men pointing their weapons at the gang. From where Mahala stood, it appeared the men had surrendered.

"We didn't mean no harm, folks," Jiggs voice echoed over the grounds.

Mahala stepped slowly to the entrance, wringing her hands and wishing the strangers would leave. One by one, the women joined her at the opening, and a stir buzzed around her.

One of the horsemen broke away from the other two riders sitting on their horses. Otis Murphy ambled his mount to the lit-up entrance of the barn. He gazed down at Mahala, his arm resting on the saddle horn. "Well, aren't you the prettiest belle of the ball?" His eyes shone with a glint of amusement.

A chorus of gasps filled the air behind Mahala as she stepped out into the yard, her cheeks on fire. "Why did you come? Didn't I tell you that you weren't welcome here?"

"And didn't I tell you I like a spitfire?" Otis held her gaze for a long moment. "Since you didn't invite us to your party, we invited ourselves." Otis touched the brim of his hat. "Good evening, Miss Shields." He rode back to his partners and the three men rode out the drive. A couple of stray shots rang through the air, but the men kept going, the horses kicking up dirt behind them.

"Well, I never," Mahala overheard one woman say. "Maybe that rustler can save Mahala from spinsterhood after all." A low murmur of laughter filled the air.

Mahala wanted to flee from these awful women! But she couldn't let them get the best of her could she?

WHEN WOODROW'S MEN HAD faded from sight, the other men shuffled back into the barn, and the room became a mixture of pandemonium and revelry as the women pressed in to give their accounts of what they'd seen. But soon families began to pack their things and make their way to the wagons. Folks just wanted to go home after the stunt the rough-necks had pulled.

Nancy appeared exhausted when John came to her side. "Are you ready to leave?" He asked.

"I am. This has been a long day, to say the least," Nancy said.

"Have Tess help you pack up the dishes, and I'll get the wagon ready. I'll be waiting out front," John said, gazing over the crowd. "I'll see if I can locate the boys to give you women a hand."

John walked out of the barn, and as he scanned the crowd, looking for the boys, his mind went back to the Woodrow gang's pranks. Where was Curly Joe? Was he the one he'd shot the other night when his barn had been raided? Is that why Curly Joe hadn't come with his comrades? There were too many questions and not enough answers about Jiggs and his men. It was high time they found out more about the rough-necks. Would they cooperate or would he need to talk to Sheriff Ford about running them out of town?

IT WAS LATE WHEN John reined the wagon into their barnyard and the older children piled out of the rig. He went around to the opposite side of the wagon to help Nancy climb down, one hand under her elbow, the other bracing sleeping Wiley in her arms as she stepped to the ground.

"Granville, unhitch Brownie and brush him down while I check on Star." John thought again about the fact that only three men had shown up at Matthews' place to cause a racket. A sense of dread washed over him—or maybe, apprehension better suited how he felt—as he headed for the barn. Maybe Curly Joe's absence at the party wasn't due to being shot.

The stable was dark and humid as John struck a match, illuminating the rafters and the ground before him. He lifted a kerosene lamp off a post and lit it, then carried it down the wide aisle between the stalls.

Blue looked out over the gate and chuffed. John rubbed the horse's velvety nose then turned to the opposite side of the aisle and gazed into Star's stall. Empty! "Dadburnit!" Heat rose to John's ears as he saddled Blue and strode out to the barnyard.

Nancy and the children were busy unloading the wagon. Calvin was pulling a blanket from the back. "Where are you going, Dad?"

"Star's not in his stall. I'm going after him." He looked over to see Nancy had stopped walking and was looking up at him.

Calvin's eyes grew wide. "Who do you think took him?"

"One of Woodrow's men." John held the reins loosely, and Blue snorted.

Calvin hugged the quilt to his chest. "How do you know it was them?"

Despite his anger at the horse thief, the corner of John's lips tilted as he eyed his young son. "You ask a lot of questions." He mounted Blue and looked down at his son. "I noticed one of Woodrow's men was missing at the festival."

"Oh no," Nancy groaned as she swayed with Wiley sleeping against her chest.

"I didn't mean to spoil the end of a good day, Nan, but I can't let that man get away with stealing my horse."

"But you don't even know for sure if it was one of those men who took Star." Her brows knit together. "Can't it wait until morning?" Nancy shifted Wiley over her shoulder. "It's late and you'd have to wake the sheriff up."

John swallowed the raw anger that engulfed him. He sat astride his mount and looked down at his family. Morning felt eons away, but he had to admit Nancy was right. He'd have to get the sheriff out of bed to visit the gang if he wanted an eye witness with the horse thieves. He stared at her for a moment. "All right. I'll wait till morning to handle this. Besides, it might be best if Charles Matthews rode out with the sheriff and me. We'd do better with numbers."

"Oh, good." Nancy let out a weary breath and turned away. "Girls, go into the house and get ready for bed while your father and brothers put the stock to bed." Nancy gave John a tired grin. "Don't take long."

John watched Nancy take Jeffrey's hand and fall in line behind the girls. Heat burned him like a branding iron. The Woodrow gang were going to wish they'd never passed through this little town. Those men had already ridden roughshod over their community too many times. It was time to put an end to it.

THE FOLLOWING MORNING, JOHN Grigsby, Charles Matthews and Sheriff Ford rode out to the abandoned ranch on the east end of town. When their horses galloped into the front yard, the shack door opened and the four outlaws stepped outside. John noted each of the men wore guns in their holsters, and their hands rested on their guns.

Jiggs squinted in the early morning sunlight. “What brings you fellas to this side of town?”

“I came to retrieve my horse,” John said in a steely voice.

“We ain’t got your horse.” Jiggs straightened and spread his feet apart as if ready for action. He stared long and hard at John.

John lifted his chin and gazed beyond the crude building to the horses grazing in the field. Star stood among three other horses, chewing grass. His head lifted at the sound of John’s voice and he whinnied.

“That black-and-white mustang is mine. One of you rode out to my ranch and stole him out of my stable while we were at the festival.” His jaw rigid, John sat astride his mount, a coiling spring tightening inside him. “Thing is, I noticed Curly Joe wasn’t with the three of you last night.”

“I found that horse wanderin’ down the road.” Curly Joe spit on the ground. “I saved him from running away.”

John held the man’s gaze, hard and long. Curly Joe flinched and bent his head to study the grass.

“Like you saved all those steers in the pasture behind the barn?” Charles Matthews’ deep voice rang out.

Sheriff Ford leaned forward in the saddle. “Cattle and horse thievery is a high crime in these parts and won’t be tolerated in my county.”

Metal clicked consecutively as four firearms were raised and aimed at Ford’s chest.

Ford wiped his face wearily. “There’s no call for foul play.”

“Mister.” Jiggs stared at Ford. “You best ride on out of here.” Black steel replaced his cool green eyes. “I’d just as soon put a bullet through your head as stand here listening to your threats.”

Charles Matthews’ hand went up. “Don’t be a fool, Woodrow.”

“We’ll oblige you fellas for now.” John’s voice boomed. “But I’m going to get my horse.” He rode Blue past the four gunmen to the pasture and grabbed Stars’ reins. He led his horse back to where Charles and Ford waited.

All the while, Jiggs squinted at the men, a match stick in his mouth, his gun still aimed at Ford. He hadn’t moved an inch and apparently, that was a signal to the rest of his men to stay put as well.

John rode Blue in front of the four men and stared down at them.

“Go on, Grigsby. I don’t want any fight with you,” Jiggs said.

"Then keep your men off my ranch."

"Will do." Jiggs held John's gaze.

John, Charles and Ford rode out, but not before John saw Jiggs reach out and knock Curly Joe's hat off his head. He half expected one of Woodrow's men to fire a slug into his back before he led his horse onto the main road.

When they were out of earshot, Charles asked, "What do we do now?"

"We wait," John said. "I won't lose any good men over this bunch. It appears those men aren't in a hurry to go anywhere. We'll get 'em."

"That's right," Charles said. "If they want trouble, they've come to the right place."

"Well," John said, pushing his hat back with a forefinger. "If I ever catch one of those men on my property again, they won't ride out alive. You can bet on that."

"That'll be all right by me," Ford said grimly. "Horse thieving's a crime. They're lucky they aren't hanging by their necks already."

"Maybe they should be," Charles said giving the men a side glance under his hat.

"Let's ride back to the office and put together a plan. I want those men gone from Grovespring—or hangin' from a noose," Ford said.

"A noose sounds fine with me," John said dryly. As the men rode back to town, John gripped the reins to Star, who trailed behind him. John's mind swirled with thoughts of Jiggs and his men. How soon could they gather the ranchers to put together a plan? Would the men vote to bring in a Marshall to take them to prison, or would the gang hang by a noose?

Chapter THIRTEEN

"HOW COME WE'RE BRANDING the cows, Dad?" asked Calvin.

"To let the world know these are our cattle, son. With an increasing number of cattle from neighboring ranches, we need to know who owns them." *And,* he thought to himself, *more cattle have been showing up at Judd Benson's deserted ranch.* But Calvin didn't need to know that.

John and fellow ranchers around Grovespring were keeping tabs on the number of steers showing up at the gang's hide out. John had put off branding his calves with so much going on. But now, with the threat of cattle being stolen, he and his cowhands had rounded up the calves and would spend the day branding them.

The past couple of days, they had scouted the range, counting stock and separating the calves and their mamas from the rest of the herd. Once again, the cowhands rode along the banks of the streams, the river, and in the low rise of hills. John wasn't surprised to find he was short several cows. He wasn't the only rancher in these parts with red-and-white Durham cattle. Two other ranchers had chosen the breed as well, as they were a sturdy beef cow. However, Herefords being a more common breed, most of the ranchers in the area had that breed roaming their land. And that's where the problem lay. Within the breed, they all looked alike.

Luke straddled a calf, holding the rope in one gloved hand and cinching it tight while positioning the bawling calve to lie still. John pulled the branding iron out of the fire pit. He could feel the heat traveling from the rod. He'd become accustomed to the heat—just like he'd become accustomed to the sound of the bawling calves and the cowhands that milled and shouted around him.

The brand singed the calf's hindquarter with a J and a dangling G to let other cattle ranchers know these cows belonged to John Grigsby.

The branding took all day in the choking dust. John had brought his brother Franklin, and his sons Granville and Calvin along. He was pleased with Granville, who watched intently but stayed back a good distance to let the cowhands do their job. He seemed to be logging the process in his brain.

Calvin, on the other hand, hung too close as the dusty red-and-white flank of the calves were exposed to the iron.

"Get back, son. Your mother will have my hide if I end up branding you instead of this squirming calf," John called when Calvin got especially close to one calf.

Calvin jumped back as John pressed the hot iron into the flank, not too deep to injure the flesh but enough to burn a clear J-G print into the hide.

John nodded to Luke, who held the frightened calf on the ground; the stench of burning hair and flesh filled the air, and the calf was allowed to stand. Once Luke removed the rope from its neck, the calf bawled and ran back to its frantic mother.

They'd been at it all day and the number of calves seemed unending as the team of cowpokes settled into a rhythm—roping, flanking, and burning the white-hot brand, then letting the calves head out to pasture with their mothers again.

John had his hands full keeping an eye on the branding process, as well as keeping an eye on Calvin. He almost regretted bringing the younger of his three boys to join them. Calvin was too eager to watch the men slap the iron into the fire, leaning too close to the hot coals and the swinging branding iron. If he'd told Calvin once, he'd told him a hundred times to 'get back' from the fire. The day had been a long one, and seeing the last calf romp out to the pasture gave him a feeling of accomplishment. Another year, another fall, and another good crop of calves made all the hard, long hours of work worth the effort.

"We're done here, fellas," John said to the cowboys as they let the last calf go. "Clean up and enjoy your evening."

"You bet, boss, Will called as the range hands slapped each other on the back in approval and mounted their horses.

"I think I'll stop by one of the horse tanks and take a bath," McDuff said as they rode away.

John threw his arm over Granville's shoulder. "That doesn't sound half bad."

"But Mom's going to have supper ready," Granville said as his stomach growled.

"I heard that," Calvin giggled. "We forgot to eat lunch."

"That's because we were too busy keepin' our eye on you." Franklin ruffled Calvin's dark hair.

"A bath by the light of the moon sounds mighty good. But you're right, Gran. We better not keep your mama waitin' on us for supper. Come on, boys, let's get back to the house."

They mounted their horses and slowly headed toward home. The four of them were too tired to kick up any dust. The boys didn't talk, seemingly lost in their own thoughts as their horses led the way.

John's mind went to his wife. She seemed overly tired these days. He'd seen her wince a few times while she worked. Was she near her time? Nancy had sent a letter asking her mother to come. Until now, he hadn't been overly concerned about his wife's condition, but the last few days had taken a toll on her. Maybe having her mother come would help the Grigsby household and give Nancy the rest she so desperately needed. Thinking of his wife, John nudged Blue into a canter. *Lord, be with Nancy. Let this baby come without any trouble. And if it be Your will, could You help Nan's mother make it here in time to be of help?*

As they rode over the rise, a glow lit the grounds from the windows of the house. It looked warm and inviting.

"We're just about done for the day," John said as he nudged Blue toward home. "We just need to get the barn cows in for the night." He and the boys rode to the west field and coaxed the cows toward the barnyard. He could smell supper as they neared the house. "We better hurry and brush the horses down. Supper's waiting."

WHILE JOHN BRANDED CATTLE, Nancy washed laundry. She set a basket of laundry on the ground near the clothesline. When she bent to pick up a wet day dress, she felt a dull ache in her womb. "Oh, Lord, not again." She kneaded her back with her fingertips, and then picked up the wad of material and shook it out. Pulling two wooden clothespins from her apron pocket, she draped the shoulders of the muslin dress over a cord stretched between two T-framed posts and then clamped the pins over the material. She pushed the wicker basket with the toe of her shoe and edged to the next space.

She pulled out a pair of John's trousers. The heavy material had been wrung out so tightly that the pants looked like an accordion. She hung them and worked to get the wrinkles out.

She pushed the basket across the ground again as she hung several more pieces of clothing and bedding. When she leaned over to pick up the next garment, another stitch pulled at her insides and she gasped in pain. Standing upright, she looked toward the clapboard house, wondering if she should abandon the job of hanging clothes. Against better judgement, she kept pinning clothes to the line.

It had been over a month since she'd sent a letter to her mother, Jane Wilson. Would she come in time to help her with the children? Not only did she need help with the family, she needed help with the chores in the house.

Nancy missed her mother, dearly. It had been four years since she and her family had moved from Tennessee to Missouri. So much had happened since they'd arrived on their ranch, and she wanted desperately to sit at the table with her mother and talk. Jane had never met her two youngest grandsons, Jeffrey and Wiley, and the older children were growing like stalks in a cornfield. A good visit was due in order to catch up on everything, both here and her extended family in Tennessee.

Nancy gazed past the clothes on the line to the east pasture where John and the boys were with the cowhands branding calves. They hadn't come back to the house for the noon meal. *They'll be tired and hungry when they get home*, she thought. *I'll cook them a good meal for supper.*

The back door slammed and Tess crossed the lawn with Mary Jane on her heels. "The boys are taking a nap." Tess sidled up to Nancy and looked at her. "Are you all right, Mama?"

"Yes, I'm fine. It's just a bit warm outside."

"Uh, there's a bit of a chill in the air." Tess stared at her mother with alarm.

"It's just me, then. It's not unusual for a woman to feel unhinged when they're as far along in her term as I am." Seeing the crease in Tess's brow, Nancy added, "Don't worry, darling. I'm fine." She brushed away the bead of sweat on her brow.

"I'll help." Tess turned to Mary Jane. "Come help Mama." The two girls stood on each side of the laundry basket. "I'll shake them out and you hand them to Mama," Tess said. She leaned down and picked up a garment and shook it out. The sun shone on her golden curls as she handed the shirt to Mary Jane, who in turn handed it to her mother. Nancy was grateful for her daughter's thoughtfulness and for a chance to spend some time alone with the girls.

"Did I ever tell you girls how much I appreciate you?"

Tess smiled at her and shrugged. "All the time, Mama."

Mary Jane hugged Nancy's side. "We love you too."

With the three working together, the clothes were hung in quick order. Still, Nancy felt exhausted and overheated.

"We should bring in another chunk of butter and some meat from the springhouse." She led the way to the small building that sat beside the barn. A tall windmill with a water pump and trough sat between the two buildings. As Nancy entered the small building, she smiled. She felt instant relief when she stepped into the cool room. The spring house was a wonderful place to go in the summertime. And though the fall weather had already set in, she was overheated.

The one-room building had a small channel built along the walls to direct the flow of cold water through a wide concrete trough inside the structure. Pumped in through a pipe from the windmill, the cold water flowed constantly. Nancy listened to the running water that moved out the other side of the building through another pipe to irrigate the garden and cornfields. The cold,-running water allowed the spring house to maintain a cool internal temperature, making it possible to keep crocks of milk, butter, meats, and fruits that would otherwise have spoiled rapidly.

Nancy checked the milk cans that stood in the cold water. Four containers stood in a row and the milk in each was fresh. John would need to take some of the milk into town in the next day or two. She had placed stoneware crocks filled with vegetables and fruits on the floor. But for now, she needed butter. Shelves lined the upper wall and thick bowls were cleaned and stacked in preparation for when Nancy would need to take more butter to the house. Taking a bowl down, she reached into the butter crock with a wooden paddle, dipped out a solid hunk of butter, and dropped it into the bowl.

Spotting a watermelon on the floor she turned to Tess.

"Grab that melon. We'll slice it for supper."

"All right." Tess scooped up the watermelon and carried it like a baby. "It's the last one, Mama."

"I know." Nancy turned back toward the house. "Your dad and brothers are going to be good and hungry when they get home. And you know how your dad likes melon."

When they went into the house, the sun was setting. Nancy stoked the fire in the kitchen stove with more wood. She set a large pot in the sink and pumped water into it. Then she added chunks of beef, along with diced onions and spices. It wasn't long before good smells sailed through the house.

An hour later, she heard the cows bellowing as they made their way to the barn. "Good, they're back. I hope they finished branding the cattle," Nancy murmured to herself. She glanced out the window and kneaded her lower back again. Another pain ebbed through her midriff. It was too early for the baby to come. She thought of her pregnancy with her last child, Wiley. There had been moments when she thought he would come early, too, and yet she finished her full term. She mustn't fret and should enjoy the next few weeks. For when the baby arrived, she wouldn't have a moment to spare. She'd have her hands full feeding and changing the child right along with rest of the responsibilities of the house.

A FEW DAYS LATER, Nancy noticed a cloud of dust and the sound of horses' hooves thundering toward the ranch house from the east. The morning breeze picked up and whipped away the dust, revealing a string of horses pulling a stagecoach down Shady Hollow Road. Standing at the window, Nancy watched the coach make its way to the front drive of the Grigsby ranch. The rig slowed and then stopped, the horses snorting and their sides heaving heavily. Nancy could see Bart, tall and wiry holding the reins as he hollered, "Whoa!" to the team.

"Someone's here," Nancy said as she dried her hands on her apron and hurried to the front door and opened it. She stepped onto the porch and watched as an elderly woman, thin and darkened from the sun, stepped to the ground. She wore a gray dress, and perched atop her head was a huge, broad-brimmed hat, tied under her chin with a white scarf.

Nancy held her breath and then hitched her skirts as she went down the steps. "Mother!"

Jane Wilson looked in Nancy's direction and arched a brow. Her broad hat glistened in the morning sun as she strode to Nancy's side and kissed her cheek before she stood back with round eyes. "Well, look at you!" She stared at Nancy's swollen belly. "You look as if you're ready to burst!"

"Shhh, Mother! Not in front of Bart." Nancy felt heat creep up her neck.

"Don't be silly. He's likely thinking the same thing." Jane waved her hand in the air as if brushing away Nancy's concern.

"I wrote you a letter, but you never answered." Nancy felt bewildered to see her mother standing there, and yet, she was relieved at the same time. "When did you leave Tennessee—"

Her mother's finger went up as if she wanted Nancy to hold her thought, and she turned to the stagecoach driver. "I need your help with the four trunks from the rear of the coach. Can you please put them on the porch?"

"Will do, ma'am." Bart climbed down and went to the back of the rig.

Sounds of a fussy baby came from inside the coach. Nancy glanced into the interior to find her sister Polly gathering a satchel and ushering a little girl toward the opening, all the while hugging a baby to her hip. Polly wore a wide-brimmed straw hat with her hair tucked inside. Wisps of curly red hair escaped the confines of the hat.

Nancy had forgotten how red Polly's hair was. Two years younger than Nancy, she had her mother's features. Nancy's arms opened wide and she giggled, "You rode out with Mother!"

"I had to," Polly said, juggling the baby on her hip. "I wouldn't have it any other way. I didn't want Mother making that long trip all the way from Tennessee to Missouri alone." She moved into Nancy's arms, with the baby squirming away. "You're so big!" Her hand flew to her mouth and she gave Nancy an apologetic smile. "I didn't mean it to sound that way." She cupped Nancy's belly with one hand and beamed. "You look ready."

Polly gazed down at the small child standing beside her and gripped the little girl's hand. "You remember Mary Annelene. She just turned four. And this"—her eyes lit up at the infant in her arms, "—is little David. He's nine months and is crawling all over the place."

"Well, don't worry. Tess is wonderful with children, and she'll help keep him out of trouble."

Filled with happiness that her family had finally arrived, Nancy hardly noticed the many trips the stage driver made from the coach to the porch with the handbags and luggage that came with them. When done, she thanked Bart before he climbed onto the seat and flicked the reins.

Bart and the horses left in a whirl of dust.

"Well, come in," Nancy said. "Let me show you to your rooms."

As Jane and Polly and the two small children entered the house, Nancy went on to say, "I'm afraid everybody's gone right now except the two little ones. The five older children are off to school, and John's out on the range with the cattle."

"And Jeffrey and Wiley?" asked her mother.

"They're in their room playing. You'll see them when we go upstairs."

"Good. Lead the way," Jane said.

Nancy took the stairs first, her girth making it difficult to climb the steps. When they reached the upper landing, the sound of children giggling filtered out to them. She opened the door to Jeffrey and Wiley's room and found them stacking blocks, one on top of the other, and letting them topple over and scatter across the wooden floor. The boys fell back laughing and ready to build the blocks again. Their eyes widened and their mouths dropped as they stared at their grandmother and aunt, who stood at the door with their mother.

Nancy pulled the two boys to their feet. "Jeffrey . . .Wiley . . . this is your grandmother." She stood holding their hands, proud as she could be.

"My oh my. Look at you," Jane said gently. "You both look like such fine young boys." Jane's eyes twinkled as she bent low to their level.

Jeffrey's finger went straight into his mouth, and he turned to gaze at Wiley. Wiley peered past the women to the little girl peeking shyly behind them.

"Oh, and this is Mary Annelene." Polly gently pushed the little redheaded child forward.

Mary brushed past the boys and sat on the floor. "Come on. Let's play blocks."

"Oh, good," Polly let out a breath. "Mary's been cooped up in that stagecoach for so long she needs to let go of all that bottled energy." She bounced little David on her hip and looked longingly at the crib by the window.

"Would you like to put David in the crib while I show you to your rooms?" Nancy asked.

"Perfect." Polly lifted her son over the wooden bar and placed the baby on the low mattress. "This will keep him out of trouble."

"I'm afraid you'll have to use the older boy's room. We're short on beds." Nancy went to a door down the hall and opened it.

"We can't put the boys out," Jane said.

"Nonsense, I won't have you sleeping on the sofa. The boys won't mind camping out in the living room for the next couple of weeks."

"If you say so," Jane said, setting her bag on one bed.

"This will be fine." Polly set her reticule and a large bag on another bed. "When will the rest of the children be home?"

"They'll arrive around four o'clock. Won't they be surprised to see you," Nancy said, thrilled her mother was finally here.

A HALF HOUR LATER, the three women sat at the kitchen table with cool glasses of water before them.

"Now, you said it was urgent that I come," Jane said as she pushed back a lock of frizzy gray hair. "How are you doing?" She reached across the table and covered Nancy's hand with her own.

The gentle touch was Nancy's undoing. Her lip trembled and she said, "I'm afraid the baby is trying to come too soon. I've still a month until it's due, but just yesterday I felt a twinge of pain on and off throughout the day and was afraid I'd go into labor."

"Have you seen the doctor about this?"

"No. There isn't anything he can do." Nancy's shoulders slumped. "The town's midwife lives a mile up the road from here. John knows to fetch her should I need her."

"Well, we're here now and you are going to stay off your feet. We'll see to everything," Jane said. She stood and tied an apron around her slim waist. "I see you've started lunch. A good thing too. We haven't eaten a thing since last night." She stirred the leftover stew simmering in a big pot on the back burner of the stove.

Relief flooded through Nancy. "I'm so glad you're here, Mother. I've needed you." A tear slid down her cheek and she quickly brushed it away. She gazed at the woman who'd taught her everything she knew. Her mother was hale and strong in body and spirit, but Nancy noticed new lines and creases in her mother's face since the last time she'd seen her. One could tell she'd lived through hardships by the tightness around her eyes. And when Jane took hold of the ladle, her fingers curled awkwardly on the spoon.

"Have you a touch of arthritis?" Nancy asked. "Grandfather's hands used to do the same."

Jane nodded. "I'm getting old. It's not so bad. It's from years of milking the cows."

"Well, you won't be doing any of that while you're here. Between John and the boys, we've got that covered."

The women wiled away the afternoon talking about everything from the past and caught up to the near future. Before long, Nancy's older children came through the front door and with them came squeals of surprise to find their grandmother and Aunt Polly had come to visit. All the while, Nancy stayed off her feet. Relief had come. She breathed a silent prayer. *Thank you,*

Father, for answering my petition.

Chapter FOURTEEN

AS THE DAY GREW colder, the Grigsby family gathered in the living room, where John stacked wood in the fireplace. Before long, he had a good fire going. The children sat at their grandmother's feet, where she sat knitting a blanket for the new babe soon to arrive. While the needles flew and the yarn took shape, Jane told stories of their mother's childhood. The children hung onto every word, as their grandmother had a way of making Nancy's childhood years come alive. Every so often, one of the children would glance at their mother as if trying to imagine that she was ever a child so full of life and adventure.

Nancy tried to relax with the family as she sat in her rocking chair, her swollen feet raised on a footstool. She watched her mother's animation as she talked, and realized her mother clearly enjoyed having the floor and the children's undivided attention.

Every so often, Nancy and Polly raised their brows as the stories seemed to have taken wings and grown a bit more advanced than they remembered. "Hmm," Polly said contentedly as she rocked baby David. "Mama always could tell a tale," she said quietly for the two of them.

"I want my babies to remember this night." Nancy smiled warmly, her heart feeling full.

Jane had parted her gray hair down the center of her head and drawn it back into a tight bun. The wrinkles on her face were proof of years gone by. Nancy's mother had raised nine children. *That would add lines to anyone's face*, Nancy ruminated. The thought startled her. *I'm about to give birth to my seventh child. I'm not far behind Mother.*

She silenced her thoughts as John finished the evening with a tune from his fiddle. The house felt warm and good inside, while the wind howled outside against the hollow of the chimney.

Later that evening, Nancy peered closely at herself in the mirror in her bedroom. She did have a few new creases in her cheeks, she noted.

She turned to John. "Do I show signs of raising children?"

He finished pulling his feet out of his boots and his height dropped a good two inches. He slipped his arms around her extended belly and kissed her temple. "No, my dear. You still look like the young bride I married."

She elbowed him away. "That's not true."

"Come to bed. I'm exhausted." John pulled her away from the floor-length mirror.

"You don't need me to come to bed." She smiled mischievously.

"Yes, I do." He unbuttoned his shirt and kissed her forehead.

"All right." She slipped into her nightgown and climbed into bed.

John shrugged out of his shirt and then snuffed out the kerosene lamp on Nancy's side of the bed. He did the same to his lamp and lowered himself into bed. The two settled against each other as Nancy turned on her side with her back to John and he spooned his body behind hers. She felt his warm breath on her neck and listened to the sound of his breathing. A smile curved her lips. He was already asleep.

She cast her gaze toward the window where shadows of the trees looked like long dark fingers stretching out to consume the house. Those shadows resembled the fearsome fingers of darkness that threatened her and her unborn child. She clenched her eyes shut. The verses from the book of Isaiah floated through her mind. *Fear thou not; for I am with thee. Be not dismayed; for I am thy God.* There was more, but her exhausted mind could not bring it to remembrance. *Help me to trust You, Lord, for in truth my spirit is willing, but my body is weak.*

A SHARP PAIN RIPPED through Nancy in the wee hours of the morning. The contraction startled her from a deep sleep. She crawled out of bed, trembling, and sat down as soon as she could get to a chair. "Oh," she groaned softly. She wondered how long she could handle the pain before she had to wake John. She knew this kind of pain. Having given birth six times before, there was no question in her mind that her time had come. Coming to grips with the truth, that this *was* not a false alarm, she had only one thing on her mind—getting through the next few hours and holding her baby.

A spasm gripped her midsection. She doubled over, clutching the edge of the chair. Cold sweat broke over her body, and she squeezed her eyes tight, gasping loudly.

John shot up in bed and looked over at her pillow and then across the floor to where she sat. The moon sent a ghostly light throughout the room.

"Is it your time?"

"Y-yes." Sweat slicked her brow.

"I'll go wake your mother!"

John fled the room.

Nancy heard muffled voices and scuffling upstairs. Moments later, bare feet padded down the stairs, the sound growing as John and her mother hurried through the hallway outside her bedroom door.

The door flew open and Jane came in. "John tells me it's your time." Her mother's gray hair hung loose around her shoulders.

Another pain sliced through Nancy and she doubled over again, gasping great gulps of air.

"Oh, dear!" Jane turned to John. "I'll need help with Nancy. Who helped deliver the other babies?"

"Our neighbor, Anne. She's a midwife."

"It's way past midnight, but I think you'd better go after her."

Nancy clutched John's arm. "Send Granville for Mahala. She can help keep an eye on the children if they wake up."

"Polly's here," her mother reminded her.

"I know." Nancy panted. "But the children are familiar with Mahala."

"If you think that's necessary—"

"I do."

John leaned over and kissed her forehead. "I'll be back as quick as I can."

Nancy heard his muffled voice in the front room as he awakened Granville. Mahala had insisted she wanted to help when the baby came, and for some reason Nancy wanted her good friend here.

JOHN SHOOK GRANVILLE'S SHOULDER on the sofa. "Granville!" He whispered loudly. "Wake up!"

Granville jerked awake and rubbed his eyes. "What's wrong, Pa?"

"Saddle Brownie and go get Mahala. Your mother needs her."

"Yes, sir." Granville sat up and pulled on his pants. He shoved his stocking feet into his boots and ran out the back door.

John strode right behind him, and the two worked swiftly to saddle their horses. Without a word, they went their separate ways. John's horse thundered a half mile down the lane to the Radburns' house. He raced down the drive, slid off his horse, and then ran up the porch steps. Drawing his hand back, he stopped. The house was pitch black inside. He hated to wake the Radburns, but Nancy needed Anne. Now. He shook his head and rapped loudly—no sound inside. He rapped again and again.

A dim light showed through the window and the door opened. "What is it?" James Radburn stared at him with his hair tousled every which way.

"It's Nancy's time!"

Anne came up behind her husband. "Lord have mercy! Let me get my bag. I'll be with you shortly."

MAHALA HEARD POUNDING ON their front door. She slid out of bed only to bump into her father on the way into the hall.

"Who'd be at our door this time of the hour!" He grumbled and stomped down the stairs ahead of Mahala.

Thinking of Nancy, Mahala ran past him and flung the door open to see Granville standing on their porch. "What is it, Granville?"

"Mama needs you quick!"

"All right. Let me get my wrap. But can you tell me if she's okay?" Mahala asked as she hugged herself from the cool breeze that seeped through the open door.

"I don't rightly know, ma'am. She's in the bedroom and moaning bad. I think it's her time."

"Goodness! Go along and tell your father I'm on my way. I'll be there as quick as I can."

"Thank you, ma'am." Granville turned on his heels and ran back to his horse. He mounted the steed and reined the horse back the way he had come.

"What's wrong with Nancy?" Mahala's mother asked. By now, she was standing behind them with a candle in her hand.

"I think Nancy's gone into labor." Mahala grabbed her wrap hanging on a hook near the front door. "You two go back to bed. I don't know what time I'll return. Don't wait up for me."

"Your shoes," Benjamin called as she threw her shawl over her shoulders and ran down the dark hall toward the back door.

"You're still in your nightgown," her mother chimed in.

"There's no time!" Mahala shut the door behind her and she ran to the stable. She knew Charlie would be asleep in the bunk room. Not wanting to wake the stableman, she opened the stall door to lead Bessy out into the open.

Bessy shook her withers and whinnied low.

"What's goin' on in here?" Charlie stood behind her. He scratched his head and ran a hand over his scruffy chin.

"Sorry I woke you. I need my horse."

"This time of night?" He took the bridle out of her hand.

"Granville just came by. It's Nancy's time."

"Step back. I'll saddle your horse."

"There isn't time, Charlie." Mahala stood in her bare feet, eager to be on the road. "Just bring her out. I'll ride her bareback."

"Like that?" Charlie pointed at her nightgown.

"Yes, Charlie." Mahala pulled her shawl closer around her.

Moments later, Charlie led Bessy out of the stall and out the double doors. "Here you go." He looked doubtful that he should be helping her.

"You're a dear." She kissed old Charlie's cheek before he leaned down and cupped his hands to help her up. Mahala stepped into his open palms, and once she sat mounted on her horse, she kicked Bessy's flanks and the horse shot forward. Horse and rider raced down the lane. *Please, Lord, let everything be all right with Nancy!*

JOHN DASHED INTO THE house with Anne on his heels. He could hear Nancy's moans.

Anne placed a hand on his chest. "You stay out here. I'll go in."

He watched the midwife slip through the bedroom door and close it.

Moments later, Mahala rapped on the front door—but she didn't wait for anyone to open it, she just sailed into the house and looked over to where John paced the floor.

"Nancy?"

"She's in there." He pointed at the closed door. "She asked for you."

"Are you all right?" Mahala hesitated.

John stared at her, his eyes roaming from the top of her nightgown to the soles of her bare feet. "I know Nancy wanted you to come in a hurry—but you could have taken the time to get dressed." He wore a look of apology on his face.

"Granville told me to hurry—" She was at loss for words. "I didn't think I should waste any time." She wrung her hands, feeling foolish now. She glanced around to assess what needed to be done right now. But it didn't take long to notice that John felt helpless. They could both hear Nancy's wails from where they stood. "Is Nancy all right?"

"I don't know. Go on. They may need your help."

Mahala headed for the closed door. She held the knob and looked back. "She'll be okay, John. She always is."

"I know. I just hate to see her like this."

Tess came down the stairs. "Daddy?"

"Go back to bed, Tess."

"Is it Mama?"

"Yes. Go back to bed." John ran his fingers through his hair. "Keep the little ones upstairs."

"I will." Tess looked at Mahala and then her father and then climbed the stairs.

"I'm going outside." John opened the door and stepped out.

The night air was cool as he walked out to the barn. The horses nickered and the cattle lowed as Granville brushed the horses down. By now, Franklin was up and out in the stable too. They all looked at each other with pensive fear etched on their faces, but none of them spoke a word. Granville and Franklin put the horses away as John stood at the opening of the stable and gazed toward the house. A dim light shone through the bedroom window and lit up the yard below. A shrill cry came from the house. His gut twisted and he slammed his hand against the wall.

John felt that this delivery wasn't normal, and gritting his teeth, he sat on a bale of hay and clamped his hands together, his knuckles white. *Lord help her. Help my wife get through this night.* He watched the house and saw movement through the window.

An hour later, it seemed quiet inside. Had the baby been born? He stretched to get the kinks out of his back and called into the barn, "Come on, boys, let's go back to the house." Granville and Franklin climbed down from the hayloft, straw poking out of their hair. The three walked to the back door silently.

John strode down the hall and entered the living room. The other children sat on the sofa near the blazing fireplace, fear in their eyes. Polly held her baby and paced the floor. When he looked at her, she shook her head.

John stopped before he headed to the bedroom. He turned to the older children. "I need your help right now. Keep the fire fed, and keep the little ones quiet."

"I've got everything under control," Polly assured him.

"I know you do." He gave her a half smile. "But the children need something to do."

She nodded. "Of course."

When he gazed at his brood, they nodded too, their eyes wide as they stared down the ominous hall. As John watched his children, he saw Granville eye the fireplace, where the flames licked high. Tess pulled Jeffrey and Wiley to her side. Franklin sat on the floor with his knees pulled to his chest.

Mary Jane slid off the couch and stood in the middle of the floor, her eyes riveted to where her mother's cries came from. "What's wrong with Mama?"

Calvin sat on the floor with Rusty. "C'mon, Mary. Sit with me by the fire. Mama's going to be all right."

John stared at his brood, his heart weighing heavy within. He wanted to believe Calvin's words, that Nancy would pull through all right. He couldn't lose her. She was the light of his life and he needed her. The children did too.

His boots clicked on the hardwood floor as he went to check on Nancy. A dull moan seeped through the door as he opened it. John dominated the room with his tall stature. His heart constricted as he walked to the foot of the bed. Nancy looked pale, and her flaxen-colored hair lay spread over the pillow, tangled and sweaty from the hours of labor. He clenched his jaw, went to Nancy's side, and reached a hand to hers.

"Oh, John," she whispered hoarsely. "Why won't this baby come?"

A chill licked up his spine and he gazed at Anne who sat at the foot of the bed.

"Some babies come at their own pace. This one's not in a hurry," Anne said.

"Can't you do something for her?" John heard his terse tone and grimaced.

Jane held a damp cloth and wiped at the sweat gathering on Nancy's forehead, while Mahala sat on the opposite side of the bed, holding Nancy's hand.

John's thoughts trailed off and became lost in a whirlwind of images and emotions. He should be holding his newborn child by now. What should be a happy moment–was now a storm of pain and regret. Each time he heard her cry, it felt as if an iron pike was being driven through his heart.

Another wave of pain broke over Nancy, and she nearly doubled over in response, groaning loudly and calling out, "God, help me!" She grasped John's hand tightly and John bit his lip in anger at the onslaught of pain that wracked his wife's body.

"This baby is not coming as God intended," Nancy whimpered. Her breath came in fast gulps. "You must be truthful with me, Anne," she gasped, continuing to grip John's hand. "Hours have passed. It is now near daylight, and I still have no child."

"You're doing fine, Nancy," her mother soothed, her voice calm. "Each child enters the world in a different manner. This child has chosen to make his entrance when the sun is out."

Jane touched John's arm. "You must have chores to do. Go on. We'll call you when the baby comes."

John stared down at Nancy, not wanting to leave.

"Go on, John." Nancy visibly trembled.

"All right. I'll come if you need me."

"I know." She closed her eyes.

He kissed her forehead and walked out the door. When he reached the living room, he called to the boys, "Come on. We've got chores to do."

John pushed the back door open and breathed in the early morning air. Every muscle in his body was taut. He knew he should trust God to take care of his wife, but somehow, he couldn't this time. Try as he might, he couldn't push back the feeling that this delivery was different. He wanted to be by Nancy's side. But every time he stepped into the room, the women chased him out. Maybe it was for the best. He walked into the barn, where the familiar scent of horse dung and hay met his nostrils. He looked toward the rafters as if God were sitting there. *If You'd keep my wife and unborn child safe, I'd be forever grateful.* Running fingers through his hair, making it stand up, he picked up a bucket and set it under Bossie. He heard the boys as they went about their chores. How long before he heard the sweet sound of the baby's cry? The sun was coming up. It shouldn't be long now. Should it?

Chapter FIFTEEN

THE MIDWIFE CHECKED NANCY again and shook her head.

Mahala hadn't missed the gesture and knelt down beside Anne. "Is something wrong?" she whispered.

"The baby is positioned wrong." She washed the blood from Nancy and checked on the baby's progress. "Babies should enter the world headfirst and crying. This baby won't enter the world in that manner." She closed her eyes briefly and took a deep breath. "The baby's coming breech." She looked at Nancy, who squirmed fretfully. "I've delivered babies like this before, and the baby and the mother were fine," she said in a low tone. But there have been times when neither the mother nor child survive the process."

By now Jane was crouched beside them, listening to Anne. She shot Anne and Mahala a look of pure fear and whispered, "Lord have mercy. Please say that isn't true!"

Mahala had been praying that the baby would come soon and for strength for Nancy, but it seemed as if her prayers were falling on deaf ears.

Anne ran a hand over her face. "She's so drained, she can hardly push. I'm going to give her a moment to regain her strength, and then we'll see where we are."

Nancy's eyes closed for a moment as if she just wanted to sleep.

Mahala leaned over the sweat-soaked bed. "Nancy?" They needed to keep her awake—and pushing.

Nancy shook her head and asked, groggily, "Why doesn't the baby come?"

Mahala chewed her bottom lip and glanced at the foot of the bed where the midwife sat. "I don't know." She couldn't bring herself to tell her friend that the baby was positioned wrong.

Nancy closed her eyes again. It seemed the need to push had left her.

Moments later, Anne checked to see how far Nancy had dilated, while Jane pressed a cool damp cloth to Nancy's forehead.

Anne gazed at Mahala and shook her head. "Let's get some pillows behind Nancy and get her sitting up more. She's too tired to walk or I'd suggest we get her out of bed and moving a little. Sometimes that helps get things moving."

"I know she's weak, but we can hold her up," Mahala said.

"All right, let's try." Anne went to the side of the bed. "Nancy, we're going to get you up on your feet so we can get your contractions going again. Mahala and I will hold you up."

"Are you sure?" Jane's brows arched high.

"I'm afraid if we don't get the contractions started again, your daughter and the baby won't stand a chance," Anne whispered.

Together, Anne and Mahala rolled Nancy to the side of the bed. Laying her arms over their shoulders, they hoisted her to her feet. She was dead weight as they walked her around the bed several times.

On one of those trips, Nancy dimly looked out the window and sighed. "I wish I could be outside instead of in this room. It's so hot in here." She lowered her hands and pressed them against the windowsill, bending forward so that her forehead leaned against the cold window pane. The glass fogged from her hot breath. Trembling, she moved away and looked at the women in the room. "My water should have broken by now."

Jane whipped off the soiled bedclothes and threw a clean sheet over the bed and then fluffed up the pillows. "This should feel a bit better."

Nancy swayed on her feet. "Put me back in bed."

Jane went to the head of the bed and held the pillow in place while Anne and Mahala carefully sat Nancy on the edge of the mattress.

"Can you lift your legs, hon?" Anne asked.

"I can't." Nancy's voice was faint.

Mahala gently lifted Nancy's ankles while Jane laid an arm under her shoulders to guide her to the pillow.

"I don't think I can deliver this baby," Nancy gasped. Sweat slicked her brow. "Something's different with this baby."

Anne turned to Jane. "All right. Change of plans." Anne lifted a thin knife from her bag and held it over a candle, holding the tip to the fire. When the next contraction came, she leaned in close to cut the sack, and water gushed onto the old towels they had laid in place.

Moments later, Nancy said faintly, "It's coming!" Her fingernails dug into the blanket. When she screamed, the sound came more like a soft mew than a healthy birthing shriek.

Mahala reached out to Nancy. "Squeeze my hand."

Nancy struggled against the pain when the contractions came again, but she was far too weak to squeeze Mahala's hand.

John stood in the doorway, looking haggard. "How's it coming?"

"It isn't—coming," Anne said, sharply. She knelt at the foot of the bed and frowned. "You need to leave."

John swung his head to gaze at Nancy's frail form, and then, dejected, he lowered his chin and walked out of the room.

It wasn't long before the contractions deepened and the time between each one came much faster.

"Come on, Nancy. You've got to push," Anne coached sternly.

Nancy tried but her pushes lessened.

"I can see the baby's bottom." Mahala felt her adrenaline pick up.

The three women coached Nancy and urged her to push, but the baby didn't come.

Nancy grew weaker and Mahala prayed harder. *Father, give Nancy the strength she needs to deliver this baby!* Mahala's request went up, hour after hour. But there was still no baby. *Did He even hear me?*

Nancy's face grew pale. Her eyelids flickered as she glanced around the room as if searching for someone. "Where's John?"

"He's outside. We'll bring him in when you bring your little one into the world," Jane said. She was pacing the floor now.

"We can't wait any longer." Anne reached into her bag again, took out the knife and nicked the skin surrounding the baby. Then, on the next faint push, her trained fingers cupped around the baby's hips to help it come.

"Push!" Anne commanded. The baby's feet cleared with a stream of blood. "Again! You're halfway there." She turned the body and eased the baby boy into the world amid a stream of blood spurting over the muslin sheets.

"The baby's here. It's a boy!" Mahala cried half-heartedly. There was too much blood, and the air felt thick with the smell of it. Weak-kneed, she stood beside the bed.

"Mahala." Nancy's breath was shallow.

"I'm here." Mahala sank onto the side of the bed. "You did it. You have a son."

"Listen to me." Nancy's head tilted to the side as if she hadn't heard a word Mahala said.

"I'm listening." Mahala's heart hammered in her chest.

"You've always been there for my babies—" Nancy's breath came in short gasps.

"What are you saying? You're going to pull through this, Nancy." Mahala could hardly swallow. "You're done. The baby's here."

Nancy turned and gazed at her mother, and then she turned back to Mahala. "Mother is going home in a few days. My children know you. Promise you will help John." A tear slid to her temple and disappeared into her damp hair.

Mahala put a finger to her lips. "Shhh! You're going to be fine, Nan." Her voice shook as she squeezed Nancy's hand. "You're done. All you need is rest. You're going to pull through this."

A second tear trickled down her temple. "No, I won't."

"Of course you will." Mahala wanted to shake some sense into Nancy, make her have the will to live.

"Promise you'll be there for them." Nancy's voice grew fainter.

"Of course, Nancy. I promise." Mahala's lips quivered.

"I know you will," Nancy whispered. Her ragged breath quieted, and her fingers slipped out of Mahala's hand and fell to the bed, for her soul had winged its way heavenward.

Mahala sat up straight. "Nancy, don't give up!"

There was no response.

Jane shook her head, and her fist went to her mouth. "Nancy?" She knelt beside the bed and pulled Nancy's limp hand into her own. "Honey. Don't go." Her voice trembled. "You're done. The baby needs you." She stared at Nancy's hand enfolded in her own. "I'm sorry you endured such a painful delivery. You're a brave girl." She rested her forehead on the bed beside Nancy's still form. She kissed her daughter's hand then said, "It's over, my girl. You can rest now."

At first Mahala didn't want to believe Nancy was gone. But when she gazed into Jane's eyes, a sad defeat met hers.

Mahala felt stone cold as she stared down at Nancy's lifeless body.

"She didn't even get to see the baby." Jane stared down at her daughter as tears streamed down her cheeks.

Mahala couldn't breathe. The air in her lungs froze. "How can this be!"

She gently laid a hand on Nancy's arm. Empty eyes stared at her and a wave of grief washed over her.

Jane ran a hand over her daughter's eyes and closed them. Then she closed her own eyes and lowered her chin to her chest as if resigning herself to the truth that her daughter was gone.

It took a moment before Mahala realized John had come into the room. His eyes were on the newborn babe in Anne's hands as she tried to help the baby breathe. He glanced briefly at Nancy, but it was clear he didn't realize his wife was gone. Instead of going to her, he went to Anne's side.

"What can I do?"

The deep timbre of John's voice shook Mahala. She wanted to scream at him that his wife was gone, that the sickening smell of the blood in the air was the smell of death. Didn't John smell it?

"He's not breathing," Anne said frantically.

"Breathe into his nose," Jane rushed to her side and patted the baby's back.

"Give me the baby," John said. He worked on the newborn, breathing into the baby's nose, rubbing the tiny back and torso, trying to make the blood circulate in the baby's body. But the baby never breathed. Never cried. He, too, was gone. A cobalt darkness flickered in John's eyes. He carefully set the baby in Jane's arms and went to the bed.

"Nancy?" John knelt beside the bed and stared at his wife, who appeared to be asleep.

"She's gone," Anne said, finality in her tone.

Jane's shoulders shook as she held the baby close to her bosom.

John's brows furrowed and he grasped Nancy's still hand. "What?" He looked at Anne, Mahala, and then Jane. She shook her head, holding the still baby, tears streaming down her face past her puffy red nose.

His steely gaze raced to Mahala in a silent plea. "Tell me Nancy's not gone," he begged.

A sob choked Mahala and she fled the room. She fetched her shawl from the wall hook and ran out the front door. She kept running until she came to the edge of the field.

JOHN GAZED IN DISBELIEF at the still form of his wife. She looked like an angel with her honey-gold hair spread over the damp pillow.

"Nancy." A guttural roar arose from his innermost being, but he held it in check, for if he let loose the crazed anger he felt, he feared he'd frighten the women and children. Instead, he touched his wife's pale cheek with the back of his forefinger and let it trail from her closed eyelids, down her mouth, and to her thin, milky-white neck.

"Nancy," he said again in a hoarse whisper, her face blurring in front of him. A tear ran off his nose and dropped onto her mouth. Blinking to clear his vision, he ran his thumb over her still-warm lips. He couldn't help himself. He leaned in and kissed them one last time, just to feel those warm lips against his. But there was no response, no heartbeat to return the love he felt for her. He squeezed his eyes shut. *She's gone!*

From the depth of his soul, a sob erupted and overpowered him. He buried his face on her lifeless form, and he sobbed and sobbed. His body shook, and he cried until there was nothing left in him to give. When he finally looked up, the room was empty save for Nancy, who was gone from him forever.

JANE FELT AS IF her heart had been ripped from her body. She needed to fall to pieces, to find a private place to cry out to God. To ask Him to help her console this family. But she had learned from life's lessons that one didn't always get what they wanted—or needed. Life must go on, and though she needed to let loose a river of tears, her son-in-law, and her grandchildren needed her to be strong. She would be the pillar of strength they needed at the moment. The tears would have to wait. Straightening her back, she faced the terrible day head on.

Jane and Polly stripped the bed and had the bedclothes boiling in the wash tub outside the back door within the hour. Jane heard the echoes of a hammer ringing as John worked in the barn. Granville shot out the door to join him.

At one point, Jane went to the stable to look in on them. She found John sawing boards, his shirt tied around his waist, beads of sweat on his brow, and storm clouds in his eyes. A tearful, Granville held the boards steady as his father worked. Rather than disturb them, she wrung her hands and breathed a word of prayer and then returned to the house.

Breakfast was cooking when footsteps sounded on the back porch. John and Granville had returned to the house. John entered the kitchen and gazed at her and the children and said solemnly, "The box will be ready in a couple of hours." He looked defeated and at a loss at what to do now that he was back in the house. Nancy and the baby lay on the clean bed in their room. Jane was sure he would avoid the room until the bodies were placed in the pine box for viewing.

"There must be an undertaker in town who would be glad to do that for you," Jane said.

"I will build it for them." A fire burned in John's eyes, and he ran a tired hand across his scruffy beard. Then he lowered his voice and said, "It's the last act I can do for my wife and child. I won't have that taken from me."

"Of course not," Jane said, sorry she'd suggested otherwise.

The children stared at their uneaten breakfast of oatmeal and biscuits; not a one of them had an appetite. A stark silence filled the air then.

Tess pushed her chair back and ran up the stairs.

Jane heard the bedroom door slam. She turned to the rest of the children. "Try to eat. Your mama would want you to."

"Don't tell us what Mama would want. She's not here to tell us what she wants." Granville pushed away from the table and strode out the front door.

"Granville!" John's voice rang out. "Get back here!"

The door slammed, leaving silence as the only response.

"Let him go, John. He didn't mean any harm," Jane said.

John gave the rest of the children a stern look. "Don't give your grandma any guff. She's doing the best she can. The least you can do is help her."

John wasn't the least bit hungry, but he sat at the head of the table and ate his breakfast to be an example for his children. When he finished eating his meal, he headed back to the barn without another word.

Jane watched him go, her throat thick with grief. How would this family get through the next few days, weeks, months?

"Mama." Polly came into the kitchen with little Mary tagging behind her and baby David on her hip. She reached for her mother, and the two clung together, their tears saying all that words could not convey.

"She's gone," Jane whispered. "The Good Lord is holding her in his arms. I just hope we can help her family get through this." She gazed at the small children sitting at the table. "They need her."

MAHALA RAN THROUGH THE tall grass as the wind tugged at her hair. The morning dew slicked the blades of grass, and the coolness somehow soothed the soles of her feet. The creek was beyond the outbuildings on the far side of the field. She kept running, great sobs working their way from her heart and into the empty spaces of the field. She wanted nothing more than to step into the cold water, to bathe the hurt from her soul.

She's gone! She cried inwardly.

The prairie grasses were not kind to her feet as she ran. Hard clumps of soil dashed her soles, but somehow that seemed right. Sharp twigs intermingled with crisp blades of grass cut between her toes. She ran, her heart rent in two. Tears flowed unchecked and her throat burned. *How can this be! It's all wrong!* Mahala kept running toward the stand of trees that now loomed ahead. Her pace slowed as she neared the path to the creek. She could hear the water dancing merrily downstream. She pushed through the trees and brush and along the narrow trail that was littered with brittle leaves and broken twigs. She crept down to the cool bank and stepped into the water, letting it wash the pain away.

Mahala waded farther in, letting the chilled water numb her senses. The day would grow warmer, but the mornings had been brisk and cold. Catfish swam in the water, scurrying away to hide from the newcomer. The hem of her nightgown flowed with the current. She watched the water ripple over the stones in the stream, remembering the times she and Nancy had waded in the creek, laughing and splashing water at each other in play. Tears streamed down her wet cheeks and her throat clogged. "Oh, God! How could this have happened? Why didn't you save Nan and the baby?" Her voice sounded hollow above the rushing water.

She wanted to lash out at God, to shake her fist at Him. The wind whipped strongly, and she hugged herself and waded farther into the stream, pushing herself farther until the water rose to her thighs, her gown tangling against her legs, making it difficult to move. "I miss her, Lord. She's not been gone more than a moment, but I already miss her." She sniffed and raised the hem of her wet skirt to wipe her eyes and nose.

A gust of wind tore the shawl from her shoulders and washed it over the fast-flowing water. "No!" Mahala sloshed through the creek and tried to catch the fading garment as it sank into the stream and floated away. She tripped on a stone and sank to her knees, and then onto her hands, the water washing over her shoulders. She pushed herself up and glanced about her, but the shawl was gone. There was a breeze blowing, and she shivered in the chill air. She looked over the creek once more, but the shawl was nowhere to be seen. Disgruntled, she waded toward the shore. The hem of her gown clung to her legs. She hadn't gone far when she heard a rustle in the bushes.

"Who's there?" Her teeth chattered as she waited.

Granville pushed through the brush and stood at the water's edge, staring down at her and then away as a flush of crimson colored his cheeks.

"Granville." She continued to wade to the bank, her nightgown heavy against her legs.

"Dad told me to find you." A storm brewed over his features.

"How did you know where to look?"

"Calvin saw you running this way."

She pulled her hair off her shoulders and trudged up the mossy bank. "I had to get away." she threw her arms over her chest.

Granville shrugged. "Figured as much."

Mahala lifted her heavy skirts and waded through the dried leaves to his side. When she reached him, she stared into his dark eyes, and she pulled Granville into her wet arms. "I'm so sorry you lost your mama. She was the best friend I ever had. We'll get through this somehow. We have to."

He clung to her and his body shook as he silently cried. "Why did God have to take Mama away?" he whispered.

"I don't know, honey. I just don't know." How could she help this family get through this terrible day? "I'm going to miss coming to your house as often as I have in the past." She sighed heavily.

Granville drew back and gazed at her. "What do you mean? You can't stay away just 'cause Mama died. We need you."

"Oh, Granville." Mahala laid a gentle hand on his cheek. "If your father agrees, I will be there to help in whatever way I can, but it won't be the same."

"Grandma and Aunt Polly won't stay long. They'll have to return to Tennessee." He looked at her wistfully.

"It will be up to your father whether he'll need my help."

"Well, he sent me out to look for you. Why would he do that if he didn't want you there?"

"I don't know." She ruffled his golden locks.

The two of them turned back toward the house, cutting through the field on the path she and Nancy had used a million times before. An ache tightened her throat as she followed Granville.

Oh, Lord God. How will we get through the next few days?

Chapter SIXTEEN

GRANVILLE LED THE WAY as Mahala padded back to the house barefoot and in her wet nightgown, feeling out of sorts dressed as such in the early morning sunlight. She glanced back at the creek, wishing for her shawl to discreetly cover her damp bodice. Mahala crossed her arms over her chest as she picked her way through the field grass. All too soon the house loomed near and grief lodged itself in her heart as she crept past Granville and went up the front steps of the porch to enter the house.

Granville came to a halt at the bottom of the steps. "Go on inside if you need to. Dad's in the barn when you're ready to see him."

"I'll only be a moment." Mahala turned the doorknob and entered the spacious hallway. She found Jane and Polly finishing up the last of the cleaning in the bedroom. A sheet covered Nancy's and the baby's still forms. Seeing the bodies covered, she stared at the bed her heart in her throat.

"If you're looking for John, he's in the barn, building Nancy's box," Jane said.

It was then Mahala heard the ringing sound of a hammer as it pounded nails into the hard wood. She clutched the front of her damp bodice, each strike a stark reminder that her good friend was gone. She gazed down at her wet skirts. "I would help you clean up, but as you can see, I'm not presentable. I need to go home and change."

"Of course," Jane said dully. "We have everything under control here."

Polly stared at Mahala, her brows knitted together. "Where's your shawl?"

"I tripped in the stream, and my shawl fell into the water. It washed away before I could retrieve it." Mahala folded her arms across her chest a little tighter.

Jane glanced back at the chair behind her where Nancy's shawl lay draped across the back. She picked up the shawl and held it to herself a rush of crimson flowing to her cheeks. "She would want you to use it." Jane held it out to Mahala.

Mahala shook her head. "I believe Nancy *would* want me to wear it, but I can't face John wearing Nancy's shawl right now. It's too soon."

"Of course," Polly said. "You can use mine. Bring it back the next time you come."

Mahala nodded. "Thank you."

Polly left the room and Mahala stared at the bed. "I don't know what I'm going to do without her," she said in a low voice.

"Me either," Jane said, her eyes rimmed in red. "And the children . . ." her voice trailed off.

Polly returned with a green shawl. "Here you go."

Slipping out the back door, Mahala draped the shawl over her upper body. She headed toward the barn and the ringing sound of the hammer. Granville had said John wanted to see her. And yet she felt reticent to interrupt his work. And though she'd rather face John later in the day, after she'd changed into something presentable, her horse was stabled in the barn. To retrieve Bessy meant confronting John and the shear pain ingrained in his features that she was sure to meet.

Granville came out of the barn, head down and his boots kicking the dirt. He didn't look up as they passed each other, and she didn't try to get his attention. The grief this family was suffering at the moment was more than she could bear. How they would get through the next few days, she couldn't imagine.

Mahala crept slowly toward the closed double doors of the barn, dirt encrusted on the soles of her feet. The doors creaked as she opened one of the doors ever so quietly. When she stepped in, she found John's back toward her, his arm lifted high to drive another nail into the wood. Seeing the pine box taking shape took the air out of her lungs. The searing sound of the next ring made her flinch. With all her being she wanted nothing more than to turn around and run out into the opening and forget about her horse. She wanted to run as fast as she could, all the way home.

Instead, she remained planted where she stood and listened to the sound of the thin nail being driven with force into the wooden frame.

John picked up another nail and stopped. She didn't miss the rigid stance of his frame or the taut muscles of his bare back. She felt him sense her presence. He set the hammer on the box and gave a deep sigh as he turned around to face her.

Mahala let out a small gasp. The work lines of his face, and the creases around his mouth had deepened and he looked years older. He hung his head, his chin to his chest, for the longest time. When he looked up, his eyes begged that the night before had all been a dream. His grim lips formed a tight line as if he feared to speak of the hurt and the anger that welled within his heart.

"Mr. Grigsby." She took a step toward him but stopped.

He flinched, as if not wanting to be consoled. His chin dropped to his heaving chest once more. What should she do? As much as her heart ached at the loss of Nancy, surely, it paled in comparison to the pain this man had to bear.

"Mr. Grigsby," she tried again in a small voice. "Granville said you wished to see me." She felt small in his presence. Not because of his stature or demeanor but because she sensed there was nothing she could say or do to lessen the absolute loss he'd endured this morning.

He cleared his throat and looked up, his hand balled into a fist. He seemed rougher around the edges. Unhinged. Tears rimmed his eyes and his face was flushed, but no words escaped his mouth. The terrifying reality that his whole world had been snatched from beneath him in the blink of an eye was revealed in his stance.

"I don't even know what to say," her voice quivered. "I'd give anything . . ."

"Don't." He shook his head.

She swallowed.

He turned to the wall beside the coffin and slammed his fist against it. The rafters rattled and a shower of dust fell to the ground. The horses stomped their feet and whinnied.

"She's gone," he growled hoarsely. "I can't get her back."

Mahala trembled. Standing there in emotional gridlock, she couldn't speak. Her throat constricted and tears burned her eyes. The image of John standing there with his back to her and the supplies for the box blurred, and she waited.

He whipped off his hat and ran his fingers through his thick mane of black hair. Then as if he'd come to a decision to speak, he shoved his hat on and wheeled around to stare at her. It seemed as if eons passed before he finally said, "I don't have the right to ask, Miss Shields." He wiped his lips with the back of his hand. "But can you stop in from time to time to check on the children?"

"Yes, of course." Mahala's shoulders relaxed and she let out the breath she'd been holding.

"Nancy's mother and sister are here for now. I don't know how long they plan on staying."

"I understand. I'll come by after they're gone." She tentatively placed a hand on his arm. "Please know that I'll help in whatever way I can."

John stared at the dirt floor speckled with hay and dirt clods. He nodded. "I appreciate that." He lifted his head and stared at her with hollow eyes. He took a step back and ran a hand over his trimmed beard.

Her arm went over the shawl that covered the thin layer of material that covered her breast. She knew John wasn't studying her, but she felt undressed in her thin damp nightgown. A sudden awkwardness consumed her as he turned away, his ears red.

"If that's all," she said quietly, "I'll get my horse and return home."

The silence ate up the air between them except for the sound of the horses in their stalls, munching their oats and molasses.

"I'll saddle your horse." John strode down the wide aisle between the stalls and opened the last gate.

"Um—" she called after him. "I don't have a saddle. I rode my horse bareback."

John's head jerked up and he gazed at her bare feet then gave her a short nod.

While he brought out her horse, Mahala went out to the yard and waited. She could barely swallow for the grief that clogged her throat. It was then that she saw that news of Nancy's death had reached the bunkhouse. The cowhands stood at a distance, their hats removed and in their hands, their heads bowed.

John held the bridle and led Bessy out to where she stood. He cupped his hands to help her up. When she was seated, he stared again at her bare feet.

She swallowed hard.

"Good day, Mr. Grigsby. I'll come back when your company is gone." She nudged Bessy into a canter. Once out of the barnyard, she let the mare take the lead and they galloped the rest of the way home. Not once did she look back. She wanted the wind to erase the chasm of pain that enveloped her, to sweep away the grief and dry the tears that escaped her eyes. She'd go back to the Grigsby house as she promised, but not for a day or two. For now she needed to let her heart cry. Her best friend was gone and she was never coming back.

JOHN WATCHED MAHALA RIDE out of the yard, her dark hair trailing behind her in the wind and her thin nightgown billowing. His throat constricted. Mahala Shields was a good woman and a good friend to his wife. He'd never seen her dressed in anything less than respectable. Yet she'd been called away in the wee hours of the morning and had obviously come immediately, with no thought for herself. Her nightgown looked damp and the hem of her skirts muddy. Had she run to the river?

He shook his head. He'd wanted to run too. Run from the reality that he'd lost his wife—forever. His thoughts returned to Mahala's retreating form. He was grateful she'd promised to come back to check on the children. He could count on her—of that he was certain. He turned back to the pine box sitting on the sawhorses. In another hour he'd be done building the last thing he'd ever make for his beloved Nancy.

He clenched his jaw and picked up the hammer again. He held the nail in place and drove it into the wood, the ringing sound echoing throughout the barn—and through his heart. Tears streamed unchecked as he drove one nail after another into the box. *Nancy—how will I get on without you? How will I breathe with you gone?*

MAHALA SLID OFF HER horse and handed the reins to Charlie without looking his way. She covered her chest with her arms and rushed through the back door, her bare feet making a dull padding sound on the floor.

Benjamin poked his head out of the study. "Is that you, Mahala? How's Nancy?" His gaze widened as he stepped into the hall. "Where's your shawl?" He glanced from her head to her bare feet. "You look like a drowned rat. What happened to you?"

Mahala shook her head wildly. "I'm fine, Father." She held out her damp skirts and dropped them with disgust. "It isn't me that you should be worried about. It's Nancy. She bled to death before our very eyes, and there was nothing we could do about it," she lashed out. "She was so weak she never even asked to see the baby."

Benjamin stared at her as if trying to grasp the meaning of what she had just said. "I'm sorry to hear that. Nancy was a good woman." He stared at her wet nightgown again. "But—why do you look like this?" he asked reluctantly, wiping a worn hand over his face.

"I fell in the creek." Mahala's lips quivered.

"What's all the noise about?" Mary came into the hallway and her brows lifted. "Why the tears, Mahala? What happened?" She rushed to where the two of them stood.

Mahala fell into her mother's arms. "Nancy's dead, and the baby—" she sobbed.

She felt her mother's arms tighten around her as she cried.

"Oh, no. That's dreadful news."

Mahala dropped her chin on her mother's shoulder, her body chilled from the cold ride home. She began to shake. "There was nothing we could do to save her. The baby came wrong," she shuddered. "Nancy never had a chance."

"Ah, my darling." Mary took a step back and gazed into her daughter's troubled eyes. Then she wrapped her arms around Mahala again and rocked her gently.

"Wh-why didn't God hear our prayers? Mahala sobbed. "Wh-why didn't He save her?" She hiccupped between sobs as she picked up the hem of her damp gown to wipe her eyes and nose. Her head felt so heavy, as if it were full of soggy moss.

Her mother continued to console her and patted her back.

Her sisters sailed down the stairs and skidded to a stop. "What's wrong?" Mary Ann asked as she strode across the floor and laid a hand on Mahala's shoulder.

"Did Nancy have a boy or a girl?" Rebecca asked, coming around to the other side. Elizabeth gaped over the banister.

The questions brought a new wave of tears. Mahala sniffed and stood holding out her soiled gown. "I-I need to change."

"Girls," Mary said, moving into action. "Ready a bath for your sister."

The girls exchanged looks and said, "All right, Mama." They backed away with uncertainty etched on their faces.

"I'll bring in the tub," Benjamin said, seeming glad to have something to do.

"Thank you, Mother. A hot bath sounds wonderful."

"I'll have your father take the tub to your room." Mary kissed Mahala's cheek. "It'll soothe your nerves. Take as long as you need."

JOHN ENTERED THE HOUSE through the back door. During the day, the downstairs rooms usually bustled with sounds of a busy household, the children harassing each other and giggling, or Tess sitting at the piano doing her lessons, or pots and pans clanging in the kitchen as preparations for the next meal were under way. When Nancy was alive, she made this house a home. But she was gone and now none of those sounds permeated the house. The children were quiet and watchful, their expressions uncertain when he walked in.

Calvin slid off the armchair and ran up to him. He threw his arms around John's waist. "Why did God take Mama away?"

John felt Calvin's body tremble.

"I don't have an answer to that, son," he said dully. "All I know is that through it all, we have to trust Him."

"I don't!" Tess jumped from the sofa and stormed up the stairs. A door slammed in the distance.

Granville stared at the stairwell, wide eyed.

"I want Mommy!" Mary Jane wailed and threw her arms around John's other side.

The interaction of the children suffocated him. He untangled their arms and bent down to their eye level. "Your mother's not coming back. We are all going to have to deal with it, and like it or not, your mother would want us to." He hated himself for being harsh—too brash in such a time as this.

Jane flew into the room from the kitchen. "Children, give your father some space. He's hurting too." She gave him a sorrowful smile. John started to back away, but on second thought, he reached for the older woman. She clung to him, her frail body quaking in his hold. She cried silently before she broke away and wiped her tears with the hem of her apron. "Thank you, John."

He nodded and backed away to escape out the back door. With long strides he crossed the yard. Halfway to the barn he heard the back door slam.

Granville strode up to him and matched his long strides. "Dad?"

"What, son?" He stopped and stared at Granville, wanting to be left alone.

Words seemed lodged in his son's throat. When he didn't speak, John continued on to the barn. He let out a deep sigh before he entered the building, having seen the wave of grief wash over his son's face. He clenched his jaw tightly, strode into the barn, and walked over to the pine coffins, flexing his hands as if he wanted to hit something or somebody.

Granville walked in and stood beside him and looked at the finished boxes, his face pale, his mouth grim.

"If you've got something on your mind, you can tell me," John said.

Granville pursed his lips and shrugged. "Are you going to give the baby a name, Pa?"

John's stance stiffened. He hadn't expected his son to broach the subject of the stillborn babe.

"No, son. I'll let your mother do that in heaven."

Granville shook his head and stuck his chin out. "I think *you* should give him a name." He wouldn't let it go.

John held his breath, a weight like an anvil on his chest. "Do *you* have a name in mind?"

"Yes, sir."

"What would you name him?"

"David."

John halted. "For your grandfather, David Wilson?"

"Yes, sir. I heard Mama talking to Grandma, and she said that's what she wanted to name him if he was a boy."

"All right." John gazed at the small pine box and made a last-minute decision not to use it. It would only be fitting to place the babe in Nancy's arms and let them rest in peace together. Still, he laid a hand on the box and bowed his head. "Lord, we give into Your hands David Grigsby—" He choked then continued, "—to be laid at his mother's side." When he gazed over at Granville, he saw a look of relief on the boy's face, and gave a short nod.

JOHN HAD SPENT THE last few days sleeping on the sofa. He couldn't bring himself to sleep in the bedroom where the image of Nancy's lifeless body seemed imprinted on the bed. In his mind's eye he could still see her flaxen-colored hair spread upon the pillow—like an angel. Her dark lashes feathered on her soft, pale cheeks as if she feigned being asleep.

Sensing he wasn't alone, John peeked through a half-opened eye to find his mother-in-law, Jane, standing over him.

"Why must you continue to sleep on the sofa, John? Your room has been cleaned and the windows are raised during the day to air out the smell of—" Jane raised her chin and gazed out the living room window, the sentence cut short.

John watched her visibly swallow. He raised to a sitting position and rubbed the sleep from his eyes. "Thank you, Jane. But another night on the sofa won't hurt."

"Polly set a basket of maple-and-cinnamon-spiced pinecones on the dresser." She gave him a small smile. "It'll give the room an autumn scent."

John rose to his feet and stretched. "I appreciate all the work you two have put into this house and the family to get us through these difficult days."

"Don't give it any thought." Jane shook her head. "I told Nancy we would help her with you and the children. I wish we could have done more."

He laid a gentle hand on her shoulder. "You've done well enough. We're grateful." Wanting to change out of his rumpled clothes and ride out to the range, John stepped past her and out of the living room and stood at the entrance to the hall.

"I've pies in the oven. I better see to them." Jane disappeared into the kitchen, leaving John in the spacious hallway where he stared down the hall toward what had been his and Nancy's bedroom.

It was time to do the one thing he'd been putting off the past two days. It was time to walk inside their bedroom and claim it as his own. *His alone.* The thought was daunting as he stood in the doorway and swallowed. He refused to look at the bed for the moment; instead, he gazed at one of Nancy's dresses draped over the chair beside the empty bed. Feeling his heart jump into his throat as a wave of nausea threatened to suffocate him, he ripped his gaze away—but only for a moment. In truth he wanted—no he needed—to be here. He found his gaze migrating back to the dress's small, lavender-flowered print, so familiar, as Nan favored that particular garment. She chose it often over the other dresses hanging in the wardrobe. The embroidered details on the white collar blurred as his eyes filled with moisture.

He stepped farther into the room. Her slippers sat on the floor at the foot of the bed and the golden hairbrush he'd bought her a few years back lay just-so on the polished vanity. Strands of hair wisped against the tabletop. He picked up the brush and fingered a strand.

Jane had wanted to set the room right by putting Nancy's things away, but John told her to leave the room as it was. He needed the remnants of what was left of Nancy to be where he could look at them when he was ready. He silently thanked Jane for adhering to his wishes.

He picked up Nancy's dress and buried his face in it, relishing the sweet scent of her, and he wept. He wadded the dress against his chest, and the room swirled. Nancy's beautiful face floated before him so real in his memory that he could hardly breathe. *I miss you terribly, Nan.* How long before the ache in his heart would dim?

NANCY WAS BURIED ON the third day on a portion of land behind the house and beneath a large oak. John led his children, all dressed in their Sunday best, to the grave site. A fresh mound rose above the ground. The earth smelled of newly-turned dirt, dark and moist. The oak tree, which had turned a wide range of colors from copper to yellow to bright red that fall, spread its branches and shaded the area.

Tess held onto Jeffrey's and Mary Jane's hands. She gazed straight ahead with red-rimmed eyes. Mahala held Wiley on her hip. She welcomed having something to do with her hands. She had felt utterly useless the past few days, as Jane and Polly seemed to have everything under control. Wiley whimpered and she patted his back. Calvin, Granville, and Franklin were in front, walking beside their father. It seemed most of Grovespring's residents had showed up for Nancy's funeral too.

Mahala heard the sound of rippling water beyond, where the creek danced downstream, oblivious to this sad day. "Your mother loved the creek. She loved taking time away from her duties to wade in the water," she said softly, turning to Tess. The memory of not so long ago, when she had held hands with her dear friend, swept through her mind and unwanted tears spilled down her cheeks. She wiped them away and glanced at the crowd who had joined them in saying goodbye to Nancy.

It was good to see the townspeople rally around the Grigsby family. John had spent the first days after Nancy's death in bleak silence. Mahala knew his silence had frightened Granville. He had come to the Shields' ranch the day before the funeral to share his own grief, and he spoke of the changes at home. She could see the young boy was lost without his father, and in some ways, he had taken over the duties in the house, trying to remain strong and supportive to his siblings and his grandmother, Jane.

Tess stared straight ahead, her mouth pressed in a tight line. If she heard what Mahala had said, she gave no indication of it. Mahala ached for the young girl.

Mahala eyed John. At the moment his shoulders were squared and his jaw set, but she sensed a trembling in his veins. Saying goodbye would be difficult for any one of them but unbearable for John. Like it or not, however, the ceremony had to be performed. News of Nancy's death had quickly spread throughout the valley and the past days, Nancy's body had lain in an open casket in the parlor for neighbors to view. Neighbors had come, bringing cooked meals to get the family through the hard days.

Now it was time to say the last rites, to have the circuit preacher pray and read Psalms over John's beloved wife and to say goodbye.

Yet she believed John could never say goodbye. But he had a tremendous amount of encouragement from the community, and an enormous amount of things to keep him busy with his 900 acres of land and over 300 head of cattle, and hopefully, staying busy would help somewhat.

Lord, please be with this man who must feel the weight of the world on his shoulders right now. Give him peace that passes all understanding. Amen.

Mahala lifted her head, letting the prayer waft its way toward heaven. When she opened her eyes little Wiley was staring at her. She squeezed him gently and kissed the nook between his chin and neck. How long would it be before this family could return to a normal life? Was it possible that she could help them in any way?

Chapter SEVENTEEN

BART LOADED JANE'S AND Polly's trunks onto the top of the stagecoach and Nancy's family headed back to Tennessee. The day they left was the same day Mahala found herself on the Grigsbys' front porch. John had sent word that Nancy's family was headed back East and if the offer still stood, he'd be obliged if she would stop in from time to time to check on the children. Mahala showed up in her fine, black buggy, and with a basket of ingredients swinging from her arm to make a stew.

Along with the food, she brought determination to break through the wall of stinging resentment young Tess had built up against her. Tess had grown bitter at the world at the loss of her mother, and she didn't want help from Mahala. The young girl resented Mahala for coming to help the first days after her mother was gone. She had lashed out, saying, "I can take care of the little ones. We don't need you or Grandmother's help!"

Mahala had not come back after the funeral, and as hurtful as it had been to hear Tess blatantly scorn her fiercely, she blamed the outburst on Nancy's death. Surely, Tess didn't want anyone to replace her mother. But in return, she needed Tess to understand that she had no intention of *replacing* Nancy. No one could fill those shoes, and she had no desire to try.

Still, the words stung. But although the words hurt, she understood Tess needed time to work through the emotions in her heart and in her mind. At eleven, Tess didn't understand that when others took care of the little ones, or when they cooked a meal, those were times that allowed Tess to sleep, to cry, and to work through her grief.

Mahala's thoughts turned to Granville. Several days before, he had ridden again to the Shields' ranch to talk to Mahala. It appeared he had a lot to get off of his chest too. He had followed Mahala to the chicken coop, where she collected eggs and deposited them in a cloth-covered straw basket. But when she'd collected the last egg, she led him to a bench under the oak tree.

"How are you all getting along at the house?"

Granville shrugged his shoulder. "Mary Jane sleeps a lot—and cries."

Mahala laid a hand over his shoulder and pulled him to her. "I'm so sorry. She's too young to understand it all, and of course, she wants her mother." The world blurred before her as tears rimmed her eyes.

"When it gets bad for Mary, Tess pulls her onto her lap and sings to her." Granville bent to pick up a rock. He rolled it in his palms.

"And Calvin—how is he doing?" She watched Granville lean his elbows on his knees and waited.

"Calvin's quiet. He doesn't feel much like exploring the ranch like he usually does. I miss seeing him bring home a hurt animal and mending it back to life." Granville threw the stone and it skidded on the dirt. "I think Jeffrey and Wiley are too young to understand what's happened to Mom. They're pretty much all right."

"And what about Franklin? Is he all right?"

"He's hurting. But there's so much going on with the younger children that he doesn't say much." Granville shrugged. "I noticed he stays out with the herd and cowhands longer." He leaned back again, his mind seeming to trail to other thoughts.

"Franklin likes working with the cowhands and the cattle. He's got a knack with the stock. It's probably best he puts his energy into them," Mahala said.

Thinking back to that day, Mahala was glad Granville felt comfortable enough talking to her, getting his cares off his chest. She'd told him to come by anytime he needed. Mahala was both grateful and disheartened by his report. It helped to know how she was needed. And with John's invitation to stop by their ranch, she intended to try setting the house in a lighter mood, and fill their tummies at the same time. John, however, was nowhere to be seen when she arrived.

Putting those thoughts aside for now, she thought maybe the sounds of activity in the kitchen would bring a feeling of normality. She deliberately made noise as she pumped water into the large pot to boil. She filled the small compartment on the stove with slim sticks of wood and struck a match to the kindling. Mahala lifted her head to listen for sounds in the other room. The children had been in the living room, keeping themselves busy when she'd arrived. But no one had come to the kitchen.

"Hmm." Mahala said to herself. She clanged the big pot onto the stove. "Well, a good stew on this cold afternoon will do them all a world of good." She hummed a quiet tune, mostly to soothe her own emotions. She wasn't used to the house being this quiet.

The sound of scuffling footsteps broke her train of thought, and she turned to find Granville standing in the doorway. "Where's your father? I've not seen him this evening."

"He's in the barn making fence posts."

She straightened from putting biscuits in the oven. "Oh."

"He'll be out there for a while."

"All right." Mahala glanced out the kitchen window that looked out over the drive. The autumn sun had long since gone down. "It's getting dark."

Granville lifted the lid on the pot and peeked in. "Smells good," he said before adding, "Dad lights the kerosene lamps so he can see what he's doing well enough."

"Well." She ran a hand down the front of her apron and picked up a wooden spoon. "Supper will be ready shortly." Lifting the lid and stirring the stew, she looked over her shoulder. "You might want to go out and tell your father to come in." But Granville didn't move. Instead, he stood in the middle of the kitchen, gazing at her. Without a word, he stepped forward and wrapped his arms around her. "Thank you, Mahala."

She kissed his forehead and lifted his chin with her forefinger. "You're welcome. Now scoot. Go get your father."

That evening, John spent time with the children. They gathered around while he played the violin. Granville usually played his harmonica when the tunes were lively, but not tonight. Tonight John played a quiet melody. Mahala cleaned the kitchen while he and the children had much-needed family time.

When Mahala finished washing and drying the dishes, she stood by the kitchen door, her back against the doorjamb and listened to the sweet melody. Moments later, she donned her shawl and pulled it close to keep out the evening chill. She stepped into the hallway and said quietly, "I'm done for the evening. I'll see you tomorrow."

John lowered the violin and stared at her, and the children leaned back against the sofa and silently waved goodbye. But nobody said a word. She walked out onto the porch and stepped down to the ground. She stood for a moment in the stream of light that glowed from the lamps within. "They're going to be all right, aren't they, Lord?" she whispered.

She smiled warmly and climbed into the waiting buggy. Feeling a satisfied kind of weary, she reined Bessy toward home. The starry night guided her down the dark road. It was cold, but she didn't hurry, and all at once she felt like taking an evening ride. Instead of going home, she turned the buggy around toward Grovespring. Bessy's clop-clopping was a comforting sound on the quiet road. Mahala rode on and on until she came to the Shady Hollow bridge and stopped. Under the bright moon, the water sparkled as it ran under the bridge, dancing over stones to far-away places. She wished she could go far away, somewhere that wouldn't remind her of Nancy's death, a place where the women of Grovespring couldn't torment her with their mean glances or tart words. It appeared that being a single woman of thirty was a criminal offence in these parts.

She flicked the reins and Bessy clopped noisily through the covered bridge. The buggy wheels rumbled and creaked to the other side where she came out again and gazed at the stars that lit up the ink-black sky. She continued on for a ways and then stopped again. She could see the distant, dim lights of town. Kerosene lamps were lit on posts on each side of the street and appeared as beacons of light in the darkness.

Yellow lights spilled from the windows of houses along Main Street. She sat on the buggy seat, trying to imagine what it would be like to have a house of her own, to have a family of her own and more than that, to have a man of her own.

Her heart squeezed tightly and her chin fell to her chest. "Lord," she whispered, "I feel as if time is running out." She swallowed. "Will I ever know what it's like to have a man's arms around me, to protect me, to love me?" Heat seared up her neck and over her scalp. "Will I ever know the urgent kiss of a man?"

Bessy stomped her hoof and nickered, seeming eager to move again. Mahala held the reins slack in her hands. Her mind went to the ad she'd answered several weeks before. Mr. Alexander Bates had seemed eager to find a wife and a mother for his children. She'd had sent him the letter answering his request for a mail-order bride. Would she hear from him soon? Did he still need a wife?

JOHN'S BROTHER JESSE SAT across the table from John. "What are we going to do about the Woodrow gang?"

John's head swung up. "We?"

"Folks are antsy. They're waiting for you to do something."

"Me? Why me? That's what we have a sheriff for." John's lip curled up.

"Come on, John. You and I both know Sheriff Ford can't physically face those men on his own."

John hesitated before he let out a deep sigh. He ran his fingers through his stiff hair. "He doesn't have to, he has us."

"Exactly!" Jesse leaned forward. "Folks around here got it in their minds that you'd best handle those men, not Ford."

"Now you're talking nonsense, Jesse."

"Am I?"

John squirmed in his chair. "I'm not the law. Ford is. He would have to deputize me . . . and Charles Matthews."

"I bet he'd do that in a heartbeat. We can't let those men tear this town apart. They've been threatening our citizens and I think everybody knows they've been stealing our cattle, not to mention stealing your horse, Star a while back."

"You're right." John stood and went to the living room to speak to his sister-in-law. "Margaret, can you keep an eye on the boys while Jesse and I ride into town?"

"Certainly. Take your time." Picking up her toddler Pulaski, she set him on her hip. Margaret gazed out of the window and stopped. "Isn't that the gang you two were talking about?" She pointed toward the road.

John pulled the heavy draperies aside and peered out the window. Four horsemen rode lazily along the road and gazed out over his ranch land. "That's them all right." He dropped the velvet curtains and stomped to the front door. "Come on, Jesse. Let's see what they're up to."

The two men reached the end of the drive just in time to see the riders had already passed by the house and were jogging lazily down the road.

"Hey!" John called, but the men rode on as if they hadn't heard him.

"Let's mount up," he said, heading back to the barn.

Moments later, the two men were trotting down Shady Hollow Road. By the time they reached the Woodrow gang, the riders were a half mile down the road and near the Shield's ranch.

John sidled up to Jiggs Woodrow and asked, "What brings you men out this way?"

Jiggs chewed on a match stick and squinted at him. "I'm surprised you keep asking me that same question." His squinted his left eye a bit. "It's a free country, Grigsby. We can ride anywhere we please."

"That may be, but one or two of your men have been hanging around my livestock— and my stable." John felt his quicken. "If that happens again, I'll shoot 'em dead."

"I wouldn't be makin' false accusations you aren't too sure about, Grigsby." Jiggs moved the match stick to the opposite side of his mouth and his hand slid to his gun. "A man's innocent until proven guilty."

The other three men halted their horses to listen, all eyes on John. Jesse rode alongside John and said, "That's true, Woodrow. But I think you'll agree that it'll be easy enough to prove you and your men are guilty of cattle rustling."

"I'm done talkin' to you fellas," Jiggs growled and the band of men spurred their horses and rode off.

"Dad blast it!" John swore under his breath. He pushed his hat off his forehead and gazed at the fading horsemen. "You're right, Jesse. It's time we see the sheriff again. Let's ride over to Matthews' place and put together a plan."

MONDAY AFTERNOON, JOHN PULLED his collar up against the wind and walked to the sheriff's office. He and Charles Matthews had talked the previous day about the Woodrow gang and all their shenanigans. They'd come to the conclusion it was time to talk to the sheriff and do something. John opened the door to find Charles already sitting in a chair before the sheriff's desk.

"Afternoon, fellas," John said. He pulled out a second chair and sat down.

"We were just talking about you," Sheriff Ford said. "About the time you had a visitor at your place a few weeks back."

John's mind went to that early, pre-sunrise morning hour. He and Nancy had still been in bed. He'd come to the conclusion that one of Woodrow's men was stalking his horses in the stable. Nancy hadn't wanted him to investigate who was out there and had clung to him to stay, but he hadn't. Instead, he had bolted out of bed and run outside. What he'd give to replay that morning again. He would have stayed and held Nancy close. Truth was, though—he couldn't go back in time, and he had to face the situation at hand.

"Like I told you, we woke up to the horses acting up in the stables. When

I ran out to check on them, the stalls were open and Blue stood in the aisle. I never found the culprit, but I heard him run out of the stable when my back was turned. Can't prove it, but I know it was one of Woodrow's men." John pulled his hat off and set it on his knees. He felt bone tired. Losing Nancy had sucked the life out of him, and he hardly had the strength to think about anything except protecting his family and his stock. He certainly wasn't in the mood to confront the Woodrow gang and wished they would simply move on.

"You've had a run of bad luck lately," Ford said. "Having to bury your woman after having trouble with that outfit at your ranch and now . . ." The sheriff waved his hand toward the window as if indicating the trouble in town.

"Truth is," Charles Matthews spoke up, "the whole community has lived in fear ever since that outfit came to town. Folks are fed up." Charles eyes grew dark.

The sheriff leaned forward and crossed his arms on his desk. "What are you two proposing we do?"

"We want to hold a town meeting with the businessmen and ranchers to discuss the Woodrow gang," John said. "Maybe over at the saloon. There's plenty of seating over there."

The sheriff stared over John's shoulder as if he were looking out the window toward the saloon. He nodded and gazed at Charles. "Let's do it. But seein' as how Grider owns the saloon, maybe you two should let him in on your proposal."

"All right," John said. "We can do that before we head home. When do you suppose we should hold the meeting?"

"The middle of the week—say, four o'clock," Charles said. "The gang generally shows up toward the later part of the evening."

"Sounds good to me, how 'bout you?" John gazed at Ford and shoved his hat back on. "Wednesday it is. We'll get the word out to the community in the next couple of days."

The men all stood and shook hands, and moments later John and Charles walked over to the saloon.

Grider looked up from behind the counter, cloth in hand and polishing a glass. "Afternoon, fellas," he said, "What can I get for you?"

John and Charles strode to the side of the bar. "Can we have a word with you—"

THE SALOON BUZZED WITH the voices of citizens of Grovespring and the ranch owners in the area. The pitch rose and fell as men waited for the meeting to begin. John and Charles leaned against the bar, watching the room fill up. Benjamin Shields and Judd Benson pushed through the swinging doors and stood in the back.

Sheriff Ford went to the front of the room and raised a hand. "All right, folks, if you'll calm down, we'll get this meeting started." He signaled to John. "John Grigsby, will do the honor of overseeing this meeting."

A low hum went through the room as the men waited.

John licked his dry lips and cleared his throat. "It's been brought to my attention—" He waved a hand over the crowd. "to all of our attentions, that we've got a problem with the outfit that ridden into town this past month."

Before he could go on, a man yelled out, "One of those men harassed my wife on the boardwalk on her way to Owens' mercantile!"

Another said, "They've been terrorizing us townspeople. I don't like it one bit!"

A third man said, "I've got four steers missing. From what I understand, they're grazing over at Benson's abandoned ranch east of town!"

Sheriff Ford spoke up. "These men said they're in our town to lay low. If Bart Clemens hadn't informed me about the bank robberies these men have been accused of, we wouldn't have known what they were probably laying low from."

Charles Matthews' hand shot up. "Since these guys might be bank robbers, we should have extra guards on hand at the bank. One at the door, and one behind the counter. We can't take a chance on the bank being robbed by these no-good outlaws."

The saloon rumbled as tempers flared, fists went into the air, and the men's voices rose.

John waited for the noise to settle down. "Well," he said, hands on his gun belt. "It seems we're in agreement that the Woodrow gang has turned our town upside down, not to mention cattle missing. If they did those bank robberies, that's an offence worthy of the federal penitentiary." John gazed at Sheriff Ford and then back to the unhappy crowd.

"So what are you going to do about it, Sheriff?" asked James Radburn. "I'm missing a half-dozen steers myself."

John pushed his black felt hat back with a forefinger. "I think it's time we lock them up and contact the federal marshal."

A roar went up along with fists. Heads nodded throughout the saloon and the room continued to buzz.

"When are you goin' after 'em, Sheriff?" a rancher bellowed.

"We haven't worked that out. But let's just say, it'll be soon." Ford ran a hand over his weary face.

Jonah Ford had to be getting on to his late sixties, John thought. He wasn't as strong and virile as he'd been in his younger years. He liked the man. Men didn't come any more honest than the sheriff and up until recently, he'd been able to handle the job of sheriff in their calm community. But now that the Woodrow gang had come to town—this was a job for someone with more strength than the old man had to offer.

While John was thinking about the sheriff, he realized the angry crowd was staring at him—waiting for him to speak.

"You're gonna bring those men to the jailhouse for the sheriff, aren't you?" one rancher asked.

Clem Owens pushed his way through the crowd and stepped to the front where John stood. He clamped a hand on John's shoulder. "I think the sheriff should deputize you and Charles Matthews. That'd give you authority to form a posse and go after those men and be within the law."

"How 'bout it, sheriff?" The banker stepped forward with fire in his eyes. "I'd just as soon see those men behind bars before they rob my bank."

Laughter rang out through the crowd and then settled down to a low rumble.

Sheriff Ford waved for John and Charles to stand next to him. He pulled two badges from his coat pocket and said, "I figured I'd just as well have these handy, seein' as how folks around here look up to you two." He looked back at the crowd of onlookers and smiled. "I hereby deputize John Grigsby and Charles Matthews as our new deputies of Grovespring, Missouri." He handed a badge to both men.

John grinned half-heartedly. "You surprised me, Sheriff." He pinned on the badge. "You came prepared."

The room filled with laughter again. The folks watched Charles Matthews pinned on his badge and a big sigh of relief filled the room.

"Go on home, folks," the sheriff said. "We'll take care of it from here."

"Thanks, Sheriff," the men said one by one and they slapped John and Charles on the back as they departed.

John felt a weight lift from the room as the folks left the saloon. When the last man had gone, he said, "Well, that takes care of that." He looked down at his badge. "Now to come up with a plan on how we're going to bring in that rowdy bunch."

A light shone in Charles' eyes. "I've been working on an idea," he said. "We know they'll never come in peacefully, but what if we make sure those boys get good and soused on Saturday night. Once they're soused, we handcuff 'em and take 'em to the jailhouse."

John slapped Charles on the back. "I gotta hand it to you, Matthews. You've come up with a good plan."

Charles looked around the bar. "Then I guess we'll meet here Saturday night?"

"I'll be here," John said.

The three men strode out of the swinging doors and went their separate ways. John stepped into the saddle and headed for home. *Thank you, Lord, for helping us with this meeting tonight. Now, if you'll give us a hand Saturday night, I'd be much obliged.*

Chapter EIGHTEEN

THE LONG WEEK FINALLY ended and on Saturday night, the Woodrow gang did not disappoint. John and Charles sat at a corner table in the saloon and kept a low profile. They had a bottle of whiskey in front of them. John picked it up and poured them each a drink. The plan, however, was to let the amber liquid sit. The men wanted to be good and sober when the moment arrived to overtake and handcuff the gang.

It had been awhile since John Grigsby had darkened the saloon doors. He hadn't had a drink in years. Yet, even though Grovespring was a quiet community, the local ranchers and cowboys found Grider's Saloon & Eatery their favorite place to hang out when they came to town. It wasn't the most magnificent place, as saloons go. The establishment was in a plain building with wooden walls and wooden floors. A long mirror hung on the wall behind the bar. The bar itself was the only thing that shone in the room, and Grider took pride in it. Oft times, the bartender could be found with a cloth in his hand, polishing the top's smooth surface.

The food was good, and a man could get a meal for half the price he'd pay at Yates Café. And Old Sam played a plunky tune on the upright piano that could be heard up and down Main Street. The lively music was often the one sound that made Grovespring feel like something was going on. It drew the men in, knowing they'd get a drink to soothe their dry throats and a meal to ease their hunger.

Across the room the boisterous outlaws were enjoying a continuous flow of whiskey coming to their table. The bartender obliged willingly, having been informed that the sheriff needed him to help set the trap. Curly Joe lacked restraint and occasionally raised his pistol and fired shots in the air. By midnight, the gang had run most of Grider's customers out of the saloon.

Grider reluctantly glanced over to the corner table where John and Charles sat. But the men shook their heads slightly. It wasn't time to approach the men yet. As the hours dragged on, the gang's boisterous whoops and hollers seemed to slow down. Still, Grider kept a constant flow of whiskey going to their table.

Finally, John tilted his head and eyed the bartender. When Grider looked his way he gave a slight nod. The bartender casually came over. "You fellas need another round here?"

John cocked a smile and asked, "You got anything stronger for those men? Something that'll knock 'em out?"

Grider nodded. "I sure do. I've got a bit of tranquilizer powder I can put in their drinks—just enough to put 'em out. If it's all right with you." He gave the men a sardonic smile. "I've had to do it a few times in the past when a customer becomes too dangerous for the crowd.

"Go easy on it, but do it," Charles said.

Grider went back to the bar and fixed four drinks. He carried the amber liquid to the Woodrow table and said, "It's gettin' late, boys, but you've livened the atmosphere around here. For that, I'm givin' you a round of drinks on the house."

"That's mighty big of you, bartender!" Curly Joe eyed the gold liquid and drank it down in one long swallow.

John and Charles leaned their elbows on the table in their corner. They were far enough away from the rowdy men that they could observe them without the gang noticing the attention. "They're wearing down," John said under his breath as he watched Otis's head hit the table and his body slouch low. "I do believe the tranquilizer is kicking in." John gave Charles an amused grin.

Charles leaned back in his chair and took a small sip of his drink, a wry smile on his lips. "Won't be long now."

Grider sidled toward their table with a disgruntled expression. "Those men have run off all my regulars except you." He carried a damp rag in one hand and a towel draped over his arm. "I may as well start cleanin' up the joint, seein' as how those men look like they're 'bout done for the night." He winked and walked away to collected empty bottles from a table.

Moments later, Jiggs' head dropped back against his chair, his legs stretched out, and he started snoring. John and Charles looked at each other, crossed their arms over their chests, and waited.

A few minutes later, Duke's head tipped forward a few times before it thumped onto the table.

Curly Joe glanced at the three men. "Hey! Wake up!" He jostled Duke, but the red-headed young man only moaned. "If yer all gonna call it a night," he slurred, "Let's flee this joint and—" Curly Joe's head leaned forward and thumped on the wooden table as well. A low moan escaped him.

The bartender motioned with his chin and nodded, a twinkle in his eyes.

"Let's get to it," John said. "We better grab Curly Joe first and then the kid. If we can get them out before the other two men awake, it'll make our job easier."

The two men quietly stood and crept stealthily to Woodrow's table. John looked at Charles and nodded. They stood behind Curly Joe, Charles lifted him out of the chair and John took his feet. They eased the man out of the saloon and crossed the street, where Sheriff Ford waited with an open jail cell. Then they returned to Grider's to get Duke.

Once they deposited the soused young man onto the cot in his cell, he groaned and rolled over, none the wiser where he slept.

John and Charles went after the next man and, finally they came to Jiggs, who was the last man at the table and was snoring loudly. John's boot scraped the wooden floor when he moved behind Jiggs. The outlaw's head swung up and he glanced around, bleary-eyed. "Where'd the boys go?" he asked and stumbled to his feet.

"Across the street at the jailhouse," Grider said, his thumbs tucked under his armpits and a tired grin on his face.

"What're you talkin' about!" Jiggs slurred and his hand went for his gun.

"Don't even think about it!" John said, jamming his pistol into the man's back.

Jiggs' shoulders slumped as if he'd given up, but in the next second, his arm shot out and he cuffed Charles' chin with the barrel of his six-shooter. Charles head shot back, he staggered, and hit the floor.

John's hand shot out and he drove the butt of his gun onto the back of Jiggs' head. The outlaw spun around, eyes wide as the shock of the blow sent him to his knees. He waved his pistol as he tried to stand, one hand on the floor, but Charles recovered from the stunning blow and kicked the weapon out of Jiggs' hand. Then he shoved Jiggs to the floor for good measure. "It's over, Woodrow!"

"You ain't puttin' me in no jailhouse!" Jiggs bellowed.

"Get up!" John said, his gun aimed at the man.

Jiggs pushed himself off the floor and swayed, then fell to his knees. Blood slowly oozed down the back of his head and he swiped at it, his hand coming back red stained. "You'll be sorry for this," he growled at John.

Grider watched from the sideline, his mouth slack and his eyes wide, but he didn't say a word. John and Charles lifted Jiggs to his feet and escorted him out of the saloon and across the street. It had taken less than an hour to get all four men safely behind bars.

Sheriff Ford, John and Charles, stood outside the jailhouse. They had them! All four of the Woodrow gang slept in the cells with a chorus of snores, and not a one of them—except maybe Jiggs—knew they'd wake up in the morning in the jailhouse.

"Goodnight," John said, stepping into the stirrup and reining Blue toward home. "I'll see you men in the morning."

"Goodnight, John," Sheriff Ford said, a pleased smile on his face. "We done good tonight!"

Charles held up a hand. "I'll ride over to the next town in the morning and telegraph the federal marshal." he said.

John touched the brim of his hat and headed for home. At the edge of town, he started whistling a tune, but farther down the road he asked himself, how long would it be before the marshal arrived to collect the gang. "I'll be glad when those fellas are sitting in the penitentiary," he told Blue as if the horse were listening. "They've stolen cattle from just about every rancher in these parts. A man's got to pay for his wrongdoings." He patted the horse's neck and put him into a gallop. Home sounded pretty good right about now.

When John stepped into the house, all the lights had been extinguished except a kerosene lamp on a table near the staircase. The flames flickered, casting shadows on the walls. John hung his hat on the wall hook, picked up the kerosene lamp, and climbed the stairs. Every night he looked into the children's rooms before he turned in. He held the lamp as he pushed the girls' bedroom door open. They were snuggled together on a full bed, the covers pulled to their chins, Tess's arm around Mary Jane. He stood at the foot of the bed and watched their even breathing.

Then he went to the older boys' room and stepped through the opening. The boys had separate beds with a table between each bed. They slept soundly, with Rusty on a floor rug at the foot of Calvin's bed. Rusty yawned and came forward. John bent and scratched the mangy looking dog behind his ears, and stroked his rough coat, glad to be home. Rusty sat on his haunches, his tongue hanging out in a wide smile. John patted his head and stepped back into the hall. As he looked back into the boy's room, Rusty circled around three times before he lay down, seeming to dismiss him.

In his youngest sons' bedroom, Wiley and Jeffrey were fast asleep in a full bed. They slept contentedly. John gazed at the ceiling as if he could see past the beams and roofing. *Thank you, God, for watching over my family. Keep them safe from the arrows of darkness. And if it be Your will, bring me a helpmate to tend to these precious children.*

John nodded and quietly went downstairs to his room. He sat on the edge of his bed, and with the toe of one scuffed-up boot, he inched off the heel of the other boot. Both boots off, he blew out the lamp. Tonight was going to be a long one, just like every other night had been. When would he get the courage to talk to Mahala? Would she be receptive to his wishes to court her? Would he ever get over the guilt of the thought of courting another woman? Nancy had been the only woman he had ever wanted. But could he live without a woman? Lord knew, he needed one, as did his children.

A TEAM OF HORSES pulled a black wagon into town. The wagon was enclosed on all four sides, with a roof on top. Two barred windows were on each side of the wagon. The words "U.S. Marshal" were emblazoned in gold above the bars, and "Missouri Territory" below the windows. The marshal, wearing a brown suede coat and felt hat, his badge prominently displayed, sat up front holding the reins in his gloved hands.

Folks stepped out of the shops to watch the ominous wagon rattle by. By the time the rig stopped in front of the jailhouse, Main Street overflowed with curious onlookers. The crowd grew as folks waited to get a look at the four outlaws to be escorted into the back of the wagon.

The marshal tied the reins to the brake post and climbed down from his perch. His hand went up, acknowledging the crowd, before he disappeared inside the sheriff's office.

From a distance, John could see some kind of commotion going on, but it wasn't until he rode in front of the sheriff's office that he realized that, after three weeks of holding the Woodrow gang in their small-town jail, the town of Grovespring would finally be rid of the nefarious men.

He tied Blue to the hitching post, his boots sounding hollow as he stepped onto the boardwalk in front of the jailhouse. He strode to the open door of the sheriff's office to find the U.S. marshal locking iron rings on Jiggs

Woodrow's ankles. He'd already clamped rings on the man's wrists with a foot-long chain dangling in between.

"Come on in, Grigsby," Sheriff Ford called to him. "This here's Marshal Dunn. He's come for the outlaws."

"Glad to meet you." John extended a hand. "You need any help?"

The marshal shook his hand, but he was all business as he released it and grabbed ahold of Jiggs' upper arm. "No thanks, pardner. I'll put these men in the wagon one at a time." He pushed Jiggs toward the open door, and the two men stepped outside. Jiggs shuffled awkwardly and squinted from the bright sun as he moved reluctantly toward the back of the fortified wagon.

He looked back at the jailhouse and at John—his eyes smoldering black coals. "You better hope I don't break outta that joint when I get there, 'cause if I do—you're a dead man, Grigsby!"

"That's enough," the marshal said pushing Jiggs into wagon.

One by one the remaining three members of the Woodrow gang scowled as they shuffled out to the wagon, their wrists and ankles in chains, while, all the while, the crowd milled close to watch justice take place. Within the hour, all four prisoners sat inside the wagon. They looked out the barred windows as the conveyance left town going back the way it had come.

John ran a hand over his scruffy beard. "It's done, Sheriff." He pulled off his badge and handed it back to Ford. "I won't be needing this anymore."

"You sure you don't want to keep that badge?"

"I'm sure. I've got a ranch to tend to, and a family who needs my time." Glancing at the Yates Hotel & Café sign, he turned back to Ford. "A good lunch sounds mighty fine before I head back to the ranch. Care to join me?"

A CHILL WIND BLEW as John built a wooden fence around the graves. He had walked out the length and width he figured would be a good size for a family cemetery and had spent every spare moment sawing wood and hewing each piece into a three-foot length with a V-shape on one end. He'd finally accumulated enough slats to begin the process of building the fence. First he would pound four sturdy posts into the ground to set the perimeter.

Nancy's death had shaken him to his core. He hadn't realized how vulnerable their lives had been until fate had taken hers. He'd read Ecclesiastes in the Good Book enough times to have memorized some of the passages. Now, as he pounded a post into the ground, those words lifted off the pages and swirled through his mind. *There is a time to live and a time to die. A time to laugh and a time to cry. A time to sow, and a time to reap . . .* oh, how those words rang true.

The sound of the hammer pounding against the post echoed through the ranch, and the truth of his wife's death drove into his soul, each strike of the hammer a searing pain in his heart. Would the days get any easier? It had been two months since Nancy and the baby had passed. The circuit preacher had said that beyond prayer, time was the healer of all wounds. How much time did he need before he wanted to live again? As it stood, he was a ghost of a man going about his business. He knew it was time for him to move on, but how did a man do that when he'd lost the love of his life?

Once the posts were in, he added the picket fencing. By late afternoon, he finished the job by setting a gate to close in the small area. When done, he gazed at his work with satisfaction. He'd left enough room for future graves. The single mound was all he could bear now.

Once John returned to the house, he built a fire in the fireplace. The living room was dark and the children weren't around. Gazing at the ceiling, he listened for sounds and heard faint shuffling and creaking on the floorboards. "Good. The children are all upstairs."

He went from room to room and lit kerosene lamps and candles to give a semblance of warmth to the house. *A semblance.* The flickering lights couldn't take the place of a wife and mother. There was something about a woman's presence that warmed every corner of a house, a warmth this house was lacking.

Without trying, his mind went to Mahala. His neighbor hadn't come the past few weeks. Had he done something to offend her? She had selflessly given of her time, cooking meals, tending to the needs of the children, and in truth, giving the house the very thing it was missing.

Logs snapped and crackled in the great stone fireplace, pulling his thoughts away for the moment.

John stared at the flames. He wished Mahala were here, that she hadn't stopped coming, but he couldn't bring himself to ask her to give up what precious little time she had from work at the shop to come again, even though he knew the children missed her.

It felt odd yet comforting seeing Mahala doing things around the house that Nancy would do if she were here. *If she were here. She isn't here!* His mind warred within him and his gut twisted. *How long, Lord, before I can think of another woman without feeling the guilt? How did a man find a woman for his children when he couldn't let go of his wife?*

THAT EVENING, GRANVILLE WENT to his room and opened a dresser drawer. He fished around under his clothes until his fingers found a small canvas bag with a drawstring. He pulled out the pouch and glanced toward the door. The family were all downstairs, talking in the living room. He didn't want Calvin to follow him to the room. A boy had a right to privacy, didn't he? He closed the door and sat on his bed. Opening the pouch, Granville poured out the change and spread it out. He'd been saving money the past five months for a rifle. Once he had enough, he'd take the money to work and ask Mr. Owens to order the rifle for him.

He divided the coins and began counting. When he picked up the last coin, he grinned. "Yes!" he said under his breath. Looking at the door as if he half expected Calvin or Franklin to barge in at any moment, Granville quickly scooped up the coins and slid them into the canvas pouch and returned the bag to the drawer. He'd take the money to town tomorrow. It wouldn't be long now before he owned a rifle just like his father's. And the best thing about it was that he'd earned the money all on his own. After he shut the drawer, Granville left the room. He couldn't wait to see the look on his father's face when he learned Granville had purchased a rifle with the money he'd earned.

MAHALA AWOKE TO THE same sounds every morning—the sound of a whisk beating against the sides of a stone bowl as her mother blended the eggs and milk for scrambled eggs. And she always awoke in time to get dressed and go downstairs for breakfast before she met the stableman, Charlie, in the barn to retrieve her horse and to ride into town for work. But in the past few weeks, her routine had taken a downhill slope.

What with the death of her best friend, all she wanted to do was keep to herself. Going to the shop and dealing with the demands of sewing for the persnickety women in town was the last thing on her mind. She just couldn't face people right now, and try as she might, she couldn't get herself into motion. And to make things worse, she refrained from going to the Grigsbys' house as she had promised.

Mahala pulled the blanket to her chin as her mind strayed to her friend's family. She had promised Nancy that she would take care of her children. And yet she had spent the past few weeks as far away from the Grigsbys' front porch as she could. Guilt ripped through her for doing so.

Feeling groggy, Mahala felt as if cobwebs had taken up residence in her head. Faint sounds from the kitchen continued to sail to her room, and her foggy mind tried to make sense of the confusion. She rolled over and pulled the covers over her ears.

She heard the back door open and close and her father's voice floated to her room.

"Is everybody still in bed?"

She heard shuffling footsteps scrambling down the stairs, along with the muffled sounds of her sisters' morning chatter. The girls were up. How was it that her family carried on with life as usual? She swallowed to stem the flow of hot tears.

She hadn't missed the worried look in her mother's eyes lately. Mahala's silence wasn't like her. In fact, quite the opposite. She was the one who usually came home full of news from town and sharing details about the next dress she was making.

Her sisters had tried every which way to wrangle Mahala out of bed to go to town, or at the least— go for a buggy ride. Mahala had resisted their efforts. She had, however, taken a walk to the creek and stood at the water's edge to watch it flow laughingly downstream. The sound of the water rippling merrily along soothed her soul. She never tired of watching the whiskered catfish swimming downstream in and out among the rocks. The days had grown cold and she refrained from removing her shoes to wade in the stream, even though it beckoned to her. But in the recesses of her mind, she heard Nancy's joyful laugh when she had waded and splashed in the cold water.—

A sharp knock on the bedroom door brought Mahala fully awake. She blinked to clear the cobwebs from her mind and ran a hand over her face. Sunshine streamed through the window. She pushed herself up and out of bed and stumbled to the door.

"Rise and shine, morning glory," Mary said as she brushed into the room. Then seeing Mahala still wearing her nightgown she gasped, "Good heavens, are you going to sleep your life away?"

Mahala sat on the edge of the bed and yawned. "Of course not."

"Well, that's good to know, because you've got responsibilities waiting for you."

Mahala clasped her hands in her lap. Her mother hadn't come to her room to chat. She was on a mission to get her up and moving and wouldn't leave the room until she'd accomplished just that. Maybe it was for the best. No amount of lamenting her friend's death changed anything. It was time to close the book on that chapter of her life—and live.

"I need you and the girls to go to town for supplies. Your father's got his hands full with the last of the cattle calving and I'm running out of staples for the kitchen."

Mahala grinned. Her mother loved to ride into town for kitchen supplies. She always came back with the latest news from the women of Grovespring. And her sisters could go into town if they had a mind to. The ruse was her mother's way of manufacturing a way to get her out of bed and into the flow of life—and she would take it.

Truth was, the moment her mother brushed into the room, Mahala didn't think she could spend another moment in bed. The energy her mother exuded made her want to shake everything off that weighed her down. She would put on her day dress and face the day with everything she had.

Mahala stood and ran her fingers through her tangled hair. "I'll get dressed and take the girls to town."

"Wonderful!" Mary said. "I'll tell Charlie to hitch Bessy to the wagon while I finish breakfast. Hurry and come downstairs." She turned to leave and stopped. With gentle eyes, she gazed at Mahala. "You're going to be all right, dear."

Tears sprang to Mahala's eyes. "I know, Mother. I'm ready to put Nancy's death to rest. The children and Mr. Grigsby need me. I've stayed away far too long."

"You needn't run to their house just yet. They've been fine without you."

"Now, how would you know a thing like that?" Mahala asked, her shoulders relaxing.

"It's been the talk of the town. Since you've been gone, the women from the community have marked their calendars to take turns taking a dish to the Grigsby house." A twinkle lit her mother's eyes. "Apparently, some of the women have encouraged their daughters to take a meal. It appears that the young girls have their sights on Mr. Grigsby as a substantial catch. There aren't that many available men in the area, and with his large ranch and all, you have to agree, John's a good catch."

Mahala felt a twinge in her gut. Why this news bothered her, she didn't know. She'd never thought of John Grigsby as anything other than Nancy's husband. She respected John a great deal. He was a good man. But he had been Nancy's man.

Had been.

"Maybe the family is doing well, and maybe not. I haven't been able to face going over to the house these past weeks."

"Even with the house full of children?"

"Yes. Even with the house full of children."

"Give it more time if you need to."

"No. I've done that. I'm ready to go back."

"Well, then, I'll see you in the kitchen." Mary patted Mahala's arm and left the room.

As Mahala dressed, she could smell the sausage sizzling in the frying pan and the biscuits baking in the oven. When she arrived at the table, there was fresh milk from the barn and Nancy's homemade peach preserves. Her appetite had awakened. When Mary set the biscuits on the table, Mahala dipped her spoon into the jar of peach preserves and spread the delicious jam over a warm biscuit. "Umm. This is good."

When the meal ended, Mahala had an overwhelming desire to get outside. What the day held for her, she didn't know, but she was eager to find out. With that in mind, Mahala went up to her room, and pinned her straw hat on, and stepped out the door. Could she put all the grief behind her and face the day head on?

Chapter NINETEEN

FALL LEAVES LITTERED THE ground as the morning sun blazed across the front yard. Mahala and the girls crunched leaves under their boots as they crossed the yard to the waiting wagon. The nippy air felt welcome after the long hot summer.

The maple tree fanned out its long brown branches, and what few leaves remained shadowed the front of the house. Glancing at her sisters and then back to the house, Mahala played with the thought that John may need her for more than just his children's needs. The thought sent her a rush of heat through her skin. *Goodness! Mahala Shields! Isn't it a might too soon to think that John Grigsby is up for grabs? Even if you have been Grovespring's longest spinster!*

Rebecca sat on one side of Mahala and Mary Ann on the other as they rode into town. Mahala had tucked her mother's list into her skirt pocket, thinking she'd need to purchase a few items of her own as well. The change of weather—crisp and clear—felt refreshing as their sleek brown horse trotted swiftly down the dusty road.

"I'll get the supplies from the feed store while you shop at the mercantile," Rebecca said, her eyes bright with anticipation.

"You don't fool me, Rebecca. You're hoping Cord Matthews will be there to wait on you like he did the last time we came into town." Mary Ann gave her sister a knowing look.

"Cord Matthews?" Mahala asked, playfully. "Do you have your sights on Charles Matthews' son?" She shook her head and laughed softly. "Where have I been?"

Rebecca's chin went up. "Now, see what you've done, Mary Ann. The secret's out." She pursed her lips and stared straight ahead. But it wasn't long before her eyes lit up again. She gazed at Mahala. "Don't you think he's the most handsome man you've ever seen?"

A smile curved Mahala's lips. "Cord is certainly good looking. And if he has his head on straight, he'll recognize that you are a good catch too."

Mary Ann leaned into Mahala, which made Mahala lean into Rebecca. "I never thought on God's green earth that I'd hear you say such a thing," Mary Ann said. 'Mama would skin Rebecca alive if she knew what a flirt she is."

Mahala gazed at Mary Ann, a giggle working its way into her throat. "Who's the flirt?" She elbowed Mary Ann's ribs. "I heard tell you got caught kissing one of the ranch hands out at the stable."

Mary Ann sat up straight. "Who told you that?"

"Mother did, and she was fit to be tied that you'd thrown yourself at that cowboy." Mahala held the reins firmly in her grip. She'd give anything to be caught kissing a man. She had no idea what that would feel like. But from the look on Mary Ann's face, she'd enjoyed it.

"Father spoiled everything. Travis won't come within ten feet of me since then. Dad threatened to fire him if he even saw Travis looking my way." Mary Ann's brows bunched up. "He can't keep us away from each other forever. And besides, at eighteen it's time I found a husband or I'll be the next spinster of Grovespring."

Mahala's cheeks burned but she kept her voice steady. "Be patient, Mary Ann. I'll talk to Father. You have every right to start letting the men in the community court you."

Mary Ann tucked her hand in the crook of Mahala's arm. "Thanks, Sis."

Mahala flicked the reins and Bessy picked up speed. Grovespring was just ahead. When the wagon rolled down Main Street, Kyle Weaver stepped out of the blacksmith stable and waved at Mahala. She waved back but turned her head away quickly.

"Mr. Weaver's got his sights on you." Rebecca crooked a smile.

"I know."

"Don't you like him?"

"He's a nice man. But I don't care for him in the way he wants me to."

Mary Ann gazed at her with incredulity, but she didn't say a word.

Mahala ignored her sister's look and pulled the wagon to the side of the road in front of Owens Mercantile. She tied the reins to the brake handle and ran her hand over her brown skirt. When she looked up both of the girls were staring at her. "Listen. Mr. Weaver is going to make some woman a good husband someday. It just isn't going to be me."

"Why not?" Rebecca asked. It appeared she wasn't about to move until she got a suitable answer.

Mahala shrugged. "I told you. He just isn't my type." She envisioned his bulky build and wide expanse of mouth under his long and narrow black mustache, waxed to perfection, which gave him the appearance of a catfish. But that didn't give her pause. The real problem was his age; the blacksmith was in his mid-fifties, twenty-five years her senior. Mahala had hopes of finding a man in his prime, a man closer to her own age.

Mary Ann rolled her eyes. "You've got to be kidding. He's the only available bachelor in town and you're a—" She stopped. Mahala couldn't tell if it was the nippy air or a blush that reddened Mary Ann's cheeks.

Mahala worried her bottom lip. "I'll thank you girls to let me handle my affairs. Mr. Weaver is not the only available bachelor in Grovespring. So let's leave it at that."

The girls gave each other a look.

"I'll be in the store if you need me." Mahala waited for Mary Ann to step down to the ground before she climbed down herself and walked away, head held high. But her heart sank low. She didn't need her sister's help when it came to finding a husband. She could do that on her own, thank you very much. She meant to fill her mother's list of staples and then find out if there was any mail. Had Mr. Bates received her letter yet? Would there be a response waiting for her?

AFTER WEEKS OF STAYING away from the Grigsbys' home, winter was settling in before, Mahala tentatively stepped onto their front porch. She hugged a warm pot of chicken and dumplings to her waist as she lifted a hand to rap on the door. But before she touched the oak panel, the door flew open.

"Oh." Mahala squeezed the Dutch oven to her side and stared at John, who stood at the opening, dark shadows under his eyes. Had he lost sleep over the past few weeks?

"I-I brought chicken and dumplings." She held up the heavy pot. "H-have you eaten?" Her cheeks burned hotly as she continued to stare at him. She feared she looked as red as a rooster. She gripped the handles tightly; if she didn't, she feared she'd drop their supper dead away.

John reached for the heavy pot. "Let me take this to the kitchen, Miss

Shields." Their hands brushed lightly as he relieved her of the load. An electrical bolt shot through her and her cheeks burned even hotter. His gaze jumped to hers, and he gave her a faint smile. "Uh, come in out of the cold."

John held the door wide as she stepped through. Mahala removed her shawl and hung it on the wall hook. All the while, she felt his eyes stayed on her. Her body still felt warm from their accidental touch.

John stood in the hallway, holding the Dutch oven, seeming in no hurry to take their dinner to the kitchen. His gaze never left her. "You've been gone a while. Are you all right?"

Her heart pounded in her ears. "Yes, I'm fine." She licked her lips and glanced to the left into the living room. The children were settled comfortably on the sofa and the armchairs, except for Calvin, who lay on his belly on the floor,—reading a book in the dim light of the kerosene lamps. She gazed farther into the room to see a fire burning brightly in the fireplace.

Mary Jane jumped from the sofa. "Molly!" She ran and threw her arms around Mahala's skirts.

Mahala bent over and gently pulled the little girl to her. "How are you, darling?" She stroked Mary Jane's long curls and gazed into her eyes.

"I don't know." Her bottom lip puckered. There was a sadness in her eyes that kept Mahala from asking anymore questions.

"That's all right." Mahala straightened and gazed at Mary Jane, then at the others in the room. "Are you hungry? I brought chicken and dumplings."

"Oh, goody!" Calvin whooped and jumped to his feet.

The children filed into the dining room, gazing at her with sheepish smiles. Tess, however, set to work bringing out dinner plates and setting them on the table. She glanced quickly at Mahala and then away as she went back to the kitchen for silverware.

John lifted Wiley and set him in the high chair. "Thank you for coming." His features lit up a bit. He set Jeffrey into a chair. Mahala watched the rest of the children find seats and sit down, all except for Tess, who continued to find reasons to exit the dining room and go back to the kitchen.

Was Tess still avoiding her?

The next time Tess came out, Mahala asked, "Do you need help with anything?"

"No, ma'am. I've got it."

"Ma'am?"

Tess avoided eye contact and disappeared into the kitchen again.

Mahala pulled her gaze away from the swinging door and back to John.

"You're welcome, Mr. Grigsby. I'm sorry I haven't come sooner. I-I—."

John came around to where she stood. "You don't have to explain. It's been difficult for all of us." He looked toward the kitchen. "Especially for her. She's taken on the role of mother and housekeeper since Nan has gone."

Mahala gazed into his blue eyes and wondered how he could speak of Nancy so easily.

She looked at the children to keep from looking into John's deep blue eyes again. "I'll be bringing meals when I can—"

"I think we're ready," Tess said curtly.

"Of course." Mahala stepped away from John.

"Will you have supper with us?" he offered.

"Um . . . to tell the truth, I haven't eaten and—." She gazed at the hopeful looks on the children's faces, all but Tess, who stared straight ahead with storm clouds in her eyes.

"I think I'll pass on the offer tonight." She stepped away from the table. She didn't miss the disappointment in John's expression.

"I'll walk you to the door." He turned back to Granville. "Say grace and start eating. I'll be with you shortly."

Mahala moved to the hallway and draped her shawl over her shoulders. She was aware of John standing nearby.

He placed a hand on the door before she reached for the doorknob. "I would have enjoyed your company, Miss Shields." He gazed at her with troubled eyes. "I'm sorry about Tess. She's having a hard time of it."

"I understand, Mr. Grigsby, and don't worry, I'm not offended. She needs more time to adjust to—"

John let out a relieved sigh. "I know I've said it a half-dozen times tonight, but it's worth saying again. "Thank you."

His features relaxed and she felt a warmth in his stance. "Mother tells me the women in the community have come often with meals for your family."

"That's true. Some of the women and their daughters *have* come by with meals. We've been blessed with plenty of food."

"Then you might be fine if I don't come as often as I have in the past."

John stared at her for a long moment. "You and Nan were the best of friends. She wouldn't want you to stay away."

"I know." *And you?* Something told her not to ask. So she said, "I'll come back to help pick up the slack for Tess."

John touched her arm lightly. "When you come— plan to stay for supper. It would be good for the children—and me."

She glanced up, seeing a warm glint in his eyes. She hadn't been here long, and yet she saw a change in his appearance and a lift to his stride. And she saw something else, as if he wanted to say more. "I will come for supper." She stared at the door.

John opened the door and lifted a hand. "Good evening, Miss Shields."

"Until next time." She waved lightly. It wasn't until she stepped to the ground at the end of the porch that she heard the door close.

She walked swiftly to the waiting buggy, the air crisp and nippy. Mahala gazed up to see there wasn't a cloud in the sky, only the big moon that hung low, lighting the ground around her. "Well, that wasn't so bad," she told herself. *Did I see a hint of interest in those dark blue eyes? Or am imagining things?*

SNOW FLURRIES CAME AND went while Mahala spent the better part of the morning cleaning her work station at Thompson's Tailor Shop. She hummed a tune while she stacked and arranged bolts of material by color and texture. This part of cleaning happened to be one of her delights. She couldn't handle fabric without her imagination running rampant with ideas for creations that could be sewn for future seasonal events.

Scraps of material and snippets of thread were scattered about the floor. Broom in hand, she swept the mess and filled the dustpan several times. When done, she sat at her table and breathed in deeply, "Good. Now to finish Gretta Matthews' dress."

The sound of horses' hooves thundered up the street and grew louder as the Wells Fargo stagecoach made an abrupt halt in front of the tailor shop. The way station sat at the edge of town, but Bart liked to unload the passengers near the hotel just up the boardwalk. The street outside Yates Hotel and Café's was usually taken with horses at the hitching post or an occasional buggy or a wagon parked in front of the structure, so it wasn't uncommon for the stagecoach to stop outside her window.

Mahala welcomed the sight of the stagecoach stopping in front of the shop. With her table near the window, she was often the first to know when a new passengers arrived in town. More times than not, the stagecoach only stayed long enough for Bart to unload his passengers, and then he moved the stagecoach down the road, where he exchanged his tired horses for a fresh team before he delivered the mail to Owens Mercantile. His last stop was a meal at Yates Café. But truth to tell, with Grovespring being such a tiny town, the stage rarely brought people to their small community. No one new had arrived since the stage brought Nancy's mother and sister a few months back.

Mahala watched Bart climb down from his seat and come around to open the coach door. He reached inside to facilitate a passenger stepping to the ground. Not wishing to be seen a spectator watching out of the window, Mahala took a step back and peered around a mannequin draped with a long dress that was a work-in-progress. She removed a measuring tape from the mannequin's neck to her own and looked over the mannequin's shoulder as she gazed out the window. Who could be arriving in the early weeks of winter?

A gloved hand appeared, elegantly extended, and Mahala leaned forward, waiting to see to whom it belonged.

With Bart's assistance, the woman stepped from the coach and shook out her gown.

"Bella!" Mahala blurted to no one. "She's back?" Mahala knew that the smart-looking woman who had just stepped out of the coach was the one and only Isabella Jean Yates—and Yates Hotel's future proprietor. Isabella, better known as Bella, was the niece of the auspicious Gertrude Yates, a rich old gal of Grovespring. Those who knew Gertrude personally, called her "Gertie."

"Welcome back, Miss Yates." Bart's deep voice sounded muffled through the windowpane. "Do you have someone coming for you?" He looked at the first tufts of falling snow and back at the stagecoach piled high with luggage.

Bella rubbed her bare arms and glanced toward the hotel. "Aunt Gertie's driver should have arrived by now." Her petite brows puckered. "He's late."

Mahala sucked in her breath.

What are you doing here? And where's your coat?

At thirty-three, Bella didn't look a day over twenty. With thick tresses of rich honey-gold hair and tea-brown eyes with tiny flecks of amber, Bella was nothing less than stunning. Her pale face had a dainty mole near her nose. Mahala continued to watch the newcomer and realized Bella was more beautiful than she remembered. And her dress, cream-colored with dainty blue and yellow flowers, featured a low-cut neckline. Mahala laid a hand to her own decidedly less—bountiful bodice and wanted to wilt right there, right now.

Holding her breath, Mahala watched Bart pull Bella's luggage from the top and the back of the stagecoach and set them on the wooden planks in the middle of the boardwalk. She counted the pieces: Eight. Two carpet bags, a small trunk, a large trunk, and a stack of four medium-sized suitcases. Her heart sank. It looked as if Bella was going to be staying a while.

She was still gazing out the window when John Grigsby, rode his horse to the hitching post and stared at the new arrival. He leaned an arm against his saddle horn as if deciding whether to dismount or stay put. Finally, he slid off his mount and tied Blue to the hitching post. On the step nearby lay a hound that the people of Grovespring seemed to have adopted as the town dog. John leaned down and patted the canine's head and swept the dust of snow off its back before he slowly strode to the stagecoach and extended a hand toward Bella.

Did John know Bella was coming to town?

Mahala ducked farther behind the mannequin. *Goodness, mercy, saints alive! Why did Bella have to show up now?*

"HELLO, MISS YATES" JOHN allowed a hint of a smile and fixed his gaze on the mole on Bella's cheek. "How have you been?"

"I must say I'm surprised to see you. Did you know I was coming?" Bella gaped at him dumbfounded.

"No. I just happened to be riding down Main Street when the stage rolled in. How was your trip?"

"I'm exhausted, John. I've been traveling in this contraption for the last nineteen days and I ache all over, but other than that—" She grinned and gave him a hug. "I'm most grateful to be out of that wretched coach and onto solid ground again." She waved a white-gloved hand. "I'm looking forward to spending time in this quaint little town. I almost feel as if I've come home again."

Bella was always elaborate when she spoke her mind, and she did it with a certain charm. John wondered, as he had many times before, why she hadn't married. Surely, it wasn't for the lack of suitors.

"I've missed you." Bella wove her arm through the crook of his. "Very much." She pressed close.

John felt himself tense. "Have arrangements been made for you to be picked up?"

"Jonas should have been here already. But as you can see, he's not."

While Bella spoke, John attempted to pull his arm back and inch some space between them—without success. She had a firm grip. He gazed across the boardwalk in the direction of Yates Hotel, and in doing so, he spotted Mahala standing near the window inside Thompson's Tailor Shop, peering over the shoulder of a seamstress mannequin. Their eyes held for a moment before she stepped away. He turned away to hide an amused smile.

Until now, it hadn't occurred to him that the stagecoach had arrived in front of Thompson's. *Dagnabbit! How'd I get myself into this predicament?* Here he stood with Bella Yates and her putting on a show right in front of Mahala. A show he hadn't auditioned for. *Lord almighty,* he groaned inwardly. He had only recently come to terms with the idea that it was time to court a woman or, should he say, given himself permission to look into the possibility of courting. Mahala intrigued him with her gentle spirit, and she was bright and smart. He meant to pursue the dark-haired beauty. Bella coming to Grovespring could sabotage his attempt to gain Mahala's trust.

Bella ran a hand along his arm. "The temperature has dropped considerably in the last hour. Perhaps you might show me to the café while we await my aunt's driver?"

While we await? John's gut twisted.

Surprised at her forwardness—and at the generous display of bosom her dress permitted at his angle—John nodded, but his gut twisted again. How would he get out of this?

Bella gave his arm a tug. "Can we go, Mr. Grigsby?"

"Yes," he said, politely. "Let's get you out of the cold. Did you bring a wrap?" He cupped her elbow as he looked past her to the pile of trunks and suitcases sitting on the boardwalk. A wool coat lay draped on top of a tall trunk. Snow fell heavier now, dappling the garment in white.

"I did. My cloak had grown a bit warm inside the coach, so I removed it. We don't have far to go. The café's next door." She tilted her head in the direction of the hotel.

"Of course," he breathed. "That will give us a chance to talk."

"And—" She smiled mischievously. "To get reacquainted again."

His collar choked him when he saw the glint in her eyes. *What has gotten into her?*

He and Isabella Yates went back a long ways. They had known each other in Tennessee, where they'd gone to school together. And though Bella was a stunningly beautiful woman, he had never taken a liking to her for more than the school girl he'd known back then. If anything, he'd thought of Bella like a sister.

Isabella's parents had died of cholera before her eighteenth birthday. An only child, she was brought to Grovespring and cared for by her aunt Gertrude. Each summer, she would travel to her uncle's home in New York City. Gertrude's brother and his wife doted on Isabella. And when she lived with them, they enjoyed the opera houses. Bella loved to sing and would come back full of stories about the big city, and how she hoped to someday be able to sing as wonderfully as the ladies who filled the opera houses.

But her grounding came from Gertrude, who opened her home and her heart to the young girl as if she had been her own. If Bella went away on travels, she always came back to her aunt's home and spent time with her for a spell before she ventured out to explore new territory again.

John felt Mahala's eyes on him and he turned to look through the window at her. She sat at her table, and quickly bent her head to her work when John turned in her direction. But she glanced up again, and for a hint of a moment, their gazes held. He couldn't look away to save his soul. As the seconds passed, he felt something akin to fear run up his spine. Would he lose his chance to court her before he had a chance to ask?

With Mahala sitting near the window, she couldn't help but see Bella throwing herself at John. She quickly averted her gaze and bent low as she threaded a needle through a button and pulled it taut through the fabric. All the while, snow fell, creating a white veil between her and the occupants outside.

"John?"

No amount of gazing her way would bring Mahala's head up to see his need for her to know that what appeared to be a happy reunion of two lovers could not be further from the truth.

"John?"

He shook his head. "I'm sorry, are you ready?"

"Is it all right to leave my luggage here?" Bella stood and eyed the array of baggage that blocked the boardwalk.

"No. We should move it."

"Maybe we can leave it by the shop until my driver arrives," Bella suggested.

Relieved for an excuse to put distance between them, John moved away and picked up a couple of bags and set them against the building. His head swung to the stage driver. "Bart, how about helping me move these trunks next to the wall."

"Sure thing, John." Bart made quick work of the luggage.

As John set the last bag against the store, he heard a wagon rattle up behind him. Jonas, Gertrude's driver, had arrived with their rig.

"Hello!" Jonas waved and jumped down, smiling. "Good to see you again, Miss Yates." He tipped his snow-covered hat. His eyes lit when he gazed the length of Bella's dress and back to her face. He cleared his throat. "These your bags over here?"

Jonas, a tall, wiry man with legs as thin as matchsticks, quickly moved to the boardwalk and began picking up luggage.

Frowning, Bella said, "Yes. I need all of them taken to the house." With a wistful glint in her eyes, she turned to John. "Might we still have lunch before I go?"

"You don't want to disappoint Miss Gertrude, Missy," Jonas said. "She's been waiting for you at the house. She has a warm meal just about ready to set on the table. We best hurry before it gets cold." He didn't wait for an answer. He and Bart loaded the trunks and bags with ease.

John assisted him with the large trunk.

"You best go along with the driver. Like Jonas said, you don't want to disappoint your aunt."

"Of course not, Mr. Grigsby." Bella stepped into the wagon and seated herself next to Jonas, her dress flowing about her. She chewed her bottom lip, seemingly vexed at what she was about to say.

John didn't wait for Bella to take her leave. If he did, he feared all hope of courting Mahala would be thrown into the river. He turned and walked away.

"Mr. Grigsby," Bella called out to him.

John stopped and looked back.

"My aunt wrote about Nancy." Her tone softened. "I'm sorry for your loss."

John stared at the spokes of the wagon wheels. His heart felt like an andiron, its weight nearly unbearable. "Thank you, Bella. I miss her . . . everyday."

"I'll come by the house at your earliest convenience. Might you send a post when I may visit you and the children?"

John ran a hand over his scruffy beard. "Our lives have been in turmoil, Miss Yates. The children are still mourning their mother. It isn't advisable for you to come to the house this trip."

"This trip?" Her brows rose. "Who said I'm leaving?"

"You're staying?"

She boldly gave him a meaningful gaze. "If I have a reason to stay—"

John swallowed. *Lord have mercy!* He tipped his hat and glanced back at the window of Thompson's Tailor Shop. Mahala was nowhere to be seen.

"Are you ready, Miss Yates?" Jonas didn't wait for an answer. The wagon jerked forward and rolled out of town. What must Mahala be thinking right about now?" John slapped his hat against his pant leg and set it back on his head. He looked down at the snow-covered hound dog who lay with its legs stretched out, observing the street. He didn't seem to mind the weather. "You got any suggestions?"

The dog whined and yawned, and then put his paws over his muzzle.

John glanced at the shop window one last time. Mahala's table was vacant.

How do I explain Bella to Mahala, Lord, when I don't know what's going on myself?

Chapter TWENTY

MAHALA PICKED UP BOOTS from the floor and set her on the bed. The kitten blinked slowly and went to the middle of the rumpled covers and curled her tail under her chin. Boots had lost the tiny fur-ball look and had become a slender kitten with long legs.

Mahala ran her hand over Boots' soft head. "Aren't you a darling?"

But her mind wasn't entirely on the black-and-white kitten. She turned her musing to a week earlier when she had observed John and Bella standing in front of the shop. Had John known Bella was coming? The woman seemed overly friendly with her hand tucked in the crook of his arm. And that low-cut dress—Mahala squeezed her eyes shut as heat radiated across her cheeks. The thought came unwanted and left a bitter taste.

"What am I to do?" Mahala bent toward the mirror and brushed her dark curls back as she splashed water on her face. She picked up a towel and dabbed the moisture from her face and stared at herself. "Girl, you're going to have to get some backbone. If you want to attract John Grigsby's, you're going to have to learn how to flirt."

But she wasn't a flirt nor a forward woman. Mahala went to her wardrobe and picked out a shirtwaist and skirt to change into and, flung the clothes on her bed. She wanted to cancel the trip to John's house.

But she had promised to bring them supper this evening. And she would.

THAT EVENING, MAHALA STARED at the Grigsbys' front door. She knew she should rap on the wood panel to let the family know she had arrived, but in truth she wanted to retreat and leave. After seeing John and Bella's exchange in front of the tailor shop, it took all her reserve to bring the meal tonight. She could just hand the meal to whoever answered the door and leave; she didn't have to stay. Thinking this was best, she raised her hand, but before she could knock, the front door flew open. There stood John—tall and handsome.

"Miss Shields." John's eyes brightened. "Please come in."

"Actually I just want to drop off the meal.—I-I won't stay—"

John relieved her of the Dutch oven and said, "Please stay. The children have been waiting for you." He gazed at her warmly.

The children have been waiting . . . Did he only want her here for the children?

"I really must go—"

"Mahala.—" John hesitated. May I call you Mahala? At her nod, he reached for her arm and continued, "*I* want you to stay . . . if you will. I'd like to speak with you after supper."

Mahala swallowed. All her reserve to just drop off the food and leave dissipated into thin air. "All right." She stepped into the warm house and pulled off her gloves. When she unbuttoned her coat, she began to shrug out of it.

"Here, let me help." John's deep voice stalled her. He gently pulled her wool jacket off and hung it on the wall hook. She felt his rough hand against her arm, and at his touch, a warm sensation shivered through her. She hesitated before she turned around. Then she heard John say, "Let's get this food to the kitchen, shall we?"

He tilted his head toward the kitchen. "The children are acting as if they haven't had a meal in months. Let's dish up their plates."

Mahala followed John into the kitchen, but she had to ask herself, *What is going on?* The quiet man she'd come to know had disappeared. She had always considered John a man of few words. But here he was, going out of his way to make her feel welcome. The change jangled her. And what could he possibly want to talk about after supper?

"Molly!" Mary Jane ran into the room and hugged her.

"Hi, darling, how are you?" Mahala gave the five-year-old a kiss on the forehead.

"Are you staying for supper with us?"

"I hadn't planned to." She looked at John, whose eyes begged her to stay. "I suppose I will this time." She patted Mary Jane's slim shoulder. "Let's set the table." She took the Dutch oven from John's hands, again brushing them lightly with her own. Heat rushed to her cheeks and their eyes met and held. His gaze didn't waver instead, those deep blue eyes moved over her face and lingered. A tingle slid through her veins—but she turned away. *Stop this nonsense!* she reprimanded herself, remembering the scene at the stagecoach. *He'll never be yours.*

As the evening wore on, the family sat around the table and talked about events in each of their lives. Mahala sensed the children needed to talk about their day, the way they had in the past. All the while, Tess looked down at her plate as if she were studying every design in the rose-patterned dinnerware. She didn't join in.

Calvin, on the other hand made up for the absence of his sister's comments. It was good to hear about his recent adventures on the ranch. It seemed he was going to be all right.

"I'll start clearing the table," Tess said abruptly, seeming to want to break up the fun.

"I'll help." Mahala scooted her chair back to get up.

"No. That won't be necessary. I can do it." Tess grabbed two plates and marched to the kitchen.

Mahala looked at John and he shook his head. He leaned his elbows against the table and stared at her as if he had something he wanted to say, but when he opened his mouth to speak, a table full of children looked his way. He closed his mouth. "This can wait. I'm going out to the barn to check on the livestock. Looks like we have a new storm coming in." When he stood, he shoved his chair under the table and asked, "Can you wait for me to come back before you leave?"

"Certainly."

"Come on, boys. Let's put the animals to bed."

The two older boys and Calvin followed John out the back door. With nothing to do but wait, Mahala leaned back in the chair, her hands in her lap. She wasn't accustomed to sitting and doing nothing, especially since the table needed to be cleared. But listening to the distant sounds of the plates rattling in the kitchen as Tess came and went, carrying two plates at a time, she decided it was best to sit—and wait.

"Are you coming again tomorrow?" Mary Jane asked as she slid out of the chair and came around to where Mahala sat. She stuck her hand through a torn seam in her dress at the waist. Her hand disappeared out of sight.

Mahala stared at Mary's dress. "Your skirt's torn." She pulled the child's hand out of the hole. "Change out of this dress and put on your nightgown. When you do, please bring the dress back to me. I'll take it home and mend it."

Mary Jane innocently looked down at the ripped seam then back to Mahala. "I'll be right back." She skipped out of the room and up the stairs.

"I could have fixed it." Tess stood at the kitchen door, having come to retrieve two more plates. She stared hotly at Mahala.

"Of course you could," Mahala said as she stood and pushed the chair under the table. She wouldn't have the young girl looking down on her. "But you've had your hands full with everything else around here. I don't mind helping you."

Tess turned away, but it wasn't before Mahala noticed her eyes were filmed with tears.

"Oh, Tess." Mahala removed the plates from the young girl's hands and folded Tess into her arms. "I know this is all too much for you. Not just the chores, but losing your mother."

Tess didn't strain against her; instead, her head fell onto Mahala's chest and her arms went tightly around Mahala's waist, and she sniffed.. "I miss her so much."

"Of course you do." Mahala said softly and kissed the top of her head.

"She's never coming back."

"No, honey. She's never coming back. But you will always have her in your heart."

"It's not the same," she said and hiccupped.

"You're right. It isn't." She gently patted the girl's back.

"I'm sorry I've been so rude to you." Tess's body trembled.

"Oh, Tess, I never let it bother me," Mahala lied in a low. "I knew you were having a hard time of it." She held Tess away to look into her eyes. "And truth to tell, I stayed away for the same reason. It's too hard coming here with your mother gone."

Tess gazed at her with pleading eyes. "Don't stay away, Mahala. We need you."

"Do you mean it?" Tears stung Mahala's eyelids. *Please take care of my children.* Nancy's words wove their way into her heart.

"I will come as often as I can—I promise."

Tess gave her a tight hug. "I need to blow my nose." She turned away just as Mary Jane arrived wearing her lavender nightgown, the torn dress draped over her arm. "Here you go, Molly."

"That's a good girl." Mahala gazed toward the hall that led to the back door. "I don't know how long your father and brothers are going to be out in the barn. But I think I'm going to go." She didn't want to paint John into a corner nor did she want him to feel responsible to explain what had happened the other day. What went on between John and Bella was none of her business.

"You said you'd wait for Papa." Mary Jane's brows drew together as she frowned.

Mahala smiled into the little girl's blue eyes and touched her bottom lip. "Tell your father I said 'goodnight' and 'that I'll return in a day or two.'"

"I will, Molly." Mary Jane gave her a big hug.

"Walk me to the door." Mahala held Mary Jane's hand as she moved to the hallway to retrieve her coat. When she opened the door, she turned back and kissed the tip of Mary Jane's nose. "Goodbye, darling."

"Don't say, 'goodbye,' Molly." The little girl's brows furrowed deeper and her blue eyes grew dark.

"Oh! Well, then—goodnight, darling. How's that?"

Mary Jane nodded enthusiastically. "See you later, Molly."

MAHALA SLIPPED ON HER flannel nightgown and lowered herself onto the edge of the bed. She pulled hairpins out of her loose knot and dropped them onto the bedcovers. Her dark hair cascaded in waves past her shoulders and midway down her back. While running the brush through her thick hair, she absently counted to a hundred and silently prayed that the Lord would give her strength for the coming days.

Setting the pins in a glass dish, she moved to the vanity and placed the dish, along with her brush, on the tabletop. She blew out the tiny flame in the kerosene lantern, and with a heavy heart, she beat her pillow into a comfortable position and climbed into bed. Shifting onto her side, she pulled the warm blanket to her chin and stared out the window. Her thoughts swirled in her head.

Bella. Had she come back to Grovespring because John was single again? Did she have her sights on him? The idea of Bella falling in love with the powerful man unnerved her. Deflated, she gazed at the moon through her window. *Please don't love him,* her heart silently begged of Isabella. *Don't be in love with John Grigsby, for I fear my heart has already taken up that pursuit.*

With Nancy gone, there was no stopping Bella, or any other woman for that matter, from staking a claim on Mr. Grigsby. And if Bella went after him, as Mahala was certain she would, it was up to John to make the call. Would he entertain Bella's romantic intentions, or would he back away? Tears burned her eyelids and Mahala blinked them away. Why did Bella have to return now?

She lay awake long into the night, her mind in a quandary. Just this evening, when John met her at the door, he truly seemed happy to see her and he had wanted her to stay. But did he want her to stay for him or the children?

He'd asked her to wait for him before she left the house, but she had been filled with so much uncertainty that it had taunted her. She'd had to leave. She remembered how tall and strong he had appeared as he turned and walked out of the room. Would her leaving change his mind? Or would he approach her on another day? Downstairs, the grandfather clock chimed three long tolls. "Go to sleep," she told herself, "or you'll be no good for anything in the morning." Mahala punched the pillow one more time, rolled over and went to sleep.

DECEMBER PASSED IN FLURRIES of snow and before she knew it, the holidays were fast approaching. With the Christmas holiday only a few days away, Mahala busied herself making blouses for her sisters and a shirt for her brother, Benny.

A slight rap sounded on the bedroom door.

"Come in," Mahala said, turning to gaze at the door.

Her mother entered and asked, "What are you working on?"

"I'm making Benny a flannel shirt."

"Hmm."

"What's that supposed to mean?"

"Gretta Matthew, came by this afternoon. She wondered if you had her dress ready for the wedding?"

Mahala groaned. "Dahlia Ford's wedding." She dropped the shirt in her lap. "I've been working on the gowns. Each of the women thinks her dress is more important than the others. I can't believe how impatient they can be. They should know I'll have them ready before Dahlia's special day."

"I thought you would have. I just thought I'd remind you, dear."

Mahala briefly closed her eyes. "I'm going to the shop in the morning. I just have finishing touches to complete on Gretta's dress."

"Good." Mary threaded her fingers together and remained standing by the door.

But Mahala paid little mind, her thoughts triggered with the images of Bella Yates coming and going to Yates Hotel, which was only a few doors down from the shop. The golden-haired woman flaunted lovely gowns she had brought with her from New York City. It didn't matter that Grovespring was a small, dusty little town. Bella acted as if she were walking the fashionable streets of her hometown back East. And of course, she'd become the talk of the town.

Mahala grew weary of thinking of Isabella. And she missed plain and simple Nancy.

"Is something bothering you?" Mary sat on the side of the bed. "Do you want to talk about it?"

"There's nothing to talk about." Mahala gave her mother a small smile.

"You don't fool me. Don't you think I know my daughter? That I don't see your world has turned upside down?"

Mahala eyed her mother and clamped her jaws tightly together. "There's nothing anyone can do about my situation."

Mary's shoulder's slumped. "Oh, Mahala. This time of year is always the hardest for you, what with families gathering together for the holidays. Don't give up. Your Mister Right is somewhere around the corner."

"Maybe. Maybe not." Mahala stood and placed Benny's shirt on a chair next to the table, where Boots sat looking out into the dark night. Mahala's reflection from the light of the kerosene lantern mirrored her image in the window. "I'm fine, Mother. Really I am."

"Well, good. I'll let you get ready for bed." Mary slipped out of the room and closed the door.

Mahala changed into her nightgown and climbed into bed. These days, her thoughts wandered to John Grigsby more times than they ought to. Lately, he seemed to measure her with his eyes, so blue that she could have drowned in them.

Just last evening, she'd left his house, feeling unusually awkward. She had lain awake far into the night, trying to put a finger on why she'd felt that way. She couldn't help but feel that John might truly be interested in her. He didn't show it directly, of course, but in little ways. He brushed against her when they cleared the table, and with their hands full when they went through the kitchen door at the same time. His muscular arms often brushed against hers sending warmth through her.

John could have easily reclined in the sitting room while she cleared the table. But he had insisted on helping. When the dishes were done and put away, he had walked her out to the buggy.

"Thank you, again for coming, Mahala."

"You're welcome," she'd said, stepping into the rig with his help. She hadn't wanted his hand to release hers when she sat in the leather seat. Truth was, with John Grigsby standing so close, it made her knees weak. His thick black hair fell across his forehead in an attractive way, something she hadn't noticed before.

John had waited until she rode out of the drive before he went into the house.—He had waited. This man—who had a thousand and one things to do at the end of the night—had waited for her buggy to roll down the lane before he stepped inside the house. She knew he waited because she swung around in her seat to look at him as the buggy left the long drive. And there he stood—gazing after her.

Was she overreacting? Could John be ready to seek a new partner so soon?

Mahala gazed out of the window into the starry night. For years she had dreamed of the day that *the right man* would come into her life. Could John Grigsby be that man? But what of Bella Yates? Didn't she have her talons in him?

Her mind drifted to what Nancy had said that fateful day. *Promise me you'll take care of my children.*

And promise she did.

If there was an inkling of truth that John had intentions to pursue her, he would have to come knocking on her door. That's the way it was done, wasn't it?

Chapter TWENTY-ONE

THE COLD DECEMBER WIND whipped at Mahala's skirts and nearly sent her hat sailing across the ground as she stepped into her buggy. She quickly clamped the top of her hat to hold it tight as she settled into the seat. The early morning cold seeped its way through her wrap as she flicked the reins, setting Bessy into a nice trot. Mahala hoped the buggy's enclosure would combat the gale.

It wasn't long before she realized she was in for a ride! The wind grew fiercer and drowned out the clip-clop-clip of the horse's hooves, and the roof of the buggy billowed and snapped. The snow clouds were gone but the wind blew fiercely.

Blinded by the soft layers of swirling snow that blew up from the road, Mahala drew back on the reins and slowed Bessy. She couldn't expect her horse to continue in this frosty wind, and yet they had another mile to go before they could find shelter. She rode on, the cold biting her skin, just when she thought she couldn't stand another moment of the frigid air, Shady Hollow Bridge came into view. She and Bessy would huddle inside the covered bridge and wait until the wind died down. The horse's hooves echoed in the tunnel as the buggy rolled to a stop.

Mahala climbed down and held onto the harness as she worked her way to Bessy's bridle. "How are you doing, girl?" She ran a hand over the horse's velvet nose. "Where did all this wind come from? I'd hoped for a couple of gentle days before Christmas." Bessy stomped her hooves and snuffled in response.

A gust of wind whipped through the tunnel and Mahala's skirts flew up, snapping and slapping. Above the noise of the wind flurry, Bessy whinnied in alarm.

"It's all right, girl. It's only the wind. We're fine." Though she spoke softly to the mare, she meant the reassurance for herself as well.

It was soon apparent that the bridge would give no relief. Mahala climbed back onto the seat and continued on. When she rode into Grovespring, the wind still blew. When she stopped in front of Kyle Weaver's livery stable, the double doors were closed. She had hoped to be greeted by the stableman so she could hurry out of the cold. Mahala waited a tad longer, but still Mr. Weaver did not show up.

"Well, Bessy," Mahala said as she tied the reins to the hitching post, "Mr. Weaver knows this is my rig and horse. I'll come check on you soon." She picked up her skirts and started to walk across the street.

"Hello!" Mr. Weaver called out.

Mahala whirled around to face him. "Mr. Weaver, I'm late for work. I wasn't sure if you were open."

"I'm open all right, but this windstorm has made the horses skittish. I'll be keeping the doors closed until the wind dies down."

Mahala held her hat to keep it from flying away, while her skirts whipped about her ankles. "Good to know. You'll see to it that Bessy gets inside and out of the weather?"

"Of course, Miss Shields. Go on ahead. I'll take care of your horse and buggy."

Mahala didn't answer. Her skirts lifted and snapped, making her hurry for cover. The snow crunched under her feet as she scurried across the street and headed for the tailor shop.

Ahead Mahala spotted Gertie's driver, Jonas, sitting in the wagon in front of the Yates Hotel. Across the street, John's wagon was parked at Owens Mercantile. She knew he delivered eggs and milk to Clem Owens' store once or twice a week. Once he dropped off the supplies at the general store, he would then cross the street to make a second delivery to the Yate's Café.

Seeing Jonas sitting in front of the hotel huddled against the chill air, Mahala wondered, *Is Bella in town?* As she walked up the boardwalk, Mahala didn't have long to find out. Bella Yates stepped out of the hotel, one hand clamped over her bulky flowered hat to keep it from flying down the street.

Mahala's skirts whipped around her, and she held onto them as she watched John Grigsby come out of the hotel, a milk can in each hand. He set them down at the edge of the boardwalk and briefly spoke to Bella, while the elegant woman clung to her oversized hat.

Mahala felt an unexpected stab of jealousy and clenched her jaws tightly. Seeing John standing on the boardwalk next to the beautiful blonde awakened an awareness of herself and Mr. Grigsby that was new to her. At that moment she knew with certainty that she really *did* care for him. Stunned by the revelation, she watched as John assisted Bella to her wagon. Were they courting?

Bella stepped onto the wagon wheel, but her foot slipped, and all at once she flew backwards. Her hands flew into the air and her hat went sailing down the boardwalk right in front of Mahala. The white felt hat with fluffy feathers and with a spray of flowers bounced against the hem of Mahala's skirts and stopped. She scooped it up and held it tightly as she watched the scene before her. Bella would have fallen to the ground, if not for John's swift movements to catch her before she landed on her fancily clad derriere.

Jonas jumped to the ground and came for Bella's hat. "Thank you, ma'am. You saved me from having to run down the street after it."

"No problem," Mahala said, her back ramrod straight as she watched Bella throw her arm over John's shoulder as he raised her to her feet. The blonde seemed breathless, but her eyes shone. Standing only a few feet away, Mahala heard Bella say, "You certainly saved me from horrible embarrassment."

Bella brushed the snow from her coat with one hand while she held onto John's forearm with the other. "You've always been there when I needed you." Her voice sailed toward Mahala with the wind as her hand rested a might longer on John's sleeve than needed.

Mahala rolled her eyes, and bit the inside of her cheek, and she moved quickly toward the tailor shop. When she opened the door, a whoosh of air sailed in along with sifting granules of snow.

Grady Thompson's head shot up from his work table. "You're here." A broad smile lit his face as he slammed a palm over the pattern-paper that lifted with the breeze.

"Yes, I'm here, wind and all!" She glanced out of the window to see Jonas' wagon rolling down the street with Bella sitting next to him. *Good!*

Grady's gaze followed hers. "She's very adept at putting on a show, I'd say. Not to mention stirringly beautiful." He watched out the window with Mahala.

That's a deadly combination when one is fighting the woman for the man she just learned she loved. Mahala turned to Grady. "That she is, isn't she?"

"Yes . . . and . . . a bit fanciful." He gave her a cheeky grin.

"That she is," Mahala repeated with finality as she pulled hat pins from her hat. She set the hat on the shelf above the wall hooks then removed her wrap and hung it up. She eyed Grady, seeing the measuring tape wrapped around his neck and dangling to his waist. His sleeves were rolled to his elbows, and his hair stood above his forehead as if he'd brushed it back more than once in frustration.

She strode to his work table and gazed down at the tweed material lying in a pattern-shape for the front of a suit jacket. Scraps of tweed fabric lay scattered on the floor. "How's it going?"

"Could be better." He eyed the material. "This is my second run at cutting out the sheriff's suit jacket for the wedding." He pointed at the hem with a pair of shears. "I knew better than to cut the material when in doubt, but be as it may, I did. I no sooner cut off the hem than I stopped and measured again." He ran his fingers through his dark brown hair just above his forehead.

Mahala kept a smile from parting her lips as she groaned, "Oh, no."

"You guessed it. Too short." Grady clicked his tongue. "All is not lost; I'll use the material for another client. It's a good thing I ordered more bolts of this tweed than I needed." He scratched the back of his neck and gave her a crooked grin.

Mahala touched Grady's arm sympathetically and pushed away from the table. "I'll be working on Gretta Matthews' dress today. I better get started."

On the way back to her own work table, Mahala eyed Gretta's dress where she'd left it hanging on a wooden hanger outside the private dressing screen. But before getting to work, she gazed out the window. Thin clouds drifted across the sky, swept along by the frigid air. Small eddies of snow swirled down the center of the road where men in wagons rolled down the street. Horses lifted their heads, and pranced and snuffled, made nervous by the howling wind. Women on the boardwalk fought to keep their skirts down and their bonnets on.

That same wild wind whistled through the small leaded panes of the tailor shop windows, but she didn't mind. Mr. Thompson had the black stove stoked with burning wood, and the shop was warm.

Mahala stopped wool-gathering and forced her mind back to the task at hand. In a few days, the sheriff's daughter was getting married. It was best she turn her attention to today's work.

Sitting down, Mahala draped Gretta's dress across her lap and threaded a needle with white thread. She'd already sewn ten tiny pearl buttons to the lower section of the gown. She had ten more to go. As she bent over her task, she listened to the whistling wind, her mind wandering again as it usually did when she had work that didn't require her attention.

Mahala was on the sixth button when Grady sauntered back to her table. "A few women have stopped by. It seems your services are in demand these days." He lifted the measuring tape from around his neck and rolled it up. "Isabella Yates came in to see you, too. It appears she wants a gown made."

"Over my dead body," Mahala murmured under her breath.

"What's that?"

"Nothing, Grady, just talking to myself."

A half smile crooked his mouth. "She's stirred up the town since she arrived."

"I've noticed. Doesn't she always?" Her tone held a snap to it.

Grady's brows furrowed and he leaned over, both hands palm down on her work table. "You didn't come in last week," Grady gazed at her. "Are you all right?"

"I couldn't bring myself to come in, Grady." Mahala leaned back and gazed at him. "Don't ask me why." Her smile quivered. "It feels really good being here now."

Grady gave her a slow grin and stood. "Well, I'm glad you're back."

The door whooshed open and the cowbell jangled. Gretta Matthews pulled her gloves off as she hurried into the shop. "Goodness sakes this windstorm is the worst I've ever seen!"

"Gretta. So good to see you." Mahala held her client's gown against her chest.

Gretta carefully worked her way to Mahala's work table. "I came to see if my dress is ready."

"Almost." Mahala stood and held the gown up. "What do you think?"

"Oh, Mahala. You've outdone yourself again!" Gretta's brows puckered. "Oh, dear. I do hope I haven't *outdone* the mother of the bride." Her eyes sparkled with a hint of mischief.

"Don't worry, Gretta. You're fine. Sherrie's dress is every bit as nice as yours."

"Is my dress ready, then?"

"Four more buttons and it will be." Mahala returned to her chair. "Do you have any shopping to do while you're in town?"

"I'm headed to Owens Mercantile. I've heard Clem got a shipment of fabric that's just come in. You might want to see for yourself."

"I will indeed." Mahala threaded the needle again and focused on a tiny pearl button.

"I'll return after I'm done shopping. You'll be ready by then. I'm sure." Gretta wove her way to the front of the shop.

"Don't let that gusty wind blow you down the street." Mahala smiled and bent over her work. She didn't look up when she heard the door slam.

It seemed every corner of the store creaked from the howling wind, but the fire in the kept the shop warm. The crackle and pop of the burning wood was comforting, and it was good to be inside knowing it was nippy outside.

A half hour later, when Gretta returned to the tailor shop, her dress was wrapped in brown paper and tied with twine. She left the shop in high spirits.

Mahala stood and stretched. Since the mercantile had a new shipment of cottons and silks, she was glad it was her lunch break. "I'll be back in a half hour, Grady. I'm going to over to the mercantile."

Grady glanced out the window. "It's crazy cold outside."

"The store's not that far. I'll be all right." Mahala pulled on her wool coat and buttoned it tightly. When she left the shop, she bowed her head low against the brisk air. She wasn't the only one out in the stark weather. A few women were on the boardwalk and they nodded hello to each other as Mahala passed them. She was glad she'd left her hat at the shop. No sense in having to chase it down the road, bringing more attention to herself.

Mahala walked swiftly past a couple of elderly women and politely lifting her chin, she said, "Good day, ladies." Not waiting for a response, she continued on, the chill wind seeping through her wool coat. She was glad she didn't have far to go and soon, she stood in front of the general store.

She gave the door to Owens Mercantile a slight nudge, and the cowbell hanging loosely above the door alerted those inside that she had arrived. Once inside, Mahala looked around the front of the store. Three elderly men sat near a wood stove just beyond the counter.

She glanced their way, only to find them gawking at her, their eyes shining. One man elbowed the other, with a silly grin on his face.

Oh, Lord. Mahala rolled her eyes and turned her back to them. Stepping farther into the store, she found two other women were already there, filling their baskets with household staples. They looked up when Mahala stepped in, and quickly glanced away.

"Good afternoon, Miss Shields." Mr. Owens nodded toward the door. "I see you braved the gusty winds."

"Yes, Mr. Owens." Mahala stomped snow from her shoes. "Gretta Matthews told me you have a new shipment of material."

His eyes lit up. "I do. Take a look over there at the long table by the counter. Seems the dry goods are all the draw this afternoon."

Mahala didn't waste any time moving to the table to peruse the new bolts of fabric. The table was piled high with a bounty of colors that teased her imagination. She loved the smell of new cloth and could never just look at the material; she had to run her fingers over the fabrics, touching this one and that, feeling the grade of the weave, some smooth, some coarse to the touch.

Mahala fingered a bolt of dark green velvet. It felt luxurious. "This would make a lovely Christmas dress for Mary Jane," she mused to herself.

While she surveyed the goods, she heard one of the old gents say in a deep voice, "I never did understood why Miss Shields never married. She's a handsome woman, and that mass of dark curls is a sight to see."

"Mind your manners, Sam," a gruff voice reprimanded.

The air suddenly felt suffocating and Mahala's cheeks burned. She stepped away from the fabric table and strode to the first aisle as, heat burned up her neck and over her scalp. When would the people of Grovespring learn to mind their own business? She felt her temper rise and feared she'd say something she'd later regret. Before she had left the tailor shop, she'd made a list of supplies she needed. She'd gather those items and give herself a moment to simmer down before she went back to the fabric table.

The door opened and shut as another customer entered the mercantile, but Mahala didn't bother to look up. When she made her way back to the front, there stood Grady Thompson.

"Mr. Thompson," she said mischievously. "If I didn't know better, I'd think you followed me here?" Mahala glanced toward the material stacked on the table.

"You aren't the only one interested in the new shipment," Grady gave her a lopsided grin and winked then strode to the table piled high with bolts of fabric. He fingered a dark tweed and gave a short nod. Bolts of navy blue, browns and black interwoven with grades of color caught his attention as he sifted through the pile of fabrics.

"Afternoon, Thompson," Owens said.

Mahala watched Grady nod his head as he examined the material before him.

Since Grady was at the table, Mahala went back to the table and resumed her own examination. She set the green velvet fabric aside and then moved to the blue chambray. It was too late in the month to make shirts for Mr. Grigsby and his boys for Christmas. But feeling a niggling of the Christmas spirit work its way into her imagination, she continued to pick up bolts of material and finger them, weighing options for their use and setting them back down again.

When Mahala came upon a bolt of cranberry-colored taffeta embroidered with tiny white flowers, she gasped. She could visualize Tess with her long, golden hair, wearing a dress in this color. Again, it was far too late to finish a dress in time for the holidays, but Tess could wear it for another occasion. Mahala picked up the bolt of material and set it on the counter.

"Will that be all, Miss Shields?"

"Is there any mail for me, by chance?"

"I don't think so, but let me look." Mr. Owens bent to look in the small cubbyholes behind the counter. He shook his head. "Not today. Is there anything else I can get for you, then?"

"I hope you still have some of Nancy's preserves."

He nodded and smiled brightly. "I've got three jars. Such a pity there won't be more. Nancy's jam always sold so well."

"I'll take two. You can set them on the counter with the material. I'm still going to look around."

"I just got in a shipment of needles too."

"Wonderful, I'll take a packet."

The door opened and the bell tinkled again. A heavyset woman stepped into the mercantile brushing light snow off her sleeves.

"Go ahead and finish your shopping," Mr. Owens said, "and I'll see to Mrs. Trubridge's needs."

"That'll be fine." Mahala stepped away, avoiding the three old gents who studied her every move.

Dixie Trubridge's voice rang loud and clear. "Good afternoon, Mr. Owens. I came to see if I have any mail."

"I believe you do." Clem stepped behind the counter again. The mercantile not only sold the basic supplies to the community, it also serviced the town as the local post office. The stagecoach delivered mail when it stopped in town every few days. Having the mail at the mercantile was an incentive for the town people to drop in and purchase supplies they needed when they came for their mail. Mr. Owens welcomed the increased business.

He handed Dixie a letter. "Here you go. Can I get you anything else? Mr. Grigsby brought in eggs and milk this morning."

At mention of John Grigsby, Mahala stopped and glanced their way, although she remained in the aisle, where she idly examined a pair of table napkins. She knew John supplied Owens Mercantile and the Yates Cafe with eggs, milk, and jam. Nancy had said they brought in a nice albeit small profit.

She didn't recall seeing John's wagon on Main Street this morning. She must have been so caught up with sewing the pearl buttons on Gretta's dress that she'd missed seeing him pass by. Why it should matter, she didn't know. But it did.

"Nancy made the best peach jam," Dixie said, as she eyed Mahala's two jars on the counter. "Do you have any left?"

"I've one jar left." Mr. Owens said.

"I'll take the last jar, please. Such a pity there won't be any more of this good jam selling in your store."

The door flew open and three women breezed into the store. They made quite a ruckus as they shook snow off their coats and stomped their feet.

Mrs. Trubridge pulled a list out of her coat pocket and handed it to Clem. "It doesn't matter how often I drop by, seems I'm always running out of something. And I need more needles. I've searched all over the house for the last one. But you know how it is," she rattled on, "it'll show up once I buy a pack."

"You're in luck. I just got another shipment of needles in, along with the fabric on the table." Mr. Owens nodded toward to the table piled high with material. "I don't suppose I've ever had as good a day as I'm havin' today despite the wind and snow and all."

Mahala couldn't help but smile at Mr. Owens remarks. The mercantile did seem like grand central station today. She listened to the quiet commotion around the store as she browsed. It'd been a while since she'd allowed herself time to shop without necessarily buying. Picking up a rose-patterned teacup, she examined the chinaware. A hum of voices filtered over from the next aisle from the three women who'd just come in.

"That John Grigsby ought to be looking for a wife soon," said one of the women in a nasal tone. "What with seven children to tend to, I bet he's got his hands full."

"Of course he should be looking for a new missus. He's got all that fieldwork and cattle. He can't be out in the field and tend to the children as well," another woman jumped in. "Whose watchin' them children while he's out working?"

Hearing the women talk so freely about John, nettled Mahala. Didn't they know that the three older children were well adept at taking care of the four younger ones while their father was out on the ranch?

The women moved from the opposite side of the aisle to the far end of the row where Mahala stood.

"My Ellie's going on nineteen next month. If she doesn't marry a man soon, she'll be the next spinster of Grovespring." The woman's words dripped with panic.

"'Course, I understand Bella Yates is in town." The nasal-speaking woman stole a glance at Mahala. "I believe she's still single. And if my eyes aren't playing tricks on me, I'd say she's got her sights on that John Grigsby."

"Why do you suppose that blonde devil ever showed up in town in the first place?" remarked another with a snicker.

"There's far too much competition going on for that good-looking man," a buxom woman said. The three women cackled.

They gazed at Mahala and haughty chins went up before they looked away. One woman elbowed ed the other and tilted her head toward Mahala. "Surely, she won't be competing for the likes of him."

Irritation nicked Mahala's nerves. She set the dainty china cup back onto the saucer with a little more fervor than intended before she moved to the front counter to tally her purchases.

"Are you ready, Miss Shields?" Clem Owens asked awkwardly. He gave her a sad smile that told her she wasn't the only one who'd heard every word those busybodies said.

Mahala's chin lifted. "Yes, Mr. Owens." She felt eyes on her while she counted out her money. When she glanced over her shoulder, the three men by the stove looked away and squirmed in their seats. Mahala bristled. It was all she could do keep from tapping her foot impatiently.

Dixie Trubridge strode to Mahala's side and spoke loudly enough for everyone to hear. "I wouldn't listen to those old hens if I were you. They don't have any more sense than a horse's you-know-what. Anyone with eyes can see you've been waiting for the right man to come along. Not like some of these old hens who've settled for any pot-bellied old Joe. But then, you're different. You'll marry for love, and for that I have great respect for you, Miss Shields."

Heat seared up Mahala's neck and to her ears! Dixie was plump and hefty, while her husband was as skinny as barbed wire, which was why folks called him 'Slim.' She could afford to make that curt statement. Still, Dixie didn't have to come to her defense and announce it to the world.

"Dixie, hush!" Mahala protested.

"No, I won't hush. If anyone should keep their mouths shut, it ought to be those women flapping their gums."

The faces of the three women flushed several shades of red.

Mahala wanted to deny that what the women said—didn't matter, but the words stuck in her throat. And—it seemed it was taking Mr. Owens forever to wrap her purchases in brown paper.

"Thank you, Dixie," Mahala said in a low tone. Their eyes held and—Mahala could see Dixie Trubridge was truly rankled by the other women's cruel words.

Mahala finished paying for her purchases and went out into the harsh wind. Her petite boots, echoing the torment of her heart, stomped all the way back to Thomson's Tailor Shop, She stopped short of the door and caught her breath. Then she pushed forward to her table—where she held back the tears and licked her wounds. "One of these days I'll be married, and then what will those she-wolves have to talk about?" A single tear stung the rim of her eye before it slid down her cheek. Would there ever come a day that she'd truly be married? Would she ever know the fullness of being loved by a fine gentleman?

THAT EVENING, AS MAHALA rode home from work, her mind swarmed with thoughts of the gossip in town. She was fully aware that the eligible young women had been—and would be—taking food to the Grigsby house and all for one purpose—to get John's undivided attention.

When Mahala turned into the Grigsbys' drive, Anne Radburn was headed out the same lane.

"Hello, Mahala!"

"Good evening, Anne." Mahala pulled on the reins. "I just came by to see if everything's all right at the Grigsbys'."

"You and everybody else." Anne smiled. "I heard you went to work today, so I took it upon myself to bring the family a meal. What with this cold weather, I figured a hot roast beef supper would make them happy."

"That's very thoughtful of you." Mahala sat with the reins held loosely in her hands. The snow flurries had died down along with the wind.

"You know," Anne said, her eyes lighting up. "John would do well to pay more attention to you." She rolled her eyes and shook her head. "Those young girls from town have been lining up at his front door."

Mahala gripped the reins a bit tighter. "I hadn't noticed."

"I don't doubt that you know Isabella Yates is back in town. She's not young like the others, but it's interesting that she's returned when she did." Anne shook her head again.

"I'm aware that Bella is back. I was at my work table at the tailor shop the day she arrived on the stagecoach."

"You get a good view of what's going on in town from where you sit." Anne bit her bottom lip. "Word has it Isabella's here on account of Nancy being gone. Isabella's still single, you know. Could be she's standing right in line with the young fillies."

"Standing in *front* of the line, is more like it." Mahala knew Anne could hear the chagrin in her voice, but she didn't care. It seemed Isabella was first in everything these days.

Anne's brows rose, but all she said was, "It's no secret Grovespring has a shortage of men, even with some of the young bucks coming of age."

"Well, I'm a testament of that." Mahala's chin jutted out. *There, I've said it.*

"Oh, Mahala. You're a fine woman. John would do well to notice you."

"I don't think he's noticed anyone or anything except the business at hand, to be truthful. He's got his plate full just keeping up with this ranch and the children. And truth be told, I don't think he's done grieving over Nancy." Mahala gave Anne a grimace. "It's only been three months."

"Well, it seems some of the mothers have put a bug in their daughters' ears. If you go inside, you'll find cakes, cookies, and pies lining the counter. They must have heard the saying, 'Feeding a man's stomach is the way to his heart.'" She smiled and picked up the reins again. "Don't stop coming on account of them."

"I won't." Mahala watched Anne drive out to the main road. She circled her buggy around and followed suit. She wouldn't check on the family tonight; she'd come another day. She wasn't up to cleaning after the new batch of prospects from Grovespring.

Chapter TWENTY-TWO

THE WELLS FARGO STAGECOACH rumbled down the road and stopped in front of Mahala's window at the tailor shop. The stagecoach hadn't stopped as frequently these past months as it had the rest of the year. Road conditions from a series of snowstorms—and sometimes blizzards—had often slowed things down for everyone. Looking out the window now, snowflakes were falling to the ground, making it difficult to see clearly if Bart was bringing new passengers to town or if he was stopping to deliver mail to Owens Mercantile. Heavy leather shades were pulled down and blocked the view of the passengers in the coach. This time of year, the window coverings were needed to help keep out the cold.

Mahala stood at her table and stretched to get the kinks out of her back. The snow fell thicker and she leaned forward to watch Bart climb down from the high seat and open the coach door.

An elderly man wearing a top hat, wool coat, and carrying a cane climbed down from the coach. When Bart stepped forward to assist the next passenger, the gentleman's cane flew out and moved Bart's hand aside. Bart stepped away and watched as a red-headed lass, looking to be in her mid-twenties stepped out onto the boardwalk. She wore a long wool coat in green plaid. A lacy white skirt peeked out below the hem and ruffled over her shiny black boots. Her green felt hat tilted to one side of her head, its plume of green feathers quickly turning white with snow.

Bart, the gent, and, the lady all turned and watched as one more passenger alighted from the coach. Mahala sucked in her breath as she watched a dark-haired young man wearing a felt top hat step to the ground. Although he had a thin mustache, he was the prettiest man she had ever seen. Pretty.

Handsome. For this young gent, it was all the same. The man was slim, moved with a snappy step, and there was a roguish look to him.

He reached inside the coach, brought out a reticule, and handed it to the woman. Bart pointed in the direction of the hotel, and the three newcomers quickly walked toward it. Then Bart went to work pulling luggage from the top and back of the stagecoach. He gazed back to see Mahala watching him. He gave a nod and then loaded one bag on his shoulder, tucked one bag under his arm, picked up a third, and walked toward the Yates Hotel.

"Bart's brought passengers, has he?" Grady stood behind Mahala.

Mahala jumped. "You sneaked up on me." She continued to gaze out the window as the snow fell. There were more trunks and bags to be hauled to the hotel, it wasn't long before Bart returned empty-handed and climbed up the back of the coach to grab more luggage.

"I don't have anything to do at the moment. I'll give him a hand." Grady pulled on his wool coat, tugged on a hat and went outside. In minutes, the men made quick work of hauling the bags and trunks over to the hotel. Mahala counted two large trunks in addition to numerous bags.

"I wonder who they are?" she murmured, her breath causing the window to fog.

When Grady returned she looked up from her work. "Well, have you learned who the newcomers are?"

He smiled brightly. "We're going to have a show in town."

"A show?"

"That's what I said." He shrugged out of his coat and sat on the edge of the table. "Seems the woman is an actress and a singer. The men are both actors."

"When will the show take place?"

"Soon. I suppose we'll learn more in the next couple of days."

POSTERS WERE PLACED IN the windows of businesses along Main Street, announcing that a female singer, Ambrosia Bustamante, and her jesters, Dante Kimball and Uncle Ezra, had come to town. Grovespring would have a live performance! It wasn't long before it was the talk of the town. With the holidays around the corner, this added to the Christmas spirit. Not only did the posters sit in the windows, but handbills were placed on counters for people to take home. It wasn't long before Mahala had her answer: the live show was to take place that coming Saturday at the saloon.

The saloon's small stage would be transformed with heavy velvet curtains, and props set up for the performance. The saloon would be cleared of tables, and chairs would line the floor. All the talk was as much about the details of the saloon as the anticipation of seeing the entertainers perform. And tickets were on sale—everywhere. Ambrosia Bustamante and Dante Kimball became household names as the community came alive with news of the upcoming entertainment.

AS MAHALA PUT ON her overcoat one evening, preparing to leave for the Grigsby house, she smiled. The children had caught the spirit of excitement for the upcoming show. John had purchased tickets for the five older children. Anne Radburn had agreed to watch Jeffrey and Wiley, saying she didn't care if she missed the show.

Later that evening, as Mahala prepared to go home, John walked her out onto the snow-covered porch. Her boots crunched on the icy flakes as he assisted her to the buggy.

"Once again, thank you for stopping by and being there for the children."

"I'm happy to do it." Mahala settled into the cold buggy and unwrapped the reins from the brake post. She could hardly breathe with John standing so near.

He gazed at her with hopeful eyes. "Might you join us for the play?"

Warmth flooded through her. Was he asking her for a date, albeit with the family? "I would love to. Thank you for asking."

"It's this Saturday night." He laughed. "Well, you know that, of course. We will pick you up."

"All right." She nodded and flicked the reins. When Bessy pulled the buggy forward, Mahala looked back and gave a slight wave. John stood in the drive, watching her leave. Her heart beat faster as the buggy rolled down the lane, making tracks on the snow-covered ground. Her mind went in all directions. What should she wear? What style should she fix her hair? On and on her thoughts went as Bessy took them home. They had gone this route so many times that she didn't need to guide the horse. Bessy knew where she was going. Mahala was free to dream!

IT WAS SOON DISCOVERED why the performers had come to town. Grady came back from lunch at the Yates Café and filled Mahala in. Gertrude had met the singer and her jesters while she was in New York City the summer before. She had invited the entertainers to come to Grovespring if they were ever out this way. Now, as the winter months were in full swing, she received a letter that the entertainers were on their way to Kansas City. "You said to come by if we were ever out this way. So here we are. We'd like to perform for you if it's all right." Gertrude mimicked the red-head as she told the small crowd how it all came to be.

"Well, now we know," Mahala said cheerfully as she cut away on the fabric of a new project.

"You're coming, aren't you?" Grady asked.

"Yes. I'll be there." She kept her escort a secret. She didn't want it made known that John Grigsby had invited her to the show. Knowing the Grovespring women as she did, if anyone found out it would soon be the talk of the town before the event even took place.

That evening, she dropped off a plate of cookies her mother had made at the Grigsbys' home. She wouldn't stay, but her mother had slaved over the baking, and she wanted the children to enjoy the cookies while they were still fresh. Upon setting the plate on the table, she couldn't help but notice a white envelope with an invitation on top of it, sitting off to the side. The invitation read, "'Please come.'" Curious, she peered more closely at the note and gasped. The note read:

Please join me and Aunt Gertie at the show Saturday night.
We'll have supper at the hotel and then walk over to the saloon.
I'm looking forward to an evening with you on this special night.
Affectionately yours,
Bella

Mahala's stomach felt like mud. Tears sprang to her eyes. She gathered her bag and left the house quickly. She was barely aware of the children asking, "What's wrong?" Before she left, she scribbled a note on a piece of paper, explaining to John that she would not be attending the show. She dropped the note next to Bella's invitation.

Tears fell all the way home. When she arrived at the house, her mother asked, "Were the children happy with the cookies?"

Mahala didn't answer. She brushed past her mother and fled up the stairs and hurried to her room. When she shut the door, she threw herself onto her bed and wept. How could Bella be so underhanded? How could life be so cruel!

Her mother rapped on her bedroom door. "Mahala?"

Mahala curled up on the bed. She didn't want company at the moment.

"Mahala. Open the door."

"Go away!"

The door clicked open and Mahala felt her mother's presence at the side of the bed.

"What's wrong?" Mary sat on the edge of the bed and patted Mahala's side.

Mahala sat up and buried her face into her mother's shoulder and cried, the salty tears searing her throat.

"Oh, dear. What has happened, my darling girl?"

"Life is so unfair!" Mahala sobbed.

"What are you talking about?"

Mahala grabbed a handkerchief and blew her nose. When she collected herself enough to speak, she said, "John Grigsby invited me to attend the show with him on Saturday night." She hiccupped.

"And you said 'yes,' of course?"

"I did. B-But that doesn't m-matter anymore," Mahala stuttered.

"But why?"

"Because Isabella Yates invited him to go with her." Tears threatened to spill again. "I-I found the invitation when I left the cookies on the table." Tears fell again. Mahala trembled as she twisted the handkerchief in her hands.

"But John may not have accepted the invitation. Was he there? Did you ask him about it?"

"He wasn't there. I jotted a note and left it for him," she said hoarsely. "I told him I wouldn't be attending the show." Mahala's chest felt heavy.

"Oh, honey. You shouldn't have done that. You should have waited to see what John wanted to do."

"It's too late. What's done is done."

JUST AS THE RUMORS had stated, the saloon was cleared of tables, and rows of chairs filled the floor. Heavy velvet curtains hid the performers while the piano player played a plunky tune. The room filled quickly, with most of the county attending. Mahala sat at the end of the middle row with her family and watched as people filed in and took seats.

It seemed forever before the velvet curtains slid open and Ambrosia Bustamonte came onto the stage with her long red hair flowing over her shoulders and her voice as sweet as an angel. After Ambrosia sang each next number, the pretty man and his co-actor, Uncle Ezra, managed to fill the room with laughter. Dante Kimball wore a brightly colored costume with an eccentric hat in a motley pattern. The uncle played his part in his jester's costume.

Together, the two jesters entertained the audience with a variety of skills, singing songs, playing flutes, and telling short, comical stories.

The audience clapped and whistled as they enjoyed the scenes. After the intermission, Ambrosia sang again and the jesters performed juggling acts and magic tricks. Much of the entertainment was performed in a comedic style, and the crowd laughed so hard they were holding their sides. At one point Mahala stole a glance to see if John and his family had come. She spotted them in the back row, sitting with Sheriff Ford and his wife.

Where's Bella? she mused.

Much to her surprise, Gertrude and Bella did not arrive until the second act, just after the intermission. Their skirts rustled as they strode toward the front past the rows of seating. To Mahala's surprise, instead of the blonde sitting with John, she sat with her aunt in the middle of the front row, their seats obviously reserved for them.

When the entertainers finished the show, the audience clapped loudly and called for an encore. Ambrosia, Dante, and Ezra came through the curtains several times and bowed low. But at last, they retreated behind the curtains.

"Encore! Encore!" the crowd called again.

When no one appeared, Bella stood and looked around at the lively crowd. A wide smile formed on her lips, and she bent and whispered in Gertie's ear. Gertie's hand went to her chest and she shook her head fervently, all the while pulling on Bella's hand as if she were trying to get Bella to sit back down.

Isabella Yates wouldn't have it. She pulled away from her aunt and walked to the piano player. She bent and whispered in his ear. The man nodded and began to play a lively tune. The crowd hushed and waited as Isabella went up the side steps to the stage and stood in the center, her fingers laced in front of her as she began to sing, "Round her neck she wore a yellow ribbon . . . ♪"

Bella sang to the crowd in pure bravery, Mahala thought, and cheers and whistles pierced the air, followed by a round of applause.

"She wore it in the winter ♪

"And the merry month of May ♪"

It was clear Bella had a gift. As if she were not beautiful and sweet enough, she sang as true as Ambrosia Bustamante.

"When I asked her: Why the yellow ribbon? ♪

"She said: It's for my lover who is far away ♪"

The roar in the saloon was deafening and the audience clapped to the beat of the song.

Mahala swallowed a sudden pang. Heavens above! Am I jealous? She didn't want to hear another phrase of the song. She picked up her skirt and slipped out of the building. Stepping off the boardwalk, she stood for a moment under the light of the moon before she escaped behind the building to a patch of dried field grass poking through the snow behind a row of bushes.

To her surprise, she spotted John standing by a grove of stark winter trees, smoking his pipe. At first he didn't move when she stepped into the open field. She stared at his back, strong and tall, and hugged herself from the cold. It was at that moment that she realized her mistake in coming here. With dread she also realized she'd have to go back inside the saloon. Holding her breath, she hung her head and stared at the dried grass poking up through patches of snow.

Before she could turn to leave, John strode to her side and gazed down at her. "Good evening, Mahala" His deep voice was low, but it broke the silence. "I see you made it to the performance after all." His eyes held hers for a long moment.

Mahala swallowed to calm her beating heart. To be standing alone with John under the vast blanket of stars and the moon shining down on them seemed like the perfect romantic setting, almost perfect . . . if she hadn't ruined everything. And now, here she stood, guilty as you please.

"Yes. The whole town has been talking about it. I decided I would come after all." She shivered and held her elbows in the palm of her hands. The chill air was beginning to seep into the single layer of her shawl.

"You're cold." John shrugged out of his jacket and slipped it over her shoulders.

"No, Mr. Grigsby. You'll be cold." She started to remove the wool coat.

"Please don't take it off." He stared down at her with an amused smile.

"You're too independent for your own good, Miss Shields."

A gust of wind blew over them, and she pulled the heavy coat closer about her. She wracked her brain for something clever to say now that the two of them were alone. "I see you needed a breath of fresh air too."

He lifted his pipe, red ashes burning in the bowl. "I stepped out to smoke my pipe."

She could smell the cherry tobacco from where she stood. In her mind's eye, she pictured him sitting at the table in the evenings, filling his pipe with the tobacco and savoring how the room smelled afterward. She cleared her throat. "Did you enjoy the performance, Mr. Grigsby?"

"I did. From what I understand Gertrude's family has known them for some time and invited them to come and entertain our little town. And you?"

"Yes, I did. Dante is quite an entertainer. Too pretty to be a man." Mahala held her ground and looked at him.

"Too pretty?" John threw back his head and laughed. "You got me there."

She loved the sound of his deep laugh. She couldn't remember having ever heard it before, and she couldn't help but smile broadly.

John leveled his gaze on her. "You should have accepted my invitation. We could have enjoyed the show together." He shoved one hand into his pocket, the other cradling his pipe, and he stared down at her with a glint of light in his blue eyes.

Seeing him gaze down at her with a look of pure delight took her breath away. She cleared her throat and stared back, not wanting to look away. They stood for a moment, gazing toward the trees that lined the river, and all was silent except the wind rustling the leaves.

"May I—" John broke the silence and stopped. He glanced toward the hedge of bushes that stood behind the building.

Twigs snapped in the darkness behind them, Bella Yates stepped into the clearing through a gap in the bushes and gawked at the two of them.

"Mahala, there you are," she said, breaking the stillness. "I thought you might have gone home."

Mahala swung toward her. "No, Bella. I came with my family. I just needed a breath of fresh air."

"But you left so suddenly. No one seemed to know where you'd gone." Bella looked past Mahala's shoulder toward John, who stood a few paces behind her. Her gaze turned back to Mahala. "I was most concerned over your safety— and your virtue as well."

Mahala's chin went up. "Mr. Grigsby and I were speaking of the performance. You had no reason for concern, I assure you. Mr. Grigsby is quite the gentleman."

"My apologies for interrupting." Seeming at a loss for words, Bella spun around and walked back the way she had come.

Bella was gone— but her presence lingered.

"I should go back in." Mahala turned and started back.

"Mahala wait."

She stopped and swung around.

"Did I ever tell you how Isabella and I met?" John asked.

She stared at him. knowing full well that he knew he hadn't shared how they met. Standing there, the chill air grew colder. Of course he hadn't told her, but somehow she was suspicious that she was about to learn their story now.

He closed the space between them and lifted her hand into his. Was that to keep her from running?

"We met when we were children in Tennessee. We went to school together. And though she has grown up with wealth, and has become a stunningly beautiful woman, I've never seen her for more than the schoolgirl I knew back then." He paused and smiled. "If anything, I see her like a sister. Her parents died when she was young. A single child, she was raised by her aunt Gertrude."

Mahala silently thanked John for clarifying his relationship with Bella. It calmed her. Now that she'd learned the truth, she could almost kick herself for not trying to learn more about Bella. The beauty had a sad past.

John continued. "For reasons unknown, I've always been protective of Bella . . . but I've never loved her like a man loves a woman. She spends her summers at her uncle's house in New York City and she comes back full of talk of how she enjoys the opera houses, wishing that someday she could sing as wonderfully as the performers. But her grounding comes from Gertrude, who opened her home as if Isabella were here own. No matter where she goes, Bella will always come back to Grovespring and her Aunt Gertrude. She spends time with the old woman and then she's off for her next adventure."

Mahala let out a long sigh and nodded. She believed John. Nancy was pretty, but not stunning in the way Isabella came across to most people. But why on earth was he telling her all of this? He owed her no explanation. And yet, the fact that he had told her, warmed her.

Had she carried the leaden weight of jealousy for nothing? Goodness, gracious! "Your story rings true, but because of your close friendship with

Bella, many of the women in town have you proposing to her any day now." Mahala smiled at him impishly.

John threw his head back and laughed again. "That won't be happening anytime soon." He still held her hand, and now he gave her a sober look. "In fact, that won't be happening at all."

"Well." Mahala drew her hand out of his. "I better get back inside or my father will be looking for me, and he carries his pistol at all times." Her tone told him she was teasing.

"I'll walk you back." The two picked their way through the field and to the front of the buildings now lit by kerosene lamps along the street. John pushed the swinging door open for Mahala to pass through. She nearly left his side until she remembered she still wore his wool coat.

"Here you go." She shrugged his coat off her shoulders and handed it back to him.

The room fell silent as all eyes went to the two of them. Mahala bit her bottom lip and gave John a small smile before she threaded her way back to where the Shields family sat. Once she sat down, the room roared with talk as some of the people continued to watch her while others craned their necks to look back to where John Grigsby sat with the Fords.

"Will wonders never cease," one woman said as she exited the saloon.

Chapter TWENTY-THREE

JOHN PULLED HIS WOOL collar up around his ears against the bitter cold. The force of the wind picked up, and made him grateful that he'd worn his heavy coat. Earlier in the fall, the ranch had been alive with the business of calving and herding his cattle to higher pastures. Now that winter had set in the fields were dry stubbles peeking through the snow.

Today, he was riding through the high pastures. His herd wandered the fields by day and often gathered near the large piles of hay the cowhands delivered by wagon-loads and which now lay in mounds that looked like small hills from a distance.

John shaded his eyes from the glare that bounced off the white snow. He needed to be busy—both physically and mentally. If he slowed down long enough, the grief of losing Nancy nearly ate him alive. He'd wished away the pain of losing her more times than he could count, but in truth, there were a few days that the pain of losing Nancy lessened. But it was being alone at night that killed him. He didn't mind days like today, when the bitter wind seeped its way beneath the layers of his clothes and numbed his body so cold that he couldn't feel his skin, his bones. It helped further numb the pain.

Seeing that the cowhands had delivered enough feed for the large herd, he nodded and circled his mount toward the naked trees of the forest and followed the ice-encrusted stream to hunt for wandering steers. Moments later, he came upon the place where he'd found the two dead cows earlier in the year. He stared down at the dry carcasses, the hollow bones and torn hides partially covered in a light dusting of snow. The gaping holes had grown since he'd last seen them. What alarmed him today were the dead blackbirds that lay strewn on the ground. Off to the sides of the steers two crows lay, pierced by slim arrows embedded in their mid-section. Empty black eyes stared up at him, dark and ominous.

Arrows? In the four years he'd lived in these parts, he'd never seen Indians. He'd been told they didn't exist in Missouri. Was it another one of Benson's tricks? John dismounted and pulled an arrow from one of the birds. The crow's body was still warm, and the arrow slid out easily. Blackbirds circled above him, cawing to let him know his presence disturbed them. Other blackbirds settled on branches overlooking the area where he stood and they cawed at the dead cows—and the ominous sight of the dead birds.

But John's eyes strayed to the cavernous holes in the dead cows. They reminded him of the immense hole in his heart. With Nancy gone, his days had changed enormously, and now the raw ache that pierced his heart decided to stay—and deepen. He'd give anything to report what he'd found to Nancy this evening. But she had deaf ears now. She couldn't hear a word he said.

John mounted his horse again and turned Blue away from the discouraging sight. He worked his way across the icy creek and through the stark forest on the opposite side. He continued to search for cattle that might have wandered too far from the herd. Having gone to the boundary line of his ranch, he studied Benjamin Shields' land on the other side of the fence. Cattle lowed near the fence line and several hunkered together under a tree that gave little protection from the falling snow. Sitting on his horse at the edge of the Shields' property, John wondered, *Would Mahala be home right now or has she traveled to town in this wicked weather?*

John turned his horse back toward his own land and nudged Blue into a canter. Once they were free of the barren stand of trees, he and Blue rode the fence line between his land and Judd Benson's. Frazzled, John's mind played back the scene of the blackbirds spread haphazardly on the ground. Had the killing of the crows been a mean-spirited prank by the Benson boy? Who else would have done a foul thing like that? And even if Benson's son had been responsible for the useless killing of the crows, why the threat? What were the Bensons trying to prove?

"Come on, Blue. Let's head back to the house. If we don't get out of this cold wind, I won't be able to feel my bones before long."

Blue snorted and threw back his head.

"You like it out here, don't you, boy?" John reached down and brushed his rough-gloved hands over Blue's silky black mane. "I'll bring you out again tomorrow. Let's go."

John had made a habit of talking to his horse as if he were human. There were times he felt his horse understood him better than anyone else. And truth be told, he spent more time with this animal than with anyone else. He appreciated the beauty of his horse and personally cared for the steed each night before leaving the stable. His cowhands or his sons could brush Blue down, of course, but it was the one thing he'd rather do himself. He crooked a smile. In a sense, he figured Blue preferred it too.

Heading back to the house, John spotted movement in the dense trees. His saddle creaked as he reined Blue to slow down, and he leaned forward. He caught sight of Clyde Benson riding his mount through the forest along the edge of the creek. "What in tarnation?" John growled low in his throat. Clyde had a bow and a quiver of arrows slung over his shoulder. John watched the horse and rider pick their way through the fallen timber and brush. What was Benson's boy doing, riding through the woods on his property.

"Hey!" John dug his heels into Blue's flank. The horse jumped forward.

Clyde Benson glanced over his shoulder and spurred his steed forward. His horse lunged into a full gallop, dodging low-hanging limbs and darting through a thick stand of trees to the right.

"Oh, no, you don't!" John shouted as he lifted off his saddle, ducking his head as he shot ahead to try to catch up with the young man. The trail narrowed and dark branches reached out making it difficult to keep the pace through the woods. John sought to catch up with the kid, but Clyde kept going, not looking back. It wasn't long before Clyde and his mount faded through the clump of trees.

"Dadburnit!" John pulled back on the reins and brought Blue to a stop. Blue snorted and stomped, seeming satisfied they'd got in a good run.

John pulled off his black hat and slammed it against his leg. "Well, I've got my answer. Bensons got a lot to answer for." Short tempered after Nancy's death, John felt he was just the man to take on Benson. He jammed his hat back on and reined Blue back the way he had come. He knew the trail that would cut through Benson's ranch from the backside of his property.

He spurred his steed through the fields and found hoof tracks in the snow that led from Benson's land to his. Benson's cattle lowed on fresh-snow-covered ground, just like his own.

Finally, John rounded the outbuildings on Benson's ranch and walked Blue to the front of the house. He slid out of the saddle. His boots scraped the wooden floor of Benson's porch. With his heart pounding in his chest, John rapped on the front door.

The door flew open, and Judd Benson frowned at him. "To what do I owe a visit from you, Grigsby?"

John whipped off his hat and slammed it against his pant leg. "I want you and your boy to stay off my land!" Stewing, he continued, "If I so much as find you or your sons on my property again, you won't live to see the light of day. You get my drift?"

"Go on home, Grigsby. I don't have any issues with you."

"I beg to differ. It wasn't enough that you or one of your boys killed two of my steers, but now I find dead blackbirds scattered on the ground around them, with arrows shot through them. The only person who'd do a foul deed like that is Clyde." John eyed Benson, his blood boiling.

Benson stormed onto the porch and stared at John. His lip curled as he shot a finger at John's chest. "I said I'm not responsible for the killin' of your steers. Not yours nor anybody else. Why you're pointin' fingers at us, I don't know, but we didn't do it!"

John studied Benson's red face. "I want to believe you, Judd, I do. But I'm curious. Have you lost any steers? And what's more, I found Clyde riding through my property with a bow and a pack of arrows on his back. I won't go light on that boy if I catch him on my land again."

"I don't know anything about Clyde being on your land. I'll talk to him. Now if you'll excuse me, I've got business to tend to."

John slammed his hat back onto his head and stormed down the steps. "See that you do!"

SITTING IN HIS OFFICE, Judd Benson rolled a pencil back and forth between his fingers. The minutes had ticked by since Grigsby rode off his land. Where was Clyde? Judd could hear his wife and daughter getting dinner in the kitchen. As far as he knew, his wife didn't know John Grigsby had paid them a visit—again.

Looking out the window, Judd thought back to his childhood days and to his father, a man who couldn't—or better yet, wouldn't—hold on to what was his: their home, their land. He'd squandered their money on whiskey and cards, and then he let the law take their land, all on account of back taxes that were due and hadn't been paid three years in a row.

It didn't matter that he'd been warned and given a chance to make his debt right. His father had been a no-account who hadn't tried hard enough to hold on to what was his. He'd let go of their home and all that they had. Who does that? He should have had enough pride in himself and his family to hold on to his property and pass it down to his sons and daughters.

Judd would never abide anyone—law or no—taking what he worked for, what he bled for. He paid his land taxes and would buy more land if he could. He'd learned a hard lesson from his father, and he'd teach his sons the responsibility of owning land.

CLYDE WALKED INTO THE house through the kitchen door.

"Where have you been? Supper's about ready." Flora, his mother, picked up a dish towel and wrapped it around the pot on the stove and carried the stew to the table. Setting it down, she looked at him. "Is Myron on his way in?"

"I haven't seen Myron all day." Clyde lifted his shoulder in an off-handed way. "He does his own thing." Looking over his mother's shoulder he reached for a biscuit. She slapped his hand. "You wait until supper with the rest of us. Now, go wash up."

As Clyde left the kitchen and headed down the hall to his room, his father stepped out of the study. "Where've you been?"

Clyde shrugged. "Ridin'."

"Riding where?"

"Around." Clyde felt his neck warm, and heat race to his face. He turned away from his father with disinterest.

Judd stomped over to him. "You look at me, you good-for-nothing son of a gun. Show respect when your father's talking to you!"

Clyde stepped back. His father was a strong man and could take him down if he wanted to. "I didn't mean no disrespect. I-I was just out riding."

Judd eyed the quiver and arrows slung over his son's shoulder. "You been on Grigsby's land?"

Clyde swallowed and took another step back. "Yeah."

"What were you doin' on his land, boy? You know you're not supposed to trespass over there."

"Just riding." Clyde stared, a nerve jerking the corner of his lip. "I saw Grigsby while I was riding along the creek. So I'm not going to lie," he said flippantly.

Judd covered the distance between them. He grabbed a wad of Clyde's shirt and asked, "Did you happen to see crows while you were out ridin'?"

Heat that had traveled to his face now burned to Clyde's scalp. "Uh, yeah. What of it?"

"You listen to me, boy. I don't need any trouble with Grigsby. I don't want to find out you been shootin' birds on his land. You hear?"

Clyde licked his lips. "It didn't hurt nothing. I was just practicing with my new bow and arrows."

Judd stabbed Clyde's chest with his thick finger. "Practice on our land. Stay off Grigsby's. I work hard to keep things straight around here. I don't need you making things worse."

"What's the big deal?" Clyde felt anger well inside him. "I thought you didn't like the man."

"I don't have any problems with John Grigsby. I just want his land. There's gonna come a day when he sells it and when he does I want to be the one he sells it to. But he won't if you go and make things bad between us."

Clyde shrugged again and clenched his teeth, wishing to be done with his father.

"Another thing, boy. Did you kill his cattle?" Judd held his gaze, and Clyde didn't miss the accusation in his eyes.

"Uh, I can't say that I did."

"What kind of an answer is that? Either you did or you didn't."

Clyde shuffled his feet. "Let's just say, I wasn't the only one who took a shot at his steers."

Judd grabbed Clyde's jaw and shoved him against the wall. "Stay off Grigsby's land. You hear me, boy?"

Clyde pushed his father's hand away. He'd had enough. "I may be your son, but don't you ever man-handle me again." He turned toward his bedroom, the air thick with tension.

"Are you men ready for supper?" Flora cut in nervously.

"I'll be there in a minute," Clyde heard his father say. But he didn't turn back to face his parents. He pushed his bedroom door open and dropped the quiver on the floor. He hadn't wanted his father to know what he'd been up to. He'd lay low for the time being.

All his life he had felt as if he were second to his older brother, Myron. And in a way he was, having been born second. A quiet young man of nineteen, Myron preferred working with the cowhands on their ranch, moving cattle from sections of their land to pastures that hadn't been grazed in a while. He often missed supper from spending so much time outdoors. When he wasn't out working, Myron's nose was in his books; books that had something to do with doctoring horses and cows.

Myron had garnered his father's approval, but he hadn't earned it. His brother did little to further his father's quest to grab Grigsby's land.

Myron wanted to be a veterinarian someday. Pfft! As if his brother could learn the trade. True, Myron had saved one of the horse's last spring when the animal hurt his leg. And he seemed to know a thing or two about the stock when it was breeding and birthing time. Still, Clyde knew his father wanted Grigsby's land. He'd be the one to help him get it. Maybe then his father would look at him like he was worthwhile too.

THE DAYS SLIPPED BY with winter continuing to dig in its heels. After a bitter cold day out on the ranch, John headed back to the homestead with Rusty running alongside. Galloping through the drifts of snow, Blue kicked up ice crystals with his hooves. Rusty barked and ran circles around them.

John had again spent the day wandering through the forest in search of stray cows or their calves that might have worked their way to the river. The cows knew where the water was and could often be found near the muddy banks. The worse thing that could happen would be a calf or its mother wandering out into the middle of the frigid water and getting stuck.

But today had been uneventful and he rode home wanting more than anything to be by the fireplace where he could warm his hands and be surrounded by his children.

Slowing his mount, John thought of Mahala—as he had a hundred times that day. He hoped she'd stop by. When he neared the house, he found her buggy sitting idle in the drive. He let out a contented sigh and stopped Blue mid-stride. His heart hammered wildly, knowing the dark-haired beauty was somewhere in his house. Leaning his elbow on the saddle horn, he stared at the black rig. He felt a familiar twinge of attraction for Mahala. He wouldn't fight it any longer.

He'd been too harsh on his brood of late—too sullen. He hadn't missed the look of sadness in his children's eyes day in and day out. Mahala was like a breath of fresh air when she entered the house. She gave gentle hugs along with home-cooked meals that not only fed stomachs but, also fed their souls.

The wind picked up and John nudged Blue forward. His stomach growled and he wondered what Mahala had brought for supper this night. Feeling the hollow behind his ribs, he knew he needed to be more attentive to food and eat more. Since Nancy's passing, he hadn't taken an interest in what he ate or where it came from. Tonight, he'd make sure to clean his plate, and before Mahala left for the evening, he'd let her know how much he appreciated her.

"Come on, Blue. We've got a dark-haired beauty waiting for us."

AS MAHALA MOVED FROM moved from the porch steps, the moon rose high, its silver stream lighting the barren peach trees in such a way that it looked as if a million subtle lights glowed in the orchard. A feeling of melancholy settled over her, and instead of climbing into the black buggy, her shoes crunched across the snow-covered drive and she strolled toward the peach orchard. A frigid breeze curled through the path between the trees, and Mahala pulled her cloak closer over her chest. "Umm. It feels good to be here, Lord, and yet, how long will it be before John finds a new wife? He and the family won't need me much longer."

The harsh wind blew as if agreeing with her, and Mahala reached up to touch a cold, dark limb. She ran her thumb over its shiny texture and gazed out over the land. It was peaceful here, even when the harsh wind blew. She had to remind herself not to get too comfortable spending time with John and the children. Surely, her days were numbered before another woman would take her place.

An owl swooped down from a branch and rose just as quickly, its wings spread wide, and it screeched an ominous, shrill call that echoed over the treetops. A chill ran up Mahala's back. She glanced up to see where the feathered foe had gone, but he was gone as swiftly as he'd appeared.

Turning toward the house, Mahala made her way back to the buggy and climbed up onto the leather seat. Light spilled out from the living room window and glowed upon the icy ground, and shadows could be seen beyond. "Let's go home, Bessy." Mahala flicked the reins and the rig moved out of the long drive. As the glow from the house grew smaller and smaller, her mind reflected over the evening. Something told her that Mr. Grigsby wanted her to come to the house for more than just the children. But she'd been coming for quite some time—only to go home with no answers for her future.

If only she could share her thoughts with her mother or one of her sisters. But a part of her wouldn't allow the possibility that a man—and not just any man—but a prominent man such as John Grigsby—might truly be attracted to her. After all, she'd waited for this for such a long time.

THE FOLLOWING DAY, JOHN'S brother Jesse and his wife, Margaret, sat at the table with John while the older children were at school. Young Pulaski played with Jeffrey and Wiley in the living room, where the adults could hear them play.

"I don't know what's come over me, Jess," John said, wiping a hand over his scruffy beard. He'd had a hard time saying it, but he finally spit it out. "Nan hasn't been gone but a few months, and yet I'm attracted to Mahala Shields." He gave his brother a disconcerting look.

Margaret lowered her eyes and seemed to take a distinct interest in her fingernails as she turned her hand up to view them. A curve lifted at the corner of her lips.

"Do you have something to say, sis?" John stared at his sister-in-law, hoping she could help him out.

Margaret dropped her hand onto the tabletop and tapped a fingernail against the wood. When she looked up, playfulness showed in her eyes and her chin jutted out. "Mahala is an attractive woman and you are a man. There's nothing wrong with you pursuing her."

"But what about Nan?"

"She's not here," Jesse broke in. "And if I were a betting man, I'd say you still love her, despite the turmoil broiling in your heart right now." He leaned back in the kitchen chair.

"I do love her. But I can't hold her—can't touch her. I can't finger her flaxen-colored tresses." John felt old beyond his years. He looked up to see a lopsided grin on his brother's face.

"I didn't know you were such a hopeless romantic, brother."

John wanted to kick the chair out from under Jesse.

Jesse changed the subject. "What about Isabella Yates—Bella?"

"What about her?" John felt irritation gnaw at him. "She's just a friend, you know that."

"Doesn't look like it," Jesse said, his brows raised.

"What's that supposed to mean?" John wanted to kick the chair out from under his brother again.

"Well, every time you go to town, you've got the belle of the town wrapped around your arm." Jesse held his gaze,—hard and steady.

John chewed the inside of his cheek. "I don't ask for that. The silly girl has lost her senses. She knows I'm not interested in her. We're just friends. "

"Tell Mahala that," Margaret broke in this time. "From the looks of her, she has all but given up on you as a future prospect."

John's head swung toward Margaret. "For your information, I did tell Mahala that. She knows Isabella and I are just friends." The conversation was moving in a direction he hadn't anticipated. "How do you know how Mahala feels?" He picked up his pipe and strode to the fireplace. He thumped the old ashes out of the bowl into the fire. Sitting back down, he took a pinch of tobacco from a pouch of cherry tobacco and filled the pipe bowl again.

He knew he was stalling, but he did want to hear what Margaret had to say. He struck a match and lit the fresh tobacco, and then he leaned back and faced her.

"Because I stopped by the tailor shop a few days ago and paid Mahala a visit, Margaret told him. "When I brought up your name, she lost interest in our conversation. It was as if she didn't want to talk about you."

John took a long drag off of his pipe and blew three perfect rings of smoke into the air. "Looks like I'm going to have to do something about that. To be honest, I can't tell if we're making strides in a relationship or not."

"You are the only one who would know. If you want her . . . tell her." Margaret gave him a pointed look and left the table. She went to the living room and picked up baby Trisa off the blanket on the floor, where the three little boys had played quietly until now. But soon shrieks of laughter filled the air.

John turned to Jesse. "What do you think?"

Jesse quirked a grin and shook his head. "You are a sorry mess, John. You've been out of the loop of the courting life for so long, you've lost your touch."

"It scares me to death, to tell you the truth. I never wanted to be in this position again. I was happy with Nancy and liked things the way they were."

"I'm with Margaret. If you're thinking you want to court Mahala, it's time you tell Isabella of your intentions so she can step aside."

"All right, I'll take care of it."

LATE THAT AFTERNOON, JOHN watched his brother's wagon roll out of the drive with his wife and children by his side. He thought back to the table conversation and Mahala. *Mahala.* She was on his mind a lot these days. He'd take his family's advice and set the record straight with Isabella. He hadn't missed her intentions on this trip. She'd made it perfectly clear that she'd stay if he gave her half a reason to believe she should. But he hadn't led her on—or at least he hadn't intended to. Problem was, would she step away? Isabella wasn't one to take a hint. She'd fight it. Maybe even think she could give Mahala a run for the finishing line. Would Mahala fight for him? The muscles in his jaw tightened. No—she wouldn't. Or would she? A slow smile tugged at his lips. Maybe she would prove him wrong.

MAHALA SET FOUR GLASSES on one side of the table as Granville did the same on the opposite side. "How do you like your job at Owens Mercantile?" She studied the young teen who seemed to have grown an inch the past month.

"I like it. Mr. Owens has recently given me the job of picking up the freight that comes on the stage."

"Really?" She saw a light in his amber-flecked eyes. "You've proven your worth, or Mr. Owens wouldn't have trusted you with the new merchandise."

"I guess so." Granville shrugged.

Mahala looked over the table to see if everything they needed was in place.

Gran licked his lips and gazed at her. "I've been saving for a new rifle." He watched for her reaction. "I've been wanting to tell somebody for a while, seeing as how I'm close to having enough money to pay for it."

Mahala's brows raised. "Does your father know about the rifle?"

"Not yet. I want to surprise him."

"Did you order it through the mercantile?"

"Yep. Mr. Owens is just waitin' on me to pay for it."

"I must say, I think your father will be genuinely surprised." She ran her hand down the front of her skirt. When she looked up, Gran looked as if a warm glow filled him.

"He will be. I'm not a kid anymore. I want to show Dad I can do this on my own."

"I'm impressed, Gran." She came around the table and gripped both of his arms below his shoulders. "You've had to grow up fast. You'll make your father proud."

Going back into the kitchen to collect silverware to set on the table,

Mahala paused to look out the window. The wind had picked up and she moved closer to the window sill and pulled the curtain aside. The sky toward town had turned a dense blue gray in the hour she'd been here. The stark trees that had been stripped of their leaves now whipped back and forth in a frenzy. The storm that had threatened to come earlier that day was arriving at a frightening rate.

Should she bid the children goodnight and head home? She had hoped to at least get a glimpse of John before she left for the evening. She worried her bottom lip and hugged herself. Some days it felt as if she were chasing the wind. Did she imagine she saw a light in John's eyes when she came to the house—or when they had a chance meeting in town? She could have sworn she'd seen a longing in those blue eyes that last time they'd seen each other. But then again, what did she know about love? Maybe she was making too much of it.

Mahala cast around her mind for answers as to where—or who—her future husband might be, but each time her thoughts ended with John Grigsby. Her conscience pricked her for even thinking about the man with his thick black hair that had a tendency to fall across his forehead, his deep-set penetrating blue eyes, and his strong jaw —a striking combination. John had a commanding presence that people who knew him respected. Handsome and rangy is what he was, and his physical vibrancy was utterly maddening—to Mahala at least.

And she knew John needed a woman to help him. He had a ranch of over 900 acres to run and a large herd of cattle that took nearly all his effort to maintain. He needed a wife, if not for him, at least for the children.

She'd seen a look of desire when he gazed at her—a long, almost hungry look. It sent an unsettling thrill down her belly. Not that anything had really happened. Not outwardly, anyway. A warmth rose to Mahala's face. She understood that look.

She'd received it on occasion from a few men in town. She hadn't, however, wanted their attention. John . . . was in a category all his own, and to think that he looked at her in that light made her dizzy. And in all honesty, it was too much to hope for.

She continued to look out the window. It was growing dark. "Where's John?" she mused. She bit her bottom lip and her brows furrowed. He'd been gone before she arrived and still hadn't come in from the range. Mahala glanced at the bubbling stew in the pot at the back of the stove. She took the lid off and picked up a wooden spoon to stir the good-smelling thickness of meat and vegetables. Steam rose, sending an aroma throughout the room. She placed the lid back on the pot. *Please hurry home, John.*

Gazing out the window at the trees bucking the wind, she wondered, *Will he be home soon? Home.* She looked around the kitchen and the familiarity of it. It wasn't her home, but could it be someday?

Chapter TWENTY-FOUR

"OUCH!" MAHALA DREW HER finger back and sucked on the rush of red blood bubbling to the surface. Bleary-eyed from sewing intricate seams for too many hours, she had just pricked her finger for the third time. She set the fabric in her lap and leaned back in her chair. Adjusting her neck and hearing it crack, she gazed out at the snowy scene beyond the window. Where had the time gone? One moment she'd been feverishly sewing garments for the holidays, and then just like that, the New Year had come and gone.

Snowstorms had driven through their little town, and snow flurries seemed to be a daily thing. Bitter wind continued to rattle the eves of the buildings as if taunting them that winter was here to stay.

With February on their doorstep and despite the harsh weather, the community unanimously decided to celebrate Valentine's Day with a Sweetheart Dance. Cabin fever had taken its toll on the men and women of Grovespring. One could only find a few things to do indoors before one became mad from being cooped up for far too long.

Mahala thought back to the morning when the party had been brought up for a vote. For some women, their saving grace was the quilting bee that took place in a back room at the Yates Hotel. The women ate lunch at the café and shared the latest news. Oft times that news included a bit of gossip.

On this particular morning, Gretta Matthews had shown up to the quilting bee with a gleam in her eyes. It hadn't taken long for the women to notice. The Grovespring women were itching to have a good conversation while they threaded their needles through the quilt. Gretta waited for the hum in the room to subside.

"Have you got something to say?" Flora Benson asked as she elbowed her sister, Cleo who sat next to her. Flora's chin lifted gravely and she eyed Gretta with a raised brow.

Mahala tried to still the agitation that quickly took hold toward the "sour-grapes" woman. Couldn't she just for once be pleasant?

"I don't know about you," Gretta began as she eyed the small group, "but I've just about gone batty with this crazy weather we've had lately."

The women nodded their heads in agreement as a buzz hummed around the room.

"So—" Gretta straightened, seemingly pleased with the announcement she was about to give. "I've asked Charles if he wouldn't mind opening the barn for a Sweetheart Dance for Valentine's Day."

The women gasped and a burst of energy, sparked by their eager responses, ignited the room. It was all Gretta needed to continue, and she explained her plans for the party. All but two seemed pleased with the announcement. Flora Benson and her sister, Cleo, sat like two peas in a pod with long faces while the rest of the ladies joined in to make plans for the list of food and games for the event. It wasn't long before the Sweetheart Dance took shape. Grovespring was going to have a community party once again!

Now Mahala's hands were busy making gowns for the affair. She sat by the window and watched the snow whistle down the road in gusts and swirls as she plied her needle in and out of the fabric. She spent endless hours creating gowns for the women, who were forever in competition to outdo one another. This was one more event that helped build her reputation as a sought-after seamstress.

Leaning to one side to peer out the window, she spotted Gertie Yates walking up the boardwalk toward Thompson's Tailor Shop. Gertie stomped the snow from her boots and pushed the door open to get in from out of the cold. The cowbell jangled as she darted in.

"Goodness, it's cold out there." Gertie quickly brushed snow off her wrap with gloved hands. Mahala pushed the needle and thread into the material one last time, tied a knot, and picked up the shears. With a quick clip, she cut the thread and waited.

As Gertie skirted around Grady's work table, her voice carried back to Mahala. "Hi, dearie. I've come to see you."

Grady glanced back at Mahala with raised brows and then to Gertrude. "Good afternoon, Mrs. Yates."

"I'm sorry, Grady. Where are my manners?" Gertrude turned back to the proprietor. "I'm just as rude as a wasp sometimes. I go barreling head on for what I'm after without giving any thought to who might get stung on the way." She looked apologetic. "How's your day going, Grady? Are the men keeping you as busy as the women are Mahala?"

"Well, I can't say they're lining up for suits to be made for the Valentine's Dance. We men tend to be more casual, I suppose." Grady lifted the tape from around his neck and bent to measure the tweed fabric on the table. He penciled a number on a pad.

"There's sure to be weddings in the spring or maybe this summer. That'll keep you busy." Gertie patted his arm and turned back to thread her way around the tables of material and mannequins standing tall.

"Gertie, what brings you to the shop?" Mahala stood to stretch her back and then reached a hand to Gertie's before she sank into the chair again.

"I'm sure you've heard there's going to be a party in two weeks." Gertie waved a hand in front of her and chuckled. "Of course you have."

"Yes, I've heard." Mahala lifted the corner of a red velvet dress lying on the table. "It's the talk of the town."

The shop door opened again and quickly shut against the gusty wind. Mahala peered past Gertie to the front entrance.

"Good afternoon, Mr. Thompson," John Grigsby said, his voice strong and deep-timbered. Mahala had to still the beating of her heart. John stood by the door, where he brushed snow from his coat-sleeves. What's *he* doing here? She watched as Grady and John shook hands and moved into easy conversation. Did he have an appointment with Grady for a fitting? Would he be going to the Sweetheart Dance? With his broad shoulders and slim waist, he'd certainly look handsome in a new suit. *Goodness! What am I thinking?*

"So what do you say, Miss Shields?" Gertie asked, looking somewhat annoyed.

"W-what? I'm afraid I wasn't listening." Mahala lifted her chin.

"I don't think you've heard a word I've said since John walked into the store."

Wishing Gertie would lower her voice, heat rose to Mahala's cheeks. "I'm sorry." She gave the older woman a whimsical smile. "You have my undivided attention."

"I said," Gertrude drew out the statement, "I want to surprise Isabella with a new gown. Do you think that's possible before the Valentine's party?"

"Oh, Gertie, I wish I could. But truth be told, I'm working overtime to finish the gowns I'm already committed to. I don't know what has come over some of these ladies. In the past many of them would never have considered using me as their seamstress. But these past months, I can hardly keep up with the demand."

"Well, that's hardly anything to complain about. You must be delighted that they've come to their senses. You have a real gift with a needle and thread." A flicker flashed in the older woman's eyes. "I'm not surprised by the extra demand after Flora Benson showed off that grand gown you made for the Harvest Festival. A dandy dress if I ever saw one."

Mahala lowered her chin and bit her tongue. "Thank you, Gertie. Some women have grander taste than I." She looked up and smiled. "I've been offered a job in Springfield. A dress shop owner has asked if I'd consider working for her."

"You wouldn't." Gertrude's hands went to her round hips.

Mahala shook her head. "Of course I turned it down. But I like having the option to take on a challenge."

"Well, don't bother feeling bad about not being able to accommodate me. I should have known you'd be up to your ears with work. I should have come sooner." Gertrude brushed imaginary wrinkles from her skirt. "Isabella does have a full wardrobe filled with charming dresses. She'll be all right."

Mahala tried to keep the giggle from working its way into her throat. She swallowed. "That's good to know, Gertie. I'm sure your niece brought several beautiful gowns with her. I was sitting right here when she first arrived, and there seemed to be an endless supply of trunks and suitcases unloaded from the stagecoach that day." Mahala felt relieved that she wouldn't be put upon to make Bella a dress, but she was certain the older woman had more on her mind than her services.

"You know—" Gertie lowered her voice and peered behind her to where John and Grady spoke in low tones. "My niece has done just about everything in her power to get John Grigsby's attention. But I think that man has taken Nancy's death harder than any of us have realized." She clicked her tongue. "He acts as if he's hardly noticed my beautiful girl is in town."

Mahala swallowed a second time and nearly choked at the words spilling from Gertie's lips. She schooled her expression to conceal the fire smoldering within. Bella wasn't the only woman in this town interested in John Grigsby.

Gertie's lips thinned. "If he were to think beyond his deceased wife, it would be my Bella he'd be thinking on." She gave Mahala a stern look.

Mahala couldn't swallow again. What could she say without biting off her own tongue? She felt as if Gertie could see right through her. Did she suspect Mahala had her sights on John? And what if she did? Gertie Yates had no control over John Grigsby or who he might court in the months to come.

A spark of hope began to kindle inside Mahala's heart. Gertie had no idea that her confession that Bella hadn't garnered John's attention was encouraging. If anyone knew how things were going between John and Bella, it would be Gertie. She felt certain the woman had put high stakes on her niece being the next Mrs. Grigsby.

Mahala fought to keep a grin from spreading across her face, and she lowered her voice as well. "I wouldn't be too concerned about Bella, Mrs. Yates. She's always had a mind of her own. And . . . she's not a quitter." Mahala wanted to pinch herself for her last remark, but then, she wasn't a quitter either.

"No truer words were spoken." Gertie's eyes sparkled. "I'd best get on back to the hotel. You never know if a drifter might need a hot meal or a room for the night." She pulled on her gloves. "Good afternoon, Miss Shields."

"Good day." Mahala watched Gertrude walk past John and Grady. The older woman smiled at both of the men and whisked out the door.

Mahala picked up her work again. She tried desperately to keep her eyes on the red velvet fabric she pulled onto her lap, but try as she might, her gaze strayed to the tall muscular man talking to Grady. Now that Gertie had gone, however, John stepped away from Grady and headed straight for her. Holding her breath, she couldn't help but feel his penetrating gaze on her as he moved farther into the shop. *Be still my heart!*

Mahala dropped her eyes and pushed the needle through the thick, red material. She pretended she didn't know John was in the store, even though she was fully aware of the aura of power emanating from him reminding her that he was a force to be reckoned with.

"Good afternoon, Miss Shields."

Mahala gripped the needle between her fingers. "Mr. Grigsby. What brings you into Thompson's Tailor Shop?" She faced him squarely, conscious of his gaze that had settled on her, an amused glint in his eyes. She wouldn't look away. She held her breath and waited for his response.

"I had business to attend to in town and I thought I'd stop by to see you."

"That's very kind of you." Mahala's gaze traveled to his work-stained boots before she looked into his deep-blue eyes.

He took off his black, wide-brimmed hat, leaving a pile of matted hair beneath. She hadn't noticed before how his hair curled on his collar. He turned the hat in his hand as if he needed to inspect it.

"Mr. Grigsby?"

He cleared his throat. "I . . . me and the children—"

Mahala straightened and peered at his handsome, rangy face. "Yes, Mr. Grigsby?"

John's chin hit his chest before he lifted it and his jaw jutted forward. "I'd like for you to come to the house Saturday. I've removed the wheels from the wagon and put the sled runners on." He fingered his hat a bit more before he finished. "I thought it might be nice for all of us to go on a sleigh ride."

Her eyes took in every detail from the crown of his cowboy hat in his work-worn hands to the dark jacket covering his muscled physique. Her gaze lingered on the rough cut of his features. She couldn't help it. A grin spread across her face as she relaxed her hands in her lap. "I would be happy to accept your invitation. Might I bring something . . . hot chocolate or a meal?"

He looked immensely relieved. "No. Don't bring anything. Just you."

"All right." Mahala stood, trying hard to conceal the beating of her heart. "I'll see you on Saturday."

"Can you come after the noon meal?"

"Of course. That won't be a problem."

John returned his hat to his head and touched the brim. "I'll see you this weekend if the weather holds."

Was he giving her a way out? "I'm looking forward to it. It's been a long while since I've gone on a sleigh ride."

"Good day then." He walked out of the shop, leaving a big hole in the room. She hadn't realized his presence had such an effect on her. Mahala quickly looked out the window to see John untie Blue from the hitching post and mount the steed in one easy step. When he rode past the window, he lifted a hand.

Mahala grinned and lifted a palm toward him. For the life of her, she couldn't wipe a silly grin off her face for the rest of the afternoon. She had no idea where John planned for them to ride. Would they travel quietly out in the countryside where no one would see them? Or would he venture into town, where they'd be seen by the people of the community? The thought of Gertie finding out she would spend the afternoon with Mr. Grigsby and the children was her undoing. *Stop it, Mahala! Bella has no claim on John. Besides, he came knocking on my door, didn't he?*

IT WAS ALL MAHALA could do to keep her head bent to her work. Her mind went to her wardrobe. What would she wear? The shop bell tinkled and looking up, Mahala sucked in her breath. There stood Isabella, glancing around the shop. Isabella gazed at Mahala and marched to her table.

"Hello, Mahala." Her voice was cold.

"Good afternoon, Isabella. What brings you to Thompson's Tailor Shop?" Mahala's sat up straight. Something in the manner of Isabella's stance told her that this wasn't a chance visit.

Isabella leaned down and looked Mahala in the eye. "I just want you to know that I have dibs on John Grigsby. I mean to make him mine now that Nancy is gone."

"But—"

Isabella's hand went up. "You need not bother going over to John's house any longer. I intend to marry the man. We've known each other for quite some time." Isabella brushed her blonde curls out of the way as she continued. "Nancy snatched John up before I even had a chance to make my intentions known." She lowered her body so that she was nearly level with Mahala, even though she stood on the other side of Mahala's work table, and her eyes grew dark. "I won't lose him a second time. I'm warning you, Mahala Shields. Stay away from the Grigsby house."

If ever there was a time to have a backbone, that time was now. Mahala clenched her jaw tightly before she answered in a steady tone, "In case you haven't learned by now, it isn't you nor I who have a say in what Mr. Grigsby does. If John Grigsby wants me to come to his house, I will—I don't need your permission. Good day, Isabella. Don't let the door hit you on the way out."

Isabella stood to her full height, her mouth slack. "You haven't seen the last of me, Mahala Shields." She turned and marched back out to the boardwalk.

Mahala leaned to look out the window to see the blonde swiftly making her way to the hotel. She realized she was trembling, but she wouldn't heed Bella's words. *John came to me with the invitation to spend Saturday with him. I'll be there if it's the last thing I do.*

JOHN RODE OUT OF town, his pulse beating a hard rhythm in his neck. Well, now he'd done it. He'd taken the first steps toward making his interest in the lovely Mahala Shields known, and there was no taking it back. Had he done the right thing? Thinking back to all the dark and lonely days he and the children had gone through since Nancy's passing he couldn't explain it but he was certain that, yes,—what he'd done was right.

Won't the children be surprised when he told them about his plans? A sleigh ride would do them all a world of good.

When he neared the entrance of his ranch, he nudged Blue in the opposite direction of where he'd planned to check on the cattle. Instead, he reined his mount toward Nancy's grave. He slowly walked Blue to the fenced-in cemetery and sat in the saddle for a long moment, staring at the single plot. A stone had been erected at the head of the grave with Nan and baby David's inscription engraved into the rock. The mound was covered with a thick layer of snow.

John slid off his horse and tied the reins to the picket fence. Walking through the gate into the bleak enclosed yard, he stood beneath the oak tree, it's brown leaves rustling overhead and standing sentry over his beloved. He removed his hat, knelt in the soft snow, and spread his hand on top of the mound. "Nancy." He paused, looking for the right words to say. "Without you, we're lost. So I'm asking permission to pursue the life I feel the children and I need."

A wave of grief washed over him. His ragged breath heaved and his eyelids closed. He wiped the tears that flowed freely. His hand grew still, his heart empty. Hanging his head, he leaned an elbow on his raised knee.

"You asked Mahala to be there for our children . . . but in truth . . . I need her to be there for me as well. Forgive me, my beloved, if it seems too soon to pursue your friend. But our home is an empty shell and aching to get back to some semblance of normalcy. I believe Mahala can breathe life back into our lives."

He kissed the palm of his hand and laid it on the grave again. "You will always be my first love." He placed his hat on his head and stood. As he untied the reins from the picket fence, he looked at the gray clouds. *Lord, I need your guidance. Show me what to do. I want nothing more than to be in Your perfect will.*

THE FOLLOWING MORNING, MAHALA arose to the sun streaming onto her bed. *The sun's shining?* She hadn't seen the sun in nearly a month. She slid from beneath the warm covers and tiptoed barefoot on the cold floor to the window. She brushed aside the lacy, white curtains to peer down at the sparkling world below. Lifting one cold foot to rest beneath her flannel nightgown and against her warm ankle, she gazed at the fields beyond the outbuildings. They glistened with sparkling snow that sprayed playfully in the gusts of wind.

Snow had fallen for days, but now it seemed the storms had passed. The dark and gloomy clouds had drifted away, leaving behind a startling blue sky. Waves of ice crystals reflected the rays of the winter sun that turned the world into a sparkling wonderland. Breathing against the cold windowpane, Mahala's warm breath caused fog to build up, blinding the brilliance beyond the square pane.

"I better quit lollygagging. The morning will be over before I know it," Mahala whispered lightheartedly. She turned away from the window and pulled off her flannel nightgown. A draft of cold air chilled her. She went to the wardrobe and opened it wide. She didn't have to second guess what she'd wear this glorious morning. She fished through the dresses hung on wooden hangers, and purposely shoved them aside, looking for her brown riding skirt and the long-sleeved white shirtwaist. Feeling a bit giddy, and quite naughty to boot, she decided to skip breakfast and go horseback-riding over the crisp fields of snow.

She mustn't delay. It had been weeks since the sun had shone so brilliantly, and just the sight of it filled her with new-found hope. She had gowns to finish for the Valentine's Dance, but they could wait. One never knew how long the sky would be open and clear. She for one would take advantage of it.

Once she changed into the riding clothes and pulled on her knee-high boots, Mahala plaited her hair into one long braid down her back and let all sense of work be thrown to the wind. She settled her wide-brimmed hat on her head and sailed down the stairs.

She quickly walked toward the back door, her boots thumping loudly on the hardwood floor. From down the hall, Boots ran toward Mahala her, greeted her with a single mew, and then rubbed her furry body against Mahala's ankles. She picked Boots up and rested her two front paws on her shoulders. "Good morning, Boots. Isn't it a lovely day?"

She wasn't surprised to hear her mother's voice fly through the hallway. "Where are you going dressed like that?"

"Riding, Mother." She set Boots on the hardwood floor. "Did you see how wonderful it looks outside? I don't want to waste a moment of it."

"But your breakfast? Your work?"

"It'll keep." Mahala whirled out the back door and made her way to the stable. She found Charlie inside Bessy's stall, brushing her briskly. When he looked up, surprise washed over his old, wrinkled face. "Don't hitch her to the buggy just yet," Mahala said. "I'm going for a ride."

Charlie's mouth made an O and he nodded. "Anything you say, Miss Shields. I guess I best be puttin' on the side-saddle instead."

"Not the side-saddle. I'll be putting Bessy into a run."

"You're going to ride astride this girl?" Charlie pulled on the bridle and brought Bessy out into the open aisle where he'd saddle her.

"Yes, I am." Mahala jutted her chin. "Please hurry before the clouds come back." She glanced out the stable doors and up at the sky. There wasn't the smallest hint of a cloud to be seen. Still, she didn't trust the weather. The north wind could bring in a string of clouds at the blink of an eye.

"Here you go, Miss Shields." Charlie brought the mare to the stable doors and cupped his hands by the stirrup.

Mahala stepped her booted foot into his palms and hoisted herself into the saddle. "Thank you, Charlie. We'll be out on the range for a while. Don't worry about us." She kneed her mount, and Bessy started out at a canter. Once they reached the gate that let out to the range, Mahala dug her heels into the mare's flanks and Bessy gleefully shot forward and galloped into the open furrows of snowdrifts, throwing ice crystals into the air with her hooves.

It felt odd to be out and about as early as her father's cowhands. The men would certainly take advantage of this clear day to hunt for their Hereford cattle who could be stranded in drifts of snow. They'd had a good many days when the snow fell, leaving numerous drifts, as high as six feet in some places. Planning to ride to the river, she would alert her father if she found stray cattle near the banks.

Mahala felt free as a gazelle as she and Bessy slowed down and rode toward the forest lining the creek. The stream would be iced over this time of year, with water flowing beneath the ice. The catfish would be hiding in rock coves. How they withstood the cold was beyond her.

Stripped of their leaves, the white oaks and sugar maples stood black and daunting. As she rode on, she found signs of wild life. The snow was imprinted with rabbit and squirrel tracks. Deer or elk had trampled the snow that led to the river. She rode on until she and her mount neared the ice-encrusted bank. She wouldn't let her chestnut mare near the frozen water;

instead, they meandered along the river's edge, and she allowed her mind to drift a million miles away from work and responsibilities.

A flutter of red drew her attention a short ways downstream, and she spotted a cardinal, the bright red feathers brilliant against the winter landscape. The bird swooped and settled by the bank, pecking its bill against the thin layer of ice. Seconds later, after drinking its fill, the bird fluttered off.

Mahala held her breath and watched in awe. It wasn't often she witnessed a red cardinal flying in the woods. To see it in action, surviving in the wild, gave her a feeling of wonder at God's magnificent creation.

Mahala was glad she'd decided to take some time for herself. It was time she allowed herself a bit of mischief. It wasn't often she tossed her work to the winds. She'd make a note to do it more often. Glancing at the clear sky, she saw the sun had risen higher, and she bit her bottom lip. Well, one did have to be responsible—she had gowns to finish. She would return to the ranch, eat breakfast, and get into town.

She sat a moment longer and gazed downstream toward the Grigsby ranch.

In the distance Mahala spotted a rider nearing the Shields' property line. She sat straight in the saddle and studied the rider. Was it one of John's cowhands looking for strays?

No—it wasn't.

Gripping the reins a bit tighter, her pulse tripped. She recognized that black felt hat and the physique of the man who sat astride the blue roan. John rode lazily along the edge of the woods, seemingly unaware that she watched him. Glad she had spotted him before he saw her, she wondered, *Will we have a chance meeting so early in the morning?*

Chapter TWENTY-FIVE

JOHN SHRUGGED INTO HIS heavy coat and headed out the back door. The skies were clear of clouds as far as the eye could see. Sheer relief surged through him as he shaded his eyes against the brilliant sun. Ice crystals glittered on the ground as he gazed to the far-reaching trees near the river and beyond the fence line where the cattle roamed. It would be a good day to search for stock and feed them.

Snow crunched under John's boots as he strode through the shoveled path his cowhands had cleared before he'd awakened. He smelled fresh coffee as he worked his way to the bunkhouse. These days, with Nancy gone, Corky had taken to fixing breakfast for him as well.

"Morning, Corky." John picked up the tin coffee pot from the black-iron stove. He poured himself a cup of the steaming brew.

Corky nodded as he wiped work-worn hands on his soiled apron. "Mornin', boss."

Luke and Brady pulled chairs out to sit down at the table. Bowls of scrambled eggs, sausage and gravy, and biscuits sat freshly made as John joined them.

Two of John's hands, Will and McDuff, ate their breakfast at home before they rode out to the ranch. Both had wives and families. But it wasn't unusual for them to show up and join in for a cup of coffee, as they did now. All eyes fixed on John as they waited for instructions for the day's work. It was evident that the bright, shining morning, lifted their spirits.

"Looks like we've got a fair day to feed the cattle and hunt for any that might have fallen in snow drifts." John took a sip of hot coffee. "We best hit it as soon as breakfast is done. We don't know how long the clouds will stay at bay."

Will scooted his chair back, the legs scraping on the rough-hewn floor. "Come on, McDuff. Let's load the wagon with hay." Will glanced at McDuff, who downed the last of his coffee, and the two men left the bunkhouse.

Corky refilled John's cup and sat down. "It looks to me that you men got a good break today."

"Um-hm," John said, setting his cup down. "Don't know how long it'll last, but after the last half-dozen cows we dug out of the snow drifts, we shouldn't waste any time before we start to look for more."

John's comment seemed to put a burr under the remaining cowhand's saddle. The men downed the last of their coffee and stood. "Good meal as usual, Corky." Brady picked up his coat and threw it over his shoulder and shoved his arms into the sleeves.

"Thanks, Corky." Luke followed Brady out the door.

John sat with the older man a bit longer. He poured gravy over his biscuit and forked a bite. Sunlight streamed in from the window and slanted across the table. The two men stared at the welcome sight.

"I been keepin' count of the days we've been hidden from the sun," Corky said. "I was beginnin' to think it were like the days of Noah—forty days and forty nights."

"That long?"

"Yep."

John glanced at the stream of light flowing across his plate and grinned. "God is always faithful."

Corky chuckled. "That He is."

John drained his cup. "I best get on out and join the men. Thanks for the good meal." He hadn't removed his hat or coat, so he just touched the brim of his hat as he pushed his chair back then strode out of the cabin. Outside, he paused and stretched. A clear bright sun shone down on him. Given enough days with the sun shining, the snow would melt enough to make the ground safer for his cattle. Deep snow was always a hazard on the ranch, both for the cattle and the horses. Men and animals both would take advantage of the break in the weather today.

Franklin strode out the back door, wearing his heavy coat and gloves. "Mornin', John," he said and yawned.

John gazed at Franklin. It took him by surprise to hear his younger brother call him 'John.' Franklin hadn't taken up calling him by his name until after Nancy died. Before that, he had called him Dad, along with the rest of the children. But maybe it was time—seeing as they *were* brothers. Franklin spent as much time out on the ranch as he could. His brother loved everything about ranching.

"Good morning, Franklin. The men are out behind the barn getting ready to head out with a load of hay to the north pasture."

"All right." Franklin headed to the stable for his horse.

When John reached the barn, he found Granville milking Bossie and Calvin filling a bucket with oats. "Morning, boys."

"Morning, Dad." Granville yawned as he pushed his head into Bossie's flank and pulled on her teats. Milk streamed into the bucket, making a pinging sound as it squirted against the side.

"Are the girls up?"

"Yeah. Tess's is getting the boys dressed." Granville didn't look up, intent on keeping the stream of milk inside the bucket.

Calvin strode up. "Can I take Brownie for a ride out in the fields?"

"No, son. I know the sun coming out from hiding is inviting, but we don't know how long it'll stay out. It's best you stay put in the yard today."

"All right." Calvin hung his head.

John couldn't help himself. He ruffled the boy's mop of dark hair. "I'm going to have to take you boys into town to the barber shop before too long."

He didn't wait for their response but headed down the stable's wide aisle to collect Blue from his stall. He found the roan munching oats when he opened the stall gate. Blue's withers shook in greeting.

"Morning, boy." John ran a hand over the horse's coat. He picked up a brush and began brushing Blue down. It wasn't long before he threw a blanket over Blue's sleek back and saddled him. Bridle in hand, John led his horse to the stable's open doors. The snow glittered across the grounds. He glanced back at the sleigh wagon sitting off to the side. *I sure hope this weather holds until Saturday.*

"Good morning, Daddy," Mary Jane called as she headed to the springhouse with a bucket in her hand. She hurried through the snow, wearing her coat and with her knitted cap pulled tightly over her ears.

"Good morning, kitten. Get what you need from the springhouse and then hurry back to the house. I don't want you catching a cold."

"I will, Daddy." Mary Jane smiled as she continued on the cleared path to the small building. It appeared that the cowhands had woken extra early and taken it upon themselves to clear a path to all of the necessary outbuildings for John's family. John knew he had a good crew. It was times like today that made him appreciate his men beyond measure.

John reined Blue to the back of the barn, where McDuff and Will shoveled pitchforks of hay onto a hay wagon until the wagon was nearly over-flowing. Brady climbed onto the hay and stomped it down, allowing room for more.

"I'm going to ride down to the river and look for stray cattle. You men go on out and feed the stock. I'll catch up with you later," John told them.

"Sure thing, boss," the men chorused.

John nudged Blue toward the thick stand of trees. The stark maple and oaks were bare, their dark limbs reaching out to each other. Deer tracks could be seen where the animals had come out to forge for food.

Rusty ran and barked behind him, wanting to join him on the ride. He ran in circles throwing up puffs of snow. "Go on back to the house, boy." John slowed his horse and turned to point at the house. "Stay with the kids. Go on, shoo!"

Rusty hunkered down and pinned his ears back. The only thing that moved was his tail, which thumped the snow.

"Go on, I said!" John tried to sound commanding, but the dog's wish to join him was welcoming. If it weren't for the deep drifts of snow, he'd likely let Rusty come along. But not today.

"Rusty!" Calvin stood at the edge of the fence line. "Come on, boy!"

Rusty turned back to the ranch yard, his feet kicking up snow.

John pulled his hat low over his eyes as he and Blue trudged slowly through the drifts. The air was brisk and cold, but the sun was bright and the sky a clear blue as far as he could see.

The land sparkled as he and the horse continued on. Before long, he came to the path that led to the fishing hole. The boys traveled this path often in the summertime. This same path, wide and worn, was used to enter the woods by man and beast. If the cattle had gone to the river for water, they would have come this way.

John kept his eyes and ears alert for sounds of his stock in the woods as he picked his way along the trail. The tree branches overhead blocked some of the snow that had fallen in prior days, their dense mass acting as an umbrella to the ground below. There was snow on the ground, but it wasn't as thick as it was in the fields.

He heard water rippling up ahead. He pushed Blue on. When he came out to the clearing, he saw the river was covered by a wide expanse of ice. But he could hear the water flowing beneath the thick, icy crust. The river ran east/west across his property, with veins of water running off to form small creeks and streams. He only allowed his sons to fish in the creeks as the river often ran fast and ferocious.

He pushed his hat up with a forefinger and gazed over the ice-covered river. He studied the surface from one side of the bank to the other. Until now, he hadn't seen any sign of cattle. Good. He didn't want to have to rope a cow off the slick ice if he didn't have to.

John followed the river to the vein that branched off to form their favorite creek. Every now and then he looked up through the high branches to the clear blue skies. "Thank you, Lord, for a break in the weather." His voice reverberated low and deep and echoed against the stark trees as he continued on, staying close to the banks, but not too close for Blue's hooves to slide into icy water.

He had pushed on for another quarter of a mile when he spotted another rider ahead. He gazed past the barren trees stripped of their leaves. Who was out there riding along the banks of the creek? He was near the Shields land now. It could be one of Benjamin's cowhands looking for stray cattle.

John nudged Blue slowly through the foot-high snow, sometimes coming to deeper drifts and carefully moving forward through the stand of naked trees several yards ahead of the other horseman.

When he stopped, he leaned his forearm on the saddle horn and took in the spectacular sight. With sheer delight, he watched Mahala Shields and her mare meander along the creek's edge, seeming unaware they had company.

"Hello." John's voice echoed along the banks.

Mahala turned in her saddle, her face red from the icy chill of the morning. Her dark hair hung in a single braid down her back, and she wore a smart riding outfit as she sat astride her chestnut mare.

And she looked wonderful.

"Mr. Grigsby! I didn't hear you ride up." A stab of guilt pressed her, but she'd never let on she'd been watching him from a distance, hoping she'd get a moment alone with him on this glorious day.

"I'm not surprised," John said. "The water's running fast under that ice. Sounds good, doesn't it?" He thought she looked stunningly beautiful on the rugged path by the banks. But he couldn't tell her that. It wasn't his right to say so. Pulling his gaze away from her, he sat up straight. "What brings you out this early in the morning? I'd have thought you'd be headed to town."

She glanced at the blue sky, the cleft in her chin more visible at that angle. "I couldn't ignore this." She pointed a gloved finger upward. "I should have been in town by now but who could pass up this kind of day?"

Her gentle laugh was refreshing and he swallowed.

"It's good to see you allowed yourself a moment in these wide-open spaces." *It's good to see you.*

John stared at Mahala sitting astride her horse. Most women rode side-saddle, but apparently not this woman. Instead of making note of it to her, he took in her red cheeks and green eyes. "Care to join me? I'm looking for stray cattle."

Mahala's eyes lit up and she looked as if she'd accept his invitation. But just as quickly, she bit her lower lip and shook her head. "I would love to, but I've spent more time out here than I should have. I've a ton of work waiting for me at the shop." She lifted her shoulders and dropped them just as quickly. "The Sweetheart Dance."

John nodded. "Of course, Miss Shields." He touched the brim of his hat and tugged on the reins. Blue took a few steps back and stopped.

"I'll see you Saturday." Her gloved hand went up and she reined Bessy toward the Shields' ranch. She slowly worked her way through the trees to the clearing that led to the fields. When she reached the opening, she kicked Bessy into a run. Snow flew, spraying a dusting of white behind her.

John held his horse steady as he watched Mahala ride away. He blew out a deep breath, and a puff of white steam filled the air. He didn't move until Mahala's horse was out of sight. He had a ranch to run and stray cattle to look for. Could he keep the dark-haired beauty out of his mind long enough to get his work done?

He turned Blue toward home. When he reached the homestead, there was a lift to his shoulders and more authority in his stride. He hadn't missed the shine in Mahala's eyes when they spoke by the creek. Was it his imagination or had he seen interest in her amber-flecked green eyes? *Lord, help me. I'm smitten.* How many days before Saturday and the sleigh ride?

JOHN'S MIND WENT TO the morning Mahala had stood wet as a beaver in her cream-colored flannel gown and bare feet in his barn. Nancy had just passed and he had been building her box. Mahala stood awkwardly, waiting for him to look up. He remembered how lost she'd looked standing there, needing her horse, but not wanting to interfere with his work. What she didn't know was that, since that day, even in his darkest hour, when he felt taking another breath would be nearly impossible, the memory of when she climbed on her horse and rode out, her dark hair flying behind her, plagued him again and again.

She'd sat straight, her slim figure sitting lightly on the bare back of her steed. The sun shone down on her wet nightgown that had stuck to her sleek waist beneath the fabric. Bare ankles hugged the horse's flanks as she had nudged Bessy to run.

That memory was no longer a plague. Now, he relished it in the middle of the night and the early morning hours. Sometimes, he could barely swallow when the scene replayed in his mind. She'd looked like an angel of mercy flying on her horse toward home. She had come when they needed her. He hoped she would be there when they needed her now. Inviting her for a sleigh ride was his first step in the right direction. He was sure of it.

There'd be no work Saturday.

Just play.

SATURDAY MORNING DAWNED BRIGHT and clear. Mahala glanced out the window long enough to see that her wish had been granted. The day looked perfect! She flew to the wardrobe and picked out a blouse and skirt for the day. She smiled to herself while she dressed, thinking what a rare breed of a man John Grigsby was. Not only was he handsome, but he faced life head on, and he did it with determination.

She remembered how he'd gazed at her the other morning when they met by the creek. He'd looked at her with what—need? Those same eyes had shown anticipation for today's outing. She was sure she'd read that in the glint in his eyes. A thrill coursed through her belly as she imagined how the day could go. And then she stopped. What were they doing—two middle-aged people— acting as if they were young adults falling in love? Could she truly believe the *sought-after* John Grigsby could really fall in love with her?

They hadn't even kissed.—The thought sent a raw heat over her flesh. She'd never been kissed—or sought after—by anyone. "Mahala Shields," she said in a firm tone. "Get a hold of yourself. Don't make more of today's outing than it really is." She buttoned the top button of her chocolate-colored shirtwaist and examined herself in the mirror.

Running a brush through the length of her hair, she decided she'd not pin it up today. She wanted to feel carefree in the fur hat she'd wear today, along with the fur-collared cloak and muff she'd worn on the few other occasions when she'd wanted to wear something special.

The smell of sizzling bacon sailed up the stairs and into her room, warning her that if she didn't get a move on, she'd be late for breakfast.

"Morning," Mahala sang as she breezed into the kitchen.

All eyes flew to her.

"Don't you look smart on a Saturday morning?" Mary Ann's brows lifted.

"Where are you going all dressed up?" Rebecca asked, sliding over to the next chair, making room for Mahala to sit down.

Their mother stood at the stove holding a plate of pancakes, and eyed Mahala with equal curiosity. "So—are you going to tell us where you're going in your Sunday get-up?" She set the plate on the table, and then her hands went to her slim waist.

Benjamin leaned back with a sparkle in his eyes. "If I didn't know better, I'd say you've got a secret you've been keeping to yourself." He jabbed a pancake with his fork and put it on his plate. "Sit down, Mother. The food's getting cold."

Benny slid into a chair next to Elizabeth and the family bowed their heads.

Mahala couldn't keep her grin at bay, and she secretly thanked God for the day she was about to experience. After all,—it wasn't every day that John Grigsby entered the establishment in which she worked to invite her for a sleigh ride. Somehow, she felt this day was going to bring a change in their relationship. One for the better—for both of them.

Chapter TWENTY-SIX

MAHALA ARRIVED AT THE Grigsby ranch at noon as promised. Jesse Grigsby's cutter sat out in front of the house and a sinking flutter filled her stomach. Would Jesse and Margaret be joining them? Not that she didn't care for John's family, she liked them just fine. It was just that she'd hoped it would only be her, John and the children.

Forcing a smile she didn't feel, she rode Bessy around to the back of the house, dismounted, and tied the reins to the hitching post by the stable.

"Molly!" The back door flew open and Calvin and Mary Jane hurried down the steps to greet her.

"We're going for a sleigh ride with you today!" Calvin's amber-flecked eyes beamed.

"That's what I've heard." Mahala laughed as Mary Jane ran up and hugged her.

"We're not supposed to tell you our surprise—"

"Mary Jane!" Calvin cut her off.

"I wasn't going to give it away." Mary Jane's brows lowered.

"Good, 'cause Dad said he wanted to be the one to surprise her." Calvin glanced up sheepishly. "He's sure been acting funny lately."

"Oh, goodness!" Mahala ruffled Calvin's dark hair and felt his cold ears. "If you're coming along, you best put your ear-muffs on."

"I'm wearing my coonskin hat. That'll keep my ears warm."

The back door slammed and Mahala looked up to see John, Tess, and Granville coming toward them.

"I didn't hear you ride up." John's eyes lit up. He wore a thick coat and gloves and his black felt hat.

Granville and Tess carried a pile of wool blankets and smiled as they trudged through the snow on their way to the barn. Just inside the building, the sleigh had been pulled forward. They dropped their load on the front seat and dusted their hands. There was a conspiratorial look in Granville's eyes as he looked at Mahala.

"Don't say a word," Tess warned as she gazed at her older brother.

John laughed softly. "The kids have waited all week for today. Are you ready?"

"Yes, I am." Mahala smiled. "I have to admit I've waited all week too." She stood with Mar Jane leaning against her.

"We painted the sleigh, Molly, just for today." Mary Jane said with a grin.

"I see that," Mahala told her. "It looks very festive. Just perfect for our day in the snow."

John eyed the two older children. "Get the rest of the things while I hitch Star and Brownie to the sleigh."

With importance to their steps, Tess and Granville eyed each other and went back to the house.

What in the world is this family scheming? Mahala giggled in her mind. Whatever they had planned, it was a family affair. Clamping her hands together, she watched—and waited.

"Jesse and Margaret are going to stay here and look after Jeffrey and Wiley." John broke into her thoughts. "They're a bit young for a full day's outing in the cold." His eyes twinkled as he hitched the horses to the sleigh.

To Mahala's surprise, both horses wore a leather strap with bells on them. The bells jingled when the horses shook their heads.

Before long, Tess and Granville returned, and Granville held a thick bundle in his arms. Tess carried a basket in hers, with their Aunt Margaret following behind them.

Did she see a secret look in Margaret's eyes as well? Mahala held her breath.

The back door slammed once more, and Jesse and Franklin strode out to the party. Franklin carried a blanket in his hands that looked as if it covered a bulky object. The air, brisk and chill, made his offering send a plume of steam rising from the woolen bundle.

"Will you be joining us?" Mahala gazed at Franklin as he held the bundle.

"I'm staying behind. I haven't seen my brother Jesse in a while."

"Well, I hope you have a good visit with him." Mahala touched his arm lightly.

"All right," John said, gazing at the family. "Climb into the back seat." He pulled the pile of blankets aside, and after the four children squeezed into the red sleigh, he tucked the blankets over their laps.

Jesse stepped up and handed John the hot bricks hidden beneath the woolen blanket Franklin held. John placed a brick at the foot of each child and then tucked the blanket under their feet. "That ought to keep you warm for a while."

"Miss Shields." John held out a hand by the front seat.

Mahala came around, and before she could step onto the steel runner, John took her elbow and guided her up. Heat flushed her cheeks as she allowed him to assist her.

"Thank you, Mr. Grigsby." She felt completely undone with his warm breath so close. It was all she could do to remain calm and collected.

"Here you go." John laid a brick at her feet and tucked the blanket around them. Their eyes met and held for the breath of a second, and an electric current ran through her body. She wished he didn't have to step away, but of course if he didn't, they'd never go on their sleigh ride. Mahala released the breath she'd been holding when he moved away and went around to the other side.

"There's a good lunch in the basket," Margaret said. "Enough for all of you. And—" Margaret grinned to the children in the back seat. "I made molasses cookies for dessert."

"And there's the—"

"Mary Jane!" A chorus of yells filled the barn.

"Sorry." The little girl hunched down as if she had wilted.

Mahala looked back to see a pucker on the little Mary Jane's lips. Mary lowered her eyelids and studied her gloved hands. When she looked up again, Mahala winked at her.

Mary Jane responded by sitting straight, but her lips thinned— as though, if she didn't keep them tightly held together,—she'd give their secret away.

John shook the reins, and the horses pulled the sleigh out of the barn. The back door of the house slammed one more time as Jesse carried out one more blanketed bundle. He set it in the back seat on the floor between Mary Jane and Calvin, who sat in the middle. Mary Jane's eyes lit up but she kept her lips buttoned tight. Only her cornflower-blue eyes spoke volumes.

A giddy excitement ran through Mahala's veins as the horses finally pranced out of the yard.

"Goodbye!" the children called to their Uncle Jesse and Aunt Margaret and Franklin.

The three waved back, and they soon faded into the background with the house and the barn.

The sleigh bells rang as the horses dashed down the lane, and the cold air brushed against everyone's faces. And all the while, Mahala was fully aware of how close she and John sat in the cutter. As they flew down the road, she wished this day would never end.

The children giggled and then quieted in anticipation for the day that lay ahead. Mahala watched the prancing horses as their breaths made a white cloud about their heads. The only sounds were the clomping of the horses' hooves on the hard snow and the rasp of the sled's runners.

Ahead, the bridge loomed up. As they went through the tunnel, the hoof beats echoed against the wooden walls and the bells jangled louder.

"Whee!" Mary Jane cried out and the family laughed.

When they came out the other side, Mahala glanced down the banks to the frozen creek. Several deer stood on the snowy slope, their ears pricked as they looked at the cutter.

The road led to their little town of Grovespring, but it would be another three miles before they reached the edge of town. Would John veer the horses off the road for a ride through the forest, or would they continue through town where the pedestrians were sure to be out and about on this glorious, sunshiny day?

On they went, the children chattering and laughing in the back and the bells jingling in the front. Mahala's chest felt tight with joy as they continued on. Every so often she and John shared a glance. Neither said a word as they took in the sounds of the ride. John's cheeks were ruddy with the chill wind and his blue eyes shone brightly.

Grovespring came into view, the sharp blades of the sleigh cutting a path along the snow-covered road as the team of horses trotted on.

"Whoa!" John called out to slow the team as they entered Main Street. Pedestrians looked to see the Grigsby sleigh, newly painted barn-red and filled with his family. A second glance displayed a look of disbelief as women gazed at the cutter and then at each other. Hands flew to their mouths and their jaws dropped.

Mahala stilled herself but her gloved hands formed fists in her lap.

"Hello!" Clem Owens called as they passed the mercantile. He held a shovel in his hands and turned back to shoveling snow off the boardwalk.

It's good to see people out, taking advantage of the bright and clear day, thought Mahala.

Charles Matthews' cutter neared as he drove the opposite side of the street. His hand went up and his dimples deepened in his ruddy cheeks. Both sleighs slowed and then stopped in the middle of the road, right in front of the Yates Hotel and Café.

Mahala stared straight ahead.

"Where you headed?" Charles asked.

"There's a nice clearing past Judd Benson's ranch. We'll eat a picnic lunch there." The timbre of John's voice carried deep and vibrant across the road.

Mahala looked over her shoulder just in time to see Gertie Yates standing on the boardwalk, broom in one hand and a fist on her hip. She appeared none too happy to see Mahala sitting in John Grigsby's sleigh.

Goodness, mercy, sakes alive! Mahala held the woman's stormy gaze. She'd not flinch if her life depended on it! And where was Bella? Mahala gazed up at the second-story of the building, just in time to see a movement behind a curtained window. Was Bella hiding behind those fluttering lace curtains?

"We best get going or the day will be gone." John flicked the reins and the sleigh-bells rang. As they rode out of town, they waved at people on the streets. Soon the sleigh went down the low grade of the road and before Mahala knew it, they came to the clearing in the woods.

"Whoa!" John called to the two horses, and the sleigh came to a stop.

Granville jumped out of the cutter and began pulling chunks of wood out of the box behind the sleigh.

The girls waited in the sleigh while John and the boys shoveled a hole in the snow, creating a space for a campfire and stacking the wood in the center. Soon a fire blazed, sending plumes of smoke into the sky and wonderful heat before them.

Tess dug old cushions out of the sleigh box and placed them around the campfire.

"I'll get the picnic basket." Mahala trudged through the snow and pulled out the straw basket.

"Can I tell her now?" Mary Jane pleaded.

"All right, kitten." John's eyes lit up.

"We made hot chocolate! Aunt Margaret makes the best chocolate ever!"

Mahala threw her hands to her chest. "I absolutely love hot chocolate!" She nearly cried at the effort the family had put into their fun-filled afternoon.

Tears rimmed her eyes, but she giggled with joy.

"Don't cry, Molly." Mary Jane stood on tiptoes and touched Mahala's cheek.

"They're happy tears, little one." She looked at John, who gazed at them with what?— contentment?

"Let's get the chocolate out before it gets cold." John's deep voice boomed in the clearing, and he threw his head back and laughed.

Mahala was amazed at the shear brightness of his features. This was a side of John she'd never seen. She hoped to see it more often.

Tess set tin cups on the ground and filled each one with the steaming brew. "Here you go." She handed Mahala the first cup in her mittened hands.

Mahala took a sip, aware that the family watched her. "Umm! This *is* good."

"Mine next!" Mary Jane sidled up to Tess and waited for her cup to be filled. She sat next to Mahala sipped on the hot chocolate, carefully blowing in the cup now and again before taking the next sip.

John didn't sit. He gazed over the clearing and beyond and then back to his family and Mahala. She felt his gaze on her, warm and welcoming. She wanted to look at him as long as she wanted, but with the children there, she didn't.

They soon opened the picnic basket and the food was passed around. They all ate with contentment, the outdoors seeming to make the meal taste better. And they whiled away the afternoon with stories by the fire.

At the end of one story, Granville drained his cup then jumped up and ran to the edge of the trees. Calvin followed and the boys began to explore the surroundings.

After running and kicking up snow for several minutes, Calvin grabbed Mary Jane's coat sleeve. "Let's make snow angels."

Mary Jane squealed in delight as he pushed her into the snow.

Calvin stretched his arms out wide and fell backward into the soft snow beside his sister. The two of them lay on their backs, waving their arms and legs, scraping the snow and making angels. When they were certain they'd made good imprints, they jumped up and checked their handiwork.

"Look, Mahala! We made snow angels!" Mary Jane pointed to the ground.

Mahala examined the imprints and hugged the two children to her. "I remember doing that when I was a child."

"You used to be a child?" Mary Jane looked at her incredulously.

"Of course, silly!" Calvin shoved her and ran off to join Granville near the trees.

"He's mean," Mary Jane said, her brows forming an angry V.

"Don't let him get to you. He's just acting like a boy. They do things like that. I have brothers too. I remember they always gave me a hard time. But I'll let you in on a little secret."

Mary Jane tilted her chin up, seeming eager to hear what Mahala had to say.

"When your brother acts that way to you, it's because he loves you. I know it doesn't seem like it, but it's true."

"Hmm. Then he must love me a lot, 'cause he's *mean* all the time." Mary Jane looked back toward the trees.

Mahala followed her gaze. Suddenly a snowball struck John squarely in the back. His attention shifted to Granville, who wore a proud expression.

"Why you—" John grinned wickedly and began packing snow into a hard ball.

"Oh, no!" Granville ran for the trees, but that didn't deter John. He threw the snowball with full force. It hit Granville's shoulder and he fell and rolled in the snow, laughing. He didn't stay down long. He packed another ball in his gloved hands and threw another snowball, barely missing his father's head. He howled and kicked the snow.

"Get him, Daddy!" Mary Jane clapped her hands.

John scraped more snow together and packed it hard. He threw it through the air.

Granville spun around and tried his best to outrun the snowball attack, but it struck him between his shoulder blades. Quickly, John shaped another. Calvin and Tess watched on the sidelines with Mahala.

Mahala laughed until her sides ached, but before she knew what was happening, she found herself in the middle of the snowball fight. She tried—unsuccessfully—to shield herself from the flying white balls. In an act of self-defense, she dug her gloved hands into the soft snow and tossed a few snowballs of her own. She had a good arm and her aim was on target.

Granville looked up, surprised at her good aim.

John scooped up another handful of snow, and with a glint in his eyes, he tilted his head toward Mahala.

Granville caught on to his father's plan, and he, too, scraped together a handful of the snow.

Mahala's mouth flew open. "You wouldn't!" Seeing there were two against one, Mahala began to run.

"Run, Mahala, run!" Tess shouted, scooping up her own ball of snow.

Mahala ran a few steps before she was pelted from behind. She stumbled and fell face-down in the snow. Startled, she began to rise, but before she could get to her knees, she felt John's hands beneath her elbows.

"Sorry. We didn't mean to knock you down." She saw a faint glint of amusement in his blue eyes.

"No worry, it was all in good fun." To avoid his gaze, she brushed the snow off the front of her heavy coat. When she finished, she looked to see that John hadn't moved. Despite the cold, her cheeks burned. She was only inches from his warm breath. Her heart raced, laughter forgotten.—She responded in a way she truly felt she had no business doing—but she couldn't stop.

Their eyes met. It was as if they were all alone. He took a step closer and thumbed snow from her warm cheeks. "You're beautiful," John said in a low, husky voice, so low she barely heard him. As an afterthought, he pressed the cleft in her chin with his forefinger, ever so gently, and winked.

"Th-thank you." She couldn't breathe. She needed to move away and take a breath lest she make a complete fool of herself. How did a woman respond to a man who'd taken—no, stolen—her heart in so short of time? She stayed put, however, her boots planted in the snow.

John's smile softened. He picked flecks of snow from her hair, letting his hand linger near her temple. She sucked in a breath— if she didn't step away now . . . Time stood excruciatingly still. *Move away, Mahala.*

"Are you all right?" John lifted her chin with a crooked finger, his deep voice cutting into her thoughts.

"Quite," she lied and stepped away, giving him a shaky smile.

"Good." He held her gaze. "We can resume this another time. For now, I think we've put in a fine afternoon in the snow. Shall we gather the picnic supplies and head home?"

Home? What she'd give to go back to the Grigsby house with the family and stay there. "That's a splendid idea." She looked up at the sky, and with mute disappointment she saw dark clouds gathering above.

John saw the ominous clouds too. He stepped away and called to the children, "Let's gather everything up. It's time to head back to the house." He strode to untie the horses from the trees.

It wasn't long before the picnic basket and cushions were stored in the back of the sleigh, and they were all seated once again. The children grew silent, as the afternoon had worn them out.

John tucked the blankets around each one, and then he retrieved the hot bricks sitting by the campfire. One by one, he placed them near the children's feet.

He handed Mahala into the front seat and laid the blanket on her lap. She tucked it around her, aware that he hadn't moved. She moved her feet, and he placed a hot brick on the floorboard. His shoulder brushed against her lap and she held her breath. Had she seen a glint in his eyes as he bent over her?

He moved away and went to the fire-pit, where he shoveled snow over the flames. Smoke spiraled toward the sky. After stowing the shovel in the box behind the cutter, he climbed in next to her. "Let's go home."

The horses tossed their heads as they merrily pranced back through the woods and to the main road that led to town. The bells on their leather straps jingled in the silence, and white steam puffed from their noses. Evening was coming on; it would be dark by the time they arrived home.

There wasn't a peep from the back seat. Mahala wondered if the children had fallen asleep, but she was too tired to look. The day had been wonderful, but it had taken a toll on all of them. She noticed that John seemed to be a million miles away as he drove the team toward Grovespring. What was going through his mind? Did he regret taking her on this outing, or would this be the beginning of a relationship?

When they arrived at the house, John saddled her horse and helped her into the saddle. She gazed down at him. "I had a wonderful time, Mr. Grigsby."

He held her eyes for a long moment. "Thank you for coming with us today. It's done a world of good for the children—and me."

"You're welcome, Mr. Grigsby."

" Call me, John, please. I think it's time to put for formalities aside. Wouldn't you agree?"

"All right." She felt her cheeks grow warm. "I best go. It'll be nightfall soon."

"Would you like me to see you home?"

"Yes. But no." She laughed softly. "Go into the house with your family. I'll be fine."

"Then I'll see you tomorrow night for supper?"

"I'm sorry, but I can't. I have work to catch up on." Seeing disappointment in his gaze, she wanted to lean down and push back his black hat back and touch his bearded face. She wanted to have the right to touch him—but she held back.

"I'm sorry to hear that. We'll miss you."

"I'll try to come the first of the week."

"Until then." John touched the brim of his hat and stepped away.

Mahala nudged Bessy's flanks and cantered out of the drive. A faint moon rose on the horizon and the wind picked up. Pulling her coat tighter around her, she leaned forward and called to her horse, "Let's go home, Bessy." As Mahala and Bessy sailed down the road, Mahala's mind ran back over the day. John had requested that she call him by his given name. Did that mean anything? She'd never been courted by a man before. She gazed at the dark sky. *Dear Lord, is John Grigsby what you have in store for me? Or should I wait for Mr. Bates?*

THREE DAYS LATER, MAHALA stood on the Grigsbys' porch with a pot of chili beans. She wouldn't stay tonight. After the wonderful weekend she'd had with the family, she wanted to give it a few days before she spent time with the family again. More importantly, she didn't want to wear out her welcome. Holding the warm pot of beans against her waist, she rapped on the front door, wishing for all the world that she could just walk in with familiarity—but she couldn't.

Tess opened the door. "Good evening, Mahala. Will you come in?"

"No, honey. I just want to drop off your supper. I've a ton of sewing to catch up on tonight."

"Oh."

Mahala took a second look at the young girl. "Is something troubling you, Tess?"

"Uh, no."

Mahala stared at Tess. She wasn't convinced the girl was okay. It appeared the twelve-year-old was struggling with something but didn't want to say.

"Theresa Evangeline," Mahala said in a slow, stern voice.

"Yes, ma'am?"

"You're holding out on me. What's wrong?"

Tears rimmed Tess's eyes.

"Oh, Tess." Mahala set the pot of beans on the porch table and tilted Tess's chin up. "Please tell me what's bothering you." Her brows rose as if waiting for an answer.

"The Sweetheart Dance is coming soon and I haven't a new dress to wear."

Mahala watched Tess swallow hard.

"Oh, darling. Is that what's troubling you?"

"Mama would have seen to it that I had a new dress for the party. Father—" She looked over her shoulder. "He doesn't think of things like that."

It was all Mahala could do to keep her secret to herself. She'd been working on dresses for Tess and Mary Jane and was nearly done. She'd bring both dresses to the house in another day or two.

"You mustn't fuss about a dress. Surely something can be done before the party."

"All right." Tess stepped outside the door and picked up the pot of chili. Before she turned back to the house, Mahala stopped her.

"I mean it, Tess. Don't dwell on the dress." She kissed the girl's forehead. "Enjoy your supper."

"Yes, ma'am." Tess went into the house and closed the door with her hip.

Mahala pulled her wrap close and climbed into the buggy. She stared at the lights in the house. Lamplight filtered out onto the ground, giving the Grigsby home a cozy look. She shook the reins. "Home, Bessy."

When Mahala reached the house, she climbed the stairs to her bedroom. Two parcels lay on a chair by the window. She pulled back brown paper back on one of them and examined the cranberry taffeta dress. Small, white, embroidered dots were woven throughout across the fabric. She held the garment to the lamplight and inspected the seams one more time. She couldn't have been more pleased with how the dress turned out. With Tess's honey-gold hair, she was certain the young girl would look adorable in the cranberry color.

"Won't Tess be surprised," she murmured quietly. She pulled a lacy sleeve out straight and danced around the room. Would the weather hold long enough so that Tess could wear the dress for the dance?

Chapter TWENTY-SEVEN

TWO DAYS LATER, AS the sun sank below the horizon, Mahala rode to the Grigsbys' house on the way home from work. She hugged two parcels wrapped in brown paper as she climbed the porch steps. Just inside the window, the multi-colored Tiffany lamp had been lit. With the heavy drapes pulled back enough that she could peer into the living room, Mahala saw the room was aglow in cozy comfort. Farther in, firelight danced in the fireplace. Granville lay on the floor, reading a book, with Rusty curled beside him. Mary Jane sat in a chair, playing with a doll, and Calvin sat on the edge of a footstool, whittling—a small piece of wood, the chips falling into a bucket at his feet.

To the right side of the front door was the kitchen. Mahala spotted Tess through the kitchen window. She rapped on the window pane, and Tess looked up to see Mahala standing there. She raised a hand and disappeared from sight. A moment later, she opened the front door.

"Mahala, come in," she smiled brightly, her eyes fixed on the packages in Mahala's hands. "What have you got there?"

"Let's go to the dining room table and I'll show you."

"Shall I take your coat?"

"No, honey. I'm not staying. I just wanted to drop these off." Mahala peered around the corner of the entrance into the living room. "Mary Jane—"

Mary Jane's head popped up. "Molly!"

"Come with me and Tess. I have something to show you."

Mary Jane slipped out of the chair and followed Mahala and Tess down the hallway and through a wide entrance that led into the dining room. When they reached the table, Mahala handed the top parcel to Mary Jane and the second parcel to Tess. Mahala clasped her hands before her, eager to see their responses. "Open them." She hoped the girls would be happy with the surprises she'd made.

Both girls carefully pulled back the brown paper, curiosity in their eyes. Mary Jane lifted her dress out first. Her eyes sparkled as she stared at the green velvet. She quickly held it up to her chin. "Ooh, Molly," was all she could say.

Tess gently flared the cranberry gown out before her and let it settle against her front. "You made me a dress for the Sweetheart Dance!" she squealed. She twirled around the room, holding the gown under her chin and smiling brightly. "It's beautiful!"

The back door slammed, and heavy boots sounded on the wooden floor of the back hallway. John stepped into the dining room and pulled off his hat. "What do we have here?"

"Molly made me a dress," Mary Jane burst out. "Isn't it beautiful, Papa?" Mary Jane twirled around with her dress, just like she'd seen her sister do.

Tess hugged Mahala. "Thank you so much. I was sure I'd be the only girl without a new dress."

Mary Jane leaned in against Mahala's side. "This is the prettiest dress I've ever owned."

Mahala looked over both of the girl's heads at John.

He beamed at her and mouthed, "Thank you." Then he verbally asked, "Will you be staying for supper?"

"No. I'm on my way home. I just wanted to drop the dresses off on my way." She kissed the top of the girls' heads and stepped out of their embrace. "Now take your gowns upstairs and hang them up right away. You don't want them to get soiled before the dance."

Tess draped her dress over her arm and reached for Mary Jane's. "Give me your dress. I'll hang them both up." Mary Jane reluctantly handed her dress over.

"Are you about caught up with the gowns for the dance?" John asked.

"I wish I could say I am, but truth is, I'm not." Mahala gazed at John's strong jaw a long moment and wanted nothing more than to reach out and touch him. She felt her gaze drawn to meet his blue eyes. She swallowed. "I best hurry on."

"I'll walk you to the door." John followed close behind her.

Mahala was aware of his nearness and tried to still the radical thumping of her heart.

When they reached the door, he opened it and stepped out onto the porch in the chill air. "Will you come by in the next day or two?"

"It all depends on when I get the dresses done. I'm on a countdown these last few days before the party. I do most of my work at the shop, but much of the time I take it home and sew into the night."

"It'll be good when the dance is over. You push yourself too hard."

"Maybe so, but I enjoy what I do. And I've nothing else to keep me busy."

John's eyes held hers, and he looked as if he wanted to pull her into his arms. A gust of cold wind blew onto the porch and she quickly hugged herself. "I best get going."

John walked her to the buggy. "Good evening, Miss Shields."

A smile stole across her face. "Miss Shields? I do believe I've asked you to call me, Mahala."

He lowered his head. When he looked up, white teeth showed in his wide grin. "You got me there. Good evening, Mahala."

She smiled. "Good evening . . . John." She flicked the reins and Bessy started out the drive. Before she got halfway to the road, Bella Yates turned into the drive in a handsome black buggy. Stunned, Mahala's hand automatically went up to wave at the blonde.

Bella wore a thick fur coat and a fur hat, her blonde curls trailing over her shoulders. She stared at Mahala with fire in her eyes. She didn't wave back but continued toward the house.

Mahala glanced back to see Bella pull the buggy up in front of the porch. "What is *she* doing here?" she groaned. Bessy pranced out of the drive and onto Shady Hollow Road. Mahala turned her head toward the house and saw Bella climb the steps and walk toward John.

He didn't move until she neared him but, instead turned his head toward the road and Mahala. She was too far to read what was in his eyes. Furious, she flicked the reins again. Had John known Bella was coming?

THREE DAYS LATER, Boots jumped onto the foot of the bed, waking Mahala from a deep sleep. It was early in the morning and a chill draft filled the room. Mahala pulled the covers tighter under her chin and rolled onto her side.

"Oh no!" came a moan from her sisters' bedroom on the other side of the wall. Mahala forced one eye open and then the second on as she gazed toward the lace-curtained window. She could see a light gray haze outside. Good, it wasn't time to get up. She gazed at the wall wondering what had brought on the distressed cries beyond it. Would she hear anything again?

"Meow." Boots trampled the bedcovers and joined Mahala at the head of the bed.

"Good morning, Boots." Mahala ran a hand down the cat's black-and-white fur. "What is all the noise about?"

Boots stretched and her back arched high. She jumped off the bed and padded to the table by the window. She leaped up to sit on the windowsill and look out at the pale white world beyond.

Mary Ann and Rebecca burst into her room. "Mahala, are you awake?" Mary Ann asked.

"Yes, I'm awake. What's going on?"

Rebecca pointed. "Look out the window."

Mahala moved out from beneath the warm covers and padded across the floor. She shoved the lace curtains aside to see a sheet of white snow pelting the house and the world below. That's when she heard it—the haunting howl of the wind whistling hard against the house. Her heart hit the floor and she, too, groaned, "Oh no! Today's the Sweetheart Dance!"

With Rebecca on one side and Mary Ann on the other, the three of them gazed out at the wretched blizzard with despair.

Mary Ann laid her head on Mahala's shoulder. "After all the work you've gone through to prepare for this dance. And now, not a soul will be able to show off their new dresses."

"Well, look on the bright side," Mahala said. "Most of the women will already be ready for the Harvest Dance this year. This may be the first time in a long while that I will not be working my fingers to the bone into the wee hours of the morning, trying to get the dresses done."

She moved away from the window and listened to the howling wind. "Poor Tess. She's going to be sorely disappointed as well. I just took the girls' dresses over to their house the other day. They couldn't wait to parade them at the party. And now look, Mother Nature has given us the biggest surprise of all."

A rustle at the bedroom door alerted Mahala that someone else was up.

Mary popped her head in and asked, "Are you all up?"

"Yes, Mother," the three of them chorused.

"A snow storm has rolled in and spoiled the Sweetheart Dance," Rebecca moaned. "It looks like we'll all be staying home tonight."

Mahala glanced back at the white world outside her window. "Maybe we'll get a break in the weather in the next few days. I'm sure the community won't mind making up for today."

"Maybe," Mary Ann said, heading out of the bedroom. Rebecca was on her heels.

"Well, since you're all up, come downstairs and help with breakfast. Your father and Benny will be plenty hungry when they get back from the barn."

"Did Dad string a rope from the barn to the house?" Mahala went to the window one more time. "We sure don't need him or Benny getting lost in the blizzard."

"Yes. He strung the rope last night. He had a feeling something was in the air."

"Good. I'll be along in a moment." Mahala waited for her mother and sisters to vacate the room and when Mary shut the door, Mahala went to her washstand. She picked up the pitcher of water and began to pour. When she ran her hand in the water she jumped back. "Land sakes! This water is freezing cold." Taking a deep breath, she cupped her hands in the water and splashed it onto her face. She quickly toweled-dried and shook her head.

"Well, if I wasn't awake before, I am now." She went to the window and stared out at the white world one more time. She wouldn't be going to the Grigsby home anytime soon.

Her mind retreated to the night she had seen Bella Yates climbing the porch steps to the Grigbys' house. She remembered wanting to turn her buggy around and go right there. But she didn't—she didn't have a hold on John. It wasn't her place to interfere. She'd been forced to swallow her pride and ride all the way home with her heart in her throat. She dreaded what she would learn the next time she saw him. *I need to know where we stand.* If John had plans for her . . . to love her, he'd best say so. And what of Bella? Did he let her stay, or did he send her packing back to town?

ISABELLA YATES PACED THE hotel room, smoldering with indignation. Her aunt Gertie looked on as she retraced her steps a dozen times from the tall windows that looked down onto the streets of Grovespring and back to the door that led down the hall.

After John Grigsby had sternly yet politely sent her back to town a few days back, she had chosen to stay at the Yates Hotel rather than her aunt's grand estate a mile away. She wanted to be closer to town, where it bustled with people, rather than sit at her aunt's estate, broiling all alone while her aunt worked. "With so much activity going on between John and Mahala, I think it's best I stay at the hotel," she told her aunt. And besides, she'd put herself to work in the café to keep her mind and body busy.

She swept her blonde waves over her shoulder. "I've got to find a way to get John's attention. I should make myself more available. Isn't that what Mahala has done?"

Isabella turned to Gertie again. "How is it that John has taken a liking to Mahala Shields?" Fire burned in her veins. She'd been jilted once; she didn't intend to let it happen a second time. "Mahala Shields has been town spinster for more years than I can count," she spat.

A slow grin spread across Gertie's face. "Well, honey, don't forget you haven't married either, and yet, you're an attractive woman in your prime."

"Don't pull that one on me, Auntie! I *chose* not to marry. I wanted to experience the adventures of the world while I was still in my youth. It's only been recently that I have grown tired of traveling. I truly think I'm ready to settle down." She gave Gertie a searing glance. "Who could have guessed Mahala would stand in my way?"

"There must be available men of credibility in New York, dear."

"Of course. There are plenty." Isabella's hands waved in the air. "But most of them are full of themselves, or they make a fool of themselves when I enter the room." She stopped pacing the floor as she glanced down at the white snow pelting the buildings below.

"I would have caught the last stage out of this god-forsaken town before this storm if it hadn't been for the fact that I thought I should pursue John Grigsby one more time. That's why I drove out to visit him." She sniffled and touched her nose with a hanky and turned her back from Gertie.

"He just isn't thinking right these days," Gertie said, wringing her hands, her brows so low she resembled a rude crow.

"Well, he certainly didn't welcome me in the least the other night—far from it. It was all he could do to keep from watching Mahala's buggy as she headed for home. At one point, I thought he was about to shove me aside and run after her." Isabella blew her nose and dabbed at her red-rimmed eyes.

"Come here, young lady." Gertie opened her arms and Isabella stepped into them.

After she'd cried herself out, she stepped back. "As soon as this wretched blizzard ends, I'm taking the next stage back to New York."

"Maybe it's for the best. You know you're always welcome to come back in the spring when the weather is more amiable." Gertie went to the bed and pulled the rumpled covers straight.

"I've got patrons who need my attention. Come down when you're ready. The cook has made a batch of chicken and dumplings. Food in your stomach should make you feel better." Gertie left the room, leaving Isabella to herself.

Isabella gazed out at the swirling snow. Not a thing could be seen for as far as she could see. Every so often the wind slowed, and she could see snow on the rooftops of buildings across the street. She felt like a caged animal having been in this room for the last two days.

"Who would want to live in this miserable town?" she moaned. "It's a good thing you didn't ask me to marry you, John Grigsby. I wouldn't want to get stuck in this despicable place."

Having voiced her decision to leave, she wondered how many days it would be before she could board the stagecoach? And when she did, was there a smidgeon of a chance that John Grigsby would miss her?

JOHN SQUINTED AS HE gazed over his land. His four cowhands held the reins of their horses as their mounts trudged through the snow. A record-breaking storm had dumped four feet of snow in parts of the county, making it difficult to ride through the pastures. Reports traveled from one ranch to the next that ranchers were dealing with heavy losses. In some cases up to half their herds had died during the four-day blizzard. John discovered a half dozen of his own calves lay dead, half buried in the snow in the east field.

"It's bad," John called out to his men. "If we don't find all the livestock, it could be catastrophic."

"It's the worst snowstorm I've seen in my lifetime," Luke said.

"Mine too." John shoved his hat back and raised a hand to shade his eyes. He gazed first at young Luke, who couldn't be more than twenty-two, a strong, dark-haired young man worth his weight in gold, and at Brady, tall and slim with a shock of bright blond hair sticking out at his ears from beneath his worn cowboy hat. John thought Brady to be in his mid-to late twenties. The two men were good cowpokes. They didn't grumble and did their jobs.

He also couldn't complain about McDuff and Will, both married with families of their own. They did a good day's work before they headed home to Grovespring each night. At the height of the branding season, John hired more men to help out at the ranch, but the four men were steady help.

The men had split up, with Will and McDuff heading to the northern section of the ranch to look for cattle while Luke and Brady stayed with John.

The bright snow nearly blinded them as they rode. In some places the snow had formed hard-crusted mounds, the top layer of snow frozen thick. In those areas it carried the weight of the men and beasts. But much of their progress was unpredictable. Blue clomped clumsily through the drifts that rippled in waves from the previous days' blizzard.

Most of the herd were bunched together in a dark mass in the middle of the field, trying to withstand the wind, but it wasn't unusual to find a stray cow stranded in a frozen snowdrift. Sometimes, a cow fell through a mound of soft snow and would be trapped in a hole until it could be rescued. If no one came, the animal would freeze to death.

John, Luke, and Brady spread out and walked their horses from west to east at a slow pace. The men strained their eyes for the slightest crack in the icy snow.

"I've got one!" Luke called out. "Over here!"

John and Brady kneed their horses and joined Luke, who sat next to a thin break in the snow. A cow's nose stuck out through the frozen crevice that imprisoned its body. When the men rode up, the animal gave a mournful cry.

John reached behind him and pulled out a shovel he'd strapped to his saddle. He dismounted and tromped through the snow.

Luke and Brady pulled out their shovels as well and began digging out the animal from the opposite end.

John chipped away at the ice crust near the cow's nose, careful not to injure the animal. Once he broke the ice loose, the snow beneath was softer. The three men filled their shovels with mounds of snow and flung them over their shoulders. The only sound was the whistling wind and the scraping of shovels. When the cow's body was visible, Luke ran for a rope and flung it around the trapped animal's neck.

"Come on, now. You gotta help us get you outta there!" Luke tugged on the rope while John and Brady kept their shovels digging into the crusty snow and flinging it away.

"Moooo!" came a wild cry from the animal.

"We got you!" Brady cried out, pushing his shovel into the snow near the animal's rump. "But you gotta help us."

Luke dug his heels into the snow, pulling on the cow's neck as the men continued sinking their blades into the snow and hefting chunks of it over their shoulders.

"Moooo!" the cow bellowed again.

"I think we got 'im!" Brady slid in behind the cow and pushed on its hind end with his shoulder. Luke pulled and Brady pushed. "Come on, you lousy cow!" Luke hollered.

John joined Luke in pulling on the taut rope. Between the two men they tugged and pulled until at last one hoof lifted out of the hole and the cow pushed forward, nearly smothering Brady,—who'd fallen behind him. In one big huff, the two men pulled the cow free. Brady quickly crawled out of the hole and stumbled before he joined the men, who were already rubbing the steer's legs down to regain circulation.

"Moooo!"

"I don't blame you, fella!" John said, rubbing the steer's side with a large coarse rag. After the red-and-white Durham staggered a few feet, he regained his footing and broke away from the men. He ran toward the herd congregating some hundred feet away.

"Whew!" Luke beat his hat against his pant leg. "How many have we freed today?"

"That makes seven," Brady said.

John watched him brush snow off his jeans before he mounted his horse. "The day's early. We best keep going. There could be more."

John felt sick to his stomach as the day progressed. More times than he wanted to count, they harnessed frozen dead cows and dragged them over the slick-iced snow drifts to the fence line. The pile of frozen cattle grew as the day continued. "We won't know until the end of the day how many we've lost."

Will and McDuff rode up. "Your cattle have been through hell this winter," Will said. "I don't remember a winter when you've been hit so hard and with such big losses."

At mid-afternoon, John paused to gaze out over the range. He judged that most of his herd were gathered in a rough circle, pushing in to each other to stay warm. Cattle could withstand tremendous cold, but this weather tried their spirits.

"Come on, boys. Let's load the wagons with hay. We need to feed these starving beasts."

The men turned their horses around and headed back to the ranch yard. John and the cowhands didn't talk. They were too beat to do more than stay in their saddles and get back to the ranch. When they reached the barn, John's legs felt like wood. It was all he could do to climb off his horse.

"We'll take it from here, boss," Luke said as he slid off his mount.

"All right. I'll tend to the stock in the barn." John watched as the four men put their horses in the corral. They would head to the barn, where the hay was stacked high in the hayloft. For the next hour, the men forked hay onto wagons from which they had removed the wheels and replaced them with runners to more easily traverse the pastures.

Finally, the first load of the day was ready to go out to feed the hungry herd. It would take several trips to deliver enough hay to feed 300-plus cattle. Off to the south side of the field lay the dead cattle they had dragged to the fence-line. When the weather permitted, they would skin and butcher them. There would be enough meat to last until summer, but John would have rather sold the stock to keep the ranch running above the red in his account books.

Ears cold, John pulled off his hat and grabbed a knitted cap off the wall hook and pulled it down over his ears. He no sooner pulled up a stool to milk Bossie than he heard the boys come into the barn.

"You're back," Granville said, picking up a pitchfork and heading for a stall.

"Yeah, I'm back."

"Find anymore dead cattle?"

"At least a dozen."

"Can we ride out and see 'em?" Calvin asked.

"Not today. Maybe tomorrow. Right now I want to get the stock fed and get into the house." He groaned. "My legs feel like tree trunks."

"Go on, John. We got this," Franklin said.

"No. I'll see this through, and we can go into the house together."

Calvin stared at him with humor in his eyes.

"What're you lookin' at?" John pulled on the first teat.

"Your eyebrows and mustache are all white. You look like an old man." Calvin stumbled backward in a fit of giggles.

"I feel like an old man right about now." John swallowed a laugh. "Let's get to work, boys."

Within the hour the cows were milked and the stock cared for. John flung his arms around his sons' shoulders, and the four of them headed for the comfort of the warm house. He wanted to spend the evening relaxing with his children, but his work wasn't done. After supper he'd go to the study and log today's losses. He'd lost too many cattle this winter. Would tomorrow be a better day? Better yet, would Mahala come by the house? He hadn't seen her since the day Isabella Yates darkened his door. Surely, Mahala knew he only had eyes for her. *You do know that, Mahala . . . don't you?*

TWO WEEKS LATER, ISABELLA Yates stood outside the Wells Fargo stagecoach, waiting for Bart to finish stowing her luggage on top of and behind the coach. While Bart worked, Isabella searched the street in hopes that John Grigsby would ride into town to make his usual milk deliveries.

"That just about does it," Bart said as he cinched the last bag behind the coach. He dusted his hands and came forward. "Are you 'bout ready for the long ride back to New York City?"

"Not really. It took me about a month after I arrived here before my derriere could be felt again."

Bart took a step back at her remark. He covered a smile by looking away, but then his eyes shot past her as if to see if anyone had heard her bold statement.

A gust of chill wind whooshed past them, ruffling the feathers on her large round hat.

"You best get seated, Miss Yates. This wind could knock you off your feet."

Clamping a hand on top of the rose-and-feathered hat that was more suited for the streets of New York City, Isabella refrained from stepping into the dark coach in hopes of seeing John ride up.

Just then Gertie flew out of the hotel, her wool coat buttoned tightly. She waved her hand as if to stop Isabella from getting into the coach. "Weren't you going to say goodbye?" She frowned.

Isabella stepped forward and gave her aunt a peck on the cheek. "I hate goodbyes, Aunt Gertie."

"You be safe and don't talk to strangers," Gertie ordered, her eyes misty.

"Don't worry about me. As often as I've traveled, I've learned to take care of myself." Isabella slid a derringer out of her furry muff for Gertie's eyes alone, and then pushed it back into hiding.

"That does quell the jitters, honey girl." Gertie winked at her.

Bart interrupted them by clearing his throat. "We best get going. We have a lot of miles to cover today and I want to be at a way station before nightfall."

Isabella stepped to the stagecoach door. "I guess I'm as ready as I'm going to be." She lifted a hand, and Bart assisted her into the coach. He closed the door firmly and climbed to his seat.

"Goodbye, Aunt Gertie." Isabella waved a gloved hand. She leaned back, her nerves in a knot. *Why didn't John at least give me a chance at a romantic relationship with him?* She had always imagined that someday he would be hers. But he only had eyes for one woman. How had Mahala stolen his heart?

"Hyah!" Bart called out as the leather whip snapped above the team of horses. The stagecoach jerked forward. Isabella watched the familiar stores from the window as the horses started down Main Street. They hadn't gone far when she heard Bart shout, "Whoa!" The stagecoach slowed to a halt.

Looking out the window, Isabella saw John Grigsby step down from his wagon and stride over to the coach. She sucked in her breath and waited.

John's gloved hand came to rest on the open sill. "You're leaving?"

Fighting tears, Isabella said, "There's no reason to stay."

John gazed at her for a long moment, his lips clamped together, and then he said, " Be safe on your journey back to New York." He stepped back.

"I will." Isabella's throat constricted. She wanted him to ask her to stay.

"I meant to tell you." John gave her a friendly smile. "You have a lovely voice. You ought to try singing at one of those fancy joints when you arrive home."

Isabella dipped her chin. "Thank you, John. And good luck to you." She turned and knocked on the coach wall. The stage started to roll easily at first, and she leaned out the window and waved. "Goodbye John." Isabella saw John's hand go up, and as the stagecoach rolled out of town, she watched as he became smaller and smaller until he was only a speck in the road.

"Goodbye John—I won't be coming back."

Chapter TWENTY-EIGHT

"HE LOVES ME . . . HE loves not," Mahala breathed softly as she set silverware on the table.

"What are you mumbling about?" Mary carried a plate piled high with pancakes.

"Oh, nothing." Mahala pushed the plate into the center of the table.

"You've been moping all winter. Why won't you share what's bothering you?" Mary went back to the stove.

"I don't know." Mahala stood by the window and stared at the bare limbs of the maple tree outside. The frigid air and the scenery of bareness and cold were reflections of how she felt this morning. "I suppose it's my love life—but that's personal."

"Love life?" Mary stopped stirring the eggs in the cast iron skillet and stared at her. "You have a love life?"

Mahala's ears burned. "I didn't—I mean . . . I don't."

Mary pushed the skillet off the fire and gently nudged Mahala into a chair. "Who is this man that consumes your every waking moment? As if I didn't already have a good guess."

"Mama." Mahala stared at her mother and swallowed. She opened her mouth to speak and then clamped it shut again. Unexpected tears stung her eyes.

"Mahala." Mary sat down opposite her at the table and patted her hands.

Mahala shook her head and quickly wiped her eyes with a table napkin.

"Morning!" Mahala's sisters called in unison as they brushed into the kitchen. "Breakfast ready?"

"Out!" Mary shooed the three girls out of the kitchen. "We're talking.

Don't come back until I call you."

"Mama!" Rebecca groaned.

"Out!" Mary pointed at the kitchen entrance. "Back up the stairs—all of you."

"All right." Rebecca groaned.

Elizabeth and Mary Ann stared at their mother with raised brows and gave Mahala an inquisitive look before they exited the kitchen.

When the sound of Mahala's sisters' feet could be heard in the upper landing, Mary turned back to Mahala. "Out with it." She smiled whimsically. "He loves me, he loves me not?"

"If you heard what I said, then why ask?"

"Because I want you to open up and talk."

Mahala let out a relieved breath. She'd held onto her fears of losing John to Isabella for far too long. In truth, she was finally ready to spill her thoughts to her mother. "If spring were here, I'd pluck petals from a flower like I've seen young girls do. I'd do anything to know my future. But unfortunately, spring is still a few months away."

"Now you're talking in riddles." Mary rested her elbows on the table.

"I've taken an interest in Mr. Grigsby." *There, I've said it.*

"That's no secret." Mary lifted her shoulders.

Mahala's head shot up. "It isn't?"

"Heaven's no, daughter. The way you primp and bake before deliver a meal to the Grigsby house. And half the time you can't wait to jump in the buggy to get over there."

"It's that obvious?"

"Quite. So what's the problem?"

"I've been wrestling over the situation with John and Bella Yates."

"You're on a first name basis with Mr. Grigsby?"

"Um, yes. He asked me to call him by his first name."

"He did, did he?" Mary's brows rose.

Mahala gave a short nod.

"All right. But what of Isabella Yates. Where does she fit in?"

"I believe the only reason she came back to Grovespring is because John is single again. She's made no secret of pursuing him." Mahala swallowed. "And then there's Gertie. She has said as much that I should step away, that Bella has her sights on John."

"Well," Mary sat back indignantly. "They don't have a say about what Mr. Grigsby wants to do."

"I know. But it seems that every time John and I take one step forward, Bella shows up, and then it's two steps back."

"Well," Mary eyed her for a moment. "Do you even know if Isabella is still in Grovespring?"

"No, I don't know. The last I saw of her, she was standing on John's front porch. I don't have any reason to believe she would leave Grovespring any time soon."

"Mahala." Mary gave her a stern look. "Don't you let Isabella stand in your way. You have to fight for what you want."

Mahala chewed her bottom lip. "To be truthful, I've decided to give the possibility of a relationship between John and me a rest."

Mary leaned back heavily against the chair. "Don't you give up. This is the first time you've finally had a chance at marriage. It's quite possible he *is* considering you for his future wife."

"If he is, he'll have to come knocking on my door. I'll not make a fool of myself any longer, and that's final."

MAHALA STAYED AWAY FROM the Grigsby ranch for the rest of the winter. Having tossed aside any chance of having a relationship with John Grigsby, she spent the remaining winter months pondering when she'd get a letter from Mr. Alexander Bates. *How long did it take for a letter to reach Pennsylvania?* And what if Mr. Bates had received a letter from another prospect? Would she ever hear from him? His newspaper ad had said he had three sons, ages seven, five, and three. If given the chance, could she learn to love his sons the way she loved the Grigsby children?

"YOU'RE DONE FOR THE day, Granville. I'll see you tomorrow after school." Mr. Owens walked behind the counter and climbed the ladder, to stack supplies on the shelves.

"Uh, Mr. Owens?"

Clem Owens stopped and gazed down at him. "You need something son?"

"Uh, yes. I was wondering if I could order my rifle today?"

A broad smile lit up Mr. Owens' face. "You finally saved enough money to buy that rifle you've had your eye on?"

"Yes, sir." Granville dug the money out of his pocket and placed it on the counter."

Mr. Owens climbed down the ladder and stepped over to where Granville stood. He reached under the counter and pulled out the paper he'd kept for Granville in a tin box. He unfolded it and read it carefully.

Granville held his breath.

When Mr. Owens told him how much he'd need, Granville carefully counted out the money. He laid it on the counter for the man to count as well.

"You did it." Mr. Owens smiled. "You've got enough to pay that rifle. I'll put in an order first thing tomorrow morning. Seein' as how your purchase will come from the town of Springfield, it won't take long for it to arrive."

"Thank you, sir." Granville's shoulders lifted as went out the back door and untied Star from the post. Riding home, he heaved a contented sigh. Mr. Owens would order his rifle in the morning. Wouldn't his father be surprised!

Granville couldn't wait for the day the rifle would be delivered to Owens Mercantile. With spring coming soon, there would be plenty of wild animals to hunt. But more than that, he'd heard his father's concern that someone had been out at the creek, stirring up trouble. Who killed those steers that now lay like empty shells by the banks? If his dad needed help catching the culprit, he'd be there to back him up.

IT WAS EARLY EVENING when John nudged Blue into a lope, eager to see his neighbor who had dug a hole into his heart. Mahala had stayed away far too long. If she wasn't going to come knocking on his door, then he'd go knocking on hers. Something told him Mahala regarded Isabella's visit as a planned event on his part. Of course, nothing could be further from the truth. But he realized it was up to him to put her misunderstandings to rest.

Truth be told, he hadn't wanted Mahala to leave that fateful day, and when she drove away, his heart dropped to the boards of his front porch. He well remembered watching Mahala's buggy leave his drive just as Isabella Yates, wearing a fur hat and coat, rode up the lane in her handsome rig.

Since that fateful day, he'd seen little of Mahala. He wouldn't wait a moment longer to put things right with the dark-haired beauty. Up ahead the Shields' two-story home came into view. His heart beat to the rhythm of Blue's hoof beats. Would she see him? Or would she send him packing back to his ranch?

John slowed Blue at they rode up to the Shields' front porch. He slid off the horse and tied the reins to the post in front of the house. Taking the steps two at a time, John rapped on the door. He could hear voices inside, and moments later the door flew open.

"Mr. Grigsby. Come in." Mary Shields stepped aside as he entered the wide hall. "How are you?"

John removed his hat and held it before him. "I'm fine, Mrs. Shields. I've come to see Mahala." He swallowed hard.

"Oh?" Mary's brows rose. "Well, she's in her room, working on a gown. Let me tell her you're here." Mary hitched her skirt and started up the stairs.

Hearing voices behind him, John turned to see Mahala's three sisters coming out of the dining room. "Good evening, ladies," he said and nodded.

"Hello, Mr. Grigsby. Would you like to take a seat in the sitting room while you wait?" Rebecca's eyes shone as she offered to lead him to the parlor. Elizabeth clenched her jaws tightly, but he didn't miss the amused light in her eyes.

"I'll wait here if that's all right." He gazed up the stairs, turning his hat in his hands as he waited.

"Of course." The girls went on into the living room, glancing at each other and then back to John.

Moments later, Mary Shields appeared at the top of the stairs. She shook her head as she came down to the landing. Folding her hands together, she gazed down at him. "I'm sorry, Mr. Grigsby. Mahala sends her regrets and says she's too busy with her work and to thank you for coming."

"But—"

"She won't come down." Mary gave John a warm smile. "I believe she needs more time."

John hung his head and then lifted his eyes to meet Mary's. "All right." He turned toward the door. "Tell her the children would like to see her—and so would I."

With that John went out into the night and mounted Blue. He wouldn't ride home just yet. He needed time alone to think. When horse and rider reached the road , John put Blue into a trot. *How do I get her back, God? I can't let her slip away.*

MAHALA STOOD BY HER bedroom door and listened to the distant sound of her mother telling John she wouldn't come down. She pushed away from the door and paced the floor. Half her heart wanted to run down the stairs and stop John from leaving; the other half was too stubborn to try. She closed her eyes and took in a deep breath when she heard the front door close. It wasn't long before she heard the sound of hoofbeats fading away. *Oh Lord,* she sighed. *I want him, but I won't compete with other woman.*

MAHALA, WHERE ARE YOU? Why do you stay away? John mused wearily. He'd seen her cross the street in town several times, but each time she had bowed her head against the cold wind and pretended she hadn't seen him. This morning, he sat on his horse and gazed down at her as she scurried to the tailor shop. She could have looked up and greeted him, but she didn't. Instead, she pulled her wrap tighter and escaped inside.

With everything inside of him, he wanted to follow Mahala into the shop and shake some sense into her, to make her see that he wanted her. But he was no good at approaching women, especially against her will. How could he make Mahala see he needed her? He had hoped their sleigh ride would be the beginning of a long and true relationship. It seemed, however, that was not to be. He wouldn't give up. He would, however, give her the space she desired. The weather had been warming and showing signs of spring. In time he would invite her for a ride in the country, just the two of them.

March and April flew by with no sign of Mahala, and before he knew it, it was the month of May. Spring had always been the season for new beginnings on the ranch. New kittens in the barn, new blades of grass popping up in the fields, and spring calving. Everything on the ranch was in full orchestra, and it wasn't long before John found himself plowing the fields and getting them ready to plant ryegrass, which would be turned into hay in the fall. The herd had also increased and needed lots of attention. John needed to keep his mind occupied, and he welcomed the extra work. Still, in the recesses of his mind, he thought about the dark-haired woman only a mile down the road. *Go after her*, his heart urged. *I will—just as soon as I get enough nerve. I will.*

GRANVILLE TOSSED HIS SCHOOLBOOKS on his bed and headed out to the barn to retrieve Star. Within minutes he was spurring his mount toward town. When he tied the reins to the hitching post in front of Owens Mercantile, he lost no time going into the store. He didn't miss the gleam in Clem Owens' eyes when he entered.

Most days, Mr. Owens was too preoccupied with the business of stocking shelves or sweeping floors to pay much attention to Granville when he arrived. But today, he seemed especially bright, and Granville couldn't help but wonder what had picked up his spirits.

"Afternoon, Mr. Owens."

"Same to you, young man. I've got a list of deliveries for you today. The boxes are waitin' in the back room. You best get to it, as old Mrs. Jensen has been in three times today, askin' when her supplies would be delivered."

"Three times? Has she lost her mind?"

Clem Owen's chuckled. "You heard right." There was that twinkle in the man's eyes again. "Today's her bakin' day and she's needin' her supplies. Go on. Load up."

"Sure thing, Mr. Owens." Granville set to work loading the boxes in the back of the wagon. After he hitched old Moses, he climbed onto the wagon seat and shook the reins. Old Moses slogged slowly down the alley. The roads were slushy from the last snowfall. With warmer days, the snow had melted leaving the back alleys and main roads a muddy mess. As the wagon rolled down Main Street the wheels caked with mud and slung it out behind them.

An hour later, deliveries done, Granville unhitched Moses, gave him his treat, and went into the store. When he walked to the counter, Mr. Owens pulled off his stiff apron.

"Get it all done?"

"Yes, sir." Granville proceeded to empty his pockets of coins and laid them on the counter.

Mr. Owens counted his share and shoved the tips to Granville. "We got a delivery today." He bent low and pulled a long narrow package wrapped in brown paper from a bottom shelf. The sparkle was back in his eyes again. He set the package on the counter and pushed it toward Granville. "Your rifle arrived this morning." His teeth shone brightly as he smiled wide.

"It came! Whoop howdy!" Granville tore the brown paper off the firearm and eyed the shiny new rifle. There it lay at last after weeks of waiting for it to arrive.

Mr. Owens reached behind the counter again and brought up a box of shells. "You'll be needin' these, too."

Granville picked up the rifle and aimed it to the back of the store, testing the weight of it. "Boy, oh boy!" He sighed with anticipation. "My dad's sure is going to be surprised when he sees this."

"Well, it's closing time. You best ride on home and show that piece of firearm to your dad." Mr. Owens pushed the ammunition forward. "This is a gift from me. You've done a good job workin' at the mercantile these past months."

"Thank you, Mr. Owens!" Granville picked up the small box. "Golly!"

Mr. Owens chuckled. "Go on now. I've got to finish closing the store."

"Yes, sir." Granville shoved the small box of bullets into his coat pocket and carried the shiny new rifle under his arm as he went out the door and climbed onto his horse. He laid the firearm across his lap and rode out. "Won't Dad be proud when he sees this gem?"

Granville patted Star's neck as they rode out to Shady Hollow Road. "Maybe Dad will let me help with the cattle this spring. What do you think, Star? I heard Dad talking about the dead steers by the creek. I'm thinking he needs a helping hand."

Franklin was allowed to work out on the range, but Granville had his job after school. But when summer came, he hoped his dad would allow him help with the cattle too.

The horse snorted as they rode through the thick mud. When they reached home, Granville stopped by the water trough and dipped a bucket into the water. He poured the cold water down the horse's legs and washed off the thick mud. Then he put Star in his stall and brushed him down. When done, Granville grasped the rifle in a firm grip and headed for the back of the house. As he strode through the back door, he listened for sounds in the house. The family could be heard down the hall. He walked into the dining room, seeing Tess setting a dish on the table and the younger siblings already seated. His dad walked in with a dish in each hand, brows raised in Granville's direction.

"Sorry I'm late." A slow grin spread across Granville's face.

His dad set the two dishes onto the table. "What's that you got in your hand?"

"My new rifle." Granville felt his ears heat up. "I've been saving money for this for some time now." He held up the firearm.

John strode to Granville and let out a slow whistle. "That's a fine-looking piece you got there."

Granville studied his father's eyes and squared his shoulders. Sure enough he saw a proud gleam.

John took hold of the rifle and turned it this way and that. "You did good, son. Never hurts to have an extra firearm on the ranch." He didn't hand it back. Instead, he gazed toward the living room. "We'll mount it with mine over the fireplace. For now, though, go wash up. Supper's ready."

"Yes, sir." Granville's shoulders relaxed. He watched his father take the rifle and set it against the door jamb.

"Um, sir?" Granville gazed at his father. "When will we get a chance to go out and practice shooting my rifle?"

"I've got my hands full at the moment, but I'll try to find time to take you out to the woods this weekend. How's that?"

Granville felt his lips stretch wide. "Fine, sir." I got that old fox with my slingshot. I hope to be as good or better with a gun."

June 14, 1842

HENRY, THE BUTLER, STOOD at the front door of the manor and watched the mail carrier climb onto the leather seat of the coach. The young man shook the reins and his vehicle started down the road. Dressed immaculately, the Negro butler shut the front door and set the envelope on a silver tray. He held the etched tray in one hand and gazed down the dark hallway. It being Friday, Mr. Bates would be in his study, looking over numbers like he always did when he sat at his elaborate desk made of cherry.

Yet, today, he heard voices coming from the study. Miss Evelyn Bates, Alexander's aunt, had come to pay him a visit. Or more to the point—to lecture Mr. Bates on his need for a wife. He had three young sons who needed a mother. Mr. Bates had hired a nanny and a tutor since his wife had passed and had figured he'd done all he could for his three boys' needs. But his aunt Evelyn thought otherwise.

Henry had heard enough from time to time between the two of them to know that Miss Evelyn's opinion about his master's need for a wife was an ongoing conversation.

Henry cleared his throat, placed one hand behind his back, and silently strode to the door of Mr. Bates' study. He rapped softy on the open doorframe. "Excuse me, suh."

Alexander wheeled around to face the butler. Eyeing the silver tray, he nodded. "Come in, Henry."

"The mail just arrived, suh."

Alexander retrieved the letter from the tray. "Who might this letter be from?" He held the envelope a moment as if waiting for his aunt to leave the room. When she didn't, he asked, "Will you be staying for supper?"

"Open the letter, Alex." Evelyn clicked her tongue. "I'm sure it's another response from your ad for a mail-order bride, is it not?"

Alexander looked at Henry and then at his aunt. "It likely is." He stared at the upper lefthand corner of the envelope. "Mahala Shields," he murmured. He glanced at the upper right hand of the letter. "It was posted a month ago—Missouri." Alexander picked up a gilded letter opener and slid it under the rose-colored wax that sealed the envelope.

Henry and Evelyn looked on as Alexander silently read the missive. While he read, Henry, not having been dismissed, kept his gaze discreetly away from his master. He had always liked the study. The dark paneled walls and polished furniture had a distinction to it. It fit Mr. Bates to a T.

When Alexander started to return the parchment to the envelope, he stopped. He tilted the envelope until a small locket slid out onto his palm. Surprised, he looked at Evelyn and then at Henry. "What have we here?" His brows raised as he stared at the picture in the tiny locket for a long moment. "A smart-looking woman." He closed his hand around the frame.

"Will you send a reply?" Aunt Evelyn stared at his hand.

"I'm not in a hurry." He gazed at the photo again. "I should give it some time before I answer."

Evelyn snatched the locket from his hand. She stared at the photo and then turned the locket over. "Mahala Shields. Just as the address said." She handed the piece back to Alexander. "She's a looker, Alex."

Alexander's nine-year-old son, Donald, walked into the study. Seeing the locket in his father's hand he asked, "Who's that?"

Alexander gazed at the portrait. "A friend." He slipped the piece back into the envelope and opened the top drawer of his desk. He set the letter amongst the other responses he'd received in the past few months. After he shut the drawer, he stared at it, deep in thought. He opened it again and pulled out Mahala's letter and held it in his hands a moment, his thumb running softly over her name in the upper left-hand corner. He shook his head, his expression grim. This time, he set the letter inside but to the right—away from the growing number of responses—and slowly pushed the drawer closed.

"Come on, Donny," Evelyn said. "Let's find your brothers. I want to take the three of you to the park." She glanced over at Alexander. "Do you mind?"

"Not at all. I've got a ton of work to catch up on. He laid his hand on a thick ledger with the inscription *Bates Western Iron Company* engraved on the cover.

"That will be all, Henry," Alexander said, nodding to the butler.

"Yes, sir." Henry bowed and left the room. As he headed for the front room the corners of the butler's mouth turned up. Would Master Bates be gettin' hisself a new wife 'fore too long?

Chapter TWENTY-NINE

THE WEEKS ROLLED BY with the promise of spring in the air, only to be forgotten when the weather grew warm and dust storms flew across the land. Cattle bawled and complained and headed to the waterholes for relief. Mahala joined her father, brothers, and the cowhands as they.drove the herds to greener pastures. Dust settled in the creases of her skirt, coating her hair, and making her eyes gritty.

But she didn't care. She needed to keep moving, finding new things to do to keep herself busy. She found she liked joining the men when they moved the cattle to new ground. She'd even helped with the birth of a few calves.

But her heart was in the tailor shop where she could create and design gowns for the women of Grovespring. Problem was, the need for new garments had diminished this summer, as she'd known would happen. Since the women had missed the Sweetheart Dance due to the white-out of the blizzard, they already had their gowns for the Harvest Festival.

Mahala lowered her wide-brimmed hat and nudged Bessy forward. Benjamin had stopped his mount to examine one of the Herefords lying on the ground. It bawled mournfully as if in pain.

"What's wrong with her?"

Benjamin slid out of his saddle and strode to the cow. "Don't know." He bent and ran a rough palm over the animal.

"I was going to ride back to the house," Mahala told her father. "Do you need me to stay?" A gust of wind blew sand into her eyes and she turned her head.

"No. Go on back to the house. This dust storm is no place for a woman."

He pulled off his hat and beat it against his pant leg. "Tell Mother we'll be late for supper."

"As soon as you figure out what's going on with that heifer, you should come back to the ranch too. The dust can't be good for your lungs."

Benjamin replaced his hat and pushed it down for good measure. "Go on and tell your mother what I said."

"All right." Mahala frowned. She turned Bessy around and galloped back to the ranch house. A mile down the road stood the Grigsby ranch. In her mind she could see the house standing tall and formidable near the road. It had been ages since she'd darkened their door. Her heart constricted as she thought of the strong man who dominated her thoughts every waking moment. She wished she could ride down the lane and visit the family, but her conscience told her to continue on home. There was nothing for her at the Grigsby ranch—except heartache and confusion. She'd stay put and wait to see what God had in store for her future.

Mahala had been aware when John tried to approach her a half dozen times over the winter and early spring. She just wasn't ready to talk to him. What could she say? *I felt slighted by you and Bella? And because of that I've decided to stay away.* It was the truth. But she couldn't say it.

THE DUST STORMS LEFT as quickly as they'd come and life on the ranch resumed to its routines. With Sunday coming, the circuit preacher would be in town. Mahala looked forward to attending church service with the community. When the service ended, she hoped to learn that the women of Grovespring were planning another event that would set her hands to sewing again.

As the Shields family entered the church yard in their buggy, they found several buggies and wagons already parked under the trees and lined up side by side. The horses were tied to picket lines. Mahala wondered if the residents of Grovespring were as starved as she was for a good, Godly service and a visit with other townspeople.

"Hello!" neighbor's called as they entered the white church.

Mahala filed into the small sanctuary with her family and looked around. The room buzzed with the sounds of people talking. She followed Mary Ann and found a seat near the front of the sanctuary. Feeling eyes on her back, Mahala turned tentatively to see John Grigsby and his family sitting in a pew a few rows back on the opposite side of the aisle. Mahala dipped her chin and turned back to face the choir.

"Good morning," Pastor Gregg said. "If you'll please stand, we'll sing the first hymn."

Mahala was hard put to pay attention to everything the preacher said with John only a few feet away. She felt his gaze on her. It stirred a warm feeling inside, but she mustn't let it take root.

When the service ended, Mahala beelined it for the back door. She had barely stepped outside and was standing on the top step when she heard her name.

"Mahala," came a deep voice—that voice she'd come to love.

She took another step.

"Mahala, please."

She stilled and then turned to face John. He stood tall and handsome—so handsome that she held her breath.

"Would you give me the favor of a Sunday ride?" His eyes begged her to say yes.

Mahala clasped her hands in front of her, and against all wisdom and imaginary control,—she said, "That would be fine." She waited for him to say more.

"Can we make it a picnic? Just the two of us?"

Just the two of us? Mahala didn't need him to say anything more. "I'll bring the buggy, Mr. Grigsby, if you'll bring the food," she said firmly.

Mr. Grigsby? John sucked in his breath. Were they starting all over? "I will bring the food."

"All right. I'll pick you up in an hour. That should give you plenty of time to put something together."

"I'll be ready." John touched the brim of his hat. He watched the headstrong beauty walk away with sure steps. She hadn't minced words with him. If he wanted to spend time with her, he'd have to work for it. A low groan escaped his throat as he walked across the yard.

When Mahala had put some distance between her and John, she nearly flew as she headed to the wagon to wait for her family. She wasn't even sure her feet touched the ground.

AN HOUR LATER, THE buggy crossed the Shady Hollow Bridge toward the other side of town and to the valley where she and John and his family had played in the snow so many months back. Though Mahala had provided the buggy, John took the reins.

The months of silence from this incredible woman who now sat beside him had turned his mind to mush. John searched his heart for a way to tell Mahala what was on his mind. Instead, he held the reins loosely and asked, "Have you had the pleasure of a country ride yet this summer?"

"Honestly, I've spent more time out on the ranch with my father than anything else."

"You've been herding cattle?"

"Yes. I love it. I never thought I'd enjoy the process as much as I do."

John gazed at Mahala with both disbelief and admiration. Time and again this woman proved to be a wonder to him. Strands of her dark hair flew in the wind as they rode on, and it was all he could do to keep his hands from reaching out to touch the silky wisps.

"You never cease to amaze me, Mahala Shields."

"Why is that?" she asked.

He didn't miss the sudden flush to her cheeks.

"It's not often one hears a woman admitting she enjoys working with cattle." He slowed the buggy to the side of the road and Bessy pranced to an open field. When they came to a stop, John stared at Mahala's lovely face.

Mahala cleared her throat. "Might we find a spot to set up the picnic?" She didn't wait for his response. She turned to alight to the ground without his assistance.

"Hold on, let me give you a hand." John climbed down and came around to her side of the buggy.

When Mahala felt his firm grip and stepped to the ground, she remembered that familiar electrical shock spread through her body. The last time she had experienced his touch seemed ages ago. Warmth spread from her neck into her cheeks. She brushed her skirts and stepped aside.

A tall mulberry tree with long branches shaded a portion of the grassy field. Wildflowers popped up here and there creating the perfect background. Mahala strode to the area and smiled. "Let's sit here."

"I agree." John's eyes sparkled as he pulled a blanket out of the box behind the buggy seat. He handed one end of the cloth to Mahala, and together, they shook the blanket until it sailed gently over the green grass. "I'll get the picnic basket." John strode back to the buggy. When he returned he placed the hamper at a corner of the blanket and said, "It was all I could do to leave the house without the children." He laughed softly. "They wanted to join us."

"You should have let them come." Mahala knew full well that she wanted time alone with this man, but during the many months that she'd stayed away, she had missed the children, too.

"No. I wanted to spend this time alone with you, without the distraction of my family." He stared at her with longing. The world stood still for that moment, except for the chirping of a mocking bird overhead. He pulled his gaze away and opened the lid to the straw basket. "Would you like to take over?"

"Yes. Find a seat."

While Mahala removed the sandwiches wrapped in a dish towel, John studied her. He'd almost forgotten how pretty she was. He watched the small cleft in her chin deepen as she concentrated on lifting food from the hamper. He relished the chance to study her more closely.

Mahala looked up delighted with everything she'd found in the basket. "You brought a feast, Mr. Grigsby."

John flinched. "Mahala . . . please call me John."

She lowered her lashes. "It's been a while."

"It's been too long. I greatly desire for our relationship to return to the way it was before . . . before you stayed away."

Mahala's eyes glistened, "Me too."

John thumbed the stray tear away and held her face in his hands.

Her cheek warmed under his touch, and though it seemed he didn't want to move away, she felt it best at the moment. "Let's eat."

Blissful hours passed as the sun edged from overhead. They nibbled and drank, talked and laughed, and watched a squirrel skitter down the trunk of a mulberry tree to beg for food. Laughing, Mahala tossed a crust of bread to the curious onlooker.

"Ugh! I'm full." Mahala sat her plate down and smiled. "Did Tess make this delicious meal?"

"She did." John watched as Mahala started returning everything to the hamper. He lent a hand, stowing the dishes and silverware in the wicker basket.

Mahala gazed at the flowers blanketing the field. "Do you mind if I pick a few wildflowers before we head back?"

"I don't mind at all," John replied lazily. The truth was, he didn't mind watching her every move.

She stepped gracefully through the grass and bent to pick a variety of flowers and lay them in the crook of her arm. The more he watched the more he wanted her to be a part of his life. Was he dreaming? Would the day come that he could bring her to the Grigsby ranch to stay?

Mahala felt more peace than she'd ever remembered. Knowing John sat on the blanket not far away, waiting for her to return, sent a warmth through her. She wanted to be needed. She wanted to be loved. Could he love her?

When she turned around, she found John reclining against the tree trunk, his long legs stretched before him and his hat on the ground near his feet. He made an altogether disturbing picture. To relaxed. Too handsome. Too . . . desirable. She clutched the armful of wildflowers in her hand and said, "I think we've made a good day of it. Might we head back?" She feared if they didn't end this glorious day, she would certainly make a fool of herself.

John stared at her with what? Desire? He stood and picked up the hamper. "Of course."

They folded the quilt and stored it in the box behind the buggy, and all too soon they were headed back to the Grigsby ranch.

When Mahala took the reins again at the house, John stood beside her. He glanced at the house and then back to her. "Don't be a stranger. We'd like very much for you to come by."

"I will, John. Look for me in a few days." She clicked her tongue and Bessy pulled the buggy out of the drive.

That evening, Mahala's mind ran rampant with thoughts of John—his voice,—his body,—the way he looked at her. She could see in her mind's eyes every detail of the man, from the dusty crown of his black cowboy hat to his worn blue shirt covering his muscled physique.

Each time she was near him, it took all her will not to let her gaze linger on the rough cut of his features. He unknowingly carried authority in the way he moved, the way he talked with his deep timbered voice, big and strong, and the uncompromising lines in his bearded face. She would go by to the ranch as he had asked but it would take will power to let a decent amount of days to go by before she ventured there. She didn't want to appear too eager, although that was the truth of it. She couldn't wait to see him again.

FOUR DAYS LATER, MAHALA took a pie to the Grigsby home. She could have taken a meal as she had in the past, but they'd managed very well without her help for several months. The days of taking meals was over. But a fresh peach pie . . . now that was another thing. It felt wonderful to be standing again in the Grigsby home. Mahala looked around and realized nothing had changed.

"Can I take your wrap?" Granville stood before her with a gleam in his eyes.

"Yes, thank you, Gran. Is your father home?"

"He's out in the barn. He should be coming into the house any minute now." Mahala noticed the sparkle in Granville's eyes remained.

"I should take this to the kitchen," she said, indicating the pie she held in her hands.

"Who's here?" Tess came around the corner of the living room. "Mahala!" Tess flew across the floor. "It's so good to see you!"

Mahala raised the pie to one side and opened her arm to hug Tess. A moment later, Calvin, Mary Jane, and the two younger boys clamored for their turn to get a hug. The front entrance echoed with the sound of joy as the children elbowed one another for their turn to speak to Mahala.

When Mahala looked down, little Wiley stood with his arms up, and she couldn't resist. "Here, Tess, take this pie to the kitchen." She relinquished the dessert, picked up Wiley, and set him on her hip. "You're getting so big. How old are you now?"

Three little fingers went up, but Wiley said nary a word. His head went to her shoulder, where he snuggled against her. Mahala's eyelids burned and she fought back tears of joy that threatened to give away how happy she was to see the children.

The back door slammed and Mahala looked up to see John coming toward them. She didn't miss the light in his eyes.

"You came," was all he said as he neared them.

"I-I brought a pie." She set Wiley on the floor.

"Children . . . can you give Miss Shields and me a moment?"

Giggles erupted as the children bounded out of the front hall and into the living room.

John stared at her with need in his eyes. "I didn't think you'd come."

"I wanted to come." She lifted a hand to his arm, allowing herself to touch him.

His face lit up. "You said you brought a pie. Let's have a look at it."

The back door slammed once more, and Franklin strode into the dining room. His deep blue eyes shone with delight at the sight of Mahala. "Good to see you Miss Shields." He found a seat at the table with the rest of the family.

The evening was full of laughter as the family sat around the table, eating the peach pie and telling stories of how their days had gone since the last time they'd seen Mahala. A rich, warm glow filled her being as she saw how eager each one of the children was to talk to her. And before she knew it, the hour had grown late.

"I best be going," Mahala said reluctantly.

The children filled the room with a chorus of groans.

"I'll come back, I promise." Mahala pushed away from the table, and the children did the same.

John came to her side and touched her elbow. "I'll walk you to the door."

"Me too." Mary Jane said enthusiastically and started to follow.

"Mary Jane!" the four older children called out.

Mahala looked back to see their eyes sparkling, but Franklin had a firm hold on Mary Jane's arm.

John reached for Mahala's wrap and draped it over her shoulders. Without a word, he opened the door and stepped out onto the porch with her. He closed the door firmly and gently touched her back, leading her toward the porch railing.

For the first few moments, John didn't say a word, he just gazed at the moon. "It's so bright we can see almost everything out here." He stalled, at a loss for words. He wanted—no, he needed—to ask her to marry him, but how could he bluntly ask Mahala to spend the rest of her life with him after the many months they'd been apart? His gut twisted, knowing he wanted her, but would she turn him down?

He had mulled over a number of ways he could ask for her hand. He even reasoned that she didn't have to love him. But as much as he rehearsed the things he wanted to say, the words wouldn't come. Instead, he stared at the moon and the starry sky, his voice mute.

Mahala lifted her chin and waited for him to speak. She sensed a tug of war going on inside his head, but did not know what was troubling him. Was he ready to make a commitment to her? And if so, why didn't he just say it?

The moment passed. "The Fourth of July picnic is coming up," he finally said. "I would very much like it if you'd join the children and me." He shook his head and started over. "I'd very much like it if you'd sit with me at the picnic."

Mahala remembered each year's fireworks display and the excitement in the air as families came to join in the activities. This would be a first for her attending the gala apart from her family. That John invited her to sit with them thrilled her.

"I would love to sit with you . . . and your family." Mahala waited for John to say more. But he only gazed at her with warmth in his eyes. If she didn't step away, she feared she'd promptly throw herself into his arms, draw his head down to hers, and kiss him squarely on his lips. Fire burned her cheeks and she stepped away.

"Good evening, John. I'll see you at the picnic." She quickly turned to stride off the porch.

"Wait!" John halted her.

Mahala turned and did just that—she waited, her heart beating in her chest so strongly that she feared he could see it.

John strode to where she stood and gazed down at her with that need in his eyes that she'd seen so many times before. "There's so much I want to say, but I can't seem to find the words." He cupped her cheek and grazed her lips with his thumb. "Forgive me?" he asked lazily, his deep voice making her knees weak.

Mahala held her breath for what seemed a lifetime as their eyes held. The door opened and light spilled onto the porch, ending the moment.

Mary Jane's head popped out. "Are you still out here Papa?"

A slow grin curved John's lips, and Mahala giggled softly. "Good evening, John."

Chapter THIRTY

DEEP IN THOUGHT, JOHN whipped a dozen eggs in the bowl while Tess flipped pancakes in the cast iron skillet. The fat in the skillet spit and sputtered as she watched over the sizzling batter.

Tess stacked the first batch of flapjacks on a plate and asked, "Is Mahala coming over this evening?"

At the mention of Mahala's name, John felt a grin tug at his mouth. With his back turned from his daughter, he gave a casual reply. "No. We won't see her until the Fourth of July picnic."

The festival wasn't for another three days. If he had his way, he see her sooner, but Mahala had already declined to see them until the appointed day. Thinking about the slender woman, it sure was a good thing he had a ranch to run. Managing the cowhands and stock took up a great deal of his time. Saturday would be here in no time.

Tess cut into his train of thought. "Will she be sitting with us?"

John turned to look at his inquisitive daughter. He didn't miss the wistful look in her cornflower-blue eyes.

He crossed the floor and poured the egg mix into the hot skillet sitting next to the new batch of pancakes Tess had frying in a pan. A third skillet had bacon in it, which sizzled and popped, sending good smells throughout the house.

He gazed at Tess, who stopped flipping the second batch of flapjacks.

"Yes. I invited Mahala to sit with us." He smiled lightly. "She agreed to join our family."

"Good. The day is going to be more fun with Mahala sitting with us." Tess wiped her hands on her apron before she took it off, a pleased look in her eyes.

John gazed at his daughter. Her shoulders had a carefree lift to them as she set the pancakes on the table. She glanced over her shoulder and smiled at him.

Dear God, my children have spent these past months mourning the loss of their mother, and the house has lost its warmth.—I have to make this work. Not only do I want Mahala in my life, but my children need her too.

It wasn't long before the rest of the children rumbled into the kitchen.

"I smell bacon!" Granville pushed past Calvin and slid into his chair.

The room grew noisy as each one found their place at the table. Franklin came in last, and he eyed the pile of pancakes. "Looks good," he said as he slid into a chair. John sat down at the head and glanced at all the children. "Good morning, my princes and princesses. Bow your heads as we say grace."

John gazed at his children as they lowered their chins and folded their hands. "Lord, we ask You to bless this bounty we are about to eat. Nourish our bodies and fill our hearts with Your gracious love. Amen."

"Amen," chorused the children. The next few moments were busy and the room was filled with the sound of plates passed around and dished up with pancakes, scrambled eggs, and bacon.

"Hold on, boys!" Tess called out. "Two pancakes each or there won't be enough for everybody." She pushed her chair back and stood to oversee the dishing out of the food.

John noticed she didn't share the news of Mahala joining the family for the Fourth of July picnic. He wondered about that as he cut up the two younger boys' pancakes. Best to keep it under a lid until the day of the event, or he'd be hard put to keep Mary Jane under control. His youngest daughter loved having Mahala around. If she knew Mahala was going to join them, she'd be asking what day it was nearly every minute.

At that thought, John studied Tess one more time He caught the secret gleam in her eyes as she ate, and he realized his daughter must be thinking the same thing. She was growing up too fast. Having to step into her mother's shoes had brought wisdom beyond her years. Without thought, he gazed at her upper chest and his ears grew hot. *Oh, Lord,* he inwardly groaned. She was developing in more ways than one.

Dear God, I need a woman to deal with such delicacies. He lowered his head and concentrated on the pile of flapjacks on his plate. Saturday couldn't come too soon.

THE GRIGSBY WAGON PULLED in front of the Shields' home. His heart racing, John set the brake, and looked over at the house, and called back to the children, "Now, you all be on your best behavior today."

Giggles followed his remark as John climbed down from the wagon. Looking over at the grand house, he strode to the front porch. He'd only gone two steps when the front door flew open. "John!" Mahala stepped out onto the porch with a basket in her arms. "I've made us a splendid meal for today!"

But John had barely heard her words, so taken was he at the beauty of her hair coiled high on her head and tendrils falling from the sides her forehead and near her ears. She wore a white dress made of some type os sheer fabric, its sleeves ending above her elbows and showing her slender arms. The dress gathered at the waist and flared out in a billowing fashion as she continued to come toward him.

It was then that he smelled the scent of lilacs emanating from her. He gulped. *Lord have mercy. I'm in trouble. How will I keep my wits about me with this beauty sitting by my side all day?*

Mahala held her basket out to him. "John?"

"Oh, let me get that for you." Heat beat a path to his neck. "I'll set it in the back of the wagon."

Mahala released the basket into his hold and turned back toward the house. "I have a quilt we can use.

"We have plenty of blankets!" the children called out, the look of anticipation written in their expressions.

"Then we're all set?"

"Yes! Come on, Molly. We gotta get to the field before all the good spots are taken!" It was plain to see that Mary Jane was eager to get on the road.

The front door opened again and Benjamin Shields stepped out. "Afternoon, Grigsby."

"Good afternoon to you, sir." The heat that had beat a path to John's neck kept going all the way to his ears. He didn't miss the twinkle in Benjamin's eyes as the older man rocked on his heels and with his hands shoved in his pockets.

"Well, I best not keep you all waiting. My Mary and the girls are just about ready to load up our wagon and get on the road ourselves. We'll see you there."

"Yes, sir." John held out a hand to help Mahala onto the wooden seat.

Benjamin stayed rooted where he stood as John climbed onto the opposite side. When he took the reins. John touched the rim of his and nodded at Mahala's father, who waved.

"Get up there, Brownie." The wagon jerked as they rolled out of the drive.

The fullness in John's chest almost choked him. It felt right having Mahala sitting beside him. The sounds in the back of the wagon were muffled to occasional giggles. Other than that, it seemed no one had much to say on the ride to town.

Mahala broke the silence. " I hope you all like fried chicken."

"We do!" the children chimed in.

The silence broken, the boys began to push and shove in playfulness, and Mary Jane exclaimed, "Look at all the wagons on the road! Woweee!" She stood to her feet and leaned her head in between John and Mahala. "Is everybody going to the picnic?"

"I believe so." Mahala brushed Mary Jane's hair out of her eyes. "You should sit down."

"All right, Molly." Mary Jane slid down to the floor of the wagon.

Mahala gazed at John and folded her hands in her lap. The wagon rumbled along and bounced on the rutted road.

It was all John could do to keep his eyes on the road instead of her. A few glances at Mahala confirmed his need to ask her to marry him. Would she oblige him and say, 'yes?'

INDEED, IT SEEMED ALL the folks of Grovespring had converged at the edge of town. The sound of clopping hooves and wagon wheels filled the air, and greetings of "Hello" and "How are you?" were shouted as people waved at one another as the wagons parked side-by-side along an imaginary fence line.

Mahala thought back to the time she and John had taken a sleigh ride with his children to this very spot. They had sat around a campfire to drink hot chocolate, and later had a snowball fight. It looked different today with the sun beating down and the heat and humidity rising as thick as a blanket.

Children whooped and hollered and jumped out of the backs of wagons. They ran around the field, while women saw to the placement of their blankets on the ground, and men set up tables for the food. A select few women coordinated how the foods for the potluck should be arranged. Everyone would share the potluck dishes to add to what they kept at their own blankets.

The field was alive with games being erected for a fun-filled day. Men set up a target on an oak tree for the ax-throwing contest, and a post was raised for the ring-the-bell-with-a-sledge-hammer competition. A favorite was the horseshoe game. One of the men walked out the distance needed to throw the horse shoes and hammered an iron bar into the ground.

As John and Mahala walked side-by-side, Mahala carrying a quilt and John the basket of food, curious eyes stared at them. It was all Mahala could do to keep from smiling. Instead, she glanced back at the troop behind them. The Grigsby children were eager to join the other children and play before it was time to sit down and eat.

"Here we are." John stopped and looked at Mahala. "Does this spot look like a good place to put our blankets?" He gazed farther ahead. "The fireworks are usually set off over there." He pointed to a spot away from the trees.

"This is fine, John."

"All right." John turned to the children. "You can set our things down here."

"Goody," Mary Jane said. "Daddy, Gracie's here with her family. Can I go see her?"

"Yes, but stay where I can see you."

Mary Jane quickly skipped away in the direction of the Williams' blanket.

For the next few moments, John and Mahala set to work setting two quilts on the ground. It took only a little time to set everything out they would need.

"I'll be right back. I'm going to take my dessert to the tables." Mahala picked up a pie and a dish of maple cookies. "Would you like to come along, Tess?"

"All right." Tess gazed at Mahala with a light in her eyes. "Thank you for coming with us. I dreaded joining the next festival without my mother here." She slipped her hand in the crook of Mahala's arm. "Mama would like it if she could see us now."

"Oh, honey. I'm more than delighted that your father asked me to join you." Mahala glanced back at John, who had taken up his rifle and looked as if he wanted to tag along with the other men headed toward the trees that had black-and-white targets nailed to them.

"We'll be right back." Mahala looked down at Wiley and Jeffrey. "You boys stay here."

"I'll wait with them." John cocked a half grin and ruffled his small sons' hair.

Women bustled around a long row of tables, pointing to dishes and moving them around. Tess and Mahala neared the area where the desserts were sitting. Flora Benson set her pies in the center and moved toward the jellies with a jar of jam in her hands. Mahala didn't miss the proud lift to her shoulders, or the watchful way Mrs. Benson looked around to see if anyone noticed her contribution.

"You can set your dish over here." Dixie Trubridge pushed some desserts aside to make room for Mahala's pie. "So good to see you again, Miss Shields." The older woman gazed over Mahala's garment and nodded. "You are a picture of summer in that lovely dress."

"Mrs. Trubridge! The pleasure's all mine!" Mahala glanced down at her attire and fingered a fold of the gauzy material. "I made this dress a year ago and hadn't found an occasion to wear it." She lowered her voice for Dixie's ears alone. "When Mr. Grigsby invited me to join his family for the picnic, I pulled it out." Clamping her lips together, her cheeks warmed. "I think he liked it too."

"Of course he did, dearie!" Dixie gazed at the gawking women on her side of the table and back to Mahala and winked.

"Well." Mahala straightened. "Let me set this peach pie right here and Tess," she turned to Tess, "let's put the maple cookies along with the others over there."

Tess set Mahala's plate on the table and then stepped back beside her. It seemed like the most natural thing for Mahala to slip her arm around the young girl's slim shoulders. Mahala eyed the tables of food. When she looked up, a half dozen women were staring at her and Tess as if they'd grown horns on their heads.

Flora Benson and her sister, Cleo, bent their heads and spoke under their breaths, but their gaze swerved to Mahala and Tess as if what they had to say concerned them.

Tess glanced up at Mahala with uncertainty in her eyes. "Uh, we better get back to the blanket." She nudged Mahala with her elbow. "Dad will want to join the men in the shooting contest."

A tightness built inside Mahala like a coiling spring. "Ladies." She brushed her hand down the front of her dress and kissed the top of Tess's head. "Come along, darling. Your father's waiting for us."

The women gasped and craned their necks to watch Mahala and Tess walk hand-in-hand back to their blanket. "Well, I'll be a cooked hen!" one women spouted.

Mahala glanced back and smiled sweetly. She could hear the women talking up a storm. When they neared the blanket, Mahala looked up at John. He had a peaceful look in his eyes.

"Did you get everything settled all right?" he asked lazily.

"Yes, we did," Mahala said. "Go on with the men. We've got everything under control here." When she plunked down on the quilt in a less than lady-like fashion, her gauzy attire spilled out around her.

Her tone alerted him. He studied the tables with the ladies lined behind them and then down at Mahala. He couldn't help but think she looked like a lily in the rough terrain. He'd known for some time that the women taunted her for having not married in her younger years. He didn't understand that kind of thinking, but in truth, he often didn't understand a lot of things about the ways of women. He did, however, appreciate this flower who sat before him with her lips puckered.

"If you need me, I'll be over there." He pointed to the men lined up at the edge of the tree line.

Wiley quickly settled into Mahala's lap. "I'm hungry, Molly." For the first time, Mahala realized the toddler had adopted Mary Jane's name for her.

Mahala gently squeezed Wiley to her. "Maybe a carrot stick will hold you off until Daddy gets back." She touched his nose with the tip of her finger.

John gazed down at them. "You can feed the boys now if you want. They don't have to wait."

"All right." Mahala watched John amble away to join the men. Charles Matthews stood in the line and clapped John on the back when he walked up to him.

Hmm, Mahala mused to herself. Of all of the men calling out and ribbing each other, John stood out to her—his physique muscled and hard. She watched the men raise their rifles to their shoulders and aim for the target. Loud *'pops'* filled the air. When John finally took his turn, he raised his rifle and held it steady. *Boom!* She couldn't see the center of the target from where she sat, but she did see John shake his head and slam his chest with the palm of his hand. The men laughed heartily and the next man took his turn.

The afternoon wore on with plenty of laughter, hoots and howls as the men competed in one contest after another. The young men joined the older ones and the contests grew testy at times. John threw the ax and hit the target this time. Ripples of muscles showed through his blue shirt. A slight thrill trickled to Mahala's stomach and she swallowed hard.

Mahala's mother, Mary, and Mahala's three sisters came and joined her.

They stood at the edge of the blanket where Mahala held a sleepy Wiley on her hip, his head lying on her shoulder.

Mahala's ribs ached from laughter as she watched Franklin, Gran, and Calvin in the watermelon-eating contest. Cord Matthews won the sledge hammer challenge. The bell clanged loud and clear and echoed over the field. A roar went up and men clapped his back, but Mahala watched as Cord's eyes sought out her sister, Rebecca. And Rebecca returned his gaze, her cheeks flushed as she touched her heart.

"Goodness, Mother. Did you see that?" Mahala bent and whispered in Mary's ear.

"I did. I wouldn't be surprised if there wasn't a June wedding next summer." She beamed at her daughter.

"Cord and Rebecca Matthews," Mahala said softly. "The name has a nice ring to it."

"I wasn't speaking about them." Mary said. She turned her gaze on John, who had been watching them from a distance. "I believe Mr. Grigsby has made up his mind."

"Oh, no, Mother. He's not said a word about anything like that." Mahala looked from her mother to John, who stood off a ways with Charles Matthews. He gave her a nod and smiled.

"But he did ask you to come with him to this event—and in front of all of Grovespring. It's clear he's sending a message to the community that he has no interest of courting anyone else." Mary Shields gave her daughter a knowing look.

"Honestly, I hope you're right." Mahala kept her gaze pinned on John Grigsby. "I love him."

DUSK SETTLED OVER THE fields and families gathered on their blankets. Night began to fall and crickets struck up their chorus. The older boys ran up to the Grigsby blanket. "Can we sit over there with our friends?" Calvin pointed to where a group of boys sat on the ground in a row at the front of the field.

"Go on ahead. But don't go any farther," John warned.

"Can we?" Tess held Mary Jane's hand, ready to follow the boys.

"No. Sit here with the little ones on the blanket." John glanced at his two youngest sons who were about to fall asleep.

"But Daddy?" Mary Jane groaned.

"Mary Jane," was all John had to say. Her shoulders slumped and she dragged her feet to the second blanket that lay beside John and Mahala.

A lull settled over the field as men prepared to light the fireworks. Mahala gazed at the millions of stars in the dark sky. She breathed in, letting the night air fill her lungs. When she looked over at John, she found him staring at her with a look she couldn't define. He drew his gaze away and then down at his rough hands in his lap. She had the feeling he had something to say, but he was fighting it.

Boom!

The first fireworks exploded in the sky. The sparks flew overhead with magnificent splendor. The crowd roared and clapped and waited for more. John's girls oohed and awed beside them. The next burst of light sprayed across the sky and the crowd cried out again. On and on it went as each burst of fireworks shot through the darkness and lit up the sky.

There was an expectancy as the crowd waited for the next flash of light. Mahala didn't want the evening to end. Sitting here, sharing all of this with John and his family, was a dream come true, and yet she feared it wouldn't last forever. Would things go back to the way they were before this night?

"Mahala," John whispered, his deep voice cutting into her thoughts.

She loved the sound of her name on his lips. She gazed over at him. "Yes, John?"

He glanced beside them to where the girls sat holding their brothers, their eyes fixed on the sparkling fireworks overhead. And then he turned toward Mahala again. He picked up her hand and gazed into her eyes. "I don't know how to ask any more simple than this." He held her gaze a long moment, searching for the right words. "Will you marry me?" She watched him swallow and his Adam's apple work its way up and down his throat. The hunger in his eyes made it clear that he wanted her.

"I—I don't know what to say." Somehow, she had expected John to pull her aside some night when they were alone on his front porch or taking a buggy ride down the lane. That he asked her tonight with the children close by took her by surprise. She felt his fingers squeeze her own.

"I should have waited till we were alone. It's just—"

"No. It's all right." She pulled her hand away, but when she looked into his handsome face, she read defeat in his expression.

"I'm sorry. I thought maybe you shared the fond affections I have for you." He straightened his back and put his elbows on his raised knees.

"John." She touched his arm and immediately felt him flinch.

"No. It's all right. I assumed too much."

"Listen to me, John Grigsby," Mahala said a bit too loudly, but her tone demanded he hear her out. "You took me by surprise. Here we are out in the field with the whole population of Grovespring around us. You proposing to me was the last thing I expected. I—"

John's shoulders relaxed. "That's just it," he cut in. "Here we are together, you, me, and my children. It all feels so right. I want more nights like tonight, lots of them—with you here with me, with us." His teeth shone in the darkness. "Don't tell me you don't agree."

"Oh, John. I love all of this too." She gave him a small smile. "May I have a couple of days to think about it?" She reached out for his hand this time, a first for her, and her heart raced in her chest.

John's gaze leapt to hers, a longing in his eyes. "Of course."

The last of the fireworks shot into the sky and flashed overhead with sparks flying brightly.

Soon afterwards, it was time to load their basket and quilts into the wagon and go home. While Mahala and Tess folded the second blanket, Gertrude Yates walked carefully through the grass to her side.

"Why, Mahala Shields. I thought that was you sitting with the Grigsby's." She gaped at the children scurrying around to help and then back to Mahala. She lowered her voice for Mahala's ears alone. "You got him, young lady." She pinned her gaze on her. "Don't let him go." She clicked her tongue and then went on toward her buggy.

Mahala held her breath and looked toward the children. All eyes were on her.

"What did she say?" Mary Jane asked.

Mahala stared at the small troop staring up at her. "Don't worry about what Gertie said, my darlings. Now let's not keep your father waiting."

As the wagon retraced its way back to her father's home, Mahala sat deep in thought, fully aware of John sitting beside here and wishing for all the world that she'd given him his answer tonight. Could she marry this man? A tickle ran up her middle. *Isn't this what I've been waiting for?*

Chapter THIRTY-ONE

FOR THE NEXT TWO days, Mahala was hard put to think of anything except John Grigsby. That he'd truly asked her to marry him put her world in a tailspin. How was she supposed to get anything done when all she could think about was a future with that handsome man and his tantalizing blue eyes?

She hummed a tune while she readied herself for work and cheerfully said, "Hello!" to nearly every pedestrian she passed on the boardwalk on the way to Thompson's Tailor Shop. When she entered the shop, she found Grady bent over tweed material at his work table. "Good morning!" Mahala sang as she unpinned her hat and hung it on the wall hook.

"You're in excellent spirits." Grady smiled with a searching look.

"It's a fabulous morning." She touched Grady's arm and threaded her way to her table.

Grady glanced out the window and then back to her. "If you say so."

"I do."

Mahala spent the morning cleaning her work area and straightening the fabric on the shelves. She glanced out the window often, expecting John's wagon to roll down the street and stop at Owens Mercantile. She turned away to carry a dustpan of material scraps and debris to dump in the trash can. The next time she gazed across the street, there sat John's rig with John hauling two milk cans into the general store. Her heart tripped as she stared out the window and she breathed in deeply. *You'll get your answer today, Mr. Grigsby.*

Not wanting to get caught staring out the window, Mahala pulled her current project onto her lap and set to work stitching the hem of the garment.

Moments later, the bell jangled and she looked in time to see John coming her way. He pulled off his black felt hat and strode to her.

"Good morning, Mahala."

She didn't miss the questioning look in his eyes. "Good morning to you, John." She set the dress aside and stood.

He pinned his gaze on her. "Have you given my request any thought?"

Mahala cleared her throat and smiled briefly at him. "I have. Can you pick me up after work?"

"At your house?"

"Yes." She swallowed.

"I'll be there." John turned and walked out of the shop with a bounce to his step.

MAHALA SAT NEXT TO John as the wagon slowed to a stop near a stand of trees. He set the brake and turned to her. "Well?"

Mahala laughed softly. "Aren't we eager?" She gave him an amused gaze and her mouth tipped up at the corners.

"I have to be straight with you," he said. "I've not slept a wink since the picnic."

"Is it truly that important that I marry you?" Her heart strummed madly in her chest.

"More so than I would have expected. I want you in my life." He took her hand and massaged her palm with his thumb. "Tell me you say yes."

Mahala stared at her ring finger. "I've given it a tremendous amount of thought." She laughed softly under her breath. "It's all I've thought of . . . to be honest." Heat burned her cheeks. She gazed at the clump of trees ahead of them and then turned to face John. "I will marry you, John Grigsby."

John heaved a deep sigh of relief and his hand cupped her chin. "May I?" He leaned his head close to hers and he watched her visibly swallow.

"You may."

John lifted Mahala's chin with a forefinger. She closed her eyes and felt a rush of uncertainty. She'd never been kissed before. The heat of his breath on her lips melted every muscle in her body, and she tipped her head to the side, heat rising within her.

John pulled her into his arms and kissed her soundly. When he drew back and she opened her eyes, she saw passion in his eyes—and she couldn't breathe.

He leaned in a second time, but this time he kissed her slowly, grazing her bottom lip with his. Too stunned to react, Mahala relished the ticklish way his beard moved against her face. Warmth spread to her cheeks and to her belly and she reveled in what had just taken place—what John Grigsby had given her—her first kiss. When they drew apart, the world spun. Mahala clasped the wooden seat with shaky fingers.

"Are you all right?" John searched her eyes.

"Quite." She swallowed again, but she pulled away for propriety's sake. With a gleam in her eyes, she said, "I believe we've sealed the deal."

Amusement played in the crook of his smile. "I don't want to put off our marriage any longer than need be. Would you agree?"

She faced him squarely, surprised that he wanted to marry right away. But from the look on his face, he was waiting for a response—and possibly another kiss.

Before John could plant another kiss on her lips, she said, "Yes, I certainly do."

John's wide smile was wide. "Then it's settled." He drew away and pulled the reins from the brake post.

Feeling utterly undone, Mahala straightened on the wooden seat. She swallowed to still the strumming of her heart.

Before John pulled the wagon onto the road, he said, "You don't need to go to all the trouble of making a fancy dress—"

Mahala's hand went up as if to say stop! "I *will* make my wedding dress," she broke in. Her skin prickled as if she'd sprouted porcupine needles, so determined was she to have her say in this. "I've told myself if the day ever arrived that I should marry, I would do it right."

"Mahala, I—"

"I will wear a fine dress and hold a bouquet of flowers fitting for the occasion." Her chin shot out and her cheeks flamed.

"All right." He gazed at her with amusement. "I may be getting more than I bargained for. It seems you've certainly got a mind of your own."

"I do." She clasped her hands in her lap. If she didn't, she feared she'd—make a fool of herself. Watching his full lips move as he spoke only tempted her to pull his head down for one more kiss. Having experienced his lips grazing on hers, even for so brief a moment, had stolen any and all sense of propriety she had left. Goodness! She had pledged to marry him; she couldn't ruin things now.

"Oh, and—" John broke into her thoughts. "Should I stop by your father's house and ask for your hand?"

Mahala stilled. At thirty, did a maiden need a suitor to ask permission for her hand? "I don't know. I believe it wouldn't hurt to pay my father a visit."

"That's settled then. I'll see to it soon." John shook the reins and clicked his tongue. The wagon lurched forward and the familiar clip-clopping of Brownie's hooves filled the air.

Moments later, John's wagon rolled in front of the Shields home. Mahala laid a hand on John's arm. "I'll help myself down." She stepped over the side of the buckboard and strode to the house. When she stood on the porch, she turned and waved goodbye.

John touched the brim of his hat and the wagon rolled out of the drive. He whistled a ditty, accompanied by the sound of the wagon wheels.

Hearing the cheerful tune she murmured to herself. "Well, aren't you full of surprises?" Mahala's face lit up at the thought that she'd just learned something new about John. She couldn't remember ever having heard him whistle. It was clear and sharp and beautiful, reminding her that she'd made the right decision to marry him. He was a good man. And John wanted her—he really did. And she was about to marry a man she truly respected.

Mahala watched him drive, her heart beating like a drum. Her mind sailed back to the moment John asked her to marry him. His deep blue eyes had held her gaze in a fervent plea. She believed she was doing the right thing. "Yes. I will marry you, John Grigsby," she murmured. She cupped her elbows and watched him ride away until she couldn't see his rig anymore. "Hmm," she said softly and for the first time she felt loved by a man.

Mahala decided against going to the Grigsby house the next few days. Instead, she spent hours at work, putting finishing details on her wedding gown. She had already spent time between clients' orders to cut out and sew the gown. At the time she had thought it would be for a marriage to someone such as Mr. Alexander Bates. If she had received a letter sending for her, she had wanted to be ready.

She was more than grateful that this gown would be worn in a marriage to John Grigsby. As her creation took shape, she found it was far from elaborate—but it was elegant. The gown of satin and in silk featured a modest neckline and flared lightly at the waist. The immediate task at hand would be to finish the delicate embroidery and beading at the front of the yoke and on the bust. It had to be perfect, didn't it?

A FEW DAYS WENT by before John drove to the Shields' ranch. The last time he'd paid Benjamin Shields a visit had been when he learned his steers had been shot by the creek. Though the Grigsby and Shields' families were friends, ranch life had a way of keeping the men on the range more often than in each other's homes.

John couldn't remember having talked to Benjamin about anything except cattle. But here he stood on his neighbor's front porch—not for ranch talk but for a completely different reason. He raised his hand and rapped on the heavy door. He stepped away and paced the porch floor until the door flew open.

"John! Come on in." Mr. Shields waved him into the front foyer. "How are you doing?" Benjamin held out his hand. "What brings you to my neck of the woods?"

John shook the older man's hand and gazed past him down the hall, grateful that they were alone. "May we speak in private?"

Benjamin's brows raised. "Certainly. Follow me to my study." Mahala's father turned down the wide hall toward a door on the left. He held the door open for John, and once the two men stepped through, Benjamin closed the door and went to his chair behind the desk.

John sank in a leather chair before the desk and held his breath.

Mahala's father leaned his elbows on the oak table and gazed at John. "What can I do for you?"

John lowered his chin and smiled. When he looked up, he gazed into Benjamin's eyes and took a deep breath. "I came to ask for your daughter's hand in marriage."

Benjamin sat up straight and studied John with a gleam in his eye. "I have four daughters under my roof. Which one might you be interested in?"

The man's response caught John off guard. "You don't know?"

A smile split Benjamin's face. "I've seen the way you look at Mahala."

John felt as if his collar was choking him. He felt his Adam's apple work its way up and then back down. "Sir . . . I'd be honored to marry Mahala."

"Ah. Will wonders never cease. I knew she'd marry the right man one day. I must admit I never expected it would be you who would give her the desires of her heart." Benjamin stood and reached a hand across the oak desk. "You have my blessings, John. I know you'll do good by her."

John squeezed his hand before he let it go. "Thank you, sir."

Benjamin's smile left as quickly as it had come. "This can't be easy, having lost your wife such a short time ago. And you most certainly need a mother for your children. But there's one thing I want to know."

John steadied his gaze on the older man.

"Do you love her? My daughter— Mahala—can you come to love her?" The look in Benjamin's eyes was sincere.

"I already love Mahala, sir. She has stolen my heart through and through." John pinned his gaze on the man.

Benjamin moved around his desk and clapped John on the back. "That's what I wanted to hear." He opened the door. "Have a seat in the parlor, John. I'll tell Mahala you're here." He turned down the hall and called up the stairs. "Mahala. You have company."

John stood under the arched opening of the parlor and waited, relieved that the hard part was over.

Moments later, Mahala appeared on the upper landing. She gazed down at him. "John." She hesitated before she came down the stairs.

"I just had a word with your father," he said in a low voice.

"And?" She gracefully navigated the steps to the ground floor.

A grin spread across his face. "He granted my request."

"To marry me?" She stepped up to him but stopped. She needed to keep space between them, or she might do the unthinkable and reach out to him.

"Yes." He gave her an uncomfortable grin.

"Then it's settled?" She walked to the fireplace then turned and gazed at him and waited.

The grandfather clock struck five times, the chimes gave them a moment to think, to hold each other's gaze. When the clock silenced, Mahala said, "My dress is completed." She folded her hands before her.

"Already?"

"Yes. To be honest, I've been working on it from time to time, so I only needed to finish some small details." She studied John, thinking he was a rare breed of a man. Quite handsome and composed indeed.

John nodded. "I went to town today. The circuit preacher is coming to Grovespring tomorrow." He gazed at Mahala's slender form and took in her beauty while fingering his wide-brimmed hat.

It was all Mahala could do to refrain from removing the hat from his hands before he crumpled it. *Is he a ball of nerves too?*

"It would be best to make arrangements to marry while the preacher is here in town."

"Yes, of course." Mahala waited.

"Then I'll speak to the minister. The ceremony can be held at the church, if that's fine with you."

"I'd prefer that." Mahala's hand went to her chest, and she fingered the pearl button near her throat.

The gesture caused him to notice the slender curve of her neck. And yet a hint of amusement shone in his deep blue eyes. "Are you nervous?"

"A tad. And you?"

"No. I want this." As he was standing in the Shields' parlor and someone entering was a real possibility, he refrained from reaching out to pull Mahala into his arms. But he held her gaze. "Then it's agreed I should make arrangements with the preacher?"

"Yes, John." She held out a hand as if to shake to their agreement. But he clasped his strong fingers over hers and pulled him to his chest.

Mahala gasped and pushed him away as she looked over her shoulder toward the entrance to the room.

John scrunched his hat. "I best get on back to the house. Tess is making supper."

Mahala cleared her throat. "Yes. You should go."

He spun around and headed toward the door.

"Enjoy the evening with your children." She cupped her elbows with her palms.

He turned back. "Would you like to join us?"

"No," Mahala said. "I've things to do to prepare for our special day."

"Well, then, good evening." John placed his hat on his head and went out the door.

Mahala listened to his fading footsteps as he stepped off the porch. She leaned against the door and grinned to herself. *Well, Miss Mahala Shields. You are getting married.* She spun around and headed for the kitchen

"Mother! I have news for you!"

The circuit preacher's in town. I may be getting married this Sunday!

MAMA HURRIED OUT OF the kitchen with Benjamin trailing close behind. From the flustered look on her face, it looked as if they'd had a spat. "Is it true?" Mary didn't wait for Mahala to respond. "Your father tells me that Mr. Grigsby has just come by asking for your hand?"

Mahala felt a knot in her stomach. "Yes. It's true." She gripped the sides of her skirt. "Is there something wrong?" She stared at her father and saw that he looked completely discombobulated.

"Well, am I the last one to learn of this?" Her mother's brows rose. "I would have thought you'd have shared this with me first after all our talks—"

"I thought you'd be happy for me." Mahala felt confusion wash over her.

"Of course I am. But you might have let me in on what you're doing without my having to find out from your father." Mary's brows tented.

The two women stood in the middle of the hall in an emotional gridlock. Mahala couldn't speak, and Mary waited for an explanation.

Taking a deep breath to settle her frayed nerves, Mahala dropped her hands. "It happened so fast, I didn't stop to think about telling you." Mahala was quite surprised by her mother's outburst. What had come over her?

Mary closed her eyes and lowered her chin. "I don't know what has come over me. It seems I have waited forever for this day to come, and now that it has, I've ruined it for you."

Mahala gazed at her mother's face, seeing a glistening of tears rim her eyes. "It's all right, Mama." She smiled and took a deep breath. "You didn't ruin it for me. I'm too happy to let anyone ruin it." She lifted her mother's chin. "I'm truly all right."

Mary nodded and took a deep breath. "I've wanted this for you for such a long time. You deserve to be happy."

"I am, Mama. John loves me. Before now, I wouldn't have been able to say that with certainty. But I know within my heart he does. And the children do too." She bit her lower lip. "And to tell the truth, I love every one of them."

Mary pulled Mahala into her arms. "He's a lucky man."

"I'm a lucky woman. All the years I visited Nancy in their home, I knew John was a prominent figure in our community. And now, I'll be his wife." Mahala held back the floodgates of tears. "And to think, I won't be the town's spinster any longer."

Mary's hand went to her lips. "Who cares what the town thinks?"

Mahala laughed ruefully. "I do."

"So when is the big day?"

"The circuit preacher is due in town tomorrow. John is going to speak with him. It could very well happen on Saturday or Sunday."

"So soon? We haven't a moment to wait. There are a dozen and one things to do before the ceremony." Mary gazed at her husband. "I'm sure you have stock to look after. We women have a lot of ground to cover if we're to have Mahala ready for her special day."

Benjamin looked relieved to be dismissed. He promptly left the hallway and strode out the back door.

Mahala's shoulders relaxed. "Well, at least my gown is ready."

"Thank goodness for that. I certainly want to see it." But her mother's mind seemed to be tallying all that needed to be done. "Do you have any friends we should invite to the wedding?"

Thinking of Nancy, who had always been her true friend, Mahala shook her head. "No—just our families. What with all the Shields and Grigsbys, there will be plenty of people to witness the ceremony."

"All right. We'd best sit at the table and make a list."

"Thank you, Mother. I so wanted your support."

"You have it." Mary kissed Mahala's cheek. "To the kitchen. We haven't a moment to waste."

I'm getting married! Am I ready?

THINGS MOVED SWIFTLY FROM that moment on. She understood John's need for a full-time mother for his children. And in truth, she relished the thought of waking up in the house and meeting each child as their day began. But as much as she cared for John and Nancy's children, she wished for some time alone with John before they wed. She knew that all too soon they would be thrown into the routine of household chores and ranch duties.

Would the children mind her becoming their stepmother? Mary Jane, as well as John's two youngest sons, surely wouldn't be an issue. They would need her no matter the circumstances. But what of the four older children? She wouldn't blame them if they weren't ready. And yet Nancy had made Mahala promise to take care of her children. What better way than to become John's wife?

MAHALA LOOKED OUT HER window to see the moon illuminating the world below. The rest of the family were sound asleep, while she lay wide awake. She couldn't still the excitement running through her. She'd never known such fullness in her heart as she felt at that moment. It was as if she could fly, she was so happy. *I'm getting married!* Pure joy rippled through her, so much so that she could hardly contain it. Had this been what she'd been missing all this time? Did every woman feel as elated as she?

Beyond the shadowed rooftops of the outbuildings, the river glimmered in the moonlight—beckoning to her. Having stayed awake well into the night, and her room stifling hot, Mahala imagined the river water would be cool and soothing to the touch. Maybe a walk in the night air would settle her—help her fall asleep. She lit the kerosene lamp and ran tepid water over her face. She stared at the rumpled bedcovers and knew she couldn't go back to bed just yet.

Not waiting another moment, Mahala stepped out of her room and quietly tiptoed downstairs. She negotiated the dark hallway that led to the back door and slipped out into the warm summer night. Once she stood on the back step, a slight breeze blew upon her face, and the treetops waved like feathered fans as the wisp of air danced through the leaves.

Light from her bedroom window dimly illuminated the ground before her as she crept through the damp grass to follow the path to the river. The night was far from silent as the crickets and cicadas droned endlessly and frogs sang their bass. A small splash cut through the stillness as a bullfrog jumped into the water.

The moon lit the way as she followed the trail through the field. Moments later, having passed through a thicket of trees, she padded barefoot to the banks of the river. She hugged herself as she listened to the dancing water rippling downstream. In a nearby cove, catfish swam in and around the smooth rocks. In the branches hovering above her, crickets silenced their chirrups, seemingly aware of her presence—but not for long. As if being led by an unseen hand, they struck up their chorus again.

Mahala dipped her toe in the water, the coolness washing over her. A few days from now she would be standing on another bank, that one at the Grigsby ranch, her new home. Tears of joy brimmed her eyes, and she let them flow freely down her cheeks. "Thank you, Lord. You didn't forget me," she whispered into the night. "I just ask that You give me guidance and help me to be a good wife to John."

The water slid over the rocks, the rushing sounds comforting to her soul.

"I hope John can love me half as much as he did Nancy." Mahala brushed the tears from her cheeks and pressed her fingertips to her lips.

A sharp snap alerted her that she wasn't alone, and she lifted her head to glance across the water. The bushes rustled across the way. She studied the dark trees about her. Had someone followed her to the river's edge?

The crickets ceased their chirping again and the bullfrogs stilled their song. A tense silence closed in around her. She waited a breath of a moment before she turned and padded back to the house, her feet swiftly pounding the worn path. When she reached the outbuildings, she slowed her steps and glanced behind her. She searched the dark woods for movement—no one was there. Still, she picked up her steps and ran through the dew-covered grasses until she came to the back steps. The horses chuffed inside the stable. Charley would be sound asleep in the bunkhouse.

"Goodness, Father. Was that your way of getting me back to the house? Or could someone have truly been out there?"

Mahala waited no longer. She turned the doorknob to the back door and retraced her steps to her room. She blew out the light and slipped into bed. She'd let sweet dreams take over tonight. Would the circuit preacher really come to town, and if so would he be available to marry them?

THE FOLLOWING MORNING, JOHN whistled in the early morning hour. He whistled while he milked Bossie and Ginger. When finished, he whistled while he filled the milk cans with the fresh warm milk. He continued to whistle while he hauled the two cans inside the small springhouse and set them into the cold, running water. And he whistled while he saddled Blue to ride to town.

Granville and Calvin set to work filling buckets with oats and fed the stock. They eyed their father and then each other. When John rode out the gate to the main road, the two boys stared at each other. "What's up with Dad?" Granville asked.

"I don't know, but he's sure been acting strange lately." Calvin swatted at the flies buzzing around his head and poured grain in Bossie's bin. When he straightened, he gazed out the barn door. "What do you suppose he's up to?"

"Don't know," Granville said. "Let's finish getting these cows fed and the horses brushed down so we can go down to the creek before it gets too hot." He picked up a curry brush and began brushing down Star's black coat. The horse chuffed and snorted as Granville ran his hand lightly over Star's velvet chin.

"Do you think Dad's got a secret he's not telling us about?" Calvin wouldn't let it go.

"If he does, we'll learn about it soon enough. Now come on, Cal, we're burning daylight." He set the brush aside and strode out of the stall.

Calvin still couldn't let it go. "Don't you wanna know what Dad's secret is?

Chapter THIRTY-TWO

THE STEADY POUNDING OF the horses' hooves and the relentless sway of the stagecoach made it hard for Alexander Bates to keep his eyes open. More than once he awoke to find his chin had dropped to his chest. He lifted heavy eyelids to glance at his fellow passengers. His gaze ran over the two women who sat across from him. A young, blonde-haired woman held her brown purse in her lap as if her life depended on it. She wore a flounced skirt that seemed to have several layers to it. An older woman sat next to her. He suspected she was the younger woman's chaperone. A heavy-set man sat to his right.

The passengers had acknowledged each other with nods and quiet greetings when they first boarded the coach. But once the team of horses galloped out of town, they all grew drowsy, words few.

The leather seats lacked cushioning, and after ten days on the road, Alexander's body ached from head to toe. Not a man to complain, he did his best to remain amiable to his fellow passengers.

Bart, the stagecoach driver, told the travelers that since the heat was unusually high, they could ride with the leather curtains pulled back. Alexander let his gaze stray out of the window, taking in the change of scenery. Once they left the city, much of it was fields, trees, and cattle.

"There it is, folks!" Bart called out from his high perch as the Wells Fargo stagecoach neared the outskirts of town. "Grovespring!" The bouncing stage eased as the horses slowed their steps. Alexander gazed at the small town ahead. *Small.* At last, the stage stopped in front of a row of storefronts. Looking out the window, Alexander read the name of the shop where the stagecoach had stopped. Thompson's Tailor Shop. Well, the town had a men's shop. Living in a small community such as this couldn't be too bad if it could support a tailor. He picked up his pinstriped suit jacket and shrugged into it. His top hat sat on the seat next to him. He reached for it and shoved it onto his damp hair.

The stage had pulled into Grovespring fifteen minutes earlier than Bart said they would arrive. When Alexander alighted from the coach, he reached for his bag at his feet. He would send the rest of his bags to the hotel. Standing on the boardwalk, he looked up and down the street and found what he was looking for. Up ahead a large sign read, Yates Hotel and Café. He set his bag on the ground, and lifting his hat, he combed his fingers through his hair. Replacing his hat he strode toward the nice-looking building, reminding himself why he was here. He hoped to find the woman he was looking for.

Pedestrians stared after him and then each other as they passed him on the boardwalk. An agreeable amount of traffic flowed on the streets. It was too hot and too gritty for sensible people to be out and about in the middle of July.

Nearing the hotel, Alexander reached for the doorknob, wanting to get settled into a room and eat a good meal. The door flew open and a tall, dark-haired man with a short growth of beard nearly bumped into to him. He held a milk can in each hand and stopped abruptly. "Excuse me, sir." He held the door open with his boot.

The two men nodded, and Alexander touched the brim of his top hat. "Good afternoon, sir."

"You just get off the stage?" the stranger asked.

"Yes. We just rode in."

The stranger set the milk cans on the ground and stretched out a hand. "Welcome to Grovespring. My name's, John Grigsby."

Alexander took his strong hand and said, "Alexander Bates." He glanced into the dark room. "Can a man get a good meal in this establishment?" He stared down at the milk cans on the ground by Grigsby's boots.

"The best in town. Gertie Yates will take good care of you."

"Good. Good." Alexander felt a trail of sweat trickle down his neck. "Good day, then."

"I'll see you around." John Grigsby picked up the two empty milk cans and strode to a wagon parked in front of the hotel.

Once inside, it took a moment for Alexander's eyes to adjust to the dimness of the lobby. The bright sun had a way of making a room seem dark when you first stepped into it. To the left there was a large opening that led to a dining room. Eager to get settled, he went to the registration desk to check in. It didn't take long for a middle-aged man to assist him with a room and a key, and Alexander soon went up the stairs to his room. He set his luggage on a chair by the bed and went to the window, which looked down on Main Street. Gazing at the street below, he had a bird's eye view of the small town. *Where are you, Mahala Shields?* Before the day was done, he planned to find out where she lived and pay the young woman a visit.

ALEXANDER SHRUGGED OUT OF his pin-striped jacket and draped it over the back of the chair. He went to the wash stand, picked up the cream-colored pitcher, and poured warm water into the porcelain bowl. It felt refreshing as he splashed water onto his face and washed the trail dust from him. He'd acquired a shadow on his chin since the trip and pulled out a razor from his traveling bag.

Moments later, he examined his features as he stood before the mirror hanging on the wall behind the washstand. Lastly, he combed his salt-and-pepper hair, trimmed close to his head, and wished the gnawing in his gut would go away. The thought of searching out the fair lady who had kept him awake too many nights in the past weeks had set his nerves on end.

Being the owner of a successful company, he met strangers frequently in order to strike deals in the iron business. Meeting people he'd never met before was common in his field of work and he seldom experienced a wave of nerves like he felt now. Yet here he stood in this small community about to search for his future wife, his mind and stomach in a tailspin.

He reached into his vest pocket, pulled out the small silver frame, and gazed at the miniature-likeness of the dark-haired beauty. Had he been a fool to think that a young woman like her would accept his hand in marriage? It had been too long since he'd courted a woman. That he'd ridden the Wells Fargo stagecoach over 600 miles to meet this lady was thoroughly out of character for him. His stomach growled as the aroma of good-smelling food wafted into his room. He'd go down to the dining room and eat before he set out in search of Mahala Shields.

The dining room had cleared of customers some since he'd last glanced into the room. A waitress led him to a table and took his order. When she turned to leave, he asked, "Excuse me, ma'am. Would it be possible to speak with the proprietor of this establishment when I finish my meal?"

The young woman smiled. "I'm sure that can be arranged, sir." She stared at his attire and paused as if she wanted to say more, but instead, she turned and headed for the kitchen.

A HALF HOUR LATER, Alexander Bates stood in the hotel lobby with Gertie Yates. "You don't suppose a man could hire a hackney in these parts, do you?"

"A hackney, Mr. Bates?" Her eyes lit up. "I've not heard that term in many years—at least since I moved away from New York. And no," she chuckled. "You won't be hiring a fancy coach like that in these parts. The best you can do is rent a buggy from Kyle Weaver's livery stable down the road. It won't cost you a pretty penny either."

"Thank you, Mrs. Yates. I believe I'll pay your liveryman a visit."

Gertie's eyes flickered over him appreciatively, admiring the top hat, striped suit and polished shoes. "If you don't mind my asking, what do you do for a living, sir?"

Mr. Bates eyed her, a keen look in his eyes. He pushed the front of his jacket aside, revealing a starched white shirt and red suspenders. He slid his thumbs under his suspenders and his chest went out a tad. "I own a company called Bates Western Iron Company. We make iron for all facets of life, ma'am. But more importantly, our current line of business is making iron rails for the railroad." He grinned with a glint in his eyes. "The railroad will be coming to your neck of the woods before you know it." He snapped his suspenders and closed his jacket.

It was all Gertie could do to shut her mouth after it had gone slack. That was some information coming from this rich man. And to think, he'd booked a room in her hotel.

"So, Mr. Bates. What are you doing in our little town—if you don't mind my asking?"

"I'm looking for Miss Mahala Shields. I understand she lives in these parts, does she not?"

"She does." Gertie stared at him, gauging his age.

"Ma'am?"

"Oh, I'm sorry, Mr. Bates. Mahala lives outside of town on her father's ranch." Gertie spent the next few minutes giving him directions to his destination. When Mr. Bates thanked her and headed toward Kyle Weaver's livery stable, she turned around and said to no one, " Well, don't that beat all!

My Isabella could sure have used a man like him!

JOHN SPURRED BLUE TOWARD town as the morning heat bore down on his back. The Shady Hollow Bridge came into view, and horse and rider crossed over the creek through the covered bridge. It wasn't long before he joined the flow of traffic in town where wagons and pedestrians filled the streets.

Searching the street for the preacher's mode of transportation, he found what he was looking for. There sat his black buggy parked outside the Yates Café. John reined Blue to the side of the road and dismounted. He tied Blue to the hitching post, then squared his shoulders. *I sure hope that's the reverend inside.*

When he entered the café, it took a moment for his eyes to adjust to the dimness of the room. But the food smelled good and his stomach rumbled. Gazing over the crowd, John made a split-second decision to have a seat and eat with the minster if the man was here.

"Good morning, Mr. Grigsby." A waitress strode up with a silver coffee pot in her hand. She tilted her head toward the room. "Find a seat. I'll be with you in a moment." She carried the pot to a table where two men sat. She filled their cups with the steaming brew, then pulled out a pad and took their order.

John stood for a moment, looking over the tables as low hum of conversation filled the room. A man sat at a table by the window, his back to John, wearing a black jacket in spite of the summer heat. John recognized the man as Reverend Fraser, and lucky for him, the seat opposite the minister was empty. John strode across the floor and stopped at the table. "Morning, Reverend, mind if I sit here?"

The slight man gazed up through round spectacles. "Good morning, Mr. Grigsby." Cup in hand, he waved it across the table. "Have a seat."

"Did you just get in?" John picked up a rolled cloth filled with silverware. He sat the utensils on the table and, with the white napkin, dabbed at the sweat on his brow.

The preacher chuckled silently and set his cup down. "You know, it always amazes me how fast word spreads. By the time I get to town, folks are waiting for me." He gave John a knowing look. "What can I do for you?"

John's ears burned and a slow grin spread across his face. "I'm in need of a preacher to marry me and my intended."

The preacher stared at him, his lips grim. "I heard about your wife dying last fall. You lost a good woman." John saw kindness in the man's brown eyes.

"Nobody will ever replace Nancy. She was one of a kind. I miss her, the children miss her—every day." The air grew thick between them.

"But you found a woman to help you and the children get through all of this." It was a statement that hung in the air.

"She's more than that, sir. She's a jewel. She'll make me and my children more than happy." He fingered the napkin and held the reverend's gaze.

"You're a lucky man then—to have found the right woman—twice."

"I have, sir."

"Well, you aren't the only one in need of a minister. That's why I'm here." He raised his glass of water and took a long drink.

John dropped the napkin onto the table and folded his hands. "Is it possible for you to perform a ceremony for us after the Sunday service?"

"Regrettably, no. I've got two weddings I'm performing after the service." He swallowed. "One right after the other."

The waitress arrived at their table and set a plate of eggs and ham before the preacher. She pulled a pad out of her apron pocket and held it before her. "What can I get for you, Mr. Grigsby?"

He stared at the dish in front of Reverend Fraser. "What he's having looks good to me. And I'll have a cup of strong coffee to go along with it."

"Of course." She scribbled on the pad and slid it back into her pocket. "I'll pour you a cup of coffee while you wait." The slim woman strode to a side counter where cups and glasses waited to be filled.

"Getting back to what I was telling you, sir, I'm full up after church this coming Sunday," Reverend Fraser continued.

John's hopes went up in smoke. "That's too bad." He stared out of the café window. "Mahala and I wanted a church wedding."

"Does it have to be on Sunday?" The reverend picked up his knife and fork and began cutting up his ham and eggs.

John's head shot up. "I don't suppose it does. What are you proposing?" Air came back into his lungs.

"I'm only here for a week. I have commitments nearly every day I'm here, but I can do it Thursday afternoon, say around four o'clock."

John let out the air he'd been holding. "That would be fine, Reverend—at the church, of course."

"Of course." The pastor lifted his cup as if to say, "'Cheers.'"

"I appreciate it, Reverend. I'll let the family know." John raised his cup to his lips and drank in the hot liquid. Setting talk of the appointment aside, the two men carried on about local affairs. An hour later, John touched the brim of his hat. "We'll see you at the church on Thursday, Pastor."

"I expect I'll see you at the Sunday service?" He pushed his wire-rimmed glasses up his nose.

"You can count on us." John left the establishment with a bounce to his step.

When he arrived home, John gathered his children together in the sitting room. Five pairs of eyes watched him expectantly, while the two younger boys played on the floor.

"I suppose you've been wondering what I've been up to lately." He studied the faces of his children.

"You're finally going to tell us?" Tess sat down on the sofa, her hands in her lap.

John opened his mouth and shut it and then cleared his throat. "I've decided to marry Mahala Shields."

"Yippee!" Mary Jane squealed and hugged herself. "Does that mean Mahala will stay with us forever?"

Granville and Calvin gave their father timid smiles at first, and then, after looking at each other, wide grins spread across their faces.

Relief flooded through John as he gauged the boys' reactions along with Mary Jane's, but he hadn't heard from Tess. He turned his gaze on her.

"Does that mean she will move in with us?" Tess asked.

"Yes, it does." John clamped his lips tightly together, his heart thudding in his chest.

"What about Mom?"

He watched Tess visibly swallow, and they held each other's gaze for the longest time. Finally, he broke the silence. "Your mother asked Mahala to look after all of you when she knew that she and baby David were going to heaven." He looked into Tess's eyes. "Mahala kept her promise when she said she would. I believe your mama would be happy knowing Mahala will always be here to look after you."

Tess stared down at her hands and nodded, and then she glanced around the room. "It'll be nice having a mother again."

Her remark sent a blow to John's heart. He let out the breath he'd been holding. "Then you all agree?"

"Yes!" came a chorus of cries.

Franklin stood to the side, seeming to observe the family. When John gazed at him, Franklin nodded as if to say he too agreed this was best.

John opened his arms and six children rushed in to hug him. Giggles filled the air as the children pushed each other out of the way. Tall and lanky, Franklin looked on with a pleased smile on his face.

When the noise and jostling settled down, Tess asked, "When will you marry her?"

"This Thursday." John stood and pulled Tess to her feet. He put an arm around her shoulder. "The circuit preacher's in town. We have to take advantage of the time he's here."

"Does Mahala know it's so soon?" Tess looked up with a twinkle of conspiracy in her eyes.

"I'm going to ride over right now and tell her. I need you to look after the younger children."

"I will." Tess threw her arms around him. "I love you, Dad."

John kissed the top of her head. "You've been a big help all these months. Your mother would be so proud."

John strode out of the house with a huge weight off his shoulders. He hitched Brownie to the wagon. *Will Mahala be able to be ready by Thursday?*

MAHALA PULLED THE CURTAIN aside when she heard a wagon pull into the yard. "John," she whispered. She went to the door and stepped out onto the porch. "Good afternoon. Have you got news for me?" She clasped her hands together and smiled at him.

"I do. I'd like to take you for a drive and talk about it."

"I'll be right back." She picked up her skirts and went to the kitchen where her mother was kneading bread dough. "I'm going for a ride with John."

"What did he find out about the preacher?"

"He hasn't said. I'll tell you when we get back." She gave Mary a peck on the cheek and went out the door.

John stood waiting beside the wagon when Mahala came outside. He gave her a hand onto the wooden seat. Moments later, they rode down the dirt road. When they neared the covered bridge, he pulled the wagon to the side of the lane and set the brake.

He turned to Mahala and took her slender hands in his. "I talked to Reverend Fraser this morning." He looked out over the fields and visibly swallowed.

"What is it?" Mahala's heart tripped as if she were about to hear bad news and she held her breath.

"The minister can't marry us on Sunday."

"Oh." She pulled her hands out of his and balled them in her lap.

John took one hand back. "The reverend's already committed to two weddings after the morning service."

"I see." Her countenance faltered and tears rimmed her eyes.

John squeezed her hand. "Not knowing how long each wedding will take, he didn't want to schedule a third wedding on the same day."

"Of course." Her voice was nearly a whisper.

"But—"

Mahala's eyes flew to his. "But what?"

"The reverend suggested we do it Thursday." His eyes searched hers.

Mahala held his gaze and life came back into her eyes. "That's two days from now."

"I know—is it possible to make that happen?"

"Do we have a choice?"

"No—but you said your dress is ready." He looked hopeful.

"It is."

"We'd have to get the word out to our families to meet us at the church at four o'clock, Thursday afternoon." John watched uncertainty wash over her features.

"I suppose it can be done. I need to get back to the house right away so I can tell my parents. Between Dad and Benny, they might be able to get the word out."

"I have family who need to be informed as well."

"So . . . has the reverend held the time for us on Thursday?"

John's face lit up. "Yes. I told him we would be there."

Mahala couldn't contain herself. She threw her arms around John. "We're getting married in two days?"

"We are," he chuckled.

Mahala moved back and smoothed the fabric of her skirt. "I need to get home right this minute. I haven't a moment to waste."

John grinned and turned the wagon around. They rode back to the Shields' ranch in silence. When they pulled in front of the house, he stepped down and went around to help Mahala alight.

She had a strong suspicion that her mother and sisters were watching them through the window. She stood on the ground and looked up into his strong face. It took all of her reserve to keep her hands to herself. She clasped them together and held his gaze. "Good day, John. I will see you Thursday."

His voice sounded husky as he said, "I'll be waiting." He kissed her cheek and climbed back into the wagon.

Mahala's knees went weak. She lifted a hand to wave goodbye.

When she turned toward the house, she said, "Holy Moses! We've got to get busy!"

July 14, 1842

ON THIS SUN-DRENCHED DAY, the buggy carried Mahala to the church. Nearly two dozen people were in attendance. In the dense heat, such a crowd caused the humidity to thicken under the rafters.

She waited in the foyer, the double doors closed to the interior that buzzed with the sound of family and friends who waited with curious fascination. How the two families got the word out in so little time was nothing short of a miracle. .

John Grigsby, in a fine cutaway coat, waistcoat, and trousers, stood at the reverend's left. Charles Matthews, his best man, stood to his right. John's demeanor was calm, but his eyes skimmed the interior of the church. Along the front row and to the right sat Mahala's mother, Mary, Mahala's sisters and her brother, Benny. To the left sat John's brother Jesse, his wife, Margaret, and John's six children. Their eyes watched his every move, and when he stared to the back of the room to the closed double doors, they turned to see if the bride would soon appear.

Dixie Trubridge sat at the pump organ and struck the first chords of the music. The wedding guests stood every eye trained to catch the first glimpse of the beautiful bride. A gasped hush spread through the room as Mahala entered on her father's arm. Her shimmering gown intensified in whiteness as the sunlight lit the room.

John's heart pounded in his throat and his nerves tightened as he eyed Mahala slowly walking toward him.

The wedding guests watched her glide gracefully down the aisle. Every eye was fastened on the beautiful bride. Her face alight from within, Mahala walked toward her smiling groom. The power of his love-filled eyes calmed her wildly beating heart.

The music faded as Mahala moved to John. He stepped forward, and she slipped her hand into the crook of his arm. Mahala turned and kissed her father's cheek. "Thank you, Father." Benjamin Shields patted his daughter's hand and whispered, "You make a beautiful bride. He stepped away to sit with his family.

"You may be seated," Reverend Fraser spoke to the congregation, and then turned his attention to the bride and groom. A rustle filled the air as the guests took their seats.

Reverend Fraser cleared his throat and looked out over the congregation, then gazed down at the little black book in his hand. "Dearly Beloved, Forasmuch as Marriage is a holy sacrament, ordained by God, and to be held in honor by all, it is fitting to weigh with reverent minds, what the Word teaches concerning it. And the Lord God said, 'It is not good that man should be alone, and I will make a help meet for him."

John squeezed Mahala's hand and she felt her knees go weak.

"We are gathered here today to celebrate one of life's greatest moments, and to cherish the words that shall unite John and Mahala in marriage. Marriage is the promise between two people who love and trust each other and choose to spend the rest of their lives together."

Butterflies took residence in Mahala's stomach as she stood next to the man she loved. In a few short moments she would be Mrs. John Grigsby.

"John Grigsby, do you promise to have this woman to be thy wedded wife, to live together after God's ordinance in holy matrimony?"

"I do," came his deep voice.

"Do you promise to love her, comfort her, honor and keep her, in sickness and in health, and forsaking all others, to keep thee only onto her, so long as you both shall live?"

John's eyes held Mahala's and he smiled. "I do."

In a haze, the reverend turned to Mahala and repeated the same words. With her heart nearly bursting, she lifted her eyes to John and she said, "I do." She swallowed hard to stem the tears of joy that wanted to fall.

"The ring?"

Charles Matthews handed the ring to the preacher then stepped aside.

"With this ring, I thee wed," John echoed the reverend as he slid the gold band onto Mahala's finger. He lifted her hand to his lips and kissed her hand where the gleaming gold band rested. "I'm yours forever, Mrs. Grigsby."

She could feel the guests holding their breath. Not a sound could be heard except the whirring of insects that flew about the room.

The reverend's eyes lit up as he closed the small book. "You may now kiss your bride!" The crowd led out their breath and laughed and cheered as Mahala lifted her face to John. He pulled her into his embrace, and Mahala felt his taut body against her own. She felt his warm breath as he leaned down and pulled her tighter. He took his time as his lips grazed hers. She wanted to savor this moment but not in the presence of these people. She leaned in to kiss him soundly and then pulled away, feeling heat beat a path to her cheeks. Still, she held his gaze and noticed his face was ruddy as well.

The reverend said his final words, "Let no man put asunder that which God hath coupled together."

John and Mahala held hands as they walked out of the church past the elated guests. Congratulations and well wishes hummed through the air, and men clapped John on the back.

Before stepping into the carriage, Mahala stopped long enough to embrace her father and mother, tears flowing freely. "I love you!"

"Daddy!" the smaller children called, their eyes bright, and the older children had smiles lighting their faces. Their aunt Margaret stood beside them, Wiley on her hip. "We'll bring the children home in a couple of days." She waved goodbye with the others.

Cheers and laughter filled the air as John and Mahala climbed into the buggy. They held hands as they rode to John's ranch by the river.

From the moment John asked her to marry him, the days had been a whirlwind. Gazing at the handsome man sitting beside her, she could hardly believe that just like that,—she was a married woman.

Chapter THIRTY-THREE

JOHN PULLED MAHALA AGAINST his side as they made the short drive home. When they came to the entrance to the drive, Mahala's heart nearly leapt from her chest, *Home!*

John drove the buggy to the backyard and began to unhitch Brownie. "You can go on into the house while I put the horse away." His ears burned a dark red.

Mahala stilled the giggle in her throat, but she couldn't stifle the grin. "Mind if I stay and accompany you?"

John's head jerked up and relief shone in his eyes. "Not at all." Moments later, he held Brownie's harness. "Right this way." He led Brownie into the barn as Mahala followed them down the wide aisle to the stall. John opened the gate and Brownie chuffed as he stepped into his cubicle. John picked up the curry brush and began brushing the mustang down. When done, he poured a small bucket of oats into the horse's feed bin.

While John worked, Mahala went from stall to stall and talked to each of the horses. Star snorted and looked over his gate and nuzzled her hand with his velvet nose. "Aren't you a handsome boy?" Mahala murmured, admiring the black mustang with the white star on his forehead.

John watched from a distance, his heart in his throat. Mahala was a sight to see in her glimmering gown, her dark hair curled softly over her shoulders, and the hem of her dress flecked with bits of straw. He swallowed. "This might not be the best place for you—dressed as you are." He gazed down at her white-slippered feet.

Mahala bent to see the hem of her skirt trailing straw and dust in its wake. Her shoes were no longer white on the sides. Her eyes grew wide.

"Goodness!" She lifted her skirts and tiptoed back to the entrance of the barn.

Mooo!

Mahala jumped and turned toward Bossie, a red-and-white cow, who leaned her head out of the gate. "Well, hello to you, too." Mahala stood her ground, not knowing if she should stay put or head to the house. She gazed from the barn opening to the back door.

She felt John's breath on her neck as he slid his arms around her waist, her back against his chest. "I'm done here. We can go to the house." He kissed her temple.

Mahala thought her legs would buckle if she didn't step out of John's embrace. "Lead the way."

John took her hand and the two went through the yard to the back of the house. He opened the door and held out a hand. "After you."

Mahala had been to this house more times than she could count but always as a visitor. To enter this home as the mistress of the house nearly took her breath away. She walked down the dark hall toward the front room, passing John's bedroom on the way.

John paused behind her, his deep resonant voice breaking the silence. "Our room is over here if you'd like to change."

Our room? Mahala turned to see John standing before the bedroom entrance. Heat traveled up her neck and over her scalp. She shut her mouth. "Of course. Um . . . but my bag is still in the buggy."

"I'll get it for you." John appeared relieved to have something to do, and he quickly turned and went out the back door.

Mahala stared at the bed in their room, her heart sinking to her feet. The last time she'd stood in this room she'd said 'goodbye' to Nancy. Could she sleep in this bed tonight?

JOHN FOUND PLENTY TO do while Mahala fixed a meal for the two of them. Neither seemed hungry, but they ate in silence as their eyes clung to each other. Before the sun went down, John stood. "I better put the stock to bed." He quirked a smile. "This may be our wedding night, but I still have cows to milk."

Mahala laughed softly, and she gently shoved him out the door. "Take care of the animals while I change for bed."

His eyes flew to hers, and the longing she saw in them sent a thrill through her. "Go on." She nudged him.

"I'll be right back." He flashed a smile.

The memory of the light in his eyes stayed with her as she unbuttoned her dress and let it slip to the floor. She gazed out the window, feeling as if she were working against the clock to dawn her nightgown before John returned.

Why she felt apprehensive, she didn't know. After all, he was her husband, but a part of her felt timid at John seeing her undressed. Would he be disappointed that she had little to no womanly curves? Her cheeks burned at the thought of John seeing her body thin as a stick. Surely this will pass, she chided herself, as she sat down at the vanity table to comb out her hair.

By the time John returned, the moon was high and anticipation shone in his eyes.

But what was it about him that she sensed? Hesitation? As she watched John slowly unbuttoned his shirt and tossed it across the end of the bed. Did he feel reluctant as well?

Mahala stared at his bare chest and then looked up to see longing in his eyes.

"Come here."

She slid her arms around his waist and lifted her face to his. She heard his low moan as he claimed her lips. When they broke away, he held her tightly, and neither moved nor spoke for what seemed an eternity.

John finally broke the silence with a heavy sigh. "Let's go to bed."

When they stepped apart, he went to one side of the bed and she went to the other side—Nancy's side. Mahala stared at the starched-white pillowcase covering the pillow. She swallowed. *Nancy . . . Tomorrow, I will ride to Father's house and bring my own pillow back here.*

They each blew out a kerosene lamp on their side of their bed, and the room grew dark. A faint haze, highlighted in the moonlight, drifted across the bed.

When Mahala pulled back the covers and slipped under the sheets, she whispered, "Do you mind if we don't—"

She felt John's warm breath against her cheek. "If you're not ready—we can wait." But when she gazed into his eyes, even in the darkness, she found disappointment in his expression.

"I just need a little time."

"Is it me?"

"No," she said truthfully. She clutched the side of her gown beneath the covers wanting to say the right thing but fearful it would come out wrong.

"It's just—"

John touched her lips with a forefinger and kissed her forehead. "No need to explain. Do you mind if I hold you?" Seeing Mahala lying next to him, her long dark hair fanning over her shoulders, it was all he could do to keep from taking her in his arms and claiming her, but his heated desire would have to wait.

In response, Mahala turned to him and lay her head on his chest. "Mmm."

"What is that supposed to mean?"

"I've wanted to do this for some time—listen to your heartbeat."

"And?"

"It sounds wonderful." Mahala closed her eyes and let the rhythm of John's heart lull her to sleep.

Moments later, John gazed down at his bride, her eyelashes fanning her cheeks. *Oh Lord, how long before I can claim my bride in every way as a new husband?*

THURSDAY AFTERNOON, ALEXANDER BATES sat in the black buggy after having knocked on the front door of Shields' home. Not a soul answered his raps, not even a servant. When he climbed back into the rig, he gazed out at the Hereford cattle grazing in the range, but no cowhands sat on horses among them.

Where is everybody?

Disappointed that no one answered the door, Alexander flicked the reins across the mare's rump and headed back to town.

The next two days, Alexander Bates rented a buggy again and familiarized himself with the territory and where the boundary lines may lie when the railroad wound its way through these parts. He didn't need to know the route, as his involvement only entailed the process of making the iron rails. But with time on his hands and curiosity on his mind, he scouted out the area.

In the meantime, he tried again to meet Miss Shields at her father's ranch, only to be told by a young teenage boy named Benny, that Mahala wasn't home, and he didn't know when she would return.

Finally, after having traveled 600 miles to meet his prospective bride, and greatly disappointed he'd made no progress, Alexander returned to the hotel. The Wells Fargo stagecoach would be arriving in Grovespring tomorrow morning, and he would have to be on it. He sat at the desk below the street-side window in his hotel room and penned a letter to Mahala Shields.

Dear Miss Shields,

I came to Grovespring in hopes of meeting you and perhaps gaining your favor in marriage. And though I have traveled to your fair town, time and circumstances have prevented us from meeting. Unfortunately, I must travel home to Pennsylvania, as I have a company that needs my attention.

If by chance, and at the reading of this letter, you have not married and may still be interested in meeting, please send another post. I look forward to hearing from you again.

Warm regards and at your service,
Alexander Bates

JOHN ROSE EARLY AS he did every morning on his ranch. He gazed at the sleeping form of Mahala and watched her steady breathing. It was his first morning to awaken to seeing her vulnerable to his eyes. He wanted to reach out and touch her dark hair and run the back of his finger over her soft cheek, but instead, he slid out of bed and silently left the room with his boots in his hands. He tiptoed out to the back steps and sat down to shove his stockinged feet into his boots. He heaved a contented sigh. *Well, Lord. I've got that beautiful woman lying in my bed. But things haven't quite gone the way I thought they would. Could You work on her a little to make her feel comfortable at the end of the day? And I'd sure appreciate it if You could make things a bit easier between us.*

John looked up at the deep blue of the vast sky. Billowing clouds sailed overhead, promising a summer rain in the next day or two. For now, John took it all in, the far-reaching cattle range and the far-reaching heavens above him. He bowed his head once more and thanked God for giving him Mahala and for his many blessings. *How can a man be so blessed, Lord?*

In the distance he saw his four cowhands moving about at the corral, getting ready to saddle their horses. John pushed away from the steps and headed for the bunkhouse. He knew Corky would have a good breakfast waiting for him, and he was ready for a cup of coffee before he saddled Blue. He may have just gotten married, but he still had a ranch to run.

MAHALA EYES POPPED OPEN and she blinked at the bright room. Had she slept the morning away? Sitting up, she turned to see that John had already left the room. For a brief moment, she felt disappointment that he had already left to start the day. She would have laid her cheek against his chest and listened to his heart and reveled in his arms as he held her close. But having grown up on a cattle ranch, she knew that a million and one responsibilities sat on John's strong shoulders. He would have gone to the barn and milked his cows before going out to check the stock, repair fences, or any of the other countless tasks required to keep a ranch running.

She moved to the side of the bed, her feet touching the cool floorboards. She stretched and then glanced down at Nancy's pillow, and then out the window, where she could see the morning was well on its way. If she were going to be the woman of the house, she'd have to get up earlier than this. She smiled to herself, though. This was only the day after her wedding, and no children awaited an early meal. John had informed her that he'd get breakfast at the bunkhouse. She was free to get up when she was ready.

Try as she may, languishing in bed was not an easy thing to do. Her mind was full of things she wanted to accomplish before the day got away from her and while John was out in the fields. First thing first, she would unpack her trunk and hang her day dresses and gowns in the wardrobe. But nature called, and she donned her robe and slippers and hurried out to the freshly painted outhouse. When she returned to the bedroom, she threw open the mahogany doors to the wardrobe and stopped.—There lined neatly on the pole, were all of Nancy's clothes—all of them. Mahala looked down to see that Nancy's shoes were lined up as well, the toes pointing toward her.

"Oh, dear," she groaned and felt the air go out of her lungs. Hurt and confused, she stared at the full wardrobe. She hadn't quite imagined that she'd find Nancy's garments still hanging.

What was she supposed to do with them? She couldn't just gather them up and toss them aside. The thought of doing so felt barbaric, and beyond that, she didn't feel as if she had the right to do it. And even if she did, where would she put them?

Mahala left the doors to the wardrobe open as she glanced back to the open trunk. Her gowns waited, tucked neatly within. She bit her bottom lip. "Well, this is a fine kettle of fish." She couldn't help it, irritation pricked her flesh, along with a dash of guilt.

She crossed the wooden floor to her trunk that sat below the window. She raised the window and breathed in the morning breeze that fluttered the white lace curtains. She gazed out at the peach grove across the drive. The trees were full of fruit, and beyond the orchard, cattle speckled the fields. John was out there somewhere, and here she stood with unfinished business.

Disappointed, Mahala dressed for the day and left the room, leaving the trunk lid open. She would wait until John came in and let him decide what to do with Nancy's clothes. As much as she loved Nancy, it needled her that she had been reminded once more that she was moving into Nancy's house—Nancy's world. Would she ever feel like this home was her own?

JOHN LED BLUE TO his stall and poured oats in his bucket. The other horses, Brownie and Star, looked over their gates and snorted. After he ate lunch he would put them out in the fields with the other horses to run.

He crossed the yard to the back door, eager to see Mahala. She was all he could think about as he roamed the pastures checking on his herd. He couldn't forget the image of her lying on his bed, fast asleep. Contentment filled him.

As he swung the back door open, he glanced down the dark hall, wondering where he might find Mahala. Much to his surprise, he found her sitting on the side of the bed, a gown draped across her lap and a sour look across her face. He stood at the entrance to the room, gaping down at her. "What's wrong?"

Mahala pointed to the open wardrobe. "I have nowhere to hang my clothes." No sooner had she said the words than tears sprang to her eyes.

John moved into the room and stared at Nancy's wardrobe. A wave of shame engulfed him and he hung his head. With chin to chest, he knew he had to rectify this mistake right away. He ran his fingers through his hair and swung his gaze to Mahala.

"You'll have to forgive me, Mahala. I haven't had to look inside the wardrobe all these months. My clothes hang in my own wardrobe." He ran a hand over his face. "Do you mind taking on the project of removing Nancy's clothes? You can give them away or do whatever you want."

It was clear she had awakened a difficult situation, but giving away

Nancy's clothes was not an option. Mahala stood and stepped up to John. She fingered the buttons on his shirt and smiled up at him. She sniffled to clear her head and tried to shove the heavy weight in her chest as far down as she could. She wouldn't dampen their first day together with a situation that John clearly didn't know had existed. "I don't mind cleaning out the wardrobe."

John let out a long breath and kissed her forehead. "Thank you." He glanced toward the kitchen. "Is lunch ready?"

"Wash up and sit down. I'll fix you a sandwich."

While preparing John's meal, a thought came to her that Tess may very well want some of her mother's things. She was sure she could cut a couple of dresses down to fit the young girl. And come to think of it, it should be easy enough to take apart one of Nancy's day dresses and use the fabric to make a dress for Mary Jane. The more she thought about it, the more she looked forward to getting started. She couldn't wait for the lunch hour to be over so she could tackle this new project.

As she watched her husband eat, she gazed at him, thoughts rolling around in her head. She had solved the problem of Nancy's clothes, but she still had one more thing she felt she needed to do. She would ride over to her parents' house and retrieve her own pillow. It dawned on her for the first time that she'd never known herself to be sensitive about such matters as Nancy's belongings. And yet she'd never claimed a man as her own either. She'd waited too long for this day to arrive, and she wanted to be the woman of the house. *Don't mess things up, Mahala. Take your stand—but do it gracefully. You'll help me, won't you, Lord?*

EARLY SUNDAY MORNING, MAHALA tied an apron over her Sunday dress. She looked for a way to broach the subject that weighed heavily on her mind and finally blurted it out when John came into the kitchen before going out to the barn.

Avoiding his gaze, she looked out the kitchen window and said, "I'll be riding over to my father's ranch after church service this morning." She gripped the hand pump on the counter and pumped water into a sauce pan and glanced back at John.

His brows rose and a worried look came into his eyes. "So soon?"

"I won't stay long. I just want to drop by and pick up a few things." She strayed from staring at him and busied herself by pulling a bowl off the shelf and setting it on the counter.

"I thought you brought everything over the other day." The corners of his lips tipped upward. "Women."

"Oh!" She smiled over her shoulder, trying to keep her nervous fingers busy. "I forgot my pillow and—"

John turned her around to face him and his lips thinned into a straight line. "There's no need to get your pillow."

"But—"

His hand cupped her chin gently. "The pillow on *your* side of the bed is not Nancy's."

Her brows rose and her lips parted, but John's forefinger went up to halt her question. "I gave Nancy's pillow to Tess months ago."

"Oh, John." The air went out of her chest and freed the weight within. "Then the pillow on the bed?"

"I made a new pillow just for you—months ago,—in hopes that you would be my new bride—and share my bed."

"You thought of everything." She touched his cheek and thumbed his soft beard.

"I wanted everything to be right for you." He opened his arms and she stepped into them. His chin rested on her head. "Happy?"

"Um-hmm." She squeezed his waist.

John relaxed his hold and stepped back. "I'd like to stay here like this, but unfortunately, I've got stock to feed."

"Go on. I've started breakfast." Hearing the back door close, she smiled to herself.

A half hour later, Mahala sat two plates on the table. It was nice that Margaret had offered to take the children, giving her and John a few days to settle in with each other. Thinking of the pillow, she realized they had a few kinks to work out before everything would feel just right.

MARY JANE JUMPED OUT of Uncle Jesse's wagon and ran to where John and Mahala pulled up in their wagon.

"Daddy! Molly!"

Mahala giggled and opened her arms. Mary Jane flew into them and hugged her neck. "I missed you so much!"

John ruffled the top of Mary's hair and grinned. "We missed you too, kitten." Moments later, all the children gathered around and chatted up a storm. Each one had their own story to tell.

"Hold up!" John held a hand up and laughed. "Let's get seated or we'll be late for church. We can hear all about your stories after the service."

"All right," the children chorused.

Jesse strode up and John shook hands with his brother. "Good morning, John." John noticed the gleam in his brother's eyes and waited for the obvious question.

"So how did it go?" Jesse asked.

"We're taking it slow," John replied, breathing in the muggy air. The two men watched the women and children work their way to the church doors, where they filed inside.

Jesse slapped John on the back in good humor. "It'll happen soon enough."

John gave Jesse a crooked grin. "I'm sure it will. Truth is, I think she needs time to get used to sleeping in Nancy's bed." John hung his head and then looked up at his brother.

"Oh, no." Jesse glanced back at the church building and then at John. "I never thought about that. I guess that would pose a problem."

"It has. But we're working through it, and she'll come around." John pushed dirt around with the toe of his shined boot.

The church bells clanged through the air. Last minute buggies and wagons drove into the church yard, and residents of Grovespring hurried inside the building.

John watched his brother Jesse climb the church steps, grateful for their close relationship.

When John stepped into the foyer, he found Mahala and the children sitting four rows from the front of the sanctuary. He removed his hat and scooted in to sit next to Mahala. A low hum of conversation filtered throughout the building. But when he sat down, the hum grew louder. John abstained from looking around. He could only imagine the rise of curiosity running through the minds of the townspeople who sat near them.

Once the voices died down, Reverend Fraser took the pulpit and preached a message on 'forgiveness.' Insects buzzed in and out of the room, as the windows had been raised in hopes that a breath of air might come through them. The July morning was already hot and muggy, promising the afternoon would grow warmer.

John's mind strayed from the sermon. With the children coming home today, maybe a drive in the country would relax his wife. Each day, he looked for ways to calm her nerves and bring back the Mahala he once knew, the woman who had always seemed in full control of her emotions and her surroundings. But just when he thought things would settle, something new brought another strain to their relationship. Just like when she'd swept the girls' bedroom and had come across the vanity brush that once belonged to Nancy. Though she assured John that it was fitting that the girls had her their mother's brush set, seeing the blonde strands of Nancy's hair locked between the bristles brought unintended tears. "The house is full of Nancy," she'd said. "And I wouldn't change it for the world."

He was grateful for Mahala's truthfulness. But he wanted to make sure everything was all right. Was there anything he could do to bring them closer together? The days were good, but the nights were lacking. *Am I missing something, Lord? Will it take an act of God to bring her around?*

Chapter THIRTY-FOUR

WHEN THE SERVICE ENDED, Judd and Flora Benson walked arm and arm out to the front of the church building and slowed their steps. The couple usually made a swift exit when the morning service ended. But today, they seemed in no hurry as they proceeded out the door. When the congregation filed outside, shaking the reverend's hand, the residents of Grovespring began to visit. After Sunday morning teachings, it was time for the folks to catch up on the previous week's news. It was a known fact, however, that the Bensons' noses were a bit high in the air when it came to the community, and they were not too keen on mixing with the townspeople.

But today, Flora Benson whispered to her daughter, Caroline, "Don't let Mahala Shields sitting with Mr. Grigsby hold you back from greeting him as we had planned. If you don't step in now, you will have lost your chance to win him."

Caroline shook her head. "I don't know, Mother. He's the one who walked up and sat with her." Caroline crossed her arms over her chest and stared out over the meadow.

"She's been taking meals to his family for months. They're just friends. Now, I'm sure those two sitting together is nothing more than plain old friendship."

This wasn't the first time Flora had tried to encourage her daughter to get in line and flirt with Mr. Grigsby. As far as she had known, none of the young women in town had caught his attention, and Caroline was a beautiful girl. She knew her daughter was interested in the man, but Caroline was not one to be forward or out of line.

Flora tipped her head and looked back at the milling crowd. "Go on, he's standing alone."

"All right, Mother. Move away please." Caroline edged over to where John stood leaning against the stair rail watching the crowd. When he looked her way, his brows raised. *Is that a good sign or not?* Caroline wondered.

JOHN RELISHED THE MOMENT to stand aside and watch his new bride mingle with her family on the lawn. When she looked his way, he didn't miss the radiant glow in her eyes. They held each other's gaze and then she looked away.

"Good afternoon, Mr. Grigsby." Caroline Benson sidled up to him and gave him a warm smile.

"Afternoon, Miss Benson." John casually took a step back.

"Would you like to join me for a walk this afternoon—by the creek? I could pack a picnic lunch." She gave him a meaningful look.

John's head jerked up and he glanced at Mahala, his ears burning red. "I don't suppose my wife would appreciate that, Miss Benson."

When Caroline stepped back, her mouth gaping and her face turning red, he said, "I'm sure this must come as a surprise to you and the community, but we're married." He stepped away and moved to Mahala's side and took her hand.

Caroline Benson's face blazed red hot as she gazed at the two of them, her mouth open, aghast. "When did you get *married?*" Her voice rose above the crowd.

The hum of conversation in the churchyard ceased at Caroline's outburst.

John pulled Mahala to his side. "This last week. We took advantage of the circuit preacher being in town."

"But you never told anyone you were getting married." Caroline's voice sounded accusing.

"I don't see that this is anyone's business but ours." John's voice took on a hard tone.

The other churchgoers gazed at John and Mahala. The men in the community could care less that John Grigsby had taken a wife. But their wives were disgruntled. When they heard that John Grigsby had married Mahala Shields just a few days ago, they had been shocked by the news. The women had hardly been able to wait for Sunday morning to see if it were true.

Now, the women stood, their heads bent together as they chattered, looking back at the couple now and again as they did. Scowls crossed their faces, and the younger women looked on in great disappointment.

"When I heard they tied the knot, I couldn't believe it," one old hag lashed out. "Miss Shields been Grovespring's spinster for as long as I can remember."

"Stop it!" Mary Shields stepped away from her younger daughters and gazed at the women. "I won't let you spoil my daughter's special day. Mahala was a beautiful bride in every sense of the imagination." Mary gazed at Mahala and continued. "Everything was just perfect." Mary held her head high. "We welcome John and his children with open arms." She gazed at John with an amused glint in her eyes.

"Thank you, Mrs. Shields—or should I say Mother?" John's eyes sparkled.

"Of course, son." She laid a hand on his arm.

Mahala didn't miss the electricity in the air. The women stared and listened to the exchange between her mother and her new husband in disgust. It was apparent she had robbed the young ladies of Grovespring of their hopes of being the next Mrs. Grigsby.

John squeezed Mahala's hand and heat burned over her body. All she wanted at the moment was to go home, away from these terrible vultures and their taunting looks. Instead of lashing out at them, she turned and opened her arms to the children. "Shall we go home and have our Sunday dinner?"

The children gathered around them in response, and the crowd dispersed.

On the way home, Mahala and John barely spoke two words. But the smiles on their faces said it all.

IT WAS AWKWARD THE first two weeks of John and Mahala's marriage. Try as she may, Mahala just couldn't relax when the evening hours came. The sun setting mean that in a few short hours, it would be time to go to bed. Each night, John pulled her in his arms, and she laid her cheek against his chest. And each night, he kissed her forehead and just held her—making no demands. But she knew in her heart of hearts that her rejection of giving in to the marriage bed was wearing thin on his emotions. He became quieter during the day—held back,—and she only had herself to blame for it. It wasn't John's fault that their bed and their room had once belonged to John and Nancy. It wasn't jealousy that kept her from him—far from it. It was just the opposite, because she missed her friend with whom she had shared her utmost dreams and fears, and now—she would share her husband.

One morning, she went to the creek and watched the water frolicking downstream. The water seemed to have a life of its own as it rippled around rocks, shimmered in the sunlight, and splashed its musical sound between the banks. Mahala wanted to feel carefree and enjoy the beautiful man God had given her. She fell to her knees and pleaded with God to give her strength to get over the wall that she'd built up between her and John. *Forgive me, Father, for I have hurt the one man I love more than anything in all the world.*

Ask you husband for forgiveness, too.

The words startled her and she stilled. *I will. He doesn't deserve what I've put him through.*

ONE AFTERNOON A FEW days later, Mahala joined John as he went to town. He delivered milk to the Yates Hotel and then to Owens Mercantile. On each of John's trips to town there were empty milk cans he picked up. He would take them home and clean them out and refill them with fresh milk. Today, he set the empty milk cans inside the back of the wagon and said, "I'll be back in a moment. I need to go to the feed store."

Climbing down from the wooden seat, Mahala stepped over to where he stood. "Take your time. I'd like to go to the mercantile and look around. I might even stop in and say 'hello' to Grady at the shop."

John gave her a crooked smile. "Then I won't hurry. Might be time for me to catch up on the town's news while you shop."

She ribbed him with her elbow. "I won't be all day. I'll only be a few minutes."

John pulled her against his side and looked up and down the road before he kissed her squarely on the lips. "Take your time, Mrs. Grigsby."

A rush of heat flared over her before he released her. She glanced up and down the road as well. Why? She didn't know. She had every right to be kissed by this man.

John walked toward the feed store, not looking back, and she picked up her skirts and headed for Thompson's Tailor Shop. Mahala hadn't shown up at the shop, nor had she gone to town since she'd married the town's sought-after bachelor. She hadn't wanted to see the sour looks from Grovespring's women and ruin the joy she felt in being a married woman at last.

But today, she rode into town knowing full well she couldn't hide from the community forever. Leaving the children with Tess, she felt free as a bird to meander and look at the new merchandise.

The cowbell jangled when she stepped inside the tailor shop. Grady looked up from his work, and a broad smile flashed across his face. "Mahala."

"Good afternoon, Grady. How's work?"

"I'm swamped. With the election for the town's mayor coming up, it seems every prominent man in the area wants a new suit."

"Good for you." Mahala tilted her head and gazed past the tables of fabric to the corner of the shop where she'd spent so many hours.

"Will you be coming back to work any time soon?" Grady set the shears on the tabletop and leaned against it.

"No. I think my time here is done."

"Please don't tell me that."

"Grady . . . I'm finally married, and I have seven children who need my time."

Grady pushed away from the table. "I know. And to be honest, I expected you to say exactly that." He nodded his head toward the back corner. "Should I put out an ad for a new seamstress?"

"I believe so." A rush of uncertainty filled her, for she loved being a seamstress, but she shook her head and said, "I can't be a mother and a seamstress, too. It would take too much of my time. And what I have now—it seems I've waited an eternity for it." She smiled at Grady. "I wouldn't trade it for the world."

"Understood." Grady's eyes shone. "I'm happy for you."

"Well, I just wanted to stop in and say 'hello.'" She backed away to the door. "I'll come by and pack up my supplies in a few days."

"Sounds good. Good afternoon, Mahala."

She waved and started down the boardwalk to Owens Mercantile. "Well, dear girl, you put that behind you," she said under her breath. She passed a few women who stepped aside when she went by. Her chin went up a degree as she said, "Afternoon, ladies."

Moments later, Mahala walked the aisles of the general store, looking for anything they might need in the coming weeks and enjoying the moment alone.

It wasn't long before John returned from the feed store and said, "I'm ready to leave when you are."

She lifted the basket on her arm. "I've found a few items I need to pay for." When she reached the counter, Clem Owens looked up and said, "Good afternoon, Miss Shields, er, Mrs. Grigsby." His lips tilted up. "Oh, by the way, that letter you've been waiting for has arrived."

Mahala's jaw dropped and she quickly glanced behind her in time to see John's head jerk up at Clem's announcement. She felt hotter than a bucket of red coals! And yet, a chill ran down her back at the thought of having to explain the letter to John.

Mr. Owens bent and searched the cubbyholes behind the counter. Then he stood straight and held out the envelope. "It's addressed to you in your maiden name." As an afterthought he added, "It isn't post marked, and it didn't come with the stage mail."

Mahala stared at Clem Owens, clearly surprised at his last remark. "It didn't come on the Wells Fargo stagecoach?"

"Theoretically, no."

"Theoretically? Um—I don't understand."

"A right proper-looking gent came into the store and left the letter for you a couple of weeks back."

"Left the letter?" She stared at the envelope Mr. Owens handed her. "Whatever do you mean?"

"The gentleman walked right in here and asked for you by name. Said he'd been looking for you. Since he couldn't find you, he told me to give this letter to you the next time I saw you." Clem Owens grinned and rocked on his feet.

Mahala glanced at the neat handwriting on the envelope and the fancy seal. Blood red. Heat crept up her neck and onto her face. "Oh, dear."

John gazed over her shoulder, and Mahala swiftly slid the letter into her skirt pocket. But he hadn't missed the way she hurriedly stashed the envelope away. He stood by her side, perplexed. "Aren't you going to read your letter?"

She cleared her throat. "Not now. I'll read it later." She set the items from her basket onto the counter. "This is all we'll need today."

"All right, ma'am." Mr. Owens tallied their purchase.

John paid for their purchase and loaded the supplies into the back of the wagon. He handed Mahala onto the wooden seat, all the while watching her peculiar response to the letter. He climbed up beside her and flicked the reins. The horses clopped at a steady gait as they rode out of town. John glanced sideways at Mahala a time or two, but he didn't say a word.

Mahala felt his gaze and heat rose to her scalp. She had no idea what the letter would contain, but she wanted to read it alone, before she confided to

John that she had answered an ad for a mail-order bride.

Now that she was married and was sitting next to her husband, she felt foolish for having answered the ad. Still, an awkward feeling slicked up her back. She'd wait for the right moment to pull the letter from her pocket to read it. Had Mr. Bates declined her offer? Or had the gentleman come for her?

The wagon rumbled down the road with the two of them deep in thought. John finally broke the silence and asked, "Who's the letter from, Mahala?"

"Nobody," she said flatly and looked away. She wasn't about to let him see her red face as hot as a kettle. Yet, when she gave him a side glance, she found his blue eyes resting on hers, a fire in his gaze.

"You got something to hide?"

"Oh, John," was all she could breathe. "If you only knew."

"May I see the letter?"

Mahala's hair bristled to its roots. "No, you may not!" Her hand went to her side, relieved the envelope was safely tucked away.

He flicked the reins and Brownie set into a trot. It wasn't long before they rode at a fast pace and all the while guilt niggled at her stomach. Reluctantly, Mahala retrieved the letter, but she didn't immediately hand it over. She gripped the cream-colored envelope and, bouncing on her seat, turned to John.

"Might you slow the horse so we can talk?"

John pulled on the reins. "Whoa, Brownie!" He brought the wagon to a halt on the side of the road. Then he turned to meet her gaze and waited.

Mahala pinched the envelope between her thumb and forefinger. "I answered an ad for a mail-order bride." She swallowed her guilt and her pride, and tried to stem the tears that welled in her eyes. "I wasn't about to be Grovespring's spinster one more year!"

John opened his mouth—then shut it. Amusement shone in his eyes, though she could tell he fought it.

Mahala turned away—wounded.

"I'm not laughing at you, my love." He touched her arm, his fingers gentle on her wrist. "I'm just happy—no relieved—that you don't need that letter."

Mahala looked up and her body shuddered, and then she fanned her face with the letter. "You saved me from uncertain circumstances, Mr. Grigsby. I couldn't have foreseen the future." A smile split her lips. "Thank you for saving me from that ordeal." She wiped a tear from her cheek.

John's strong arms enfolded her around her waist, and he pulled her tightly against him. "*I* didn't save you." He kissed her forehead. "*You* saved me."

His last words were barely above a whisper. She turned her face to his and he claimed her lips. When they drew apart he said, "Let's go home. We've got unfinished business to tend to." He flicked the reins and the wagon jerked forward.

Goodness, Mahala sighed. *What have I gotten myself into?*

John parked the wagon in front of the house. When the two of them stood on the front porch, he opened the door and it swung wide. Mahala started to step through, but John held her back. "I didn't carry you over the threshold on our wedding day. It's about time I do." He scooped Mahala into his muscular arms and stepped into the hallway.

Six pairs of eyes swerved to stare at them as if the couple had grown extra heads.

"Granville. Calvin." John said, still holding Mahala in his arms. "Take the wagon back to the barn and unload it. Then unhitch Brownie and brush him down." He looked at Tess. "There are supplies for the kitchen. You might want to follow the boys out to the barn and retrieve them. When done, keep an eye on the little ones."

Mahala felt hot blood rush into her face. "You can put me down now."

"Not on your life." John edged the front door closed with his boot.

Granville, Calvin, and Tess gave the two of them raised eyebrows and their eyes lit up.

"Yes, sir," Granville said and opened the door. The three older children quickly moved out onto the front porch, giggling.

John carried Mahala down the hallway to their bedroom, and again, he closed the door with his boot. Wide-eyed, Mahala watched his every move. He crossed the floor to the bed. "We have a lot of time to make up for." His breath sent a delicious chill up her spine. His lips claimed hers and a moment later, he set her on the bed and began unbuttoning his shirt.

Mahala cleared her throat and asked, "In broad daylight?"

John's fingers stilled and he cupped her chin. "You're my wife. Any time of day or night is all right with me."

"But the children?"

"They'll be fine."

"Really?"

"Really."

John pulled Mahala to her feet and began unbuttoning the row of tiny pearl buttons down the back of her dress. His hands slid to her waist and he kissed her neck. "Are you all right, Mrs. Grigsby?"

Fully aware of his closeness, her body warmed, the heat traveling to her midsection. She did not know what it would be like to be claimed by this man, and now that the moment had arrived, panic struck her cold. "Y-yes. I-I'm fine." She swallowed. "Um—" She turned out of his hold to face him. "I've never—I mean—I don't know what—" Her jaw went slack. "I've never been with— a man."

"That's a known fact, Mrs. Grigsby." Amusement played in his eyes as he pulled her against him.

"I—I don't know what to do."

A smile spread across his handsome face. "That's all right, Mahala. I do." He kissed her forehead and then turned her back around and finished unbuttoning her dress.

She closed her eyes and felt his hands caress her. The next hour flew entirely too fast. And before she knew it, she woke up to early dawn.

"DADDY! SOMEONE'S COMING UP the drive," Mary Jane hollered.

At the sound of Mary Jane's announcement, Mahala looked out the kitchen window in time to see her father coming up the drive with her horse, Bessy, trailing behind him. "Bessy!" She started to turn away from the window and head toward the hall, but at second thought, she turned back to the kitchen window again. *What was her father carrying in front of him? Is that Boots in the crate?*

Mary Jane flew out of the living room and moved toward the front door.

"Hold up, kitten. I'll see who it is." John laid a hand on Mary Jane's shoulder.

"It's my father," Mahala announced as she followed John onto the porch. Benjamin Shields rode alongside the front of the house with a lead rope in one hand and Bessy trailing behind him. "Hello," Ben called out.

"Hello, yourself," John said. "What have you got there?" John took the lead rope from Ben's hand and ran a hand over the horse's coat. The mare was a rich reddish-brown, the mane and tail black, a white diamond shape on her forehead.

"Bessy! Father!" Mahala called out. "What a wonderful surprise to see you." Mahala dried her hands with a dish towel and stepped off the porch steps to stride over to where her father waited. "And what have we here?" Mahala raised her hands to take the wicker crate. "Boots?"

"That's right. Your mother wouldn't let me leave the house without bringing Boots too. She said you'd be wanting her." Benjamin dismounted and shook John's hand and smiled at Mahala. "Your mother's been fussing the past couple of weeks that you'd be wanting your cat and your horse."

John stepped over to join them and asked, "Is that true?" He glanced at Mahala. "Yes, it's true. I haven't thought to bring it up just yet. I didn't think you'd mind if I brought my horse, but I wasn't sure how you'd feel about having a cat."

He slipped a hand around her waist and pulled her against him. "I don't see any problem with having a cat." He kept his arm possessively around her waist. "If you don't mind, I'll take your horse on back to the stable. I have a stall waiting for her."

"You do?" Mahala blinked, and gazed at her husband.

"Of course I do." He winked and pulled on the lead rope. He turned the horse around to follow him to the barn.

Mahala watched John lead Bessy away before she peeked inside the cage. "Well, little Miss Boots, welcome to your new home." She picked up the crate and gazed at her father. "Would you like to come in for a cup of coffee and a piece of cake?"

"Thanks for the invite, Mahala, but I should get back to the ranch. Your mother will have supper ready before too long." He looked up at the house. "Everything all right?"

"I couldn't be happier, Father." Mahala held the crate on her hip and leaned forward to give her father a kiss on the cheek. "Thank you."

The door swung open and the children filed out. "What's that?" Mary Jane pointed at the wicker crate.

"That," Mahala said as she set the crate on the ground and unhooked the top lid, "is little Miss Boots." She grinned.

"Can I hold him?" Mary Jane squealed as she leaned in with her arms out.

"Boots is a girl," Mahala said. "Let's bring her into the house first. Everything is new to her, and we don't want to scare her." Mahala lifted her head to see her father had already mounted his horse. "Thank you," she mouthed, holding Boots close to her chest.

Granville came down the steps. "I'll take the crate to the stable."

"Thank you, Gran." She watched Granville pick up the crate and stride around the corner of the house. She lifted Boots and touched the cat's nose with her own. "Well, isn't this a pleasant surprise," she said to the children looking on.

"Let me see," Jeffrey crowded in to see the kitten.

"Let's go into the house. Come on, all of you." Mahala carried Boots into the house and set her down on the living room floor. Mahala felt like the rest of her was there as well, with her horse and kitten at her new home. She was pleased as she could be. "Meet your new family, Miss Boots."

Chapter THIRTY-FIVE

Early Fall 1842

ONE EVENING, MAHALA STRUGGLED to stay awake as John read to the family. The scent of tobacco filled the air as John filled his pipe and settled in to read. Gran and Franklin stretched out on the floor before the fireplace. No wood burned in the fireplace, as the weather hadn't grown cold enough to burn logs to keep them warm. Tess and Mary Jane sat on one end of the sofa, with Calvin sitting on the floor before them. He whittled away on a narrow piece of wood with his sharp knife, making a pile of chips on his pant-legs. On the opposite end of the sofa, Jeffrey leaned against Mahala while Wiley snuggled in her lap.

Mahala listened to John's voice, deep and rich, as the family gathered around. He had taken to reading to the family after the supper hour, and each evening, the children took their respective places—except for Mary Jane and Jeffrey. Mary Jane's lower lip had puckered for the right to sit next to Mahala the first few evenings, but early on, Mahala settled the skirmish by saying, "Wouldn't it be fair if you took turns?" Jeffrey was quick to agree, but Mary Jane resigned herself with a slow nod and thin lips. "All right, Molly. We'll take turns."

When John read aloud, Mahala lost herself in the deep resonance of his voice. The words washed over her like a warm blanket and she drifted, exhausted, fighting to stay awake as he read the stories of Abraham, Elijah, and Moses. Their new routine as a family filled her every waking moment. The days were long, giving little time for simple pleasures such as taking

Bessy for a run to the river. But she was fine with that. She was finally living her dream of having a family of her own.

John closed the Bible. "All right," he said, breaking the comfortable silence of the room. "Time for bed."

The room buzzed with disappointed groans. The children enjoyed sitting and listening to their father read. But they had school tomorrow, and the morning would come soon enough.

"Already?" Calvin groaned. He looked down at the pile of chips scattered around him.

"Don't move," Mahala said. She set Wiley on his feet and went for the dustpan. Between the two of them, Calvin and Mahala made quick work of cleaning up Calvin's mess.

"What are you making, Cal?" John asked.

"Oh, nothing." He held out a rough figure of an animal.

"A deer?" his dad asked.

Calvin nodded, his ears burning red. "I'm not done with it yet."

"It's a good likeness, son. It looks like you're getting there."

Calvin looked at Franklin, who had turned on his side and leaned on his elbow. "Franklin's giving me some lessons."

"He's a good teacher. Your uncle has a knack for carving."

Mahala looked on, seeing that no one was in the mood to end the night.

Surprisingly, Mary Jane was the first to make a move to go upstairs. "Good night, Daddy." Mary Jane yawned and hugged his side.

"Good night, Molly."

The curly-headed little girl squeezed Mahala's neck and promptly headed to bed.

Franklin, Granville, and Calvin were next to jump up. They tromped out of the room and headed up the stairs, making a lot of noise on the way. Tess followed as Mahala took Jeffrey's and Wiley's hand and led them up to the second-floor landing.

Mahala checked on each of the children after they'd changed into their pajamas and helped them say their prayers. When done, she descended the stairs and found John waiting at the landing, a pipe in one hand and his eyes alight with a warm glow.

"Care to take a walk with me?" He held out his hand.

"I'd love to." Mahala stepped out onto the porch and before long, the two of them were strolling down the drive. A cool breeze ruffled the hem of her skirt as they walked.

Mahala slipped her hand in the crook of John's arm and gazed at the harvest moon. She enjoyed walking beneath the moonlight. There was something magical about its soft light. A distant flash zipped above them. "Did you see that?" Mahala' brow lifted as a meteor traced a brilliant path across the velvet sky, reminding her how fortunate she was to be standing here with John. He loved her. She didn't wonder if he loved her. She *knew* he did.

John seemed lost in his own thoughts as the two of them walked slowly down the road. Mahala had fallen into deep thoughts of her own. They'd been married a month, but there was no sign that she was with child. She loved John's children, but she ached for a child of her own. She had voiced her concern a few nights ago, and John had assured her that there would be a child on the way soon enough.

John broke into her thoughts. "Are you happy?"

"Oh, John, how can you ask me that? Can't you see that I am?"

He stopped strolling and looked down at her. "I just want to hear you say it. You've made me a happy man, Mahala." He pulled her into his arms and kissed her under the stars.

In the distance they could hear the cattle lowing, and other than the soft breeze that sailed about them, the night was still. And for the moment, it belonged to them. They took their time as they walked a little farther. When they turned back, she could see the soft glow of the yellow lights streaming out of the living room window. *Her home.* Something she'd waited a lifetime for. But she also wanted a child of her own. No sooner had the thought entered her head than she admonished herself. She wasn't going to start wishing for the moon now.

ALTHOUGH TESS AND MARY Jane had said their prayers and climbed into bed, Tess couldn't sleep. The moon lit their bedroom as she stared, wide awake. She sensed she wasn't the only one who couldn't sleep and asked Mary Jane, "Are you awake?"

"Yes," Mary said. "I can't sleep."

"How come?"

"I don't know. I guess I didn't want the evening to be over."

Tess could hear the rustle of Mary Jane's covers as she turned to face her.

After a moment Tess said, "Me either. I like having Mahala here. It feels right." Tess turned her face toward Mary Jane and a small goose-down feather from her pillow tickled her nose. The pillow's cover had bunched away from the edge just enough that the feather was peeking out. Tess idly plucked the feather from the seam and puffed it into the air with a soft blow from her lips. The feather drifted in the air, highlighted by the moonlight filtering into the room.

Mary Jane asked, "Do you think Mama minds that we have Mahala now?"

"No," Tess answered as the feather glided to the floor. "I think she's glad we have her." As she spoke, Tess felt another feather peeking out from the seam of her pillow, and this time she punched her pillow to flatten the seam away from her nose. But all at once the seam burst open and a cloud of feathers flew out into the moon's beam and floated through the air.

"Oh, Tess!" Mary Jane shot out of bed. "You're gonna be in trouble!"

"No I'm not. I didn't do it on purpose." Tess sat up and placed her feet on the floor.

Mary Jane looked down at her pillow and gave it a good punch. The seam burst open on her pillow as well. Feathers billowed out and powdered the floor.

"Rats in a poke! What did you do that for?"

"I don't know." Mary Jane's bottom lip went out. "Because you did."

"You silly goose!" Tess picked up her pillow and raised it over her head, darting to her sister's side of the bed. At the same time, Mary Jane jumped out of bed and grabbed her pillow and raised it over her head. The two girls met in the middle of the room and clobbered each other over and over with their downy pillows. The room filled with shrieks of laughter and shrill screams.

The door flew open and Granville and Franklin stood in the doorway, their eyes wide. "What are you doing?"

Calvin ducked under Franklin's arm to see what all the noise was about. He didn't laugh—he didn't speak. They all stared at the white room that looked as if snow had fallen inside the house. Feathers covered the beds, the chest-of-drawers, the small table under the window—the room was covered in goose-down feathers. The girls stopped laughing and held their limp pillow cases in their hands. As the two of them stared at each other, Mary Jane's mouth went slack.

"Uh . . . we were having a pillow fight," she whispered.

"Come on, Mary Jane," Tess said, falling to her knees. She tried to scoop up the soft feathers and stuff them back into the pillowcase. "We've got to get this mess cleaned up before Dad and Mahala get back. If Dad comes in, this will be a fate worse than death."

Tess saw Calvin unsuccessfully struggle to keep a smile from his lips and a giggle from his throat.

Laughter broke out from the boys, but neither Tess nor Mary Jane were smiling.

"You're in trouble for sure," Granville said, and the boys backed out of their room.

"Aren't you going to help us clean up this mess?" Tess called after them.

"No," the boys giggled.

Tess heard their door close down the hall and she stared at the mess around her—feathers seemed to have worked their way into every inch of the room. And looking at Mary Jane, with feathers stuck in her curls, Tess knew she must look the same. She wanted to disappear into thin air. But like it or not—there was no getting out of this.

JUST THEN THE DOOR clicked open, and there stood Mahala and their father. Neither said a word, they just looked on in disbelief.

John broke the silence. "Who's responsible for this?"

"Uh . . . I am, sir," Tess said.

"And what is the meaning of this?" He shot Tess a dark look.

"John." Mahala touched his arm lightly.

John let out a long sigh. "I'll let you handle this. If I do, it might not end well."

"All right." Mahala watched as he backed away and retreated down the stairs. The full moon filled the room with plenty of light. She could easily see the room was filled from stem to stern with feathers. She fell to her knees. "Come on, girls. Let's get this mess cleaned up."

The three of them worked for several minutes, but it was soon evident that they were fighting a losing battle. The feathers had a will of their own. Mahala sat against the foot of Tess's bed, feathers plastering her skirt and blouse. She puffed a feather off her shoulder. "We'll have to clean this up in the morning. For now, like it or not, you two are going to have to climb back into bed and get some sleep." She stood and watched the girls edge to their beds.

"In feathers, Molly?"

"In feathers." Mahala held back a giggle and tried to restrain her smile.

Tess groaned and slid into bed. "I'm sorry, Mahala."

"Go to sleep, Tess. We'll talk about this in the morning."

Mahala closed the door and looked down at her clothes. White goose-down feathers speckled her skirt, some falling to the floor. A trail of feathers speckled the stairs as she descended. It had been all she could do to keep a stern look on her face while in the room with the girls. It tickled her to see that Tess and Mary Jane had had some fun. It seemed that as the days wore on, the children were healing from their mother's death. She couldn't be angry at them. But how in the world would they get all those feathers picked up?

THERE WAS NO HOPE for them. Mahala and the girls spent days finding feathers in every nook and cranny of the bedroom. They kept a gunnysack in the corner of the room, as Mahala had promised to make new pillows with the goose-down feathers they collected.

When the day came to put the newly made pillows, stitched from blue-and-white, striped ticking on their beds, Mahala noticed that the girls' pillowslips were worn out. While she finished making the beds and straightening the room, new plan formed in her mind.

Mahala thought back to when John had told her she could remove Nancy's clothes from the wardrobe. Tess had helped, and the young girl had pointed the dresses she wanted. After Tess picked out her favorite frocks, Mahala examined the condition of the rest of the garments before setting them aside for future use. She already knew a couple of them could be taken apart to make a couple of new dresses for Tess. And she found a flower-printed dress she could cut down for Mary Jane. But there would be enough flower-printed material left that she could salvage to make new pillowcases for the girls. Eyeing a blue-and-white plaid material, Mahala tapped her chin with a forefinger. She'd make new pillowcases for the boys as well.

Days later, when she sewed the last seam, she held the pillowcase up to examine it, and sighed, "I hope the children like these." A dash of doubt plagued her at the thought of presenting the pillowcases to the children. It would be another reminder that their mother was gone. But she quickly brushed that thought aside.

Mahala carried the stack of pillowcases up the stairs and proceeded to change out the pillow slips on all the beds.

She changed out the boys' room first and then proceeded to Tess and Mary Jane's bedroom. She quickly dumped the goose-down pillows out of each old case and replaced them with the new covers she'd made from their mother's clothes. When done, she placed her fists on her hips and gazed about the room.

What time was it anyway? The morning seemed to drag. She usually liked the hours the children were at school. It gave her time to catch up on much-needed sewing and baking. But with this special surprise waiting for them, it felt as if the day was especially longer. All morning, Jeffrey and Wiley had played on the floor while Mahala had sewn. The afternoon finally came and went and soon the brood stormed into the front hall and then into the kitchen. The sound of noisy chatter filled the house as they each shared news of the day.

Franklin, however, watched for a moment and then said, "Thanks for the cookies." He held one up to Mahala. "I'll do my homework after I see to the cattle." He didn't wait for permission to go. It was understood that this was how it was with him. Franklin loved going out to the pasture and spending time with the cowhands and the cattle. He barely tolerated the time he spent at school and doing homework. John had said this would be the last year of school for Franklin. He'd get more learning on the ranch than he would in a classroom. He was certain Franklin spent more time staring out of the school windows than he did at the chalkboard at the front of the classroom.

Granville, on the other hand, enjoyed learning. And he kept up his work at Owens Mercantile.

Tonight, as usual, the children headed for bed at the end of another long day. But it wasn't too long after they had gone upstairs that the stairwell bustled with the sound of the children coming down to the first-floor landing. Gran and Tess held their new pillows in their hands. Tess held hers up. "You made pillowcases from Mother's dresses." It was a statement rather than a question.

"Yes I did." Mahala was aware that John had come up and stood behind her. She went on, "Now, when you lay your heads down to sleep, you can all be a little closer to your mama."

Tears welled in Tess's eyes. When Mahala looked at the rest of the children, she found tears in their eyes as well.

John stepped over to Granville and fingered the material. He hugged his son to him, looking as if he was coming undone.

Calvin and Mary Jane flew to Mahala's side and hugged her. "Thank you so much!"

Looking over their heads, Mahala gazed at John. He stood with a look of thanksgiving, his eyes brimming with unshed tears. He mouthed, "Thank you."

In Mahala's mind, there was no greater feeling of achievement than to have one's work appreciated. Her heart was full as she gazed at the family before her. She cleared her throat and said, "Now, it's time for all of you to go to bed. Tomorrow will be here sooner than you think."

The children clamored up the stairs and soon the house was quiet. John stepped up to her and held her to his chest. "You never cease to amaze me, my love." He kissed the top of her head.

"Thank you, John. It's been a long day. Might we go to bed?"

He squeezed her tighter. "You bet we can." His eyes lit up. "Then I'll show you how much you're loved."

Heat traveled to the top of her neck. She wondered if she'd ever get used to the way John boldly spoke to her. But then, she had the rest of her life to find out. She led the way to their room and lit the kerosene lamp on her side of the bed. John did the same on his side. They made quick work of undressing. Mahala slid her nightgown over her head. When she turned around, she saw that John watched her from under the covers. He had already slipped into bed.

Mahala blew out both lamps and then she lay nestled against John's chest. She listened to the night sounds outside as the moon hid behind a cloud.

John's hand cupped her chin, and he grazed her lips with his thumb. A moment later, her kissed her softly, but it wasn't long before his kisses grew ardent. The night was theirs for the taking. She would revel in his arms, as she knew the morning would come all too soon. John would go out and spend the day with the cattle, and she would start another day of cooking, baking, laundry, and cleaning. How long would it be before the thrill of being held in John's arms would settle and become old?—Never, she hoped. She would embrace each day as if it were her first.

THE FALL WEATHER HAD grown colder as John and his men covered the pastures, caring for the cattle. The herd had grown, making it a good year for the Grigsby ranch.

As John headed back to the ranch yard, he saw a horse standing at the edge of the cemetery where Nancy lay. He nudged Blue toward the tall oak tree that hovered over the ground and found Tess kneeling beside the mound that cradled her mother.

John stepped out of the saddle and tied Blue's reins to the fence. When he opened the gate, Tess looked back, tears streaming down her cheeks. John quickly pulled a handkerchief out of his back pocket and gave it to her.

"Are you all right?" His heart thundered in his chest.

"No." She sniffed. "I miss her."

John knelt down beside Tess.

"Do you ever try to talk to Mama?" Tess's eyes gazed at him and back to the marker with her mother's name on it.

"Every day, Tess. Every single day."

"Even though you're married to Mahala?"

"Marrying Mahala does not change the fact that I loved your mother. Mahala loved her too, you know."

"I know." Tess stared at the gray stone and then gazed up at him. "It's okay that you love Mahala. She saved you. She saved all of us."

John pulled Tess into his arms. "She did, didn't she. For the longest time, I was a mess. I couldn't think right, or eat right, or do anything right." He patted Tess's back as he held her to him and rocked her. "I'd lost all sense of direction. But all that time, Mahala came to the house to take care of us. She fed us food, but more than that, she tended to our souls."

He let Tess go and said, "It's wonderful to have someone who is solid and can bring you right back down to earth."

Tess pushed off the ground and kissed his cheek. "I love you, Daddy."

"Oh, Tess," He breathed deeply and stood as well. "God did a wonderful thing when he brought you into our lives." When he looked down at Tess, her cheeks were wet. "I'm going back to the house. You can stay longer if you need to."

"I'm going back too." Father and daughter walked back to the yard, the horse trailing behind them. Tess went on to the house while John put the horses away. Before he strode out of the barn, he lowered his chin to his chest, his eyes closed. *Thank you Lord for all Your blessing. Each one, dear Lord.* When he looked up he saw lights glowing within the house. He picked up his steps. He'd read to the family again tonight. It brought them all together for a little time. And it filled them with the Word. Life couldn't get any better than this, could it?

Five months later . . . January 1843

MAHALA LAID SLABS OF bacon onto the hot iron skillet. While the bacon sizzled and popped, she whipped a batter of pancakes in a large bowl. Wiping her hands on her apron, she closed her eyes while yet another wave of nausea gripped her.

Tess stepped groggily into the kitchen and reached for an apron off the wall hook. "Good morning."

"Good morning, Tess." Mahala pushed away from the counter and grabbed a glass of water to take a sip, but the nausea was too great. She pulled the skillet off the flames and fled the kitchen. Once outside the back door, the chill air smacked her full force. The cold, however, was not enough to remove the awful need to wretch. Throwing open the door to the outhouse, Mahala rushed in and bent over the dark hole. She wretched and wretched and then coughed, gagging from the putrid smell of the outhouse.

Moments later, she pushed the door open to find John waiting for her with her wrap. "Are you all right? You gave Tess a fright the way you ran out of the house."

"Oh, John." Mahala wiped her sweaty brow with the hem of her apron. "I don't know what's come over me. Every time I start to make breakfast, nausea hits me full force. I can barely make it to the outhouse in time. This has been going on for weeks." She felt hot tears flood her eyes. When Mahala looked up, it was to find John smiling down at her with a crooked grin.

"What's so funny?" She brushed past him and clamped her jaws tightly together.

John reached out and grabbed her arm. "Hold up there, sweetheart." He pulled her against his chest.

Mahala pushed him away but he did not let go. "I have a houseful to feed." She tried once again to move away from John.

"I think I know what's making you so sick." He wouldn't relinquish his hold on her arm.

Mahala turned back to face him. "So what is it? Is there a flu going around?"

"Not that I know of." He couldn't get the silly grin off of his face.

"Well, mister-know-it-all, why do you suppose I'm so sick that I cannot make a breakfast without racing out to this awful outhouse every morning?" Irritation licked up her back and she stepped away. This time she crossed her arms over her chest and glared at the lazy smile on John's face. "It appears you think my plight is quite amusing."

Her urge to snap at the drop of a pin was another thing she noticed these days. One moment she felt like crying, and the next moment she felt like lashing out at the family. But in truth, nothing had changed at home. John and the children were carrying on as they always did. It appeared she was the only one who had changed with these sudden mood swings.

Mahala gazed at the amusement dancing in John's eyes and wanted to stomp back to the house, but instead she asked, "So, are you going to tell me what you think is going on with me?" The nippy air made her want to huddle against John again, but she was too stubborn to make the first move.

Thankfully, John pulled her into his arms, and his warm breathe settled on her cheeks. "I think we're going to have a baby."

"We . . . what?" Startled, Mahala thought of all of the obvious symptoms she'd been having these past weeks. It made perfect sense. But still, she had to ask, "I'm with child?"

"I believe so."

"We're going to have a baby?"

John threw his head back and laughed. "You're shaking like a leaf. Let me get you inside the house before you catch a cold." He took her hand and the two of them walked back to the house. When she entered the kitchen, she found herself in a daze. *I'm going to have a baby?*

Once inside, Mahala removed her wrap. The day had barely gotten underway, but she had a houseful to feed before the morning got away from them. Tying her apron back on, Mahala eyed the skillet of bacon. Tess was nowhere in sight and the fire had gone out under the front grate. She quickly set to work lighting the kindling in the wood box. She was determined that the morning sickness would not get the best of her. After all, she wasn't the first woman to experience this awful stage of being with child, and she certainly wouldn't be the last.

Before long, the kitchen smelled of sizzling bacon and warm hotcakes. The sound of rumbling feet coming down the stairs told Mahala the children were up. She never tired of hearing them coming down the stairs first thing in the morning.

No sooner had the younger children gathered at the table than she heard Franklin coming in the back door.

"Morning!" he greeted everyone as he entered the kitchen and slid into a chair at the table. "I'm hungry as a wolf, and breakfast smells awful good." His voice wobbled between high and low, and the younger children giggled. Franklin's face grew red. His voice was changing, and he had no control over it. Yet each day his voice took on a deeper tone.

"Did you help John in the barn?" Mahala asked.

"Yes. Calvin and Granville are on their way in too." The back door slammed just then.

Mahala and Franklin eyed each other. Franklin shrugged. "The pancakes look good."

"You sound as if you don't get a decent meal around here." Mahala stepped back as John and the boys slid into their chairs.

"I'm just hungrier these days. Maybe it's the cold weather," Franklin said.

Mahala set a plate of pancakes before Franklin. "I think it's because you're growing by leaps and bounds." She gazed at John for confirmation. "Say grace, and you can all eat." She looked around to make sure everything was on the table, and seeing it was, she settled into her chair next to John. The family bowed their heads and John said grace. During the next few moments, plates were passed around and filled with pancakes and bacon. All the while, Mahala felt a giddiness she couldn't explain. *The older boys' voices were changing with their maturity, and she was going to have a baby! So many changes were occurring around her.* A warm glow filled her.

An hour later, five tin pails lined the counter. Two homemade cookies sat on the bottom of each pail, and Mahala had wrapped a cheese sandwich in a cloth napkin for each of her school-age children. She had just placed the last sandwich in the pails when the troop came into the kitchen.

"We're ready to go," Tess said as she reached for her pail.

"You must hurry or you're going to be late." Mahala handed the other pails to the children and followed them out to the wagon.

Granville took the reins while Tess and Franklin sat beside him on the wooden seat. Calvin and Mary Jane sat in the back of the wagon on a rolled-up quilt. They were all bundled in their coats, hats, and mittens.

Mahala waved goodbye as the wagon rolled out of the yard. She wanted to share her secret of the babe lying sweetly in her belly, but first she waited to get the children off to school and then she'd pay her mother a visit. *Won't Mother be surprised when I tell her the good news? I'm going to have a baby!*

Chapter THIRTY-SIX

Early April 1843

TIME HAD A WAY of slipping away right before their eyes, John mused. The year 1842 had breathed its last breath and 1843 was upon them. Spring brought green buds to the stark bare trees in the forest. It wouldn't be long before leaves would unfurl in the stand of trees by the river and around the ranch. Pink buds lined the thin branches in the peach orchard, promising a good yield of peaches in the summer. The ground was covered with a thin layer of snow, but purple and yellow crocuses peeked through the ice-encrusted soil below the front porch rails.

John hunkered in his coat with the collar pulled up around his ears and his hat pulled down tightly around his ears. The air was crisp as he and his men rode their horses over the pasture, checking on the cattle. He thought about next month, which was just around the corner. The town would fill up with wagons again. Folks would be traveling west. He had played with the idea of talking to Mahala about moving to Oregon. Most of her family lived in Missouri, although scattered in different counties, but her mother was just down the road. Could he talk his wife into picking up their roots and joining the adventure of finding new land to settle in? If he were a betting man, he'd bet he'd have to plead his case on why the move would be advantageous.

Grovespring was a nice little town, but that is just it. The town was small. Selling cattle from a remote place had been difficult—except for when the wagon trains came through. He knew there was a demand for his breed of cattle. But getting them into the right hands was not an easy task. The

Durhams were good for beef, they were hardy in all kinds of weather, and their milk was the best in the land—at least in his mind anyway.

Thinking about milk, he'd set milk cans in the springhouse until he could take them to town. After he checked for straying cattle down by the river, he'd take the milk, along with some eggs, and load them in the wagon. Clem Owens and Gertrude Yates had both complained they were getting low on both items. Thinking about the peach jam Nancy had made in the past, he wondered, if he could he talk Mahala into putting up peach jam this summer.

BOOTS LAY ON THE bed and watched as Mahala dressed for the day. The sun peeked over the horizon, and the first rays dappled the black and white cat. Mahala walked around the bed and sat down to scratch behind Boot's ears for a moment. Boots had grown to be a healthy, fat cat. Her long white whiskers fanned out from her cheeks, eyebrows, and ears. Mahala had never seen such long whiskers on a cat. And the kitty had a black dot on her pink nose. With the white patch of fur covering her chest, Boots looked as if she wore a tuxedo, and to Mahala—she looked majestic. The cat purred as Mahala ran her hand over the black and white fur.

Sitting there, it was tempting to crawl back into bed. Mahala's mind was encumbered with thoughts that swirled in her head. John had brought up the subject of moving to Oregon once again. What was he thinking? His children had roots here in Missouri. And how could he think of leaving their beautiful river full of catfish? In her mind's eye, she could see the boys heading to the river with their fishing poles. The thought of leaving their beautiful home left a dull ache in her heart. Furthermore, she didn't want to leave her mother and sisters. The ache deepened at the very thought of leaving her family behind. She wanted this baby that was growing inside of her to know its grandparents.

A slight kick in her belly made Mahala smile. "Do you want to stay here too, little one?"

"Meow." Boots raised to her feet and stretched.

"Well, it looks like the two of you are telling me to quit lollygagging. The morning will slip away before we know it."

Boots jumped off the bed, her tail extended in the air like a walking cane. Mahala followed the cat to the back door. When she opened it, a crisp breeze blew in. She let Boots out and headed for the kitchen. It wouldn't be long before the boys would be up to do their chores.

At least she didn't have morning sickness anymore. Being in her fifth month of gestation, her tummy had settled. She lifted an apron off the wall hook and tied it around her waist then stopped and gazed around the familiar kitchen. *Lord, help me know what to do. I want to stay here on the ranch where life is good. But if it's Your will that we travel west, I need you to show me.*

Mahala opened the wooden insulated icebox that stood next to the counter and pulled out a bowl of eggs and bacon wrapped in brown paper. It wouldn't be long before the kitchen sent tempting smells throughout the house. When it did, the children would be scrambling down to start another day.

Early May 1843

"THANK YOU FOR BRINGING in the milk and eggs today." Gertie Yates said to John. "With the town filling with the wagons from the east, it's all I can do to keep up with my supplies. I've never seen so many wagons coming through these parts. Where do you think they're going?"

John set the milk cans down and gazed out the glass window in the hotel's doors. A stream of light streaked down the hall that led to the kitchen. John and Gertie stood just outside the bustling kitchen taking a moment to talk.

"I'm guessing most of the wagons are headed to Oregon. But some folks have families living in states on the way, like Wyoming and Nebraska. Kansas is growing, too. The land are calling them, as the wheat grows well there." He ran a hand over his short, scruffy beard.

Given his longing to move to Oregon, John often talked to the immigrants. He'd learned a lot about their reasons for moving, and in turn he was able to give advice for when they reached Independence. The big city would be fuller, with wagons coming from all over. He'd learned of a few good scouts to lead the way.

"And what about you?" Gertie asked, bringing John's mind back to the present. " Have you thought about making that trek out west?" Gertie eyed him with a knowing look. "Sometimes, I see a wistful look about you when this town fills up with wagon trains."

"Well," John said, eyeing the older woman with a crooked smile. "I guess there's no hiding it. I wouldn't mind moving my family to Oregon."

"What's in Oregon that you can't find here?"

"More land, for one." He bent and picked up the milk cans again. "And the ocean, for two. It'd make it a lot easier to sell my cattle."

"Speaking of cattle. We're running low on beef again. Did you bring a hindquarter of beef to the back of the store like I asked?"

"I did. Your cook is already working on the cuts of meat. You'll have more steaks and roasts before the end of the day." He nodded to Gertie. "I best get these milk cans loaded onto the wagon. Owens is waiting for me and I've got a long day ahead of me at the ranch."

"I'll see you tomorrow?" Gertie asked.

"You bet." John strolled to the door and started to set a can down to open it. Before he did, the door opened and a stranger stepped into the lobby. Seeing John's hands were full, the man held the door open for him. "Thank you, sir," John said as he strode onto the boardwalk.

John stepped out of the hotel in time to see two horsemen ride up to the building and dismount. The strangers tied their steeds to the hitching post and looked up and down Main Street, and then at John.

"Good day, sir. We've ridden a fair distance today," said one of the men. He gazed at the hotel then the stranger shifted his gaze to John. "Is this the only hotel here in Grovespring?"

"It is." John stayed rooted where he stood, an empty milk can in each hand.

"We're looking to stay a few days. I hope the proprietor has a couple of rooms available."

The man doing all the talking turned to his saddlebag and withdrew a worn, leather wallet. He shoved it into his pants pocket and then combed back his steel-gray hair behind his ears. He adjusted his large-brimmed hat and turned to his companion. "Let's see if we can get a room, Joseph, and maybe a good meal."

John stepped toward the edge of the boardwalk and nodded. "Good day, gentlemen."

"Excuse me, sir. Would you happen to know of a man named John Grigsby in these parts?"

"As a matter of fact, I would." John set the milk cans down and narrowed his gaze on the red-headed man who had a red beard to match.

"We've traveled all the way from California to have a word with this gent." The man stroked his trimmed beard.

John's head shot up. "All the way from California?"

"Yes, sir. How can we find this man?"

“You’re speaking to him.” John reached out a gloved hand.

Both men stared at John in disbelief.

“Well, I’d say this is a strike of luck!” said the other man. His bushy brows rose. “I’m George Yount.” He stepped forward and took John’s hand and shook it hard. He stared at John as if a miracle had just taken place right before his very eyes.

The bearded man stepped forward and extended his hand as well. “I’m Joseph Chiles. It’s a pleasure.” He shook John’s hand with less exuberance but with a firm grip. He glanced at the door of the hotel. “Would you care to join us for a meal after we’ve checked in?”

John stared at the milk cans sitting on the boardwalk. He’d already spent more time in town than he’d intended. But knowing these men had traveled 2,000 miles to meet him, how could he resist? “I’ve got a couple of deliveries to make. Why don’t you get settled in and I’ll meet you in a half hour.”

The men gazed at the milk cans, brows raised. “You get that milk from your Durham cows?”

“I do,” John said, curious that the strangers knew his cattle were Durham. “Durham cows make the best milk around.” He picked up the empty cans and stepped off the boardwalk. He headed toward his wagon and didn’t look back.

“We’ll wait for you in the dining room,” Joseph called.

John kept walking. He lifted the cans into the wagon and stared back at the hotel. The two men had disappeared inside the building the door had closed behind them.

Why would those men be looking for me? And how in ‘tarnation do they know I have Durham cattle?

John gazed down the street at the wagons parked along the sides of the road. People bustled around, taking things out of the back of their wagons and shuffling through them. Children ran around the wagons seeming to be glad they were in town. Men stood in circles, talking and glancing at the stores. John watched them wistfully. Might there come a day he and Mahala and the children would be on their way to Oregon?

He pulled out two full cans of milk and made his way to Owens Mercantile. As he crossed the street to the boardwalk, he couldn’t help but wonder why those men had traveled 2,000 miles to see him? The thought had plagued him from the moment they met.

THE LOBBY AT THE Yates Hotel was busier than John had seen in a while. The concierge turned the registration book around for a crude-looking man to sign in. John wondered if the gentlemen he spoke to earlier had been able to find a room and check in.

Thinking about the two men, John stood at the entrance from the lobby that led to the dining room. The café bustled with people. He panned the room to see if the two men sat at a table. A hand went up across the floor and John spotted Yount and Chiles seated at a table.

As John neared the table, both men rose and shook his hand. Mr. Yount waved him to a chair. "Have a seat, Mr. Grigsby. We were just talking about you."

"I can't imagine why, but I assume I'm about to find out." John removed his wide-brimmed hat and hung it on the wall hook by the table. He pulled out a chair and sat down, curiosity getting the best of him.

"There's a lot of commotion going on in this town," Yount said, and he glanced out the window by their table, before he gazed at John.

John nodded. "This happens every year about this time. Folks come through from back east. There's a lot of miles between towns. By the time they get here, the people on the wagon trains are needing supplies and fresh stock."

"And your general store has enough supplies to help these people?" Chiles asked.

"Clem Owens stocks up on everything well ahead of May. He's ready when the wagon trains come through—all in hopes that the folks will buy everything he has." John leaned back in his chair and crossed his arms over his chest. "So far they haven't disappointed him yet."

"But they still need to change out their stock for fresh ones," Chiles said.

"That they do." John took a sip of the water the waitress set before him. She took their order and left.

"Which brings us to you," Yount said as he leaned his elbows on the table and narrowed his gaze on John.

"I have to admit I'm wondering why you'd come all this way to see me?" John leaned forward as well.

"Well, you see, folks have been coming to California with your stock. After several groups have arrived, it's come to our attention that the cattle you are selling to these folks make it a lot farther on the trip than other breeds who don't have the stamina."

John leaned back and looked at George Yount and Joseph Chiles. He gazed at the men taking in their features. Both men were older, seeming to be in their fifties. And both men had high foreheads, their hairline reaching to the middle of their heads.

George Yount's forehead had a row of creases as if the man did a lot of thinking. Another set of creases were set between his brows. His face was full, and the man seemed somber and with kind blue eyes. When he spoke, his voice was deep in a soothing kind of way.

Joseph Chiles' face was long with high cheekbones, a strong nose, and a grim mouth. His forehead protruded just so, and his brows lowered when he spoke. To all appearances, he seemed disgruntled. But when he smiled, everything about him changed. His green eyes lit up and softened the contours of his face.

John cleared his throat and asked himself, *Is it my cattle they're after?*

George Yount grew serious. "We started asking the groups that made it through the summit where they got their Durham cattle. We were told that many of the immigrants come out to your ranch and purchase their stock from you."

"That's true," John said. "This is a busy time of year for me and my ranch hands. Folks will come out to purchase a couple of cows and, sometimes calves."

Everyone stilled as the waitress came to the table with plates lined up on her arm. She set a plate before each of the men. While she set their plates on the table, John's mind ran with questions. He'd been wanting to travel out west for the last three years. But he'd always considered Oregon as his destination. He knew little about California.

"Can I get you fellas anything else?" the waitress asked.

The men eyed their plates filled with steak, mashed potatoes, and green beans. A bowl filled with buttered rolls was set in the center of the table. Yount looked at the young waitress and said, "I think we're all set. The food looks delicious."

"I second that," Chiles said. "We haven't eaten this well since we left California."

"I'm glad to hear it!" the waitress said brightly. "I'll come back and check on you." She left their table and went back to the counter, took up a coffee pot, and headed to another table.

"Where were we?" Yount asked.

"You were asking Mr. Grigsby about his cattle," Chiles said.

"Oh, yes." Yount tilted his head toward John. "We're just wondering if you'd consider relocating to California with your stock. California has mild weather for the most part, with plenty of green pastures for livestock."

"I have to admit it sounds enticing, but I don't know a thing about California. The thought of moving there has never crossed my mind."

"You aren't the first immigrant to say that." Chiles eyes lit up. "But I have to tell you, it's beautiful country."

"That may be, but I've had it in mind that if I decided to go west, it would be Oregon."

"Why's that?" Yount asked.

"I don't just want land," John said flatly. "I want a lot of land."

Both men smiled and gazed at each other with a knowing look. Yount gave a rich, low laugh and took up his fork and knife. He cut into his steak and took a bite.

John glanced at Chiles to see the man had a pleased look as well. Neither spoke as they chewed their food. Seeing they decided to eat rather than talk, John took up his knife and fork and sliced into his steak. Before he took a bite, however, he gazed at the men again. "Do you have something to say to me?"

Yount nodded and wiped his mouth with a napkin. "This is a fine piece of meat." He chewed a little longer, seeming to enjoy the flavor.

John cracked a smile. "That comes from my ranch too."

"This meat is from your steers?" Yount looked at Chiles.

"I'm not the only one who provides beef to the Yates Hotel. There's another rancher in these parts, a friend of mine, Charles Matthews, who provides beef as well."

"Durham?" Chiles asked.

"No. Hereford," John said.

"Can you tell the difference?" Chiles asked.

"Certainly."

"And this is?" Chiles held a piece of steak on his fork.

"Durham," John said.

The two men looked at each other again.

George Yount swallowed a bite and pointed his fork at John. "You should really consider moving to California. We need your beef."

"You don't have cattle in California?" The idea struck him as incredulous.

"We do. But they're not hardy animals like your stock, and the meat pales compared to this." George cut another slice of meat and held it up to Chiles. "Am I right or wrong?"

Joseph Chiles gazed at John. "He tells you the truth. And to be frank, Mr.

Grigsby, we'd like to make you an offer."

John's heart started to beat hard in his chest. As often as he had thought about moving out west, there was always doubt in the back of his mind that the move might not be in the best interest of his family. What if he sold his property and made the 2,000-mile journey across the prairie only to find that he had made a mistake. But here he sat with these two men who had traveled all the way from California, wanting to offer him a way to get to their land. He stilled himself and asked, "How long have you lived in California?"

Yount spoke first. "I came to Sonoma, California in 1834. I was employed as a carpenter under General Mariano Vallejo when I first arrived." He smiled and continued. "Vallejo is a generous man. As governor he had permission to give land grants to the people, meaning the Mexican population and the Indians if he chose, but to the Americans as well. Vallejo felt it would benefit the Mexican government by settling people in the northern territory of California. In 1836, Vallejo granted me a large portion of land in Napa Valley. It's beautiful country. I had first seen the land in 1831, but never dreamed there would come a day that I would bring my family to live there." He smiled again. "I've named my place Rancho Caymus." He touched his lips with his napkin and continued, "And wouldn't you know, our family became the first Americans to settle in Napa Valley."

"You say you were the first Americans to settle there—"

"Yes. Alta California belongs to Mexico. The land Vallejo granted to me is rich land, and not only that, there's every kind of wild life you can imagine roaming the land.

"I noticed that you called your place, 'rancho'. Why is that?"

"It is what the people call their ranches in that territory," Chiles said. "Remember, the people are predominantly Mexican and Indians, and they speak Spanish. There are few white people in that part of the country. But there are settlers arriving every year, and more Americans are settling in the territory," Chiles said.

"Do you speak Spanish?" John felt discomfort dampen his spirit. The thought of moving to a land and not knowing how to speak to the people seemed a real challenge.

Vallejo speaks both English and Spanish. And there are English settlers that have come into the valley and have stayed. You will find plenty of people who speak English, but—" Yount's chin hit his chest before he looked up. "You would want to learn their lingo. It would be to your advantage to learn their language as soon as you could."

John listened as the men spoke, uncertainty building a wall in his mind.

"I had to improve the land in order to keep the grant," Yount continued. "I built a cabin and a grist mill. I've been able to help the community with flour for bread and tortillas."

"Tortillas?"

"It's a flat bread the Indians use for just about everything they eat," Chiles said.

"With Americans flooding into California, it is necessary to be able to build homes faster than we have in the past," Yount went on. "I recently built a sawmill that helps buildings go up faster now that we can cut the trees down and saw them into boards. But that's another story." Yount waved his hand. "What I'm trying to point out to you is that California is an open frontier. You would do well there."

John gazed at Chiles. "And you? Do you live in California as well?"

"I'm a widowed man, Mr. Grigsby. I left my children with relatives and joined the Bartleson-Bidwell Party in 'forty-one. Our wagons were the first to enter Alta California over the Sierra Nevadas."

"Sierra Nevadas? Where's that?"

"It's a tough summit for wagons to go through, but I've led seven groups into California. It can be done. And I might mention, there are places where, at times, you cross the same river several times because of the trail."

"But you haven't settled in California?" John asked.

Joseph Chiles gazed at George Yount and then at John. "I haven't become a citizen yet, but it is something I will do. I'm ready to settle down."

"You men have given me a lot to think about, but you said you wanted to make me an offer. What would that be?"

George Yount checked his pocket watch. "Might we come to your ranch and take a look at your cattle?"

John gazed at the men and said, "Come for supper. You can look at the cattle while you're there."

LATE THAT AFTERNOON JOHN came through the back door. Mahala heard the clomping of his boots on the hardwood floor. He'd been gone all day, which wasn't like him, and she couldn't help but wonder what had kept him in town so long? Of course, that was a ridiculous question; she knew beyond a shadow of a doubt that the town was full of wagons. Folks had been coming out to the ranch to buy cattle, meat, and even some of their chickens. But today, he hadn't been home to meet the immigrants who came out to buy stock. William and McDuff had set aside steers, heifers, and calves in pens for the people until John got home. The immigrants would come back tomorrow. So where had he been?

Mahala pushed a tray of biscuits into the oven and set the dish towel aside. She'd already set the table in the dining room and was just about to call the children in to eat when John appeared at the kitchen door and said, "Add two plates to the table, honey. We've got company."

Mahala's brows went up. "Company? Who might that be?" She darted a look out the kitchen door and down the vacant hallway, and then back to John. "Who did you bring home?" She bit her lower lip, a frown on her face.

"They're travelers I met in town. Is that a problem?"

"You brought people home from the train?"

"No, hon. A couple of men showed up at the hotel this morning. I'll explain later, but for now, set extra plates on the table. Our company should be coming up the drive any minute."

"I made leftovers for supper. You know I usually do on Thursday nights." She glanced at John as dread washed over her.

"The men won't care what you put on the table. They'll be grateful for a home-cooked meal and your wonderful cookin'." John kissed Mahala's forehead and wheeled around to head out the back door.

Mahala grabbed two more plates off the shelf and moved into the dining room, where she stared at the table she'd already set. "Well, isn't this a fine kettle of fish!"

"What's wrong?" Tess asked as she entered the room.

"Your father's invited company for supper, and all we have is leftovers." She ran a flustered hand over her face.

"Don't worry, Mahala. Your leftovers are always good." Tess glanced about the room and picked up a chair setting against the wall. Holding it against her chest, she carried it across the floor. "I'll help you get ready." She set the chair down and maneuvered the other chairs to make room.

"Thank you, Tess. I best put some extra biscuits in the oven." She started out of the room but turned back. "Call the children down for supper, please."

"All right." Tess disappeared from the dining room, stood at the base of the stairs, and called, "Supper's ready!"

Mahala grinned and shook her head. "I could have done that," she murmured. Mahala looked out the window to see two men riding horses into their front drive. They wore nice clothes and their hair was slicked back. *Whatever is John up to now?*

Chapter THIRTY-SEVEN

AS JOHN AND MAHALA sat at the table with their guests, George Yount and Joseph Chiles, the evening dragged on much longer than Mahala had expected. She made several trips to the kitchen to heat more coffee. As the hour grew late, she sat at the table, doing all she could to keep from yawning and falling asleep in front of their guests.

On the other hand, she wanted to hear every word the men had to say. They painted quite a picture of a land called, California. Apparently, from the comments they made, this land flowed with milk and honey. It seemed that settlers had bragged about John's cattle and his knowledge of scouts who traveled out west. And of all things—they wanted John to uproot the family and move out west too!

It was all she could do to keep from drumming her fingers on the table or from giving John an agitated look. They would talk later. She noticed, however, that Franklin and Granville leaned forward, listening to every word the men spoke as if they were intensely interested. It appeared that the two older boys would jump at this wild adventure if given the chance. She had long since put Jeffrey and Wiley to bed. But the rest of the children begged to stay if they kept quiet. She would give them a moment longer—but only a moment. She didn't for the life of her understand what they saw in this conversation that held their attention.

"We want you to come to California, Mr. Grigsby. There's plenty of land for you to have a nice spread for your cattle and horses. And should you come, I would offer you land south of my rancho."

John's head jerked up. "I have nearly a thousand acres here in Missouri. How much land are you proposing to offer?"

Mr. Yount leaned back in his chair and drew out a cigar. "May I?" He glanced first at John and then Mahala.

Mahala couldn't speak if her life depended on it. Her stomach roiled just listening to this outlandish conversation. She eyed John, wishing he would send these men packing.

"By all means," John said, pulling out his pipe as well.

"Having ridden our horses over your pastures and seeing the wealth of water you have with a river running through your property, I can see you are doing very well for yourself."

Mahala held steady—at least the men noticed that John didn't need their land.

Yount continued, "Obviously, you wouldn't journey to California without assurance that you could expect to receive land that is at least comparable to what you have—and who could blame you?"

Chiles broke in saying, "Having traveled the two thousand miles it would take to get there, I agree with Mr. Yount. We would have to make it worth your while to spend six months of hardship in all sorts of weather and crossing land that can be ruthless—"

"Not to mention Indians," Mahala broke in. She had not intended to spill out her thoughts, but she could not stop herself.

All eyes went to her. A woman didn't usually interject her point of view in a meeting meant for men. But a smile cracked Yount's face. He gazed at John and Chiles with a glint in his eyes and cleared his throat. "Your husband tells me that the two of you have only recently married."

Mahala's chin went up. "That's true." It was the first words the man had spoken to her all evening. She wasn't invisible after all.

Yount stared at the stub of his cigar and said, "He also told us that you're a seamstress and quite sought after from as far as Independence." His brows went up. "Impressive."

It took every ounce of effort not to squirm in her seat. She didn't want a compliment from this man—or the gent sitting next to him. But etiquette begged that she at least force a smile. "I worked for Mr. Thompson until John and I married. I no longer hold that job." She looked at the children, who sat patiently at the table. "I'm needed here with these lovely children." She winked at Mary Jane and smiled at the other children, whose eyes were turned on hers.

Joseph Chile's eyes lit up. "It looks to me that both you and John have a lot to offer in our neck of the woods in California. Your cattle can be sold far and wide from northern California. You would have the ships that come into the bay at your disposal. The cattle could easily be shipped up and down the West Coast."

Yount leaned forward, and the chair creaked under his weight. "Your family would be quite an asset to the Valley."

"The Valley?" John lowered his pipe.

"Napa Valley. Yountville, New Helvetica, Sonoma. These are a few of the essential towns in the area." Yount looked at Chiles. "We, along with John Sutter, have dreams of opening the land to Americans."

John added tobacco to the bowl of his pipe and lit, it deep thought. "But you say that California belongs to Mexico and is made up of mostly Mexicans of Spanish decent. How would my children strive in an environment like that? In your honest opinion, is there any problem with the Americans fitting in with the Mexican people?"

George Yount blew a ring from his cigar. "The people are open to the Yankees, as they call us, coming to California. They are hard workers. When an American family settles in the area, they hire the natives to help build their homes and set up the ranches. Many of the natives stay on, their wives becoming cooks or housekeepers. The Americans provide income for these people. And you need a lot of men to help break the land."

John lowered his pipe and eyed the cinders in the ashes.

Yount's chair scraped the floor as he pushed away from the table and stood. "Think about it, Mr. Grigsby. The mild weather would be suitable for raising cattle and your prized horses."

Mahala's grogginess took flight. She sat up straight and stared at John willing him to look at her. To her dismay, he showed intense interest in what Mr. Yount had to offer.

"You could be a wealthy man with that herd of cattle you've got on your ranch." Yount bowed low toward Mahala. "We have taken up a fair part of your evening, Mrs. Grigsby. I apologize for that." He gave his partner a nod. "We should go and let them go to bed."

John stood as well and stretched out his hand. "I have to say I've enjoyed the evening very much. I will give your offer some thought."

Yount shook John's hand. "We'll be heading back to California day after tomorrow. Until then, we're holing up at the Yates Hotel. We'd like to see your cattle once more before we go."

"Of course," John said.

Mahala hugged herself and tried to keep her inner turmoil from showing.

She listened to the men, wanting to hurry them out the door.

The men nodded toward her. "You're a wonderful hostess, ma'am." Mr. Yount told her.

"And the food was delicious," Chiles added. "Your husband's a lucky man."

Mahala cleared her throat before she spoke, feeling some shame for her reaction to the evening's events. "Thank you, sir."

Chiles smiled wide. "Thank *you*, ma'am." The men headed toward the entrance to the hallway with John on their heels.

Mahala could hear George Yount at the front door as he said, "Look me up when you get to the Valley, Grigsby. You'll need a place to stay while you set up your rancho. Mahala and the children are welcome to stay at the hacienda until you're ready for them to join you at your ranch."

Mahala started clearing the table with a little more fervor than needed. "Hacienda, my foot!" she said under her breath. "We're not going anywhere!"

JOHN LED GEORGE YOUNT and Joseph Chiles to the stable to collect their horses. When he returned it, was to find Mahala waiting for him in their bedroom. She'd already changed into her nightgown and stood barefoot before him, her hands on her hips and her brows raised in question. "You aren't really considering their offer, are you?"

"As a matter of fact, I am."

"You would uproot the children from their home?"

"Is it the children you're worried about?" he countered. "When Nancy and I came west from Tennessee, the traveling was hard on the family, not to mention the animals. But we have done well here in Grovespring. I don't look forward to uprooting the family to go farther west, but—"

"Let's not talk about it tonight." Mahala blew out the kerosene lamps, leaving her and John standing in the dark. She needed to step around him to move to her side of the bed. When she tried to slip between him and the bed, John's hand went out to her waist, but she side-stepped him and moved to her side of the bed with her back straight. The air behind her practically bristled. John crooked a smile and began unbuttoning his shirt. Was this there first spat? He tried not to let the sparks flying from her side of the bed burn him.

He lay awake long after he heard Mahala's even breathing. He thought about the visit this evening with Yount and Chiles. Excitement grew in him at the thought of moving to a warmer climate and new beginnings, but he had his work cut out for him. It was clear Mahala didn't share his interest in a move west. Could he convince Mahala that uprooting their family and moving out West would be in their best interest? His lip turned up on one side, and he held his sleeping wife. His heart softened as he held Mahala in his arms. He loved her. *Good Lord, if she only knew how much.*

Early August 1843

MAHALA LEFT THE HOT kitchen and strolled through the peach orchard. The fruit hanging on the trees would be ripe soon. She reached out and plucked a peach from a low limb and gently squeezed it. A pang went through her heart as she remembered that it had only been two summers ago that she and Nancy had spent hours making peach jam. Nancy had made the best peach jam in all of Grovespring.

She knew John and the children would want the pantry replenished with the good-tasting jam, along with canned peaches, for the winter.

Mahala tossed the peach in the air and caught it with her right hand. "I'll do it," she murmured. "Maybe I can talk Rebecca, Elizabeth, and Mary Ann into coming to the house and helping me." She dropped the peach into her apron pocket and walked back to the house.

A FEW MORNINGS LATER, the scent of peaches hit Mahala the moment she entered the kitchen. "Hmm." Had the boys brought in peaches before they went to the barn to do their chores? She cradled her large belly with her fingers as she stared at the bushel basket sitting on the floor. "I guess I'm making peach jam today," she murmured.

The pitter-patter of bare feet announced that Jefferson and Wiley were awake and had descended the stairs. The boys bounded into the kitchen with rumpled hair and wide yawns. "I'm hungry," Jefferson said, rubbing his eyes with his small fists.

"Me, too," Wiley chimed in, which he often did when he followed his brother. The two boys started across the floor to the table and stopped. Seeing the baskets full of peaches, they glanced at each other and headed toward the baskets.

"No peaches before breakfast, boys." Mahala turned the boys around and moved them out of the kitchen. The three stood at the foot of the stairs, and Mahala called up the stairwell, "Tess, are you up?"

Mahala heard the muffled voice, "I'll be right down." A moment later, Tess stood at the top of the stairs, looking down at them. Her hair was mussed up from just getting up.

"I need to start breakfast," Mahala told her. "Can you get the boys dressed while I get started?" Her brows rose. "Do you mind?"

"Of course not. Come on, Jeffrey and Wiley. Let's get you dressed."

Mahala gave the boys a gentle nudge, and they climbed clumsily up the stairs on their short, stubby legs.

After breakfast, Mahala shooed everyone outside except for Tess. "I need you to help me today. The boys have already picked peaches, and I guess that means your father wants us to make peach jam."

"Uh . . . I'm not so sure he wants *us* to make peach jam. I think he wants *you* to make it."

"I can't do this all by myself." Mahala bit her bottom lip as a thought occurred to her. "Wait a minute. We don't have to do this by ourselves. Let's hitch up the wagon and ride over to my mother's house. I'm sure I can convince my sisters to come and help us. And if I can't—Mother can." Mahala took a deep breath. It was only last week she'd thought about inviting her sisters over. She wasn't sure she could convince them to do it, though. Those girls had minds of their own and often treated life as if it were one continuous ball.

"Can I ride Star over?"

"I don't know why not. Why don't you hitch Bessy to the wagon. I'll meet you outside in a moment."

"All right. Do we have to bring Mary Jane?"

"You don't want your sister to come?"

"We never do anything alone—just the two of us."

It warmed her to know Tess wanted to spend time with her. Mahala made a quick decision. "I'll see if Cal will watch the little ones while we're gone."

Tess smiled widely as she left the kitchen. "I'll be waiting outside."

"Send Calvin in if you see him."

"I will."

Moments later, the back door slammed and Calvin came into the front room. “Tess said you wanted to see me.”

“I do. I need you to keep an eye on the three little ones while Tess and I pay a visit to my mother.”

Calvin stared at her as if she had horns growing on her head. “But I was going to go down to the river.”

“You still can after we get back.”

“How long will you be gone?”

“Calvin Grigsby, you will not question my whereabouts or how long I’ll be gone. Don’t be disrespectful.”

“Sorry, ma’am.”

“That’s more like it. Now do as I say and keep an eye on your siblings. I won’t be long.”

Calvin hung his head and stared at her. “All right.”

“The children are playing in the back yard. Don’t let them out of your sight.”

“I won’t.”

“Good.” Mahala followed Calvin out the back door and found that Tess had the wagon ready. “Shall we go?”

“Molly! Where are you going?” Mary Jane ran up.

“I’m going to visit my mother. You be a good girl and stay in the yard with Calvin.”

“I want to go!”

“Not this time, Mary Jane. Tess is riding over with me. We won’t be long.”

“Why does she get to go?” Mary’s finger went into her mouth.

Mahala just stood there and stared at all of the children. All she wanted to do was pay her mother a visit. This was becoming more of a fiasco than she’d seen coming.

Just then, John rode up the drive from the pasture. “Hello, there. Going somewhere?”

Heat rose to the top of Mahala’s head. “Yes, I’m riding over to my mother’s house to invite my sisters to help me put up the peach jam.”

“By yourself?”

“No. Tess is coming along.”

“Molly won’t let me go with them,” whined Mary Jane.

John stared down at Mary Jane and then over to Mahala.

“I promised Tess that just the two of us would go over today. Calvin is going to watch the children while we’re gone.” She gave John a meaningful glance that said, "'Help me with this.'"

"That's an excellent idea." John gave Mahala a warm look. "Mary Jane, you help your brother keep an eye on your little brothers."

Mary Jane's brows lowered, and her lip did, too. With a dark look in her eyes, she turned and marched back to the side of the house where the two little boys played.

"Go on," John said with amusement in his eyes. "She'll be okay."

Mahala flicked the reins and Bessy started down the drive. Tess passed her on their black horse with a white star on its forehead. It seemed that Tess was spending more time in the corrals with the horses these days. Watching her turn the horse down the lane, she could see that Tess sat on the horse with ease. She rode just ahead of Mahala, looking back every now and then and smiling. It was nice having just the two of them paying her mother a visit. They should do it more often.

MAHALA AND TESS SOON turned into the Shields driveway and pulled up in front of the front porch. Tess slid out of the saddle and tied Star to the hitching post. Mahala climbed down from the wagon more slowly, her girth making simple movements more difficult these days. The two of them went up the steps, but before they reached the door, her mother opened it and looked out with surprise on her face.

"Look who's here." She turned to glance back into the house.

The girls came out of the living room and cried in delight, " Mahala!"

"And you brought Tess with you," Rebecca added.

"Come in and have a seat."

"Is everything all right?" Mary asked.

"Everything is just fine. I'm getting ready to put up peach jam." Mahala looked down at herself. "But I don't think I can do several bushel baskets of them by myself." She gazed at her three sisters. "How would you like to come over tomorrow and spend the day with me. We can make peach jam and catch up on each other's news."

All Mahala got back was stares from all three of the girls. "What's wrong? Did I say something wrong?" She glanced at her mother.

"Well, that's a fine how-do-you-do, girls." Mary gave each of them a stern look. She glanced back at Mahala. "Of course they'll come."

"Mother!" the three girls groaned.

"You'll be going over to the Grigsby ranch and help your sister out and that's that."

"But—we were planning on going to Libby Matthews' house tomorrow," Rebecca said. "We've already made plans to pack a picnic lunch and go for a ride."

"Oh, for crying out loud. Sometimes you girls are as useful as a fork in a sugar bowl. You can go another day. I'm sure Libby won't mind."

Mahala watched her sisters and her mother going back and forth, and something shifted inside her. "Never mind," she said and rose out of her chair. "I thought you'd enjoy coming over to help. But I can see I was terribly wrong." She turned to Tess, who sat gazing at her aunts in discomfort. "Come on, Tess. Let's go home."

"Mahala." Her mother's voice stopped her. "Please don't go."

"I'll come back another day." Mahala continued to the door, feeling for the first time that she needed to run from her parents' house.

"Mahala, wait!" That was Elizabeth's voice. Mahala didn't turn around. "I'll come. I don't have anything else to do. I wasn't planning to go to Libby's with my sisters."

"That's not necessary." Mahala continued to leave, her hand on the doorknob.

"Don't be a dunderhead," Elizabeth said. "I really do want to come and help."

"Me, too," said Mary Ann." When Mahala looked back, Mary Ann had a sheepish look on her face. "We can be quite selfish sometimes. I'm sorry. I really want to come."

Mahala's fingers continued to grasp the doorknob. She didn't know what to do. There was no way she could put up all those peaches by herself, and yet she didn't believe her sisters honestly wanted to come. She let out an exasperated sigh. "I've always kept from giving you girls a tongue lashing over the years. But, yes, you are selfish. I truly didn't think you'd turn me down, or I wouldn't have come. I'll figure something out. Good day." She held the door open for Tess to pass through and stepped out behind her. She closed the door with her heart in her throat. Tears stung her eyes as she stepped into the wagon.

Tess stared at Mahala, a grim look on her face. She led the way out of the drive, and they retraced their way back to the Grigsby ranch. When they reached home, Tess put the horses away, and Mahala went into the house. At first she didn't know what to do with herself. She had never expected the reaction she'd witnessed from her sisters. She'd always believed that, through thick or thin, they would always be there for one another. She went to her bedroom and closed the door. She didn't want to talk to anyone right now. It had been a long time since she'd had a good cry, but at that moment, she sat on the edge of the bed and threw her face into her hands. Sobs shook her as she let go of all her emotions.

She heard the click of the doorknob as John came in. She felt his presence standing behind her as tears streamed down her cheeks. She sniffled but she couldn't look up. She knew her nose was red and swollen and she looked a ridiculous mess. She continued staring down at her hands, but from the corner of her eye, she saw his hand reach out with a handkerchief. She kept her head bowed and accepted it. She blew her nose, but her head still felt clogged from the hurt in her heart.

"Do you want to tell me about it?" John asked soothingly.

"No."

He cleared his throat and walked to the window. She hadn't looked up, but she saw his boots and knew that he stood by the window that looked out over the peach orchard. The silence was loud. And somehow, she felt she owed him an explanation for the tears she cried.

"Take your time," John said. "I'll be out in the barn, putting the stock to bed."

She felt him walk past her, a wisp of air waving past her as he went out. The door clicked again.

"Oh, Mahala," she said, her nose stuffy. "Let it go." She blew her nose and stepped over to the wash stand in the corner of their room. She splashed tepid water onto her face and towel-dried it.

The baby kicked her rib and she could hear the sounds of the children somewhere in the house. "I best get supper started." She shook her head, squared her shoulders, and opened the door. She no sooner stepped out of the room than Mary Jane walked up and said, "Molly! I'm glad you're back!"

A wave of gratefulness filled her and she bent to kiss Mary Jane on the cheek. "Me, too, darling. "Me too."

THE NEXT MORNING, TWO wagons pulled into the front yard. One held her sisters, the second held Margaret, her sister-in-law. Mahala stepped out onto the porch and gazed at the women as they made their way to the front porch. Margaret hugged her and said, "The Peach Brigade is here."

"What is going on?" Mahala watched her sisters come forward, sincere regret on their faces.

"We've come to help, Mahala, and you will not turn us away," Mary Ann said, giving Mahala a peck on the cheek. "We were truly naughty yesterday, but we're going to make it up to you." She walked past Mahala and went into the house.

Elizabeth and Rebecca gazed at Mahala and gave her sheepish looks with a hint of playful tease in their eyes. "We really didn't mean to upset you. Put us to work. You won't regret it." Elizabeth said. She hugged Mahala and stepped aside for Rebecca to squeeze in.

"Forgive me?" Rebecca asked.

"Oh! You girls! Just come in. My kitchen is full of peaches, and we've a long day ahead of us!"

The house soon filled with the sweet smell of peaches. Never had Mahala had so much fun as she did that day. The girls were their usual noisy selves and laughter filled the air. But fun aside, they had a regular system going with the peeling, cutting, boiling and stirring as the sugary aroma of peach jam spilled out the open windows and into the yard.

Mahala had no idea what John had done with the children, but the women had the kitchen all to themselves all afternoon.

Several hours later, Mahala gazed down at her swollen belly filled with a rambunctious baby kicking her ribs and remembered the last time Nancy had made jam, Nancy had been just as big but with swollen feet. The chore of making jam had been an overwhelming, and Mahala was grateful for all the helping hands.

"You look like you need to sit down," Margaret said, pulling out a chair. "Sit!"

"All right," Mahala said. "My back's killing me." She looked down at her stomach. Movement could be seen on one side of her belly. It raised and lowered in one swift move.

"Will you look at that," Rebecca said, staring with wide eyes. "I don't think I've ever seen a baby push a stomach out like that."

Mahala beamed. "I believe this little one is going to be a boy." She cradled her tummy with her hands. "He can't lie still for a moment these days."

Tess came into the kitchen just then and said, "I hope you're wrong, Mahala." She watched Mahala's tummy too. "We have enough boys in this family. We need another girl."

The women all laughed.

Mahala saw the wistful look in Tess's eyes. "Well, darling, we don't have any say in this. This little one is going to be whatever God intended." She pushed away from the table to check on the women's work.

"Back into that chair," Elizabeth said. "We've got it here."

Mahala's hands flew up. "I give up."

By late afternoon, the girls had cleaned up the kitchen and were waving goodbye. Margaret had chicken and dumplings cooking on the stove. "Goodbye, Mahala. Stay off of your feet as much as you can. You look like you're about to pop."

Mahala watched Margaret's wagon disappear out the drive. When she was sure she was gone, she turned toward the house. *Well, now, she wondered. Where is John?* She was certain he was responsible for the women showing up today. It would be improper if she didn't let him know how much she appreciated him, wouldn't it?

Chapter THIRTY-EIGHT

THE EARLY MORNING DEW evaporated by mid-morning as John and his cowhands moved the cattle to the east pasture. The morning had already heated up and Blue chuffed a few times, seeming to want to run. But John held him at bay. They walked slowly while John whistled a tune and took in the scenery about him. He had a good spread, and he knew that some of the ranchers in their community envied him for it. Yet, here he was, his head full of ideas for moving out West.

Ever since George Yount and Joseph Chiles came into town, his every waking hour was consumed with the idea of taking the offer the men had made on moving to California. They had promised him land. And not just land but good land and more than he had here.

It was a strange feeling to change course in his thinking, seeing as how until now he'd planned to move his family to Oregon. He'd heard a lot about the land that Oregon had to offer and very little about California—until now.

"Hup! Hup!" one of his men bellowed, chasing a stray yearling back to the herd. Luke shrilled a whistle and his horse kicked up dirt.

John slowed his mount to a stop, and leaned his elbow on the saddle horn, watching Luke bring the young steer back to the herd. Contentment filled his chest. He not only had a good spread of land, but he had good help. His men were the best. If he pulled out of Grovespring and moved out West, could he talk any of his men into coming along?

He would need men to help herd his stock on the trail. Which brought him to another thought. How many cattle should he take to California? And how many cattle should he sell? He couldn't bring the whole lot of cattle with him, but he could sell a few to the members of the wagon train. He pushed that particular thought aside. He'd deal with that when the time came.

Sweat trickled down his temples, and he pulled off his wide-brimmed hat. He ran a hand over his face and head. There wasn't even the slightest hint of a breeze in the air to cool him off. It was going to be a hot one today.

With the days warming up quickly under the hot August sun, the men had taken to riding out earlier in the mornings. John and the hands carried canteens of water with them as they rode out to the pastures, but he'd already drained his. "May as well go refill my canteen and check on Mahala," he said aloud, and Blue's ears flickered. John leaned forward and rubbed Blue's neck. "You thirsty, boy?"

Blue snorted and stomped his hooves on the prairie grass.

"All right, let's head back to the ranch yard." As he loped toward the house, John saw two horses coming up the road from town. A second glance told him the riders were Yount and Chiles. He urged Blue toward the ranch yard at a gallop. By the time he reached the drive, the two men were riding slowly toward him.

"Morning, Grigsby," Yount said.

"Morning to you." John touched the brim of his hat. "You fellas getting ready to ride out?"

"We are," Chiles said. "We just finished a good breakfast at the hotel and bought a few supplies to hold us over for a few days on the trail." Chiles glanced back at his saddlebag, which looked fuller than it had when they first rode in.

"You give any thought to our offer?" George Yount asked. He pushed his felt hat back and looked at John with expectancy in his eyes.

"You know I have, Mr. Yount. As a matter of fact, that's all I've been thinking about since you two rode into town."

"So we should expect to see you and your family riding into Fort Sutter next fall?" Yount asked.

"Don't be surprised if we show up." John crooked a grin. He straightened in his saddle. "Can I offer you gentlemen a glass of cold water before you head out?"

Chiles pointed to his canteen, the strap looped across his saddle horn. "We're good, my friend. We just wanted to stop by and tell you we're leaving, and we hope to see you next year."

John nodded and eyed the two men. "There's nothing keeping me here except my wife. But I think she'll come around." He looked over at the house as if Mahala could hear his exchange with the men. He felt his ears heat up.

George Yount moved his mount alongside John's and reached out a hand. John took it and the two men shook hands.

"See you around, Grigsby."

"You can count on it," John said.

Yount moved his horse aside and Chiles moved in. His green eyes lit as he pumped John's hand, but he'd already had his say. He touched his hat and the two men turned their horses out of the long drive and onto the main road. They both waved and then went on, not turning back this time.

John sat astride Blue in the shade of the house. He watched the men disappear down the road until they were two small dots. A smile spread across his face and he gazed at the clapboard house as if he could see through the walls. "I've got my work cut out for me for sure," he said in a low tone. "But we'll make that move to California. You don't know it yet, my love, but it'll be one of the best moves we'll ever make."

Blue sidestepped and snorted, eager to get going again. "Hold on there, Blue. Let's get you some water at the trough while I check in on Mahala."

John walked Blue to the barn, where the trough sat, and slid off his mount. He tied the reins to the hitching post by the trough and glanced at the house. How was Mahala doing this morning? It was late enough in the morning that she should be up. He headed to the back door, eager to see her. In the recesses of his mind, he remembered feeling anxious about Nancy when it was close to her time. He didn't want a repeat of that worry. Mahala was healthy and she hadn't shown any sign of trouble. Still, he'd check on her and maybe get a kiss while he was at it. His neck burned as he entered the house.

MAHALA PUNCHED THE BREAD dough down once again and began to knead the dough with a rhythm. She pushed down with the heel of her palm three times, then folded the dough over and pressed down again.

She had already filled the stove's fire box with wood to heat the oven. Between the stove's heat and being in the throes of the summer heat, sweat poured down her back and beaded her forehead.

She had worked herself into a dither ever since she'd looked out the kitchen window and saw the two men from California riding up their lane and into their drive. The men disappeared at the side of the house.

At first she thought John might invite the men into the house, but he hadn't. However, it wasn't long after the two men left that John came in through the back door.

He looked as hot as she felt. His blue shirt was dark, stained with sweat, and his hair was matted from his hat. But he was still handsome. And if she weren't so upset at the sight of the strangers, she might have welcomed him into the kitchen.

As it was, she couldn't put the two men out of her mind, and she felt threatened by their presence once again. Would those men convince John to pull up stakes and move their family out West?

"Good morning," John smiled sheepishly, seeming to sense her mood.

"Morning yourself." Mahala moved away when he reached out for her.

"Did I do something wrong?" he asked.

She didn't look back. She couldn't look back. If she did, she'd walk right into his arms and let him hold her, something she relished with every new day that broke. But today, she couldn't put the sight of those two men out of her mind and for reasons unknown, she blamed John for it.

"You want to talk about it?" John had moved up behind her and had reached his arms around her, pulling her against his chest and his lips near her ear.

"Oh, John." She turned to face him. "What were those men doing here?"

John heaved a long sigh. "They came to say goodbye. They're headed back to California."

"Good." A weight dropped from her. "If I never see their faces again, that would be all right by me."

"You're being too hard on them, Mahala. They only have our interest at heart."

"Humph! They only have their interests at heart. Don't pull that one on me." She pushed him away and started for the table, where a bowl of bread was rising, and the ingredients to make two more loaves of bread were waiting.

John pulled her back into his arms. "Mrs. Grigsby. I came in for a glass of cold water and—to look at your face."

"I'll get you some water." Mahala tried to pull out of his wonderful arms.

"Not so quickly, honey—"

She turned out of his arms and reached for a glass. She pumped water into it and held the glass out to him. "Here you go." Her cheeks felt hot.

"Thank you." John downed the water, letting the coolness fill him. Then he gazed at Mahala again. "Don't be so put out. We're not going anywhere for a while."

"For a while?"

"Yes." He set the glass on the counter, but he kept his distance. "We can't go anywhere just yet. There's too much to do. I have to see if Charles Matthew still wants to buy our spread, and if so, I have to sell off some of the cattle too. And once that's done, there's a hundred other things that need to be done to be ready to go. And we haven't even begun to start yet."

"Yet?" Mahala said with a lifted eyebrow.

John stared at her and then hung his head. "We won't go if you don't want to, Mahala. I won't make you do anything against your will. I think it would be a good move for us, but if you're dead set against it—we stay."

Mahala stared at him. Why was it that, even though he had gifted her with the decision to stay, she still felt weighted down with the thought that they wouldn't be here a year from now? After all, she *could* tell him she wanted to stay.

John kissed her forehead. "I'm headed back out to the south pasture." He touched the crease in between her brows tenderly. "Don't fret about it, honey." He turned and walked out the back door.

The room felt empty without his presence. She stared at the table and said, "I've bread to make. Thoughts of California will have to wait."

August 23, 1843

MAHALA PUNCHED THE BREAD dough down and began kneading it with more energy than needed. She felt an urgency to get the bread made. Why, she didn't know. They still had a loaf sitting in the bread box. But something told her to get more loaves made and that had been her priority this morning. She enjoyed the process of making bread. She liked the softness of the dough as she kneaded it and rolled it into a ball. She would repeat the process several times before she would set it aside. She sucked in her breath—there it was again—a tightening of her abdomen and a deep ache in the pit of her stomach.

She stopped kneading the bread dough and stood straight, her fist going to the small of her back and sweat beading her forehead and upper lip.

If she didn't know better, she'd think the kitchen was hot enough to bake the bread without having to put it in the oven.

The tension in her belly let up and she leaned forward again to punch down the dough. After she rolled it into a ball, she lifted the dough, and placed it in the bowl, and covered it with a dishtowel to let it rise one last time.

Mahala reached for a glass off the shelf and pumped cold water into it. If there was a chance of a breeze outside, she needed it. Picking up the glass, she strode to the front porch and sat on the porch swing. To her dismay, not the slightest breath of air stirred. She couldn't help that. She needed to get off her feet and rest awhile.

In the distance she could hear the children playing in the back yard. Squeals of laughter from Wiley and Jeffrey filled the air. She could only imagine what they were doing. On a hot summer day like today, they were likely playing in the wash tub filled with water from the well.

Mahala listened to the pleasant sounds and wiped beads of sweat from her forehead. She felt her tummy tighten again. It was the strangest feeling in the depth of her being. She looked down to see that her belly had hardened into a tight ball. And that tight, dull ache rose in her again.

She pushed the swing with her toe on the wooden floorboards of the porch, and the springs at the sides squeaked with each push. A fly buzzed around her head and she swatted it away. All the while, her tummy felt tight. Mahala gazed out over the front yard and waited for the firmness of her belly to subside.

She tried to squash the realization that the baby was trying to come. As far as he knew, they always came in the wee hours of the morning. Yet, here she was, feeling something going on inside—clear as day. Would this baby make its appearance in the middle of the day?

She was grateful Tess had taken the younger children out to the yard. Mahala needed to stay focused and see if she was truly going into labor. She concentrated on the minutes in between each hardening of her stomach and each dull ache. Her mother had given her a few pointers on what to look for when the baby started to come. Her mother had warned, "With this being your first child, it won't come quickly. Unfortunately, the first child usually takes many hours of labor before it arrives. And you will think you can't live through the pain—but you will."

It was too much information in Mahala's frame of thinking, but her mother reminded her of one more thing. "Even though the hours of labor are long, when that baby comes into the world, all that pain and suffering disappears into thin air, as if it never happened. Hang onto that, Mahala."

Her mother being the kind of woman that she was, she wouldn't spare her any piece of information if she could help it—all for her own good.

Like it or not, she took her mother's words to heart, for the contractions had only begun about an hour ago, and if her calculations were right, she still had the rest of the afternoon to go. *Good heavens! Can I do it?* Mahala smiled grimly. *I don't have any choice. It's the only way I'll see my baby's beautiful face.*

A TWINGE SHOT THROUGH her womb and another contraction hardened her belly. It had been several hours now, and through it all, she had managed to put the bread into the oven and had even taken it out and set it aside, all along keeping the contractions to herself. No need to worry the children. There was nothing they could do. But all afternoon, the children went about their business, looking at her strangely at times, but they hadn't questioned her. When she felt their look on her, she smiled patiently at them and pretended all was well.

But the afternoon wore on and John and the older boys were still out on the ranch. Tess had taken the children outside again after their naps, and Calvin and Mary Jane played in the middle of the yard.

Mahala stood at the back door, checking on the children, and trying to make up her mind whether she should send one of them for John or to wait and take a nap. She tried to knead the pain away from her lower back. Maybe if she took a nap some of the ache would ease. She watched Calvin disappear into the barn, and Mary Jane came to sit on the step with Tess.

"Girls," Mahala called when she stepped onto the back step. Two heads swung around to look up at her. "Keep an eye on the boys a little longer, would you? I'm going to lie down for just a little while."

"Mahala," Tess said, jumping to her feet. "You don't look so good."

"I'm fine. I just need to lie down for a bit."

Tess and Mary Jane looked at each other, and their brows went up and their lips thinned.

"You're quite flushed, Mahala." Tess tried again.

"That's from all the heat, Tess. I've been working in the kitchen all morning making bread." She gazed at the girls wistfully. "Do you mind keeping an eye on the boys a little longer?"

"I don't mind," Tess said, but her brows drew together. "Go lie down."

Mahala closed the door and headed for the bedroom. The bed looked so welcoming. She sat on the edge of the mattress and allowed herself to fall back onto the pillow. "Oh," she said softly. "Sleep sounds so good." And before she could think of anything more, the world drifted away and sweet comfort filled her—but there it was,—that hardening of her belly and the dull ache,—only this time it was harder than before.—Was it her time?

Try as she may, Mahala couldn't lie in bed. It didn't do anything to relieve the discomfort and ache that drilled through her body, and thoughts of things that needed to be done flooded her mind. She had supper to make, and the boys needed to be cleaned up, and the table needed to be set . . .

Mahala swung her feet to the floor and rose. She was restless and decided she would tend to the boys first. When she opened the back door once again, Tess and Mary Jane still sat on the top step, and their heads turned to look up at Mahala.

"I can't sleep. Bring the boys in, and we'll get them cleaned up before I start supper. You—"

A warm and wet sensation ran down her legs, and when Mahala looked down, she found a puddle of water at her feet. When she looked at the girls, they stared back at her in horror.

"What have I done?" Mahala stood there, stunned that she didn't have any control over what had just happened. And she didn't know what to do next.

"Mahala," Tess said in an unusually stern voice. "Go lie down. I'm going after Dad!"

"No . . . don't do that—"

"The baby's coming." Tess announced. "I'll send Granville after the midwife."

"But—"

"Go to bed!" Tess insisted. "I've seen Mama do this enough times before to know that when her water broke, it wasn't long before the baby came."

"But—"

"Mary Jane. Go tell Calvin to go fetch Mrs. Shields!" Tess turned back to Mahala. "You want your mother here, don't you?"

Mary Jane couldn't move. Her brows creased and she stared at Mahala with tears brimming her eyes. "I don't want Mahala to have the baby." Her lips protruded and her chin hit her chest.

"Mary Jane," Mahala said. "You don't really mean that, do you?"

"I don't want you to die!" Mary Jane threw her arms around Mahala, and her shoulders shook as she cried.

Mahala brushed her hand over Mary Jane's curls and lifted her chin.

"Don't worry, darling. Everything will be all right."

"Really?" Mary Jane gazed trustingly into Mahala's eyes.

"Yes, really," Mahala said, and she kissed the top of Mary Jane's head. "Now do as your sister said, and go after Calvin. I do want my mother here for when the baby comes."

"I'm riding out to get Dad. Go lie down, Mahala." Tess ran to the barn.

"All right." Flustered, Mahala raised the hem of her dress. "But what about the water?"

"I'll get it later. Go to bed!" Tess called back.

Mahala stilled herself as another contraction came. She watched as Mary Jane disappeared into the barn, with Tess flying right behind her. Moments later, Tess came out of the barn with Star behind her. She stepped into the saddle and rode out of the yard.

Mahala turned to go into the house. *The baby is coming, and of all things, in the middle of the day!*

ANNE WRAPPED THE NEWBORN in a soft blanket and handed the bundle to Mahala. "You have a baby girl."

Mahala held her breath as she looked down at the dark-haired infant, and she nuzzled her close to her heart. Tears slipped down her cheeks as she looked over the baby's head at John and her mother. "Can you believe it? She's perfect."

John sat on the side of the bed and watched Mahala kiss the baby's soft, tiny head. "What are you going to name her?"

"You mean, what are *we* going to name her?"

"Of course, but to tell you the truth, I thought you might want to do the honors. I haven't even tried to think of a name for the baby."

"Well, I have." Mahala gazed at the tiny infant in her arms. "Nancy Ann."

"What did you say?" John gazed at Mahala and saw the twinkle in her eyes, a twinkle that glistened into tears. "Nancy was my dear friend, John. And I think the children would love it if we named the baby after their mother."

"Are you sure, Mahala. You don't have to—"

"I want to." Mahala smiled contentedly and kissed the baby's soft, downy head again.

"All right. Nancy it is."

"Nancy Ann Grigsby."

"All right," John swallowed.

Mahala held the baby up to him. "Nancy Ann, meet your father."

John lifted his newborn daughter into his arms, still wrapped in the warm blanket, and for a moment he gazed into the baby's eyes. Little Nancy Ann wriggled beneath the cloth and stretched a toe out of a fold. A grin spread across his face as he kissed the soft, tiny flesh. Love for this newborn made his heart swell and he could hardly breathe.

"Well, aren't you going to show her to the children?" Mahala asked.

"You bet I am." John opened the door to find his children waiting there. He leaned forward and showed baby Nancy to them. "What do you think?"

The children gazed at the baby, their eyes fixed on her ruddy cheeks. They held their breaths for a beat, and then Mary Jane asked, "Can I hold her?"

"Not yet, kitten. She's a bit fragile at the moment."

Mary Jane's mouth formed an O, and she stared longingly at her new little sister. "I'll wait then."

John glanced at Tess, who hugged herself as she looked on. "She's cute as a button, Daddy."

"I'd say you're right about that." John glanced over his shoulder and saw that Mahala had closed her eyes. "We better put the baby back in her mother's arms. I think they both could use some rest now."

Granville shuffled on the hardwood floor. "We best get on out to the barn and tend to the animals."

"All right, son." John saw a light in his son's eyes.

Granville threw an arm over Calvin's shoulder. "Come on, Cal. Let's go."

John watched the boys go out the back door. Franklin stopped at his side and touched the baby's forehead. He smiled, but he didn't say anything. The moment seemed awkward for the boys, seeing a fresh newborn in the evening hours. It warmed him to see the love in their eyes, even though little Nancy wasn't even an hour old. "I'll join you boys in a minute."

"All right," Franklin said.

John returned to the bedroom and pulled down the covers. He lay the new babe in the crook of Mahala's arm, and she instinctively turned on her side and brushed a kiss on the baby's soft, downy head. John heaved a relieved sigh as he stood for a moment and watched mother and child. He hadn't realized until now that he'd been afraid that the delivery wouldn't go well. He couldn't lose Mahala, too. But here she was, looking up at him with tired eyes. He kissed her forehead. "You did good. Get some rest."

"Hmm." Mahala sighed softly and she closed her eyes. "I will."

"COME QUICK!" MARY JANE burst into the living room. "There are thousands of fireflies in the yard and in the field!"

"What on earth?" Mahala said, holding baby Nancy to her chest as she rose from her chair.

"Let's see what she's talking about," John said as he followed Mahala and the children out to the front porch. "We don't usually see them this late in the year."

But sure as the world, thousands of fireflies winked all across the lawn and the fields in the distance. Their quiet presence added a sense of magic to the summer night.

"Would you look at that!" Mahala giggled, watching the children bound off the porch and run among the lightning bugs that winked on and off, some in unison and some seeming to follow their own patterns. The boys tried to catch them, while the girls just danced among the twinkling bugs. Rusty barked and ran in circles, chasing after the children. There was laughter on the lawn for the next half hour, but soon the twinkles died down and only a few lightning bugs flickered here and there until there were none. Their absence set the mood for quietness, and the children wandered around the lawn, searching for one last flicker. And finding none, one by one the children went back into the house and closed the door.

John and Mahala lingered a little longer, baby Nancy tucked in Mahala's arms. The evening was so humid that after the fireflies had disappeared, the katydids struck up their chorus and the bullfrogs croaked their song. Boots stretched out on the porch rail, her tail swinging back and forth.

What a difference a year made. This time last year, Mahala had dreamed of having her own home, her own family, and a man to love her. And here she stood with John's arms wrapped around her, holding her tightly, and with the baby safe in her arms. Life couldn't get any better than this, and Mahala realized for the first time,—she felt deep in the heart of love.

The End

To the Reader . . .

"A work of Fiction inspired by Truth."

Writing historical fiction is one of my favorite genres. I have found that the lives people led in the 1800s is truly inspiring. I must say though, that working against the backdrop of real history is truly a challenge. When I decided to bring John Grigsby and his family from the dust, I went to great lengths to remain true to their history. I did, however, take the liberty of creating a personality for each character, as there were no records of their essential characteristics.

I have spent years researching the life of my third-great-grandfather, John Grigsby, and his family. As the story unfolds, I set them in the small town of Grovespring, Missouri. Research records show that the Grigsbys and the Shields lived in several counties in Missouri. And in many cases the resources that explained where these two families lived contradicted other sources. I was left with only one thing to do—I chose a location that best described where the families lived—Grovespring in Wright County. And though I have used Grovespring, Missouri, for the setting of this story, all of the names of the roads, bridges, and creeks leading to the town are completely fictional, as well as the names of the buildings in town.

Till We Meet Again,
Marilyn

With gratitude . . .

I owe so much to those who helped make writing *Deep in the Heart of Love* so rewarding. To my husband, Bob—for understanding when I'm "in the zone," for being the first to read and edit each chapter, and for making time for me to write. To Bonnie Kiser, who sent information about our family and, more importantly, our third-great-grandfather, John Grigsby.

To Bob Shields, who sent a multitude of information about the Grigsbys and Shields. You helped get the facts straight and you answered endless emails and questions.

To Jenny Margotta, my editor, for your insight, encouragement, and patience as this story took shape. You are indispensable to me.

To the Inkspots critique pals, Beckie Lindsey, Patty Schell, Karla Luther, Rebekah Koontz, and Kassidy Ridenour, for doing what you do so well, and for your prayers and support. To John Garner, my critique partner, after the pandemic—for the many hours you spent editing the book and for the selfless time you spent throughout the process.

To my family, who over the years talked about my third-great-grandfather, John Grigsby, and inspired me to write his story. To my readers, for loving these historical characters—some real, some not—with a passion that rivals my own. You encourage me in ways I cannot begin to describe. Just know I'm so grateful to you.

To my Lord and Savior, Jesus Christ—for being there every step of the way. Mold my heart, Lord, and let me hear you call my name. You were the One who ultimately held me up when I was down and encouraged me to finish this novel.

Affectionately,
Marilyn King

Grigsby Family Tree

Third-Great-Grandfather
Captain John Etchison Grigsby - Grandmother: Nancy Weir Wilson

Second-Great-Grandfather
Granville White Grigsby - Grandmother: Sarah Ann Rector

First-Great-Grandfather
Henry Frances Grigsby - Grandmother: Charlotte Augusta White

Grandmother
Tilly May Grigsby - Grandfather: Martin Peter Le Roy

Father
Jack Henry LeRoy - Mother: Verdean Gwendolyn Fisher

Me
Marilyn Vernay LeRoy (King)

Thank you for reading!

I hope you enjoyed *Deep in the Heart of Love*—Book One in The Call of the West. I loved writing about my ancestors, Captain John Grigsby and his family.

As an author, feedback from my readers is indispensable. mailto:Marilynking6318@gmail.com

If you're so inclined, I'd love a review of *Deep in the Heart of Love*. Leave a review on Amazon. Go to Marilyn King Books and find Review.

I invite you to visit me at:

Website: www.marilynking.net.
Facebook: www.facebook.com/marilynvking
http://goo.gl/qXSY2Dhttp://www.marilynking.net.

Stay Tuned for Book Two!

The Far Side of the Mountain

Look for these other books by Marilyn King, Available on Amazon.com

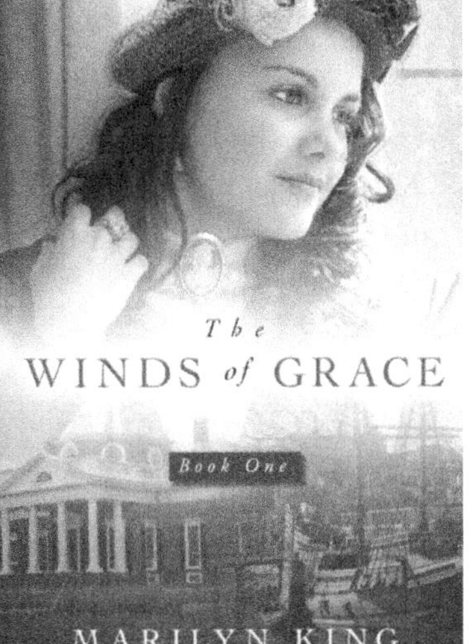

1830s' Jamaica, Grace Cooper must trust God to help her find acceptance from a father she never knew, fulfillment in a place she's never been, and safety from those who would rather see her dead. Can she hope to find love as well?

One story of two sisters who struggle to realize their dreams. Kindra and Grace's lives are hanging by a thread. Can they persevere in the challenges they face? They must put their faith in God and forge ahead to their true destination

Two sisters on two different plantations. One man stands between them. Can they survive in a world turned upside down?

In 1841 one man's revenge sets out to steal another woman's freedom, but two young hearts set out to restore it. Is it too late to bring her home, or does love conquer all?

Made in the USA
Coppell, TX
03 June 2022